Internet Starter Kit

Windows™

Internet Starter Kit for Windows™

Adam C. Engst, Corwin S. Low,
and Michael A. Simon

Hayden
Books

Internet Starter Kit for Windows™

Library of Congress Catalog No.: 94-75729

ISBN: 1-56830-094-8

96   95   94   4   3   2

Interpretation of the printing code: the rightmost double-digit number is the year of the book's printing; the rightmost single-digit number the number of the book's printing. For example, a printing code of 94-1 shows that the first printing of the book occurred in 1994.

Dedications

To my lovely and talented wife, Tonya, without whose patience and editing skills I would certainly have gone stark raving mad.

—Adam C. Engst

To Mom and Dad, whom I love more than I ever get around to mentioning.

—Corwin S. Low

For my Mom and Dad, whom I owe more than just a dedication.

—Michael A. Simon

Credits

Publisher

David Rogelberg

Acquisition Editor

Karen Whitehouse

Development Editor

Dave Ciskowski

Copy Editor

Mary-Therese Cagnina

Publishing Coordinator

Stacy Kaplan

Cover Designer

Jay Corpus

Interior Designer

Barbara Webster

Production Team

Gary Adair, Brad Chinn,
Kim Cofer, Meshell Dinn,
Mark Enochs, Stephanie
Gregory, Jenny Kucera,
Beth Rago, Marc Shecter,
Kris Simmons, Greg Simsic,
Carol Stamile, Robert Wolf

Indexer

Rebecca Mayfield

*Composed in Palatino
by Hayden Books*

To Our Readers

Dear Friend,

I want to thank you on behalf of everyone at Hayden Books for choosing *Internet Starter Kit for Windows*™ to learn more about the Internet and how to get connected to this great "information superhighway." It can be challenging to learn something new without the benefit of the right book to help you. We have carefully crafted this book to make it as helpful as possible.

What our readers think of our books is important to our ability to better serve you in the future. If you have any comments, no matter how great or small, we'd appreciate you taking the time to send us a note. Of course, great book ideas are always welcome.

David Rogelberg
Publisher, Hayden Books and Adobe Press
201 West 103rd Street
Indianapolis, IN 46290

(800) 428-5331 voice
(800) 448-3804 fax

Email addresses:

Internet	hayden@hayden.com
America Online	Hayden Bks
AppleLink	hayden.books
CompuServe	76350,3014

About the Authors

Adam C. Engst

Adam C. Engst is the editor and publisher of *TidBITS*, a free electronic newsletter distributed weekly on the world-wide computer networks. After graduating from Cornell University with a double-major in Hypertextual Fiction and Classics, he worked as an independent consultant in Ithaca, NY, where he started *TidBITS* in April of 1990. He now lives in Renton, Washington with his wife Tonya and cats Tasha and Cubbins, but seems to spend most of his time corresponding via electronic mail with friends and associates around the globe. Like anyone who attempts to condense the immensity of the Internet into a single book, he is certifiably crazy. His favorite quote (which reportedly comes from Alan Kay, an Apple Fellow and Xerox PARC alumnus) is: "The best way to predict the future is to invent it."

Corwin S. Low

Corwin S. Low is part owner of Conjungi Corporation, a consulting firm providing network design services in the Seattle area, specializing in Internet access and related issues. Corwin has been using computers since 1980 starting with a PDP-11/03, and was first exposed to the Internet, then ARPAnet, at the University of Washington in the early '80s. He has worked for IBM Corporation and Asymetrix Corporation before branching into computer and network consulting in 1991.

Michael A. Simon

Michael A. Simon is also a part owner of Conjungi Corporation, a consulting firm providing network design services in the Seattle area, specializing in Internet access and related issues. Mike has been involved with networks and the Internet since his participation in connecting the University of Idaho to global networking in 1986.

Contents at a Glance

Contents

Part I

Introduction and History

In part one of *Internet Starter Kit for Windows*, I introduce myself and give you a look at what the Internet is, why it's so neat, and its history. These four chapters convey the proper mindset for thinking about the Internet. If you don't like reading about history, you can skip chapter 4, "The Internet Beanstalk." Don't blame me, however, if you find yourself condemned to read it at some later time. This history provides the background information that puts the Internet's current size and growth rate in proper perspective.

Chapter

1

Welcome!

Welcome to the *Internet Starter Kit for Windows*. I have two purposes in mind for this book—at least one of which I hope applies to you, the person glancing at this first chapter in the bookstore or first delving into your new book. First, I want to tell you about the Internet, what it is, why I think it's so wonderful (and I mean that in all senses of the word, especially the bit about becoming filled with wonderment), and look at a number of the services and resources that make the Internet one of humankind's greatest achievements. Second, I show how you can gain access to the Internet and look at many of the Windows tools available for working with the Internet. But for now, let's avoid the awkward small talk about the weather and introduce ourselves.

Who Are You?

I haven't the foggiest idea who you are. That's not true, actually. I hope you have a PC running Microsoft Windows, because if you don't only about half of this book will hold your interest. I hope you're interested in the Internet; otherwise, only about 2 percent of the book is worth your time. Given these two minor requirements, this book should provide hours of educational entertainment, just like Uncle Milton's Ant Farm. The major difference is that the Internet Ant Farm is worlds bigger than Uncle Milton's, and if you go away on vacation, all the Internet ants won't keel over, although you may be tempted to do so when you get back and see how much you have to catch up on. The Internet never stops.

I'm aiming this book at the individual. In the process I undoubtedly may disappoint the die-hard UNIX system administrators and network gurus who probably talk about X.400 and TCP/IP in their sleep, which doesn't come often because of the amount of Jolt cola they consume. I'm aiming this book at students and staff at universities who often have wonderful connections to the Internet, but who seldom have any guidance or information about what's out there. I'm aiming at user groups who can teach their members about the Internet and need a good resource in terms of both the book and the disk. And, I'm aiming at ordinary people who have a personal computer, Windows, a modem, and the desire to learn more about the Internet.

What Do You Need?

First, you need a personal computer running Microsoft Windows. That's not actually true because you can use any sort of computer to access the Internet, but to get the most out of this book, you should use Windows. You don't need a fast PC, although they're always nice.

Second, you need some type of a physical connection to the Internet. This connection may take the form of a local area network at work or, more likely, a modem. A 2400 bps modem works, although barely, and the faster, the better.

Third, I recommend that you use Windows 3.1 or later, if only because I have no idea if this software works under previous version of Windows including version 3.0. In addition, all of my instructions assume that you use Windows 3.1. If you need to upgrade, talk to your dealer. I've included a representative sampling of the best of the Internet access software on the disk cleverly attached to the back cover, and I'll show you where to get most of the rest of the programs I talk about as well.

Fourth, you need an account on a host machine somewhere. Later in the introduction to section III, I talk at length about how to find an appropriate account for your needs.

This stuff is not for the Windows novice. If you don't know the difference between a menu and a window, and haven't figured out how to tell applications and documents apart, I recommend you visit your local user group and ask a lot of questions. Bookstores are also becoming a good source of information.

I also want to talk about expectations. The Internet is not a commercial service like America Online or CompuServe. Customer service representatives are not available 24 hours a day via toll-free call. The majority of people on the Internet have taught themselves enough to get on or have been shown just enough by friends. The Internet is very much a learning experience, and as much as I hope to provide a whole slew of information that you need to know, there's simply no way to answer every question that may come up, or to hand-hold everyone through those first few days. The Internet is what you make it, so don't be shy. No one greets you on your first dip in but, at the same time, people on the Internet are some of the most helpful people I've ever had the pleasure of knowing. If you are struggling, just ask and someone almost always comes to your aid. I wish that were true outside of the Internet as well.

Evolution

One of the things that has made Windows so immensely popular is that it provides consistency—not only to the user in the form of menus, dialog boxes, buttons, and toolbars, but it also provides consistency for the programmer.

When there were only DOS-level applications (you know, those character-oriented interfaces), every programmer had to support every printer, video board, input device, and network board known to man in order to get wide-spread acceptance. For the entrepreneurial individual trying to make his mark on the business world by writing the next greatest productivity application, this was a most daunting task.

Microsoft Windows provides what computer marketing people like to call an Applications Programming Interfaces (API) to help kick-start the programming effort. For instance, if someone already knows how to print to a printer, why should every programmer have to include printing code? Why reinvent the wheel? And with the bulk of code already written the programmer then can concentrate on specific widgets.

The kicker here is that Windows with an Internet compatible API (later we'll refer to this as Windows Sockets—or WinSock for short), has only been around for a year or so. This book describes many applications written specifically for this API, with releases occurring daily. Numbers are expected to grow astronomically in the next year.

Who am I?

"Who am I?" is a question that I often ask myself. In the interests of leaving my autobiography for later, I must limit the answer to the parts that are relevant to this book. My name, as you probably figured out from the cover, is Adam Engst. I started using computers in grade school and had my first experience with a mainframe and a network playing Adventure over a 300 baud acoustic modem (you know, where you dial the number and stuff the receiver into the modem's rubber ears) on a mainframe my uncle used in New York City. I used microcomputers throughout high school, but upon entering Cornell University learned to use their mainframes. In my sophomore year, I finally found the gateway to BITNET (the "Because It's Time" Network) in some information another user had left behind in a public computer room. Finding that initial bit of gateway information was just like finding a clue in Adventure, but don't worry, it's not that bad any more. From BITNET I graduated to using a computer connected to Usenet (the User's Network, generally synonymous with "news") and about the same time learned about the vast Internet, on whose fringes I'd been playing.

After graduating from Cornell in 1989, I set up my own Internet access using CE Software's QuickMail for Macintosh and the UMCP\QM gateway from Information Electronics. QuickMail was overkill for a single person because it's designed to be a network electronic mail program, so I eventually switched to uAccess from ICE Engineering, now called UUCP/Connect and marketed by InterCon Systems. Several years ago, my wife and I moved from Ithaca, New York, where we had grown up and where Cornell is located, to near Seattle, Washington, and in the process I learned more about finding public-access Internet hosts in an area where you know not one person. In many ways the Internet kept me sane those first few months.

Throughout this Internet odyssey, which has gone on for about seven years now, I've used the Internet for fun, socializing, and general elucidation. In the last three years, I've written and edited a free, weekly electronic newsletter called *TidBITS*, which focuses on two of my favorite subjects: Macintosh and electronic communications. *TidBITS* is both a product and a citizen of the Internet, and it has grown from a 300-person mailing list that once crashed a Navy computer running old mail software to an electronic behemoth that lives on every network I can find, and boasts an estimated 50,000 readers in some 44 countries.

So that, and the incriminating photographs of important people in the publishing industry that I have digitized and poised to distribute to the net at large are the reasons I'm writing this book. Any questions? I hope so, but hold off until you've finished the rest of the book. And for those of you already marking things up with those nasty yellow highlighters, don't; I promise there is not a quiz.

Who Are We?

You may have noticed the title of this section uses the plural. Who are we? And why is there more than one? Excellent questions; let me explain. Depending on how your friendly local bookstore has organized their computer books, this book may have sitting next to it a similar-looking book entitled *Internet Starter Kit for Macintosh*. I initially wrote that book during 1993. It became quite popular, and I received numerous requests for a Windows version of the book. Unfortunately (major confession time here), I know very little about Windows since my PC expertise stopped at the 386 and the 640K RAM barrier. However, a large portion of *Internet Starter Kit for Macintosh* covers only the Internet, and makes no mention of the Macintosh at all. So in early 1994, Hayden Books decided to create a Windows version of the book and asked my friends Mike Simon and Cory Low to make the book relevant for Windows users by editing and rewriting the portions of the book that were Macintosh-specific.

I have a somewhat eccentric style, and since I believe strongly in talking directly to the reader and not avoiding or concealing my limitations, Mike and Cory's sections may read slightly different from the rest. Don't worry about it—just consider it a presentation with multiple presenters. As we move from the areas of my expertise in the Internet to the areas of their expertise in Windows, we'll simply switch places at the podium and I'll pass the microphone on to them (this is especially true in Chapter 10). Sure, it's not the traditional method of doing this sort of thing, but few people have accused me of being traditional. I suppose that's good.

In any event, I want to offer my heartfelt thanks to Mike and Cory for all their help, and I want to welcome you to the book. I sincerely hope you enjoy reading it and find it useful in your personal and professional lives.

Changes

Keep in mind that the Internet changes quickly and constantly, and trying to capture it in a snapshot requires high-speed film. I've got that film, so the image of the Internet that I present here isn't blurry or out of focus; but it's impossible to cover, or even discover, everything that deserves to be in the *Internet Starter Kit for Windows.* If, in the course of your travels on the Internet, you find a truly neat resource or piece of software that we overlooked, send us electronic mail (email) at cory@conjungi.wa.com, and we'll take a closer look for future editions.

Thanks

To not thank someone at the beginning of a book is extremely bad form and, luckily, many people have helped me throughout the writing of the book. I certainly want to thank my wife Tonya, who edited everything and put up with me during the final few weeks; Karen Whitehouse, David Rogelberg, and David Ciskowski of Hayden Books who have gone out of their way to help make this book a success. Thanks also to my mother, who went from WordPerfect 5.0 on an aging IBM PC to using a Quadra 700 and running a Gopher server, and to my father, who has become quite fond of Eudora on his LC II and is contemplating a PowerBook 160. I'd also like to thank all the readers of *TidBITS*, because they have kept me going these last three years.

Thanks are due as well to all the people who reviewed portions of the book, including the following:

Bill Dickson, for general comments and Internet kibitzing

Brian Hall, for general comments and communications lore

Chuck Shotton, for the World-Wide Web sections

Geoff Duncan, for his UNIX comments and Internet discussions

Mark H. Anbinder, for general comments

Mark Williamson, for providing much needed information about LISTSERV

Steve Dorner, for checking the Eudora section

And, of course, thanks to those people who provided text for the Appendices, including the following:

Gene Spafford, creator of the newsgroups list

Peter Kaminski, author of the PDIAL list

Phil Eschallier, author of the nixpub list

Ed Morin, Craig Suhadolnik, Scott Anderson, and Ralph Sims of Northwest Nexus

Finally, although I don't have room to acknowledge individually the programmers of all the software I mention in the book, I do want to thank those people who graciously allowed me to include their programs on the disk, including the following:

Steve Dorner, for Eudora

Mark Riordan, for WinVN

Robert Williams, NetManage, Inc., for Chameleon Sampler

Separately, I want to thank Ken Stuart for creating the resource section. It was a major help and is greatly appreciated.

Chapter

Why Is the Internet Neat?

Unless you idly picked up this book based on its cool cover while waiting for your spouse to finish buying the right present for Aunt Millie's birthday, you probably have some sense that you should be interested in the Internet. I'm sure you've heard the occasional drooling report on the radio about how the Internet is a massive BBS (bulletin board system), and with the Clinton administration's emphasis on a national data highway system (pushed of course by Vice President Al Gore), many print publications have forced some poor reporter to write a story on this Internet thing.

Those stories almost always make those of us who live and breathe the Internet cringe, because they almost always miss the point of the Internet. The stories crow about the technological achievement and vast worldwide coverage of the Internet, while failing to explain that the Internet is definitely not a commercial service staffed by friendly nerds in white coats and ignore the interesting human interactions on the Internet. Sometimes the stories can provide a gratuitous human interest story about how two people meet on the Internet and get married eleven days later, because typing to each other was such a moving experience. Sure, this stuff happens (and it's the last time I mention an Internet marriage because I don't think it's any stranger than many of the ways couples meet), but such gee-whiz stories never touch on the commonplace parts of the Internet: the discussion groups, the information databases, the selfless volunteer work that keeps the whole thing running. That's a shame and I promise to avoid that slippery slope.

Oh right, I should be talking about why the Internet is neat and why you should be interested, not ragging on the mediocre attempts made by people who don't use the Internet. Keep in mind that I may miss your favorite reason to use the Internet—one woman's Brownian motion generator is another man's cup of tea. In addition, remember that technology is seldom used for its intended purpose. The Internet started as a method of linking defense researchers around the country and it has grown beyond that use in ways unimaginable at the time it was created.

Software

For Windows and even DOS users, some of the most interesting things about the Internet are the file sites. File sites are several computers on the Internet that are accessible to everyone (more or less) and that store thousands of the latest and greatest freeware and shareware (where you pay the author if you use the program). An equal or greater number of file sites exist for other platforms, UNIX and Macintosh, for example. But you probably don't give a hoot about them. Finding specific numbers is difficult, but I think it's safe to say that thousands of people download files from the most popular archive sites (just another name for file site).

Electronic Mail

For many people, electronic mail, or email, is the primary reason to get on the Internet, because they want to send mail to someone else on the Internet. Once you're on, though, it is likely that you can strike up many new friendships and end up with a long list of electronic correspondents. Email is an excellent way to stay in touch—even with people who you regularly talk to on the phone—because it's quick and easy. Even though

I often talk to my parents, I often send them email because it's more appropriate for quick notes. Email messages are seldom long and can be even better than an answering machine for merely conveying simple information. For example, at one point a local user group held steering committee meetings at my house. I could have called everyone on the steering committee the night before to remind them, but because all I wanted to say was, "Don't forget the meeting tomorrow night," contacting them was easier via email.

Email sometimes gains the least likely converts. One friend of mine is best described as a telephobe. (He hates talking on the telephone and has only one at his house out of necessity.) He was equally disparaging of computers and email until he was forced to try it—after which he became an instant email proponent. He discovered that with email he no longer had to play telephone tag with coworkers or make numerous calls to arrange meetings. With email he was able to work more flexible hours because it didn't matter when his coworkers were present and their email was waiting whenever he wanted to read it.

Discussion Groups

Many people read and participate in the hundreds of discussion groups about specific computers; and many more people read other discussions that aren't as technical. For example, I took a bike trip several years ago and when my computer refused to work—citing a simple error code—my wife couldn't reach me to ask about it (and I wouldn't have known what the problem was then anyway). So she posted a help message on one of the discussion groups and within a few days had received numerous answers from experts around the world, telling her that the code indicated a bad memory card. (Luckily, the card was only badly seated.)

Similarly, when in the process of buying a car, I started reading appropriate messages on one of the car discussion groups. The messages were of some help, but I wish I had known then that an entire discussion group talked about Hondas (the make we were most interested in).

Information at Your Electronic Fingertips

The popularity of email and news notwithstanding, some people are impressed most by the massive information databases. Recently, a friend came over to watch a movie of the Knowledge Navigator film clip. The Knowledge Navigator is former Apple CEO John Sculley's idea of what information access will be like in the future—an anthropomorphic "talking head" that acts as an information agent, searching through massive databases of information on the user's command. The Knowledge Navigator film portrays a professor preparing for a class discussion about deforestation in the Amazon rainforest by looking at data retrieved by his electronic agent.

The film is fairly neat, but after watching it I remembered that I wanted to show my friend WAIS (or Wide Area Information Server). Using the WAIS software, we connected to WAIS and typed in our query, "Tell me about deforestation in the Amazon rainforest," and after thinking for about 15 seconds, WAIS returned a list of 15 articles from various sources that dealt specifically with that topic, sorted by relevance. Talk about knocking someone's socks off—my friend was staring, mouth open, tongue lolling, and completely barefoot, so to speak. Although WAIS doesn't have an infinite number of databases, it does have several (including *TidBITS*), and more appear all the time. I list some of the more popular databases later in the book where you can look at WAIS in more detail.

The Lemming Factor

Aside from the personal communications, the discussions on every subject under the sun (and some that never see the light of day), and the databases of information, Internet is neat for yet another reason. It's related to what I sometimes call the "lemming factor." That is, if so many people from so many cultures and walks of life are connecting to the Internet, something has got to be there. Don't scoff. No one makes all these people log on every day and spend time reading discussion lists and sending email. People aren't forced to increase Internet traffic at a whopping rate of 20 percent per month. They use the Internet because they want to, and few people are happy when they lose Internet access for any reason. And as much as the "lemming factor" may make it sound as though people are getting on Internet because their friends are, they aren't doing it from peer pressure. (Well, okay, so I hassled my parents into getting connected, but they love it now.) People are connecting to Internet because the Internet is becoming more than just an elite club of technoweenies—it has become a virtual community in and of itself.

The allure of the Internet sets it apart from other communities like religious, charitable, or humanitarian groups. No implied theological punishment exists for avoiding the Internet, and although its allure somewhat resembles the way people devote their lives to groups like the Red Cross, those organizations depend on people's belief systems. The Internet continues to thrive because of the volunteer labor pumped into it; but also important in its growth is the fact that it provides as much information as an individual can handle and in this day and age, information is power.

The Decision Is Up to You

Whatever advantage you want to take of the Internet, remember two things. First, the information available on the Internet generally has avoided the processing introduced by the mass media. If you want some real opinions on both sides of any issue ranging from the death penalty to abortion to local taxes, people usually are discussing the issue at length somewhere on the net. Because of that lack of processing, you may read a bit more about any one subject than you do in the mass media. Second, you get only the information you want.

When we get the Sunday *Seattle Times*, my wife and I always compete for the funnies and then for the "Pacific Magazine," which has in-depth articles. Then we settle down, and I read the sports section and the business section and maybe glance at some of the others before ripping out the job listings for my uncle, the ex-MIS director. My wife proceeds to the Home & Garden section. Good little stereotypes, aren't we? My point is that I'm completely uninterested in reading at least half of the two-inch thick stack of paper we get each Sunday. The same goes for my wife. So why should we pay for the entire thing when we're only going to bring it home and recycle half? A good question, and one that newspaper publishers should get their duffs in gear and answer. The same applies to junk mail. I instantly throw out about 90 percent of the snail mail (the Internet term for paper mail) I get, whereas almost all email I get is at least worth reading.

On the Internet, however, that's just the way it is. I read a small set of the several thousand newsgroups and I subscribe to a few specific mailing lists. When all is said and done, I get only what I ask for. Periodically, my interests change, so I switch things around. But I don't have to read, or deal with in any way, topics that either bore or irritate me—like anything unpleasant that happens in Northern Ireland or Beirut. Try avoiding such topics in the mass media—it's impossible.

I hope this chapter has instilled some curiosity and enthusiasm in you because we are moving on to the harder stuff now: that ever-popular and seldom-answered question, "What is the Internet?"

What Is the Internet?

What is the Internet? That question is tremendously difficult to answer because the Internet is so many things to so many people. Nonetheless, you need a short answer to give your mother when she asks, so here goes. The Internet consists of a mind-bogglingly huge number of participants, connected machines, software programs, and a massive quantity of information, all spread around the world. Let's see if I can put the size of various parts of the Internet in context.

In Context

People: The Seattle Kingdome seats 60,000 people for a sell-out Seahawks football or Mariners baseball game (once-in-a-lifetime experiences for those teams). That's about the same number of people who read a single, mildly popular newsgroup. If all 22,000,000 people on the

Internet were to get together, they'd need almost 300 stadiums the size of the Kingdome. I could calculate how many times that number of people would reach to the moon and back if we stacked them one on top of another, but it's a silly exercise.

Machines: In the infancy of the computer industry, IBM once decided that they did not need to get into the computer business because they felt that the world as a whole needed only six computers. Talk about a miscalculation! Many millions of computers of all sizes have been sold in the decades since IBM's incorrect assumption, and an estimated 2.2 million computers (2,200,000 for those of you who like the digits) are currently connected to the Internet.

Information: I can't pretend that the Internet offers more pieces of useful information than a good university library system, but that's only because a university has, in theory, a paid staff and funding for acquisitions and development. Information on the Internet is indeed vast, but finding your way around in it proves a daunting task. One goal of this book is to provide pointers to the best information sources. Also, keep in mind that Internet information is more personal and fluid than the sort of information in a library. Although you can't look up something in a reference work on the Internet, you can get 10 personal responses (some useful, some not) to any query you can pose.

Geographical size: Explaining how large the Internet is geographically is difficult because, in many ways, messages traveling over network connections don't give a hoot where they are physically going. Almost every industrialized nation, however, has at least one machine on the Internet, and more countries come online all the time. Geographical distance means little on the net. I mail issues of *TidBITS* to the mailing list on Monday night, for example, and people down the road from me find it in their mailboxes on Tuesday morning, as do subscribers in New Zealand and Finland (accounting for time differences, of course).

Perhaps the best way of wrapping your mind around the Internet is to think about the old joke about blind men all giving their impression of an elephant based on what they can feel. Like that elephant, the Internet is too large to understand at one mental gulp (see figure 3.1).

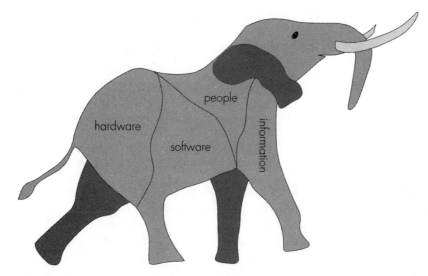

Figure 3.1   *The Internet Elephant—Elephantidae internetus.*

Information

More so than any other human endeavor, the Internet is an incredible, happy accident. Unlike the library at Alexandria (the one that burned down) or the Library of Congress, the Internet's information resources follow no master plan (although the Library of Congress is working on putting its catalog and some of its contents on the Internet). No one works as the Internet librarian, and any free information resources that appear can just as easily disappear if the machine or the staff go away. And yet, resources stick around; they refuse to die in part because when the original provider or machine steps down, someone else generally feels that the resource is important enough to step in and take over.

Andy Williams at Dartmouth, for instance, runs a mailing list devoted to talking about Frontier, a scripting program from UserLand Software. Andy also originally made available sample scripts and other files pertaining to Frontier, but he was not able to keep up with the files and still do his real job. Luckily, Fred Terry at the University of Kansas quickly stepped in and offered to provide a Frontier file site because he was already storing other files. (Fred also rescued the mailing list for Nisus, a word processor, when the original administrators had to bow out and he's probably a sucker for stray dogs, too.) Fred felt that keeping the information available on the Internet was important and the sacrifice was sufficiently small that he was able do it. Such is the flavor of the Internet, and damming the Internet's flow of information is harder than damming the Amazon with toothpicks. Next, let's look at the main rivers of information that flow through the Internet.

Information Rivers

Information flows in four main rivers through the Internet: *electronic mail* (generally known as email), *Usenet news* (generally abbreviated as Usenet or netnews, or just plain news), *Telnet*, and *FTP* (File Transfer Protocol). Each river carries or provides access to different sorts of information and most people dip into one or more to quench their thirst for knowledge. You've learned a little bit about how each of these rivers makes the Internet a neat place to be; now you're ready for more detail.

Electronic Mail (Email)

Email is the most prevalent of the four rivers. Almost everyone who considers himself connected to the Internet in some way can send and receive email. Most personal exchanges happen through email. Email handles most *directed information*, or information that is directed only at the recipient. Email also carries a great deal of *undirected information*, or information that is meant for a group of people, but for no one person in particular. Most of this undirected information travels in the form of *mailing lists* or LISTSERVs (a special form of mailing list software used by numerous discussion lists). In these discussion lists, all the readers can post questions, answers, and comments, and everyone can read everyone's postings. Again, these exchanges occur in email.

Email is also the medium for automated requests for information. For example, I've set up my computer to send an informational file about *TidBITS* automatically to anyone in the world who sends email to a certain address (which I give later in the book, after I explain how to read addresses). A number of similar systems exist on the Internet, dispensing information on a variety of subjects to anyone who can send them email.

A variant of these auto-reply systems is the *mailserver* or *fileserver*, which generally looks at the Subject: line in the letter or at the body of the letter and returns the requested file. Mailservers enable people with email-only access to retrieve files that otherwise are available only via FTP. (I explain about FTP later in this chapter.)

Usenet News

Like email-based discussion lists, Usenet news is undirected information aimed at thousands of people around the world. Almost everything on Usenet is a discussion of some sort, although a few groups are devoted to regular information postings with no discussion allowed. The primary difference between Usenet news and mailing lists is that news is more efficient because each machine receives only one copy of every message. If two users on the same machine (generally, multiuser mainframes or workstations, at this point) read the same discussion list via email, getting the same information in news is twice as efficient. If you have a large mainframe with 100 people all reading the same group, news suddenly becomes 100 times as efficient, because the machine stores only the single copy of each message, rather than each individual receiving her own copy.

In some ways, you can think of Usenet as the kitchen table of the Internet—the common ground where no subject is taboo and you must discuss everything before implementing it. In great part because of the speed at which Usenet moves (messages appear quickly and constantly, and most machines don't keep old messages for more than a week due to lack of disk space), finding information on your own can be difficult in Usenet. It really is a river and you must dip in to see what's available at a specific point, because that information may disappear downstream within a few days.

You can, of course, ask your own question and you usually get an answer, even if it's the sort of question that everyone asks. Common questions are called *Frequently Asked Questions*, or FAQs, and they are collected into lists and posted regularly for newcomers. Luckily, the cost of disk storage is decreasing sufficiently that some people and organizations are starting to archive Usenet discussions so that you can go back to them later and search for information that flowed past a long time ago.

Telnet

Both email and news can operate in a *batch mode*—that is, you can write a bunch of email, reply to news postings, and then have your machine connect to another machine to send your messages and bring in new ones. You need not be connected all the time for email or news (although they work just as well if you are connected all the time). Telnet and FTP, on the other hand, require a direct and constant connection because you actually run a program on the remote computer when you use them (you will learn about FTP later in this chapter). Although it sounds as though I'm talking about software in a section that should be about information, you cannot separate the software from the information to which it provides access. I'm talking about the information Telnet and FTP make available.

You run Telnet on your local machine, giving it the address of an Internet machine, usually a mainframe or UNIX workstation. (You have to know what you're looking for beforehand—one of the reasons for this book.) Suddenly, you're connected to that host machine just as though you were logging on locally. This process is neat, for example, because it can enable me to telnet to the mainframes at Cornell University and use them just as I did when I was actually in Ithaca, and not 3,000 miles away in Seattle.

Most people don't have personal accounts on machines around the world (and I never use the Cornell mainframes any more, either), but a number of organizations have written special programs providing useful information that anyone can run over the Internet via Telnet.

Say you want to search for a book that's not in your local library system, Ted Nelson's *Computer Lib/Dream Machines*, (an excellent book). You can connect via Telnet to a machine that automatically runs the card catalog program. You can then search for the book you want, find out which university library has it, and then go back to your local library and ask for an interlibrary loan. Pretty cool, especially if you live somewhere with a less-than-capacious public library.

File Transfer Protocol (FTP)

You can think of File Transfer Protocol (FTP) as a conceptual subset of Telnet, in that you run a special program called FTP when you FTP to a file site. As you may expect, FTP enables you to transfer files back and forth from your machine to the remote machine—although most people use FTP primarily to get files from other machines.

Telnet and *FTP* can serve as nouns that describe the program and as verbs that can describe the act of running that program.

Probably millions of files are available via FTP on the Internet, although you may discover that many of them are duplicates because people tend to want to give users more than one way to retrieve a file. If a major file site goes down for a few days, it's nice to have a mirror site that has exactly the same files and can take up the slack.

Several sites that have lots of disk space (several gigabytes, actually) store a tremendous number of DOS and Windows freeware and shareware programs, along with commercial demos and other types of computer information.

Special Services

Along with the standard information services of email, news, Telnet, and FTP, several new services have appeared in recent years. These special services usually cut across the standard services, so they can be hard to categorize. In addition, even more so than the others, these special services inseparably meld the software you use and the information they provide.

Archie takes the grunt work out of searching numerous FTP sites for a specific file. You can ask Archie to find files with a specific keyword in their names, and Archie searches its database of many FTP sites for matches. Archie then returns a listing to you, providing the full file names and the address information you need to retrieve the file via FTP.

Gopher, which originated with the Golden Gophers of the University of Minnesota, is an information browser. Numerous sites on the Internet run the host Gopher software, placing information in what are colloquially called "gopher holes." When you connect to a Gopher site, you can search databases, read text files, transfer files, and generally navigate around the gopher holes.

WAIS, which you learned about earlier, originated from a company called Thinking Machines, but has now split off into its own company, WAIS, Inc. Using the tremendous processing power of Thinking Machines' Connection Machine supercomputer or other powerful computers, WAIS can quickly (within a few seconds) return a number of articles to English-language queries, sorted by relevance. WAIS is limited only by the information that you feed into it.

The still-evolving *World-Wide Web*, or WWW is the most recent of the special services. WWW provides true hypertextual links between documents and suffers primarily from a lack of good ways of searching for documents. For those people unfamiliar with *hypertext*, it's a powerful concept that enables the reader to navigate flexibly through linked pieces of information. If you read a paragraph with a link word of WWW and then click on it, you immediately get more detail on the WWW.

People

The most important part of the Internet is the collection of many millions of people, all doing what people do best, short of reproducing. I mean, of course, communicating.

Communication is central to the human psyche; we are always reaching out to other people, trying to understand them, trying to get them to understand us. As a species, we can't shut up. But that's good! Only by communicating can we ever hope to solve the problems that face the world today. The United Nations can bring together one or two representatives of each nation and sit them down with simultaneous translations, but via the wires and satellite transmissions of the Internet anyone can talk to anyone else on the Internet at any time—no matter where in the world he or she may live.

I regularly correspond with friends (most of whom I've never met, but I still consider them friends) in England, Ireland, France, Italy, Sweden, Denmark, Turkey, Russia, Japan, New Zealand, Australia, Singapore, Taiwan, Canada, and a guy who lives about four miles from my house (although my wife and I finally broke down and went to visit him). I've worked on text formatting issues over the networks with a friend in Sweden; helped design and test a freely distributable program written by a friend in Turkey; and co-wrote software reviews with a friend in New Zealand who had been one of my Classics professors at Cornell. On the nets, when everything comes down to the least common denominator of ASCII text, you don't worry about where your correspondents may live. Although people use many languages on the nets, English is the *de facto* language of the computer industry, and far more people in the world know English than English speakers know other languages.

During the Gulf War when people in the U.S. were glued to their television sets watching the devastation, people in Israel with access to the Internet sent reports to anyone who would listen, describing the terror of the air raid sirens and the worrying about the SCUD missiles launched from Iraq. No television shot of a family getting into their gas masks with an obligatory sound bite can compare with the lengthy and tortured accounts of daily life that came from the Israeli net community.

The Internet also helped disseminate information about the attempted coup in the former Soviet Union that led to its breakup. One Internet friend of mine, Vladimir Butenko, said that he spent all of those nights during the proceedings near the Parliament (which is the equivalent of our White House), and when everything seemed to be clear, he went to his office and wrote a message about what he'd seen and sent it to the Internet. His message was widely distributed at the time and was even partially reprinted in the *San Jose Mercury News*.

Although no one can pretend that people on the Internet aren't often argumentative and contentious, an incredible sense of community and sharing transcends all physical and geopolitical boundaries. How can we attempt to understand events in other parts of the world when we, as normal citizens, have absolutely no clue what the normal citizens in those other countries think or feel? And what about those simple facts of life like taxes and governmental services? Sure, newspapers print those info-graphics comparing our country's tax burden to those in other countries. However, that information doesn't have the same effect as listening to someone work out how much some object, say a PC, costs in France once you take the exchange rate into account and add an 18 percent VAT (value-added tax), which of course comes on top of their already high income taxes. It makes you think.

If nothing else, that's the tagline I want to convey about the Internet. It makes you think.

Maybe with a little thought and a little communication, we can avoid some of the violent and destructive conflicts that have marked world affairs in recent years. Many of the Internet resources stand as testament to the fact that people can work together with no reward other than the satisfaction of making something good and useful. If we can translate more of that sense of volunteerism and community spirit back into the real world, we stand a much better chance of surviving ourselves.

The Hardware

Getting down to the technical bits, more than 2.2 million computers of all sizes, shapes, and probably even colors make up the hardware part of the Internet. In addition to the computers, there are various types of network links: ranging from super-fast T-1 and T-3 lines, all the way down to 2400 bps modems (and you thought T-3 was a movie starring Arnold Schwarzenegger). T-3 also was one of the code names, for Microsoft Word 6.0. But I digress; that often happens when I'm talking about relatively boring things like networks because what's important is that it works and you don't notice it—just like your phone service.

The Computers

The computers that form the Internet range from the most powerful supercomputers from Cray and IBM all the way down to your personal computer. You can split these machines into two basic types: *host* computers and *client* computers. Host computers are generally the more powerful of the two and usually have more disk space and faster connections. I don't want to imply that host machines must be fancy, expensive computers. You won't always know when you're downloading files from an FTP site that the host isn't a lowly 8086 or 80286 computer. Client machines also can be large powerful workstations, but because their tasks are more limited; they require less processor power or storage space. Microcomputers make the best clients, in my opinion. Why spend lots of money and a large amount of configuration time when an inexpensive, simple-to-set-up personal computer does the job as well or better?

I look only at client hardware and software in this book because the gritty details of setting up an Internet host and the many programs that run it aren't all that interesting to most people, not to mention the fact that I haven't the foggiest idea of how to configure a UNIX workstation to be an Internet host. I'll leave those tasks to the wonderful people who are already doing them. (First rule of the Internet: Be extremely nice to your system administrator.) If you want to get into the administration end of things, O'Reilly & Associates publishes a long line of books on UNIX and network administration.

As a friend pointed out, you don't absolutely need to use UNIX on an Internet host and, in fact, you can run a Gopher or FTP server on a PC with no trouble. But this setup requires a fast and constant connection to the Internet and, again, this book is aimed more at users of Internet information, not provider wannabes.

The Networks

In basic terms, two computers attached together form a *local area network*. As that network grows, it may become connected to other independent local area networks. That configuration is called an *internet* (with a small "i"). The Internet (with a capital "I"), is the largest possible collection of inter-connected networks. I could talk about the gory details of the networks that are connected to the Internet and whether they are true parts of the Internet (as defined by using a *protocol*—which is a language that computers speak among themselves called *TCP/IP*, or Transmission Control Protocol/Internet Protocol—the language that Internet machines speak). But those details are generally pointless these days because many machines speak multiple languages and exist on multiple networks. For instance, my host machine speaks both TCP/IP as an Internet host and *UUCP* (UNIX to UNIX CoPy) as a Usenet host. My old machine at Cornell existed in both the Internet and BITNET worlds. The distinctions are technical and relatively meaningless. (Although Telnet and FTP require TCP/IP connections, whereas Usenet news uses UUCP or NNTP (Net News Transport Protocol) connections, and email works almost no matter what.)

If you use microcomputers, a *modem* makes the necessary link to the Internet. Modem stands for modulator-demodulator (glad you asked?), and it enables your computer to monopolize your phone, much like a teenager. You may not need a modem if you study or work at an institution that has its local area networks attached to the Internet, which is usually true of businesses and large universities. If you are at one such site, count yourself lucky and ignore the parts of this book that talk about finding connections and using the modem. But remember those sections exist because one day you may leave those connections behind, and nothing is more pitiful than someone pleading on the nets for information on how to stay connected after graduation.

It's beyond the scope of this book to tell you what sort of modem to buy, although most reputable modem manufacturers make fine modems with long or lifetime warranties. Suffice it to say that you want the fastest modem you can lay your hands on and, as of this writing, the fastest means that you want one with the magic word *v.32bis* stamped prominently on the box. That word, which says that the modem supports a certain standard method of transmitting information, ensures that your modem talks to most other modems at a high rate of speed, although nothing approaching a local area network. There's not much point telling you what theoretical speed a v.32bis modem talking to another v.32bis modem can reach, because real speeds vary based on several variables such as phone line quality and the load on the host. The main point to keep in mind is that it takes two to tango, and the modems on either end of a connection drop to the slowest common speed (usually 2400 bps) if they don't speak the same protocols. Just think of this situation as my trying to dance with Ginger Rogers—there's no way she and I could move as quickly as she and Fred Astaire did.

Modems connect to phone lines and residential phone lines are generally self-explanatory, although you may want to get a second line for your modem at some point. Otherwise, those long sessions reading news or downloading the latest and greatest shareware can irritate loved ones who want to speak with you. Of course, those sessions also keep telemarketers and loquacious acquaintances off your phone. I also thoroughly enjoy searching the Internet for a file, downloading it, and sending it to a friend who needs it, all the while talking to him on the phone.

One caveat to phone lines. If you connect from home, you may not want to be too forthcoming about why you want a second line. This is because business rates are higher than residential rates, although they provide no additional quality or service. Some phone companies can be sticky about using modems for non-business purposes, which is why this point is worth mentioning. If you connect to the Internet from your office, there's no way around this situation.

The Software

As for the software, the programs that probably come to mind first are the freeware and shareware files stored on the Internet for downloading. You can discover those files for yourself. This book will concentrate on the software that is available for connecting to the Internet (much of which is free). Other programs are shareware or commercial, although most of these programs don't cost much. The software for Windows will be discussed in greater detail later in the book.

For the time being, I want to hammer home a few key points that may help you understand at a more gut level how this setup works. First, these Internet machines run software programs all the time, so when you use electronic mail or Telnet or most anything else, you actually use a software program. That point is important to understand because as much as you don't need to know the details, I don't want to mystify the situation unnecessarily. The Internet, despite appearances, is not magic (although you can find a newsgroup for magicians). Second, because it takes two to tango on the Internet (speaking in terms of machines), a software program is always running on either side of the connection. Remember the client and host distinctions for machines? That's actually more true of the software, where you generally change the term host to the term *server*. So, when you run a program—say something like Fetch, which is an FTP client that retrieves files—it must talk to the FTP server program that is running all the time on the remote machine. Third, FTP and Fetch are the high-level programs that you interact with, but low-level software also handles the communications between Fetch and an FTP server.

So, if you cram the idea into your head that software makes the Internet go 'round on both a high level that you see and a low level that you don't see, you'll be much better off in the future. Some people never manage to understand that level of abstraction and, as a result, they never understand anything beyond how to type the magic incantations they have memorized. Seeing the world as series of magic incantations can be a problem because people who do that find it difficult to modify their behavior when things change.

I've tried to answer one of the harder questions around, "What is the Internet?" The simple answer is that the Internet is a massive collection of people, machines, software programs, and data, all spread around the world and constantly interacting. That definition, and the explication provided about the various parts of the Internet elephant, should serve you well as you look next at the history of the Internet.

The Internet Beanstalk

Unlike the Greek goddess Athena, the Internet did not spring from the head of some Zeusian computer scientist. It was formed by a process of relatively rapid accretion and fusion, keeping in mind that this industry is one in which computer power doubles every few years. In 1980 there were 200 machines on the Internet; now over 2.2 million are on the Internet. The grain of sand that formed the heart of this giant electronic pearl came from the U.S. Department of Defense (DoD) in 1969. I'm pleased to be older than the Internet, having been born in 1967, but I'm not that much older to talk authoritatively about world conditions at that time. Bear with me and my second-hand recounting.

Cold War Network

In the 1950s, the Soviet Sputnik program humiliated the United States. The U.S. space program, at the time under the auspices of the military, then received major government funding to better compete in the space race. That funding came from the DoD under its Advanced Research Projects Agency (ARPA). In the early 1960s, the space program left the military to become NASA, but ARPA remained—and as with many government programs that have seemingly lost their reason to exist—so did its funding. What to do with the money?

The DoD was at that time the world's largest user of computers, so J.C.R. Licklider and others proposed that ARPA support large-scale basic research in computer science. ARPA didn't originally require that the research it supported be either classified or directly related to military applications, which left the door open for far-reaching research in many fields. In 1963, ARPA devoted a measly $5 to $8 million to its computer research, the Information Processing Technologies Office (IPTO), first under Licklider, and then subsequently under the 26-year-old Ivan Sutherland, who had developed an early (perhaps the earliest) graphics program at MIT. After Sutherland, a 32-year-old named Robert Taylor headed IPTO. Taylor managed to double IPTO's budget in a time when ARPA's overall budget was decreasing and even admitted to diverting funds from military-specific projects to pure computer science.

About this time the ARPAnet (Advanced Research Projects Agency Network) got its start, connecting various computers around the country at sites performing research for ARPA. Computers were expensive and sharing them was the only way to distribute the resources appropriately. Distribution of cost via networks proved to be an important force in the development of the Internet later as well. Proponents like Taylor ensured the early survival of the fledgling ARPAnet when it was all too vulnerable to governmental whimsy.

In 1969, Congress got wind of what ARPA was up to in terms of funding basic research with money from the defense budget. Three senators, including Edward Kennedy, pushed through legislation requiring that ARPA show that its programs were directly applicable to the military. In the process, ARPA's name changed to reflect its new nature; it became the Defense Advanced Research Projects Agency, or DARPA. Bob Taylor became entangled in some unpleasant business reworking military computers in Saigon during the Vietnam War and left DARPA shortly thereafter. He was succeeded by Larry Roberts, who worked in large part to get the then two-year-old ARPAnet up and running. Stewart Brand, founder of *The Whole Earth Catalog*, wrote at the time:

At present some 20 major computer centers are linked on the two-year-old ARPA Net. Traffic on the Net has been very slow, due to delays and difficulties of translation between different computers and divergent projects. Use has recently begun to increase as researchers travel from center to center and want to keep in touch with home base, and as more tantalizing sharable resources come available. How Net usage will evolve is uncertain. There's a curious mix of theoretical fascination and operational resistance around the scheme. The resistance may have something to do with reluctances about equipping a future Big Brother and his Central Computer. The fascination resides in the thorough rightness of computers as communication instruments, which implies some revolutions. (Stewart Brand, in *II Cybernetic Frontiers*, Random House, 1974)

So if ARPA, now DARPA, had to justify the military applications of its research, what survived? Well, the ARPAnet did, and here's why. As leaders of the free world (pardon the rhetoric briefly), we had to have the latest and greatest methods of killing as many other people as possible. Along with offensive research must perforce come defensive research; even the DoD isn't so foolish as to assume we could wage a major war entirely on foreign soil. For this reason, the tremendous U.S. interstate highway system served double duty as distribution medium for tanks and other military hardware. Similarly, the Internet's precursor was both a utilitarian and experimental network. ARPAnet connected both military research sites (hardware was expensive and had to be shared) and as an experiment in resilient networks that could withstand a catastrophe—including, in the imaginations of the DoD planners of the day, an atomic bomb.

Gateways

As a result of the preceding machinations, thus was sprung the Internet Protocol, or *IP* (the second half of TCP/IP). Essentially, the point behind IP systems is that each computer knows of, or can determine, the existence of all the others and thus can route packets of information to their destinations through the quickest route, taking into account the section of the network that was bombed out or merely chopped by an over-enthusiastic telephone repairperson. This design turns out to work well and, more importantly, it makes for an extremely flexible network. If your computer can get a properly addressed packet of information to a machine on the Internet, that machine will worry about how to deliver it, translating as necessary. That's the essence of a *gateway*—it connects two dissimilar networks, translating between them so that information can pass transparently from one to the other.

In the early 1980s, the military began to rely more and more heavily on the ARPAnet for communication. However, because the ARPAnet still connected a haphazard mix of research institutions, businesses doing defense work, and military sites, the military wanted their own network. And so the ARPAnet split in half, becoming the ARPAnet and the Milnet (Military Network). The ARPAnet continued to carry traffic for research sites, and even though the military now had their own Milnet, traffic passed between the ARPAnet and the Milnet through gateways.

The concept of gateways proves important in the history of the Internet. Alongside the development of the Internet came the development of a number of other, generally smaller networks like BITNET, JANET, and a host of others, including ones like Usenet and CSNET that didn't care what transmission protocols were used. These networks were regional or dedicated to serving certain types of machines or users. Perhaps the longest running story on the Internet is the need to connect with other people and other networks. The grass is always greener on the other side of the fence, and gradually gateway sites sprung up so that email could pass between the different networks with ease.

Usenet

I'm going to take a brief break from the Internet itself, because at about the same time as the ARPAnet split, a whole host of other networks came into being, probably the most interesting of which was Usenet, the User's Network.

Usenet started in 1979 when two graduate students at Duke decided to link several UNIX computers together in an attempt to better communicate with the rest of the UNIX community. The system they created included software to read news, post news, and transport news between machines. To this day, that simple model continues, but whereas once two machines were on Usenet, today hundreds of thousands are on the network. The software that transports and displays Usenet news now runs on not just UNIX machines, but on almost every platform in use on the networks. The topics of discussion have blossomed from UNIX into almost any conceivable subject under the sun. Like all the other network entities, Usenet quickly grew to be international in scope and size.

Unlike many of the other networks, Usenet truly grew from the bottom up, rather than from the top down. Usenet was created by and for users, and no organization—commercial, federal, or otherwise—has had a hand in it. In many ways, Usenet has provided much of the attitude of sharing that exists on the Internet today. In the past, you usually got a Usenet feed (that is, have another machine send news traffic to your machine) for free (other than your telephone charges) as long as you were willing to pass the feed to someone else for free. The days of the free feeds are on the wane due to commercial pressures, but the attitude of cooperation they engendered remains in much of what happens on the Internet.

BITNET

Shortly after Usenet took its first faltering networked steps, Ira Fuchs of City University of New York and Gleydon Freeman of Yale University decided to network their universities using IBM's then-new NJE communications protocol. Although this protocol later expanded to support Digital Equipment's Vaxen running VMS and even some implementations of UNIX, the vast majority of machines on BITNET (the "Because It's Time" network) have always been IBM mainframes. Fuchs and

Freeman made their connection in the Spring of 1981, and BITNET grew rapidly encompassing over 100 organizations on 225 machines by 1984, and reaching the current level of 1,400 organizations in 49 countries around the world. Most BITNET sites are at universities and colleges and other research institutions.

BITNET has always been a cooperative network; members pass traffic bound for other sites for free and software developed by one has been made available to all. Unlike Usenet however, BITNET developed an organizational structure in 1984 in the form of an Executive Committee made of up representatives of all the major nodes on the network. Also in 1984, IBM made a large grant that provided initial funding for central-ized network support services and this grant, coupled with the fact that most of the machines on BITNET were IBM mainframes, gave rise to the erroneous rumor that BITNET was an IBM network. In 1987, BITNET became a nonprofit corporation, and in 1989 changed its corporate name to CREN, the Corporation for Research and Educational Networking, when it merged its administrative organization with another of the parallel educational networks, CSNET, the Computer+Science Network. Today, BITNET isn't on the decline, but it isn't growing at anything approaching the rate of the Internet as a whole, in large part due to the nonstandard NJE protocol in an increasingly IP world.

NSFNET

The next big event in the history of the Internet was the creation of the high-speed NSFNET (National Science Foundation Network) in 1986 to connect five supercomputer sites around the country, one of which was Cornell's Theory Center. There were only five supercomputer sites around the country at that time because supercomputers are terribly expensive, so the NSF could afford to fund only five (and even then they received some major financial help from companies like IBM). With only five supercomputer sites, it made sense to network them so that research-ers everywhere could use the supercomputers without having to travel to one of the sites. At first the NSF tried to use the ARPAnet, but that attempt quickly bogged down in bureaucracy and red tape.

The NSF therefore decided to build its own network. Merely connecting the five supercomputer sites wasn't going to help the vast majority of researchers, of course, so the NSF created (or used existing) regional networks that connected schools and research sites in the same area and then connected those networks to the NSFNET.

To quote from W.P. Kinsella's *Shoeless Joe*, "If you build it, they will come." Perhaps not surprisingly, once all of these networks were able to communicate with one another, the supercomputer usage faded into the background and other uses, most notably email, became preeminent. One important feature of the NSFNET was that the NSF encouraged universities to provide wide access to students and staff, so the population of the net increased dramatically and along with it, the traffic on the net.

In 1987, the NSF awarded a contract to a group of companies to manage and upgrade the NSFNET. This group was made up of IBM, MCI, and Merit Network, which ran the educational network in Michigan. The group dealt with the massive increase in traffic by replacing the old lines with much faster connections.

Eventually the NSFNET had entirely supplanted the ARPAnet and in March, 1990, the ARPAnet was taken down for good, having played the starring role for 21 years. Similarly, another national network, CSNET, which had connected computer science researchers around the country, closed its electronic doors a year later, all of its traffic having moved to the faster NSFNET.

NREN

The NSFNET is all fine and nice, but in many ways it discriminated against "lower" education (two-year colleges, community colleges, and the much-maligned K-12 schools). Then-Senator Al Gore sponsored a bill passed in December, 1991, called the "High-Performance Computing Act of 1991." Gore's legislation created a new network on top of (and initially using) the NSFNET. This new network is called the Interim NREN, for National Research and Education Network. Along with even faster speeds when feasible (at which point the "interim" will go away), the NREN specifically targets grade schools, high schools, public libraries, and the two- and four-year colleges. I see a lot of email addresses while working with the thousands of people who subscribe to *TidBITS*, and it's clear that these educational institutions are joining the Internet in droves. A day barely goes by when I don't see something from someone whose address clearly labels him or her as a teacher at a grade school or even a student in a high school.

Alert readers probably have noticed that NREN looks a lot like CREN and, in fact, the acronyms are similar and with reason. CREN recognizes the need for an integrated National Research and Education Network and as the IBM-created NJE protocol gradually disappears in favor of the more powerful and popular IP protocol. CREN has said that when NREN exists with access rules, funding, and usage policies that allow a clean transition to NREN from CREN, CREN will disband, merge with NREN, or cooperate with NREN as is appropriate. Currently, CREN feels that the interim NREN, the NSFNET, does not provide consistent policies regarding funding, access, and usage. And, of course, what happens if commercial organizations end up running some large part of the NREN?

Commercialization

Along with the NREN taking over the part of the Internet that was the NSFNET, more and more of the Internet is being created and run by commercial organizations. All a commercial provider needs to do is pay for its part of the network, just as universities pay for their connections and government departments pay for theirs. The difference is that unlike universities or government organizations, commercial providers want to make money, or at least break even, so they in turn sell access to their machines or networks, to other providers or end users.

The gut reaction to the commercialization of the Internet from the old-timers who remember when you could get a Usenet feed merely by asking is often negative, but most people believe that the Internet must accept commercial traffic. In part, this response is true because the alternative to accepting commercial traffic is actively rejecting it, and no one wants to sit around censoring the Internet, if it were even possible.

Commercialization also allows small organizations to create the equivalent of wide-area networks that previously only large businesses were able to afford. A company such as Microsoft can spend the money to install an international company network, but few companies are so large or so wealthy. Many companies may not need a wide-area network but may need enhanced communications. For the reasons I mentioned earlier, email can be a powerful medium for business communication just as it is for personal communication. And, if transferring a file via FTP or email can save a few uses of an overnight courier, the connection can pay for itself.

In addition, whereas in the past you had to work at a large business or university to gain Internet access, it has become easier for an individual to get access without any affiliation. Gaining easier access couldn't have happened without increased participation by commercial interests.

The commercialization issue has another side. The U.S. government still runs the NREN, which is a large portion of the Internet and connects many of the major educational sites. As more commercial providers get into the business and see the massive interest in the Internet, the more they think that the government should turn the public portions of the Internet over to them. This thought has much support because commercial providers could make money—which is what they want to do—and the government could save money, which is what many people want the government to do.

In fact, as I write this book, an impassioned plea is zapping around the Internet. This plea, poorly worded and ambiguous, claims that the government is indeed proposing to sell off the Internet—lock, stock, and barrel—which, the message claims, may result in 15 million people losing free Internet access. Such messages—some real, most not—appear every few months and it's difficult to determine whether they are real and whether you should do something about it. My advice is to do nothing until you have sufficient facts to cause you to believe that the danger is indeed real. In this instance, no contact information or pointers to current legislation exist, which makes it hard to believe without more corroboration.

The trick is to remember that someone always pays. If you have a free Internet account thanks to your school or business, remember that the institution is paying for that connection. And an increasingly large number of people, like me, pay directly (usually somewhere between $5 and $30 per month). Sure beats cable television.

So if the Internet does indeed move from governmental to private control, most people would not see the difference because their organizations would continue to foot the bill, especially if the costs don't change. The danger is to poorly-funded organizations such as grade schools and public libraries, which may be able to afford their Internet connections only with help from the government. Oh, and where do you think the government gets the money? Taxes, of course. So you end up paying one way or another.

Politics

After all this discussion, you're probably confused as to who runs what on the Internet. Good, that's the way it should be, because no one person or organization runs the Internet as such. I prefer to think of the Internet as a collection of fiefdoms that must cooperate to survive. The fiefdoms are often inclusive as well; so one group may control an entire network, but another group controls a specific machine in that network; so you as a user must abide by what both of them say or find another host.

I don't mean to say that there aren't some guiding forces. The NSF exercised a certain influence over much of the Internet because it controlled a large part of it in the NSFNET. Thus, the NSF's Acceptable Use policies (which state that the NSFNET may not be used for "commercial activities") became important rules to follow, or at least keep in mind.

Several other important groups exist, all of which are volunteer-based, as is most everything on the Internet. The Internet Architecture Board, or IAB, sets the standards for the Internet. Without standards, the Internet wouldn't be possible because so many types of hardware and software exist on the Internet. Although you must be invited to be on the IAB, anyone can attend the regular meetings of the Internet Engineering Task Force, or IETF. The IETF's meetings serve as a forum to discuss and address the immediate issues that face the Internet as a whole. Serious problems, or rather problems that interest a sufficient number of volunteers, result in working groups that report back to the IETF with a recommendation for solving the problem. This system seems haphazard, but frankly, it works.

Other networks undoubtedly have their controlling boards as well, but the most interesting is Usenet, which has even less organization than the Internet as a whole. Due to its roots in the user community, Usenet is run primarily by the community, as strange as that may sound. Every network administrator controls what news can come into his or her machine but can't control what goes around his or her machine. The converse applies as well. If a sufficient number of network administrators don't approve of something, say a newsgroup creation, then it simply doesn't happen. Major events on Usenet must have sufficient support from a sufficient number of people.

Of course, some people's votes count more than others. These people are sometimes called "net heavies," because they often administer major sites or run important mailing lists. The net heavies consider it their jobs (who knows how they manage to keep real jobs with all the work they do on the nets), to keep the nets running smoothly. Even though they often work behind the scenes, they do an excellent job. When I started *TidBITS*, for instance, I searched for the best ways to distribute it. I wasn't able to run a mailing list from my account at Cornell, and *TidBITS* was too big to post to a general Usenet group every week. After I talked with several of the net heavies, they allowed me to post to a moderated newsgroup, `comp.sys.mac.digest`, that had up to that point been used only for distributing the Info-Mac Digests to Usenet.

If you want to get involved with what organization there is on the Internet, I suggest that you participate and contribute to discussions about the future of the nets. Gradually, you'll learn how the system works and find yourself in a position where you can help the net continue to thrive.

You should keep one thing in mind about the Internet and its loose controlling structure: It works, and it works far better than most other organizations. By bringing control down to a low level, but requiring cooperation to exist, the Internet works without the strong central government that most countries use and claim is necessary to avoid lawlessness and anarchy. Hmm...

It makes you think.

The Future

I hope this chapter has provided a coherent view of where the Internet has come from, along with some of the people and networks that were instrumental in its growth. After any history lesson, the immediate question concerns the future. Where can we expect the Internet to go in the future?

I'm an optimist. I'm sure you can find someone more than happy to tell you all the horrible problems—technical, political, and social—facing the Internet. I don't hold with such attitudes about the Internet, because something that affects so many people around the world didn't appear so quickly for no reason. In one way or another, I think people understand on a visceral level that the Internet is good; the Internet is here to stay; and, if they want to be someone, they would do well to get access today. Of course, books like this one only encourage such utopian attitudes.

In any event, I predict that the Internet will continue growing at an incredible rate. You may make an argument for the rate of growth slowing from its 20 percent per month rate based on the fact that it's silly to assume that anything can continue to grow at such a breakneck speed. A naysayer also may point out that the Internet is almost out of the numbers that uniquely identify every machine. But I feel that such growth is self-propelling: that bringing more people and resources onto the Internet only further fuels the expansion. I think that growth is good: the more people, the more resources, the more opinions, the better off we all are.

I also expect to see the Internet continue to standardize, both officially and informally. At lower levels, more computers will start to use IP instead of BITNET's NJE, or the UUCP protocols. It's merely a matter of keeping up with the Joneses, and the Joneses are running IP. At a higher level, I think that using various network resources will become easier as they start migrating toward similar interfaces. Just as it's easy to use multiple applications under Windows because you always know how to open, close, save, and quit—so it will become easier to use new and enhanced services on the Internet, because they will resemble each other more and more. Even now, people rely heavily on network conventions.

And yes, I fully expect to see the Internet become more and more commercial, both in terms of where the service comes from and in terms of the traffic that the Internet carries. However, we must remember the old attitudes about commercial use of the Internet. In the past, commercial use was often acceptable if it wasn't blatant, was appropriately directed, and was of significant use to the readers. In other words, I'll be as angry as the next person if I start receiving automatically generated junk email every day, just as I receive junk mail via snail mail. If such things start happening, the course of action will be the same as it always has been—

politely ask the originator to stop once and then flame away (send back an outrageously nasty message).

I don't believe that the Internet will be governed to a greater extent than it is now in the U.S. (other countries are different), simply because I don't believe that most governmental organizations understand the Internet well enough to do so. Even then, how can you govern something that spans the globe or police something that carries gigabytes of data every day? The way the government as a whole currently views the Internet reminds me a bit of the joke about how to tell if you have an elephant in your fridge. The answer is by the footprints in the peanut butter—it's the middle of the night, and the government is standing at the open door, yawning and blinking at those massive footprints. Luckily, portions of the government are starting to wake up, which should help dispel the dangerous ignorance that has marked certain past government actions on the Internet.

Part II

Internet Foundations

So far we've looked at the Internet only in the abstract, and it's important that you have an overview of the world that you are entering. Like all things electronic, however, the Internet is terribly picky about the details; you must know exactly what to type and where to click. Unlike on your friendly local Windows PC, though, on the Internet real people see what you type, so I also talk about the social customs of the Internet, the manners, and mores that everyone eventually learns. And, because I hope the Internet becomes something about which you talk with friends, I try to pass on some of the jargon and modes of speech. First, you will look at names, addresses, and email in chapter 5, followed by an exploration of Usenet news in chapter 6, and end in chapter 7 with a look at the services that are available only if you have a full connection to the Internet: services such as FTP, Telnet, Archie, WAIS, Gopher, and the World-Wide Web.

Keep in mind that this information is all background—I don't tell you the specific details of how to deal with programs on the Internet or the like until Part III.

Text Styles

As a convention, I write all network addresses, whether they are only machine names or full email addresses in this `monospaced font`. Note also, that any punctuation following the address is not part of the address itself; instead it's required by my seventh grade English teacher, who was adamant about ending clauses with commas and sentences with periods. Every now and then I leave off a period when it confuses an address that ends a sentence, and the thought of her beet-red face (I'm sure she was very nice, but she reminded me of a lobster) looming over always makes me add that period. So remember that addresses never have punctuation at the end.

I indicate commands that you type exactly as written in this other **typestyle**, and when there is a variable that you have to fill in, I'll put it in italics. So **TYPE** *this* means to type the word **TYPE** followed by whatever is appropriate for this: a file name, a directory name, a machine name, or whatever.

Finally, any text that shows up as though it scrolled by on a terminal window connected to a UNIX machine appears in its own monospaced font on lines by itself, much like the following two lines.

```
To: The Reader <reader@tisk.book.net>
Subject: Style conventions...
```

Chapter 5

Addressing and Email

Before you learn about email or retrieving files via FTP, or much of anything else, it is beneficial to have a discussion about how email addresses are formed, where they come from, and that sort of thing. After an addressing discussion, the wide world of email is explored in greater depth, relating some of the uses and customs that you will encounter.

Addressing

A rose may be a rose by any other name, but the same is not true of an Internet computer. Not surprisingly, all Internet computers think of each other in terms of numbers; people think of them in terms of names, also not surprisingly. The Internet uses the *domain name system* to make sense of the millions of machines. In terms of the numbers, each machine's address is composed of four numbers, each less than 256. People are notably bad about remembering more than the seven digits of a phone number, so a *domain name server* was developed. The domain name server translates between the numeric addresses and the names that real people can remember and use.

Despite the fact that Internet numeric addresses are all sets of four numbers, the corresponding name can have between two and five sets of words. After five, it gets out of hand—so although it's possible, it's not done. The machine I use now is called `tidbits.com` (two words), for instance. The machine I used at Cornell was called `cornella.cit.cornell.edu` (four words). The domain style addresses may look daunting, but in fact they are quite easy to work with—especially when you consider the numeric equivalents. Each item in those addresses, separated by the periods, is called a *domain*. In the following sections, you are going to look at them backward, or in terms of the largest domain to the smallest.

Top-Level Domains

In any machine name, the final word after the last dot is the *top-level domain* (although, to no one's surprise, British addresses are reverse, though usually translated when sent out of the country) and a limited number of them exist. Originally—and this shows the Internet's early Americo-centric view—six top-level domains indicated to what type of organization the machine belonged. Thus, we ended up with the following list:

```
com = commercial

edu = educational

org = organization, usually nonprofits

mil = military

net = network

gov = government
```

That setup was all fine and nice for starters. However, as the number of machines on the Internet began to grow at an amazing rate, another solution became necessary. The new top-level domains are based on countries, so each country has its own two-letter domain. Thus, the United Kingdom's top-level domain is uk, Sweden's is se, Japan's is jp, Australia's is au, and so on. (Check the news.answers newsgroup for a regularly posted list of country codes. Every now and then another country comes on the Internet, and I see a domain code that totally throws me, as Iceland's is code did the first time.) The United States has this system as well. Thus, The Well, a popular commercial service with links to the Internet, is `well.sf.ca.us`. Unfortunately, because so many sites already existed with the old domain names, it made no sense to change them. So we have both types of top-level domain names here in the U.S., and you just have to live with this system.

You may see a couple of other top-level domains on occasion: `bitnet` and `uucp`, as in `listserv@bitnic.bitnet` or `ace@tidbits.uucp`. In both of these cases, the top-level domain indicates that the machine is on only one of the alternative networks and doesn't also exist directly on the Internet (otherwise, it would have a normal top-level domain such as `com` or `uk`). This setup isn't a big deal these days because so many machines exist on both networks that your email gets through just fine in most cases. In the past, few connections existed between the Internet and BITNET or Usenet, so getting mail through one of the existing gateways was more difficult. Keep in mind that because a machine whose name ends with `bitnet` or `uucp` is not actually on the Internet, you cannot use Telnet or FTP with it.

My current machine name, `tidbits.com`, is as simple as it gets: a machine name and a top-level domain. Many other addresses are more complex because other domains are in the middle. Think of an address such as `cornella.cit.cornell.edu` as one of those nested Russian dolls. The outermost doll is the top-level domain, the next few dolls are the mid-level domains, and, if you go all the way in, the final doll is the userid (see figure 5.1).

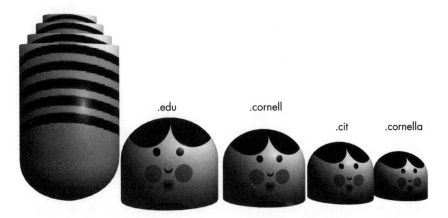

Figure 5.1 *The Russian doll approach to Internet addresses.*

Mid-Level Domains

What do these mid-level domains represent? It's hard to say precisely because the answer can vary a bit. The machine I used at Cornell, `cornella.cit.cornell.edu`, is an example of one way to set up the mid-level domains. As a recap, the machine name is `cornella`, and the top-level domain is `edu`, (because Cornell claims all those undergraduates are there to get an education). The `cit` after `cornella` is the department, Cornell Information Technologies, that runs the machine known as `cornella`. The next part, `cornell`, is obvious; it's the name of the overall organization to which CIT belongs. So, for this machine anyway, the hierarchy of dolls is, in order: machine name, department name, organization name, and organization type.

In the machine name for The Well, `well.sf.ca.us`, you see a geographic use of mid-level domains. In this case, `well` is the machine name, `sf` is the city name (San Francisco), `ca` is the state name (California), and `us` is the country code for the United States.

Middle-level domains spread the work around. The Internet obviously can't have machines with the same name; otherwise, chaos would erupt. But because the domain name system allows for middle-level domains, the administrators for those middle-level domains must ensure that everyone below them stays unique. In other words, I can actually name my machine `cornella.com` because that name is completely different from `cornella.cit.cornell.edu` (why I'd want to, I don't know). And, if they want, the administrators at CIT can put a new machine on the net and call it `tidbits.cit.cornell.edu` without any trouble for the same reason. More importantly, the administrators don't need to bother anyone else if they want to make that change. They control the `cit` domain, and as long as all the machines within that domain have unique names, there are no problems. Of course, someone must watch the top-level domains because it's all too likely that two people may want `tidbits.com` as a machine name. (But I've already got it, so they can't have it.) That task is handled by the Network Information Center, or NIC. You needn't worry about naming problems as a user, because you should have a system administrator who knows who to talk to about naming.

There is yet another way of handling the mid-level domains, this time in terms of intermediate computers. Before I got my current address, I had a feed from a machine called `halcyon`, whose full name was `halcyon.com`.

My machine name was `tidbits.halcyon.com`. In this case, `tidbits` was my machine name, `halcyon` was the machine through which all of my mail was routed, and `com` indicated that the connection was through a commercial organization. I realize that this example is a bit confusing, but I mention it because it's one way that you can pretend to have an Internet address when you really have only a UUCP connection (a different sort of connection that transfers only email and news). All my mail and news came in via UUCP through `halcyon`, so by including `halcyon` in my address, I created an Internet-style address.

The other way of pretending that a UUCP connection is a real Internet connection for address purposes is to have your host set up an *MX record*, which stands for Mail Exchange and is a pointer on several true Internet machines to your site. That's what I use now. However, because `tidbits` is truly a UUCP site, theoretically you also can reach me by sending email to `ace@tidbits.uucp`. Mail sent that way isn't generally as quick or reliable, however.

Machine Name

The next part of my machine name is the machine itself, `tidbits`. In my case, the machine is a Macintosh SE/30, but people use all sorts of machines. Because the system administrators often are a punchy, over-worked lot, they tend to give machines silly names. Large organizations with more centralized control lean more toward thoroughly boring names, such as the machine at Cornell which was called `cornella` (as opposed to `cornellc` and `cornelld` and `cornellf`). One reason for boring names in the early days was that machines on BITNET were required to have names with between six and eight characters. Coming up with a meaningful unique name within that restriction became increasingly difficult. Usenet doesn't put a limit on the length of names, but requires that the first six characters be unique.

If you remember that machines often exist on the Internet as well as one of these other networks blurring the distinctions, you'll see the problem. Internet machines don't, as far as I know, have any rigid limitations on names, so any alternative connections dictate what names are acceptable. Although possible (another machine at Cornell was called `crnlvax5` on BITNET and `vax5` on the Internet), most machines have only one name. This naming convention makes life easier.

There is one caveat to this multiple name issue. Often, special services keep their names even when they move to different machines or even different organizations. Because of this situation, a machine that runs a service may have two names: one that goes with the machine normally, and one that points solely at that service. The anonymous FTP site that I use to store all the software I talk about in this book, for instance, is called `ftp.tidbits.com`. But in fact, it runs on a machine called `halcyon.com`, and I could move it to any other machine while still retaining the `ftp.tidbits.com` name. This situation is not a big deal one way or the other.

To summarize, you can have multiple domains in an address. The farther you go to the right, the more general they become, often ending in the country code. Conversely, the more you go to the left, the more specific the domains become, ending in the userid because that part of the address is the most specific. Time to talk about the userid, I guess.

Userid

Now that you've looked at the machine name, you can move on to the *userid* or *username*, which identifies a specific user on a machine. Both terms are equally correct and commonly used. If you set up your own machine or work with a sufficiently flexible provider, you can choose your own username. Choosing your own name is good because your correspondents can then more easily remember your address, assuming, of course, that you choose a userid that makes sense and is easy to type. If I made my address `ferdinand-the-bull@tidbits.com`, I would be disliked by people who typed the address slightly wrong and had their mail bounced back to them.

Internet userids cannot have spaces in them, so convention dictates that you replace any potential spaces with underscores, dashes, or dots, or omit them entirely. Other reasonable userids that I could use include `adam_engst@tidbits.com` or `adam-engst@tidbits.com` or `adam.engst@tidbits.com` or `adamengst@tidbits.com`. All of these names are more difficult to type than `ace@tidbits.com`, and because I have good initials, I stick with them.

Unfortunately, there are a limited number of possible userids, especially at a large site. So Cornell, for instance, with its thousands of students and staff, has opted for a system of using initials plus one or more digits—

because initials aren't all that unique either. (In fact, I once asked for my initials as a userid on one of Cornell's mainframes and was told that ACE was a reserved word in that machine's operating system, but no one could tell me for what it was reserved.)

Microsoft uses a different scheme yet: first name and last initial (using more than one initial to keep the userids unique). As Microsoft has grown, the common names like David have been used up, so the company has started in on other schemes such as first initial and last name. Why am I telling you this? Because knowing an organization's scheme can prove useful at times and so that I can note a societal quirk. At places like Microsoft where people use email so heavily, many folks refer to each other by email names exclusively. Every now and then I must ask my wife to translate when she starts talking about someone from work in terms of her userid, and I don't recognize it. My wife, Tonya, also had a problem with her username, tonyae (first name and last initial) because it looks more like TonyAe than TonyaE to most people.

The real problem with assigned userids comes when the scheme is ludicrously random. Some universities work student ID numbers into the userid, for instance; and CompuServe userids are mere strings of digits like 72511,306. I believe the scheme has something to do with octal numbers or some such technoweenie hoo-hah. I don't speak octal or septal or any such nonsense, and as a result I can never remember CompuServe userids.

Remember that email addresses point at an individual, but when you're using Telnet or FTP, no individual is involved. You simply want to connect to that machine and you have to connect sans userid. This restriction may seem obvious, but it often trips people up until they get used to it. For example, it seems that you could just FTP to anonymous@space.alien.com. The system doesn't work that way, though, and you FTP to space.alien.com, and once there, log in as anonymous.

Punctuation

Enough about userids. What about all this punctuation? Better known as Shift-2 on U.S. keyboards, I imagine the @ sign came into use because it's a single character that generally means "at" in traditional usage. The @ sign is generally universal for Internet email, but not all types of networks have always used it. For instance, some BITNET machines once required that you spell out the word, as in the command TELL LISTSERV AT BITNIC HELP. Luckily, almost everything uses the @ sign with no spaces these days, which reduces four characters to one, and has probably saved untold person-hours of typing over the years.

As long as you're learning about special characters, look at the dot. It is, of course, the period character on the keyboard and it serves to separate the domains in the address. For various reasons unknown to me, the periods have become universally known as dots in the context of addresses. When you tell someone your email address over the phone, you say (or rather I'd say because it's my address), "My email address is ace at tidbits dot com." The other person must know that "at" equals the @ sign and that "dot" equals the period. If he's unsure, explain yourself.

Alternative Addresses

You may see two other styles of addressing mail on the Internet, both of which work to sites that aren't actually on the Internet itself. The first is the older of the two and is called *bang* addressing. It was born in the early days when there were relatively few machines using UUCP. Not every machine knew how to reach every other machine, so the trick was to get the mail out to a machine that knew about a machine, that knew about a machine that knew about your machine. Talk about a friend of a friend! So, and this setup still works—sort of—today, you may be able to send email to an address that looks like uunet!nwnexus!caladan!tidbits!ace. This address then bounces the mail from uunet to nwnexus to caladan to tidbits and finally to my userid on tidbits. This approach assumes that your machine knows about the machine uunet (run by the commercial provider UUNET) and that all of the machines in the middle are up and running. All the exclamation points are called "bangs," appropriately enough, I suppose. On the whole, this style of addressing is slow and unreliable these days, but if you use a machine that speaks UUCP, you occasionally can use it to your advantage. For instance, every now and then, I try to send email to a machine that my host, nwnexus, can't reach for some reason. By bang-routing the mail appropriately, I can make another Internet machine try to send the mail out, sometimes with more success.

The other sort of special addressing is another way to get around the fact that your machine, or even your network, isn't connected to the Internet as such. In this case, you must provide two addresses: one to get to the machine that feeds your machine, and one to get to your machine. The problem here is that Internet addresses cannot have more than one @ sign in them. You can replace the first @ sign with a % sign, and the mailers then try to translate the address properly. My old address, `ace@tidbits.halcyon.com`, also could have been `ace%tidbits.uucp@halcyon.com`. These tricks are ugly and awkward, but sometimes necessary. Luckily, as the Internet grows and standardizes, you need fewer and fewer of these addressing tricks.

Electronic Mail

Electronic mail is the most pervasive application on the Internet, and for good reason. What better way to communicate with so many people so quickly? But to use and understand email properly, you should know how it's constructed, the social mores and pitfalls, and the uses to which you can put it.

Email Construction

What makes up an email message? Most messages have two important parts, with a third part that doesn't have to appear. The first two parts are the *header* and the *body* of the message, and the third—non-essential part—is the *signature*. For simplicity's sake, let's work backwards.

Signature

Many email programs—including Eudora which is included on the disk—provide a facility for creating signatures. Signatures are just about what you'd expect—some text that goes at the bottom of every message you send. Most people include their names (real or pretend) in their signatures, and it's considered good form to include your preferred email address in your signature as well (just in case the address in the header isn't useful for some reason or another). After you get past the basics of name and email address, however, you can put anything you like in your signature. Many people lean toward the clever quote or manage to express some sporting partisanship of their favorite team, usually with an erudite "Go Weasels '93" or some such. It's hard to grunt in ASCII. I prefer clever quotes. Especially if they are changed once per day—not that I have time or energy to think them up or type them in every day. Here is a signature that must have taken some time to create because all the lines and dashes had to be typed in the right place:

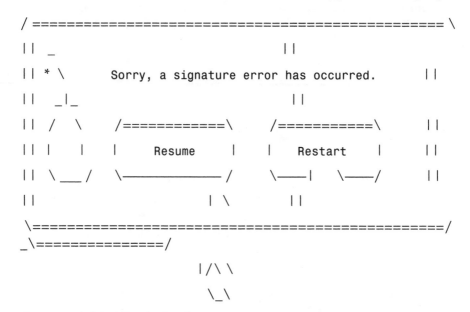

Courtesy of A. Marsh Gardiner, `gardin@harvarda.harvard.edu`

Many people also use signatures to disclaim their messages. The signature acts as a disclaimer. It usually states that the opinions and facts stated in the preceding message have no relationship to the organization paying for the account or employing the individual. Disclaimers are important online because readers have no context in which to take postings. If Ferdinand the Bull posts a glowing review of a specific species of cork tree, for example, he should also note at the bottom of his review that he is a paid consultant of Corking Good Times International and is therefore biased. More common are glowing reviews from users who "have no relationship with Corking Good Times International, other than as a satisfied customer." Disclaimers also serve to ensure that no one takes the words of a single employee as the policy of the entire organization. Marketing departments hate that. "But Joe said online that Microsoft was going give free copies of Flight Simulator to everyone whose birthday falls on the second Tuesday of odd months this year." "Yeah, sure buddy."

One warning, however, in mailing lists that are *digestified*—that is, lists in which a moderator collects the day's messages and concatenates them into a single file—postings with multiple line signatures are frowned on or even rejected. This suggestion makes sense, if you think about it. A big digest file can have 50 messages in it, and if every person has a four-line signature, the digest suddenly becomes 200 lines longer than necessary.

Body

What you put in the body of your letter is your business. I can recommend several practices, however. First, get in the habit of pressing the Enter key twice between paragraphs to insert a blank line between paragraphs; that additional white space makes email messages much easier to read. Nothing is harder to read than page after page of unbroken text.

Actually, something is worse than unbroken text, and that's page after page of unbroken text in capital letters. DON'T USE ALL CAPS BECAUSE IT LOOKS LIKE YOU'RE SHOUTING! No one uses all capital letters for long because everyone hates reading it and will tell you (nicely the first time), to stop.

I suppose now is a good time to talk about manners in terms of the sorts of things you should consider when writing email. Email differs from normal mail in many ways. Think of the difference between a short note to your mother, a memo at work, and a formal business letter. Most email falls in between the short note and the memo, and seldom do you ever see an email message with the formality and rigidity of a business letter. Although I'm giving this information in the context of email, it applies equally as well to postings on Usenet; if you like, reread this section, substituting posting for email everywhere.

How do you start these messages? In many ways, email acts as the great equalizer. Most of the time, you know someone's name and email address when you send email to him, nothing more. JoeSchmoe@alien.com could be a janitor, a summer student intern, or the president of what is actually a Fortune 500 firm. Similarly, any address ending in edu can link to a student, some member of the staff, a world-renowned professor of underwater basket weaving, or the president of the university. You have no way of knowing, unless that fact somehow comes up in conversation.

Most people react to this lack of context by treating everyone with the same level of polite, but informal, respect. Seldom do people use their titles, so equally seldom do correspondents use those titles in email.

Everyone is on a first-name basis. I once took a class with the astronomer and science advocate Carl Sagan while at Cornell, and the first day of class, an awed undergraduate (but braver than the rest of us) asked, "How should we address you, Dr. Sagan?" He replied, "You can call me Mr. Sagan, Professor Sagan, Dr. Sagan, or Herr Doktor Professor Sagan," he paused, "or you can call me Carl." Carl it was then, and the class benefited greatly from that level of informality, just as the Internet does.

In light of this knowledge, when I started using email I thought about the differences between email and paper mail (hereafter called by its true name in the Internet community, snail mail). The standard salutation of "Dear" sounds inappropriately formal and stilted to my ears (apologies to Miss Manners) and because email more closely resembles spoken communication than written, I opted for the less formal and more colloquial "Hi," which has served me well since then. Some people forego the salutation completely, relying solely on the first name, but that approach feels abrupt to me, as if someone called me on the phone and stated my name without a "Hello" or so much as a questioning tone. Do what you like though; no one has laid down rules on this matter.

What you say in the letter itself deserves more thought, however. Because email is so quick and it's so easy to respond without thinking, many people often reply hastily and less politely than they would had they taken a moment to consider. Remember, you want to achieve a certain effect with an email message, just as you do with any form of communication. If you just whack your first thoughts into an email message, they probably don't properly convey your true wishes. If you want information from someone, phrasing your request politely only increases your chances of getting that information, and if you wish to comment on someone else's words, doing so in a reasoned and level-headed manner ensures that that person doesn't immediately consider you a serious jerk.

You also must remember that informal as email may be, it lacks most of the nonverbal parts of communication that we seldom consider in normal speech. All inflection, body language, and facial expressions disappear, and it doesn't help one whit if you make them while composing the letter. Email is ASCII text only, and only two ways exist to convey inflections such as sarcasm or irony that would be obvious in spoken conversation. First, polish your writing skills. There is no substitute for clear and coherent writing. Many people find writing difficult, but I recommend that you don't think of composing email as writing, but as speaking to someone who sees your words but cannot see or hear you. Most people who claim they can't write have little trouble making themselves understood when speaking.

Second, utilize *smileys*, or as they are sometimes known, *emoticons*. Smileys are strings of punctuation characters meant to be viewed by tilting your head (which is usually easier than tilting your monitor) to the side. People have come up with literally hundreds of different smileys, and you can find lists containing hundreds of them on the Internet. Seth Godin has even compiled many of them into a book, *The Smiley Dictionary*, published by Peachpit Press (and there is at least one other book, published by O'Reilly & Associates, on the same topic). I take the view that only two, or maybe three, smileys are at all useful in normal email. The first is the happy face **:-)**, which implies that what you just said was meant as humor or at least shouldn't be taken too seriously. I often use it to imply that I would have said that bit with a smile. A variant of the happy face uses the semicolon instead of the colon **;-)** and (because of the wink) implies that the preceding sentence was somewhat sarcastic or ironic. Finally, the frowning face **:-(** implies that you aren't happy about whatever you just said.

I use smileys heavily in email, when I don't have time to craft each letter as carefully as I would ideally like. I miss not being able to use them (I could, but no one would understand) in snail mail occasionally, and I actively try to avoid using them in *TidBITS*, favoring instead words that convey my feelings without the smiley crutch. When in doubt, use smileys. If I say in email, "Well, that was a stupid thing to do," the message carries a lot more weight than if I say, "Well, that was a stupid thing to do. :-)." Believe me, it does.

I may have given the impression that the Internet is this utopia where everyone always behaves nicely and ne'er is heard a discouraging word. That unfortunately is not the case. In reality, you see plenty of *flaming* on the nets. Flaming can happen when you innocently mention that you like your Macintosh in a PC discussion list and seventeen people immediately jump on you in email and in the discussion and pummel you within an inch of your electronic life for saying something so obviously stupid and incorrect. Everyone knows that only weenies, wimps, and little wusses use those toy Atari computers, which are good only for paperweights—and expensive paperweights at that—because you can buy three completely configured top-of-the-line 486-based PCs for the same price as a used Atari 520ST without a hard drive. And by the way, did I mention that your mother wears combat boots and your father wears ballet slippers? :-)

The preceding paragraph is flaming (except for the smiley, which I threw in to indicate that I was kidding about your parents' footwear), and if you must flame, do it in the special newsgroup that is specially lined with asbestos, alt.flame. If you must respond to an inflammatory message, which I don't recommend, do it in email. No one else wants to read your flames. Think before you lower yourself to flaming; it never solves anything. I have found in almost every case that replying calmly and clearly embarrasses anyone (assuming that person is normal and rational, which is not always a good assumption) so thoroughly that she immediately apologizes for being such a jerk. And yes, I know how hard it is not to just tee off on someone. Restrain yourself and rest assured that everyone who sees your restraint will think more highly of you for it.

Often, people flame companies or large organizations that are doing stupid things. The government is a favorite, slow-moving and unchallenging, target. This sort of flaming is more acceptable, although you may start a *flame war* if other people don't share your opinions on some major topic, such as whether the Mac is better than Windows. As a spectator, you may enjoy watching the occasional flame war, as I do, but again, they never solve anything and they waste a huge amount of *bandwidth* (which is composed of transmission time, people time, and disk storage throughout the world).

Keep in mind that no matter what you say, it may not be private. Always assume that gobs of people can and do read every message you send. These people include your coworkers, your system administrator, system administrators on other machines through which your email travels, random pimply-faced fools who like poking around in other people's email, and last, but certainly not least, the government, probably in the form of the CIA, FBI, or the National Security Agency. I realize this news sounds alarming, and it is most certainly not completely true, but the possibility exists for all of these people to read your email.

In reality, email carries significant privacy, but because you have no guarantee of that privacy, you should stay aware of what you're saying. This suggestion is especially true if you send email at work! This lack of privacy carries over to mailing lists and Usenet news (where you want people to read your messages, but you may not want the government to keep tabs on your postings). In fact, some people have gone so far as to include inflammatory keywords in otherwise innocuous postings, just to trip up the rumored government computers scanning for terrorists, assassins, space aliens, nudists, vegetarians, people who like broccoli, and other possible undesirables.

Header

Okay, I admit it; I've been avoiding talking about the header so far. That's because the message header generally looks like a lot of gobbledy-gook to the novice user and, in fact, it should. The header exists for the computers, not for the users. You're lucky that you can read it as well as you can. In some programs you can see an abbreviated header, which is good; in some programs you can ignore the header altogether, which can be a little dangerous because it may not be clear who receives a reply to that message.

As much as the header is technoweenie information that exists primarily for the computers to route mail to you, I recommend that you choose an abbreviated header display if you have one. An abbreviated header shows you information that can be useful, such as who sent the email to you, when it was sent, what the subject of the message is, and to whom it was sent (not always just you—it's easy to send the same piece of email to multiple people).

Take a look at a typical header, culled from one of my archived pieces of email:

```
From TC.Cornell.EDU!baka!mha Mon Jul 19 07:08:08 1993
Received: by tidbits.com (uA-1.6v2); Mon, 19 Jul 93 11:04:17 PDT
Received: from THEORY.TC.CORNELL.EDU by nwnexus.wa.com with SMTP
id AA18636
    (5.65c/IDA-1.4.4 for <ace@tidbits.com>); Mon, 19 Jul 1993
08:32:37 -0700
Received: from baka.UUCP by theory.TC.Cornell.EDU with UUCP id
AA02180
    (5.65c/IDA-1.4.4 for ace@tidbits.com); Mon, 19 Jul 1993
11:32:32 -0400
Received: from BAKA (QM 2.6) by baka.ithaca.ny.us (UMCP\QM 2.1.3)
 id AA05891; Mon, 19 Jul 1993 11:32:36 EDT
```

The preceding lines are merely routing information that tell you where a message went and when it arrived there. You have to read it backwards to follow the flow. This message traveled from the QuickMail server at BAKA Computers to the UMCP Bridge (`baka.ithaca.ny.us`), which acts as a gateway for QuickMail messages destined for the Internet. From there it traveled to Cornell's Theory Center, `theory.TC.Cornell.EDU`, and from the Theory Center, the message bounced almost instantly to `nwnexus.wa.com`, which is my Internet host, and then several hours later to my machine, `tidbits.com`.

You generally can ignore this part of the header, although it can be fun to see where your message went at times. If your message *bounces*—that is, if it fails to go through for some reason and comes back to you—looking at this part in the header helps you determine how far it got and which machine didn't like it.

```
Message-Id: <00192.2825926356.5891@baka.ithaca.ny.us>
```

The Message-Id: line uniquely identifies each message. Only once have I found this information useful. For some reason, one of my hosts was duplicating some files that went out, and often the only difference between the messages was that at a certain point they started having different Ids. Of course, I never figured out how to solve the problem; I just switched to another host.

```
Organization: BAKA Computers Inc.
```

The Organization: line identifies the organization of the sender, as you may suspect. Individuals often have a good time with this line because they don't have real organizations to put down.

```
To: ace@tidbits.com (Adam C. Engst),
        Rick_Sutcliffe@faith.twu.ca (Rick Sutcliffe)
```

The To: line can have one or more entries, and it specifies, reasonably enough, to whom the mail was sent. The recipient may not be you because you may be the person mentioned in the Cc: line or even the Bcc: line (which you don't see because Bcc: stands for Blind Carbon Copy). Most of the time you see a name before or after the email address, but it's not mandatory.

```
From: mha@baka.ithaca.ny.us (Mark Anbinder)
```

The From: line indicates who sent the email and is self-explanatory.

```
Date: Mon, 19 Jul 1993 11:08:08 EDT
```

The Date: line lists the date that the email was sent originally, not the time you received it or read it, and should usually indicate the time zone in which the sender lives. Even then I find it difficult to keep track of what time it is in other countries. Do you know the local time in Turkey right now? Some messages use a number, either positive or negative, and the acronym GMT, which stands for Greenwich Mean Time. Unfortunately, this use requires that you know what time it is in Greenwich, England, and that you know how your local daylight savings time is involved. Times zones always throw me.

```
Subject: Terminal Compromise
```

The Subject: line should give a clear and concise description of the contents of the email message. In practice this description often isn't true, especially after a discussion proceeds, changing topics occasionally, with everyone using the Reply function to keep the Subject: the same. After a while the Subject: line bears no resemblance to the contents of the message, at which point it's time to change the line.

```
Cc: werner@rascal.ics.utexas.edu (Werner Uhrig)
```

The Cc: line lists all the people who received copies of the message. There is no functional difference from being on the To: line or the Cc: line, but in theory if you receive only a copy, the message shouldn't concern you as much. In practice, I don't notice a difference.

An abbreviated header probably just shows the last five lines and certainly avoids displaying the routing information at the top of the header.

You also may see other lines in the header that identify which program mailed the message, to whom the recipients should reply, the type of data included in the message, how the data is encoded, and the like. In general, you don't need to worry about anything in the header very much, but it's worth taking a look every now and then to see if you can tell what's going on in there.

Using Email

All email programs share some basic features that you need to read quickly and efficiently, reply to, and to store your email. However, after these basic commonalities, the differences between email programs mount quickly, so I concentrate on those differences when I talk about each program later in the book. For the moment, though, look at what an email program must do at a minimum.

Reading Mail

An email program should enable you to display and scroll through an email message easily. Because you're using Windows, you should be able to do all the standard editing things to text in a window, such as copying and pasting into a different program, resizing the window to display more text, selecting all the text with a single command, and that sort of thing. Although you usually can choose the font and size in which you view messages in Windows email programs, I recommend that you stick to a monospaced font such as Courier New or System. This is because people on the Internet must format tables and graphics with spaces and monospaced fonts such as Courier New and System in order to display these tables and graphics properly. Proportionally spaced fonts such as Times New Roman and Arial don't work as well because the characters in these fonts can have different widths, with a lowercase "i" being thinner than an uppercase "W". Obviously, few of these features are easily available with a UNIX mail program; that's one of the major advantages of using Windows.

Navigating and Managing

Another important feature of an email program is the manner in which it enables you to move between messages, save messages in different mailboxes, and delete unwanted messages after you've read them. Most email programs display a list of the messages in an In Box area, and some indicate which messages you have already read, replied to, or saved to disk. Opening a message usually opens a new window to display the message, and sometimes closing the window opens the next message to be read. The capability to sort the list of messages is useful on occasion, and you should be able to select multiple messages at once to move them to another mailbox or delete them.

Speaking of multiple mailboxes, all email programs should support them, although unfortunately not all do. Most people want to save some of the messages they receive, so a program should enable you to create your own mailboxes for filing away messages on different topics. Of course, you can create a new mailbox. Your email program should enable you to do everything that you can do in your In Box to the messages stored in a personal mailbox.

While you're managing your email, you will undoubtedly want to delete many of the messages you receive. This area may seem straightforward, but the better email programs enable you to throw away a file without actually immediately deleting it. The easier it is to delete a message (and it should be easy), the more likely you will eventually delete something accidentally and, if the email program deletes immediately, your message is toast. The other advantage of the two-stage (where a message is put in a wastebasket can before being deleted later) or a delayed delete (where a message is marked as being deleted but isn't actually deleted until you close the mailbox) is that you then don't have to put up with an annoying confirmation dialog box each time you delete a message.

Some of your messages may, in fact, contain programs or other files that you want to save to a normal DOS or Windows file. A few email programs automatically detect programs encoded in a certain format (more about that later) and decode such messages on their own. But one way or another, you need a simple way to save the message you're looking at without copying and pasting the entire thing into a word processor.

Replying

Much of the mail you receive requires a reply of some sort. An email program should make replying extremely easy, either with a command key shortcut or a single click on an icon. An email program also should facilitate *quoting* the original message, or prefixing each line with one or two special characters, usually a greater-than sign and a space. Using quoting, you can easily include some of the message you're replying to so that the recipient has some context to know what you're talking about. A nice feature is the capability to select a certain part of the original mailfile and have the email program quote only the selected text in the reply and ignore the rest of the original message.

Because email may have originally been sent to several people, an email program should give you the option of replying only to the sender or to all the people to whom the message originally went. At the same time, an email program should ideally ensure that you see the salient lines in the header. I've spawned a couple of embarrassing scenes by forwarding a message to a friend, and when my friend replied to me, his email program saw that mine had included the original message's address in the Reply-To: line in the header. So his reply, rather than going only to me, went back to the sender which was a mailing list that went to thousands of people. Oops! Luckily, I didn't say anything embarrassing and neither did he. That's a good example of how two computer professionals, who know better, could have been thoroughly embarrassed in public. Think of this situation as standing up in a crowded restaurant and shouting loudly that your underwear has holes. You get the idea.

More powerful email programs provide features that automatically can mark or reply to email based on the contents of the header or the body of the incoming message. They often generalize these features so that you can essentially run a *mailserver*, which sends out requested information automatically via email. You also can use this sort of feature to run a mailing list, which takes a message to a certain local address and forwards it automatically to a list of subscribers.

New Mail

Both when replying to email and when creating new mail, an email program should provide all the features you're used to when you're writing in a Windows word processor. In my opinion (which is by no means universal), the editors in the character-based DOS or UNIX world stink (yeah, I know those are fighting words), and I spend so much time writing and editing my email that I couldn't possibly put up with anything other than a decent graphical editor. However, because every email program implements text entry and editing on its own, none of them compare to a full-fledged word processor, and a few barely even compete with the free Notepad. My dream, which isn't all that far off, is to be able to use my word processor for all of my email. With the growing acceptance of Object Linking and Embedding (OLE), this change will happen. I just hope it happens sooner rather than later.

I may be odd in this respect, but I think that any email program should make it easy to save a copy of everything you write, preferably automatically. I send more email than most people, some 600 messages last month, but I like to be able to go back on occasion and see what I said, forward a message to someone who lost it, or just browse through the thoughts that appeared in my writings at that time. Why bother to keep a diary if you're writing about most of what happens in your life in email to friends?

Finally, whenever you create email, your email program should enable you to send the mail to a *nickname* or *alias*, which is merely another, easier-to-remember, form of an email address. So instead of typing `ferdinand-the-bull@cork.tree.com` every time you want to send that person email, you can type the shorter `Bull`. You have to be careful with nicknames because it's easy to create more than you can remember easily, at which point they don't particularly help any more. Defining nicknames for everyone you may ever send email to is a waste of time; settle for defining a nickname only after you decide that you are likely to send that person email frequently.

You also want to be slightly careful with nicknames because occasionally the recipient sees the nickname as well as the address. A friend once created a nickname DA BOSS for our supervisor, who fortunately thought it was funny when she saw it. I could think of some less humorous situations.

Finding People

Now you know how an email program should work, how to read email addresses when you see them littering up this book, and the nets in general. But how do you find people to write? Finding people to write to depends on what you're looking for. Hmm? What does he mean by that?

Assume that there are two types of people: those you already know and those you haven't yet met. The latter group makes up most of the world and, in some respects, are the easiest to find and talk to because you don't really care who specifically you end up talking to. After all, you don't know any more about one person than another, so who you talk to makes no difference.

Friends

When I first started using the networks way back when, few of my friends had accounts and, of them, only my best friend from high school ever managed to send me email more than once. I think I got a total of three messages from him. I tried to convince them, but I just couldn't get my friends to use email. Finally, I decided they all truly hated me (a logical conclusion for a 17-year-old college freshman) and gave up on them. My ego has recovered some since then because I've found that convincing people to start using email just to talk to me is actually almost impossible. This argument worked with my parents after a while, and especially after my sister also started using email heavily at Cornell. But otherwise? I can't think of a single person who I've convinced to use email for my sake, and I don't even attempt to convince my grandparents. The moral of the story is that you should assume that you can talk only to people who already use email.

Okay, so once past that reality check, how do you find the address of someone you know who uses email? The simplest and most effective method seldom occurs to many net denizens—use the telephone and ask them. This method, low-tech as it may be, has the advantage of being quick, accurate, and easy. Of course, it does ruin the surprise value of that first email note. Such is life. You do need to know your friend's telephone number, or failing that, her address so you can call the all-knowing information computers at the phone company. If you don't even know where your friend lives, she may be trying to hide from you anyway after that ugly incident a while back.

"Aha!" you say, "If the all-knowing phone company computers can give me my friend's telephone number, aren't there all-knowing computers on the Internet that can give me my friend's email address?" Nice try, and good question, but the answer is unfortunately, maybe. Most computers know what users they support, and you can find some information via a program called *finger*, but that information doesn't help unless you already know what machine to search. Several attempts have been made at linking various directory services on different machines, but frankly, I've never found them the slightest bit useful. The problem is twofold. First, hooking a local directory of users to an Internet-wide directory requires some effort and certain standards, and inertia being what it is, that effort isn't always made and the standards don't exist. Second, many organizations shield their users from the outside world for reasons of security and privacy. These shields also make it difficult to determine how many people actually use the Internet because one machine name may have a single user, like `tidbits.com`, or around 14,000 users, like `microsoft.com`.

That said, I know of several services you can use to find people. However, because using these services relies on details you have yet to look at, you must wait until later in the book. Patience is next to something, if not godliness.

Acquaintances

As I said earlier in this chapter, finding new friends is easy on the Internet. You don't know people beforehand, so communicating with them in a discussion list via email or news requires nothing in terms of opening lines or trivial small talk about the fallibility of weather forecasters. If you have something to contribute to a discussion, or perhaps if you merely want to make a private comment to one of the people in the discussion, meeting him is as easy as replying to his message. Whether that first contact grows beyond a one-time message depends on many variables, but with so many people, finding correspondents on the net doesn't take long.

As much as meeting people may be easy, finding them again after some time often proves more difficult. You may not remember where a person lives, if you ever knew and if it's in the United States at all; you probably don't know his telephone number; and frankly, you may not even remember how to spell his name. And yet, all too often I've had long, involved conversations that eventually trail off after several weeks or months, and then I don't hear from that person again. If I haven't saved a message (which contains the all-important email address in the header), or recorded his email address somewhere, I must hope that my friend has better organizational systems than I do.

I suggest then that you figure out some way to keep track of your correspondents' email addresses. Nickname features work well, although they may prove unwieldy as a storage mechanism later. If that's true, I recommend using a standard database or address book program that can handle an extra field for email address. This advice may sound obvious, but I can't tell you how many times I've lost an address that I wanted several months later. These days I keep a copy of every piece of email I send, often as many as 1,000 per month. I can search that file, large as it may be, for email addresses that have escaped my short-term memory.

Mailing Lists

There's no accounting for taste and, similarly, there's no accounting for different interests. I may be interested in electronic publishing, tropical fish, and competitive distance running; whereas the next person may favor "The Simpsons," aviation, and Irish culture. As a result, discussion groups have sprung up around almost every imaginable topic, and if your area of interest isn't represented, it's not too hard to start your own group. These groups take two forms: mailing lists and Usenet newsgroups. I talk more about Usenet in the next chapter; for now I concentrate on mailing lists.

The beauty of mailing lists is that they cover specific topics and they come straight to you, without any extra work on your part. If you find yourself interested in a topic, you can subscribe to the appropriate mailing list and all the traffic comes directly to your electronic mailbox. This system makes participating in many mailing lists easy, even if you have only email access to the Internet; Usenet access may require more money and effort. Luckily for those of you who cannot get Usenet access, many mailing lists and newsgroups mirror each other.

Mailing lists have several other advantages over Usenet news. Email is ubiquitous on the Internet, whereas access to news is far less common (although certainly extremely widespread). Because of the way Usenet news propagates throughout the nets, mailing lists often arrive faster than any given posting in a newsgroup may. Because mailing lists arrive in your electronic mailbox, they may seem less intimidating than large newsgroups with many participants. And, frankly, many of us who lead busy lives find mailing lists easier to keep up with because we don't have to run another program to read the list. Whereas reading news always requires leaving that ubiquitous email program and running a newsreader.

You can split mailing lists into groups along several different lines: moderated versus unmoderated, individual messages versus digests, and LISTSERV versus UNIX mailing lists. Each of the possibilities changes how you interact with the list. Let's look at each in turn.

Moderated vs. Unmoderated

I suspect many mailing lists started out *unmoderated*, which means that anyone was able to send a message on any topic (whether or not it was appropriate to the group) to the list, and the list software distributed that message to the entire list. You see the problem already—no one wants to read a bunch of messages that have nothing to do with the topic or discussion at hand. Similarly, if a discussion is spinning out of control and turning into a flame war, it's just a waste of bandwidth and time.

Thus was born the concept of the moderated mailing list. To stem inappropriate postings, a moderator (always a volunteer), reads all the postings before they go out to the group at large and determines which ones are appropriate. Moderated groups tend to have less traffic, and the messages that go through are guaranteed by the moderator to have some worth. This system is good. On the downside, moderated groups sometimes run into sticky issues of censorship, because the moderator may not always represent the wishes of the majority of the readers. Moderator positions are volunteer only; I've never heard of a mailing list that elected a moderator—although it's certainly possible, particularly among lists that carry traffic associated with a professional organization.

I see no reason to choose to read or not read a mailing list based on its moderation until you've seen what goes on in the group for a while. I subscribe to various lists (some moderated, some not), and on the whole, both have their places. Keep in mind that if you post to a moderated list, the moderator may reject your posting. Don't feel bad, but do ask why so that your future submissions stand a better chance of reaching the rest of the group. On the other hand, when posting to an unmoderated group, try to stick to appropriate topics because people hate hearing about how you like your new car in a list devoted to potbellied pigs. Too many misdirected postings to a list, and the list members may start agitating for a moderator to limit the discussion.

Individual Messages vs. Digests

When the number of messages in a mailing list increases to a certain level, many lists consider creating a digest version of the list. A *digest* is simply a single mailfile that contains all the individual messages concatenated in a specific way. Why bother with a digest? Depending on how your email program works, you may find it awkward to receive and read as many as 30 messages a day (especially if your email service charges you a per-message fee to receive email). Just think how many messages you may have waiting after a week of vacation. If the messages are sent in digest form, a mailing list becomes easier to handle for some people because you get one big mailfile rather than lots of little messages. Often, it's not an either/or decision, since many mailing lists have a digest setting that you can toggle on and off, depending on which form you prefer.

Unfortunately, digests have problems too. Some email gateways to commercial services limit the size of incoming email messages. Thus, digest mailing lists can range in size from just a few bytes to over hundreds of kilobytes, so very few issues of the digest sneak through the gateways with size limitations. In addition, you may find it easier to read (or skip through) small individual messages, whereas scrolling through a 100K file can take quite some time and be extremely awkward with some email programs. To add to the complication, certain email programs can break up a digest into its individual messages for easier viewing. I'm talking the email equivalent of digestive enzymes here.

You have to decide for yourself whether a digest is easier or harder to work with, but only with some groups do you have a choice. That's the breaks. If you feel that a group should have a digest, consider volunteering to assemble and distribute one. The Internet works this way: if you see something you don't like, fix it.

LISTSERV vs. UNIX Mailing Lists

Two main types of mailing list software exist on the Internet. The first is the Revised LISTSERV program, created by Eric Thomas of LSoft. The second, and arguably less powerful, mailing list software is an extension to the UNIX mail software. You may wonder why LISTSERV doesn't have an "E" at the end and why it is spelled with all capitals. LISTSERV software has existed for some time, originating on (and still requiring) IBM mainframes attached to BITNET that run the VM/CMS operating system. The operating system these IBM mainframes use limits userids to eight characters (hence the missing "E"), and because the operating system itself is not case sensitive, all commands and program names traditionally have been typed in uppercase only. The name also may have had something to do with early computer terminals not supporting lowercase, but I can't prove that theory. Just believe me. By convention, LISTSERVs are always addressed in the uppercase, although it doesn't really matter any more.

The LISTSERV program sports many sophisticated features for managing large mailing lists, and these features have made the LISTSERV software popular among the people who start and run mailing lists (you didn't think they just worked on their own, did you?). For instance, you can easily and automatically subscribe to and sign off from a LISTSERV-based mailing list without bothering a human (in most cases), which significantly reduces the amount of work the list administrator has to do. In contrast, mailing lists based on the UNIX mail software usually have no such automatic subscription facilities—although some list administrators have automated the process to a certain extent. LISTSERVs also have provisions for tracking the subscribers to a list and for those who want to remain unknown, concealing certain subscriptions.

LISTSERVs can prevent unauthorized people from sending messages to the list. The *TidBITS* list works this way in theory because only I can send a message, in this case an issue of *TidBITS*, to the list. I say "in theory" because in practice the safeguards have broken down twice, resulting in confusing messages going to the entire list. The LISTSERV also knows to route all replies to postings on the list to me directly (which is normally good), but when these two accidental postings got through the safeguards, I received hundreds of messages from confused readers who didn't know why they had gotten this message. It was a major hassle.

Finally, LISTSERV software knows about other LISTSERVs running on other machines around the world and uses this knowledge to limit network traffic. For instance, I send a single message from my machine to a mainframe at Rice University in Texas that runs the LISTSERV handling the *TidBITS* list. Once the message arrives at Rice, the LISTSERV software checks to ensure that it came from me and then sends it out to the thousands of readers on the *TidBITS* subscription list.

The LISTSERV is smart, however. It doesn't blindly send out thousands of mailfiles, one per user, because that would waste network bandwidth, especially on expensive trans-oceanic satellite or cable links. Rather, the LISTSERV determines how to enlist the help of certain other LISTSERVs running around the world. If it knows of a LISTSERV site in Australia, for instance, it sends a single copy of the message to Australia along with the distribution list of Australian readers. If 100 people in Australia subscribe to the *TidBITS* list, only one message crosses the Pacific instead of 100 identical copies of the same message. That's elegant.

UNIX mail-based mailing lists don't have nearly as many features as the LISTSERV software, but they are easier to set up and run for an individual user with an account on a UNIX machine and a bit of UNIX knowledge. And, more importantly, they run under UNIX, which is more prevalent on the Internet than IBM mainframes (which are generally considered to be dinosaurs). Of course, not all IBM mainframes are dinosaurs, and UNIX programs inspired by, and to a certain extent compatible with, Eric Thomas's LISTSERV software have appeared. In addition, other mailing list programs run specifically under UNIX, although they are generally less prevalent than the LISTSERV software. Don't worry about it one way or another; you have no choice when picking mailing lists to which you are subscribing. And despite all the added features of the LISTSERV software, the thing that makes the administrative details of a list easy to deal with is the administrator, not the software.

Using LISTSERVs

Most people find dealing with LISTSERVs quite easy; however, you should watch out for a few common pitfalls while working with LISTSERV-based mailing lists.

Every LISTSERV list has two email addresses associated with it: the address for the LISTSERV itself and the address for the mailing list. Why the dichotomy? Well, the LISTSERV address handles all the commands (things like subscriptions and requests for lists of subscribers and the like), and the mailing list address is where you send submissions to the list, assuming of course that it's that sort of list. Here, I use the *TidBITS* list as an example for my illustrations of the basic tasks you do with a LISTSERV-based mailing list. The only difference between the *TidBITS* list and many others is that if you send mail to the mailing list address, it doesn't go to everyone else on the list because the *TidBITS* list is dedicated to distributing *TidBITS*, not to discussion, as are most lists. Any mail sent to the mailing list address comes to me, which is fine, because such messages are usually comments on articles.

If you want to send the LISTSERV that handles the *TidBITS* list a command, such as your subscription request, you send it to `listserv@ricevm1.rice.edu`. Notice that nowhere in the address is *TidBITS* mentioned, which is a hint that you have to specify *TidBITS* somewhere else. LISTSERVs ignore the Subject line entirely, so don't worry about filling it in at all. In the body of the message, however, you can put one or more commands, each on its own line.

To subscribe to the *TidBITS* list, you send the preceding address a message with the following command on one line in the body of the message: **SUBSCRIBE TIDBITS** *Jane Doe*, where you replace "Jane Doe" with your real name, not your email address or some cute nickname. If the list administrator needs to contact you about a problem, she probably doesn't appreciate having to address you as "Dear Swedish Chef Fan Club Ork Ork Ork." To clarify the preceding command, to subscribe to any LISTSERV mailing list, you send the **SUBSCRIBE** command, a space, the name of the list to which you want to subscribe, a space, and then your full name (which should be at least two words). I don't know how Cher or Prince manage with the LISTSERV.

The LISTSERV always returns a welcome note after you have subscribed successfully. Keep that note! It lists various useful commands, such as how to sign off from the list and it usually provides the address of the list administrator. You can contact the list administrator to handle any problems that the automated program chokes on.

After you have subscribed to a list, you mainly want to post messages to the rest of the people on the list. Once again, to post a message you send it to the mailing list address, which is always the name of the list at the same machine. If, for example, you want to send mail to the *TidBITS* list (which comes only to me), you send the email to tidbits@ricevm1.rice.edu. I realize I've almost beaten this particular horse to death, but I can't emphasize enough the difference between the LISTSERV address and the mailing list address. You send commands to the LISTSERV and submissions to the mailing list address. Perhaps the most common problem I see on LISTSERV mailing lists is that people forget to send commands to the LISTSERV address and fill up the mailing list with the electronic equivalent of junk mail that no one wants to see. And, of course, sending commands to the mailing list address isn't just annoying and flame-provoking, it's futile because the LISTSERV doesn't respond to them there.

After you've been on a list for some time, the LISTSERV may ask you to confirm your subscription. I set this option with the *TidBITS* list to clean the deadwood from the list every year. Students graduate, employees move on, bulletin boards close up, and those addresses don't always go away, so the LISTSERV wastes network resources sending to a non-existent person, much like talking to a politician. After you have received *TidBITS* for a year from the LISTSERV, it sends you a nice message asking you to confirm that you still want to get the newsletter. If you don't respond within seven days, the LISTSERV removes you from the list, assuming that you don't want to continue receiving email from it.

If you respond, you must respond with a command so that you send it to the LISTSERV address, not the mailing list address. The command is simply **CONFIRM TIDBITS** (or the name of the list you are asked to confirm). A significant portion of the time this confirmation process fails. If you noticed in the preceding paragraphs, nowhere do you provide your email address to the LISTSERV, which is supposed to determine it from the header of your message. This idea seems excellent at first because the header should, in theory, have your email address correct and it doesn't suffer from typos or simple human mistakes that you make if you type it in by hand. However, depending on the routing that your mail takes and how you or your system administrators have set up your system, your address as it appears in the header may change from time to time. Those changes play havoc with the LISTSERV, which is a very literal program. Therefore, when you confirm a subscription, if that confirmation comes from an address the LISTSERV doesn't recognize, poof, it doesn't work. You probably still receive mail to the original address just fine because the address is usually merely a variant on the theme, so many people sit helplessly by as the LISTERV asks for confirmation, rejects it, and then calmly deletes them from the list.

This situation is a perfect example of why computers should never be given direct control over human lives. If you don't properly match for some reason, you're just another file to be deleted.

There is a simple fix. Just resubscribe as soon as the LISTSERV sends either the confirmation rejection or the message saying that it has deleted you from the list. You may get duplicates of everything for a few days, but then the LISTSERV deletes your old address and continues to send to your new one.

If you blow it and misspell your name while subscribing or perhaps decide to change your name for one reason or another, you can always change just your name with the LISTSERV by sending another **SUBSCRIBE** command. The danger here, as discussed above, is that if your address looks at all different from when you originally subscribed, the LISTSERV happily adds you to the list again, and you receive duplicates of everything. Now is a good time to ask the list administrator for help because the LISTSERV recognizes only your new address, so you can't delete your old address. Bit of a Catch-22 there.

This Catch-22 can apply to trying to sign off from a list normally as well. Under standard circumstances, if you send the command **SIGNOFF TID-BITS** to the LISTSERV address, it removes you from the list. If your address in the header has changed, however, it doesn't recognize you as a current subscriber and thus doesn't let you sign off. Once again, if you need help beyond what the LISTSERV program can provide, don't hesitate to ask the list administrator—but ask nicely. These people don't get paid to take abuse and, in fact, they don't get paid to administrate a list at all. See the following paragraphs for details on how to contact a list administrator.

The reason for this seemingly irritating address feature is that administrators realized early on that it would be way too much fun to sign up other people for mailing lists, if you really don't like someone. You can, for example, sign them up for all the special offers in the back of *The National Enquirer*. Some friends of mine once had a war with that game, but one was declared the loser when he received bronzed baby shoes and a free subscription to a white supremacist newsletter, or some such nonsense. I'm sure it would be great fun to sign Bill Gates up for a really far-out mailing list, but it gets old after a while and is generally considered abuse of the networks.

Some LISTSERVs can send you files if you send them proper commands in a message. The LISTSERV at Rice, `listserv@ricevm1.rice.edu`, is one of these sites. You can find site-specific information by sending a **HELP** command to any LISTSERV, and for the standard LISTSERV information, send **INFO REFCARD**.

LISTSERVs support a number of other commands, of which only a few are generally useful. If you want to see a list of all the people who have subscribed to a LISTSERV list, you can use the **REVIEW** command. For instance, if you want to receive a 300K message listing all the subscribers to *TidBITS* (and I don't really recommend you do so unless you like reading lists of names and addresses), send email to the LISTSERV address, `listserv@ricevm1.rice.edu` with the following line in the body of the message: **REVIEW TIDBITS COUNTRIES**. I threw in the COUNTRIES modifier (it's not necessary) because it instructs the LISTSERV to sort the subscribers by country and to include a count of subscribers for each country at the bottom, which is neat.

The other utility of the REVIEW command is that it includes the address of the list administrator at the top, so it's a good way to find out who to ask for help. Using the REVIEW command is a good way to see what address the LISTSERV thinks you used to subscribe and then ask the administrator for help. For just the administrator address, you can change the command to **REVIEW SHORT**.

Budding direct marketers should be aware that if you request a bunch of subscriber lists and use them for nefarious marketing purposes, (a) that feature is immediately turned off in most lists, and (b) I personally lead the flamethrower crews on a mission to turn you into a fine electronic ash. That sort of opportunism doesn't fly on the Internet.

Most of the other commands that LISTSERVs support aren't as interesting, or as much fun to write about, so I refrain and move on to Usenet in the next chapter.

Chapter

6

Usenet

Enough about email. It's time to turn now to Usenet. I've talked generally about how we now have thousands of newsgroups (my host machine carried almost 4,000 at last count) on every imaginable topic. How is this different from the mailing lists we've just looked at? I see two primary differences between mailing lists and Usenet news, neither of which has to do with the information that flows through.

First, although mailing lists may be faster to propagate because they go directly to the subscriber, think of how inefficient that system can end up. If only one person on a machine reads a mailing list, one copy comes in. However, if 100 people on that machine all read the same mailing list, then 100 identical copies of each posting must come into that machine, eating up disk space and slowing down the communications for other tasks. This setup is bad. In contrast, only one copy of every Usenet message goes to each machine, and any number of people can read that single message. So in the preceding example, you can reduce the load on your machine by 100 times by reading the Usenet newsgroup rather than the mailing list that provides the same information (if that is indeed true, which is not always the case). If you keep in mind that nothing is free, even though you may not see any money change hands, you also see the financial advantage of Usenet over a mailing list.

Second, many people like mailing lists because they always read their mail, but they may not always run a separate program to read news. This situation is true, but works in favor of news as well. Most email programs are designed for a relatively small number of messages, each completely different and unrelated. In contrast, most newsreaders concern themselves with large numbers of messages, many of which are related, or in a *thread*. So, if you read the news and come across an interesting posting, reading the next posting in that thread is trivial (or at least it should be), whether or not the posting is the next one in the list. Following threads in an email program is generally difficult or impossible.

Given those advantages, how does Usenet work, what do the messages look like, and what are the basic types of information?

Usenet Plumbing

For the most part, you don't need to know how Usenet actually works because it isn't in the slightest bit important to daily life. However, the basic principles may help you understand some of the quirks and limitations of Usenet.

The entire concept of Usenet is based on one machine transferring the postings to another. Scale that idea up so that any one machine carrying Usenet talks to at least one other machine carrying Usenet. You start to see how an idea that has remained simple can become an immense and powerful reality with the addition of thousands of machines and millions of people and megabytes of data per day.

If you post a message in a Usenet group, your machine passes the message on to all the machines it talks to, both *upstream* and *downstream*. Upstream loosely refers to the machines that your machine generally gets all of its news from, and downstream loosely refers to the machines that get all of their news from your machine. In either case, those machines continue to propagate your message throughout the network, with the Usenet software that controls this system ensuring your message isn't duplicated *ad infinitum* (Latin for "a hell of a lot of times, which irritates everyone").

The actual process by which your message travels is equally simple. The Usenet software creates a batch of messages to go out and compresses the batch to reduce transmission time. When the next machine receives the batch, it unbatches the messages and places the files in directories in which the news reading software knows where to find them. One testament to the simplicity of this scheme is that not all implementations have to use this technique (and in fact, another common method of transferring news sends only the text of articles a specific reader requests while reading news). Some Windows news readers create a single file for each newsgroup and appends new messages to that single file. However, most UNIX machines store the messages as individual files within specific directories and those directories are directly related to the names of the newsgroups, which you look at next.

Newsgroup Innards

Just as email addresses make sense after you know all the parts, there is a reason behind the rhyme of the Usenet newsgroup names. They look a little like email addresses, with all the dots, but the principle is a bit different. Let's dissect the name of a popular newsgroup, say `comp.os.ms-windows.misc`.

First, here is a quick note on the punctuation. Usenet newsgroups use periods, or dots, to separate the different parts of the name, just like different domains are separated by dots in email addresses. For some reason, people tend not to use the dots when speaking about newsgroups. If you were to tell a friend about an interesting discussion on `comp.os.ms-windows.misc`, for example, you'd say "Check it out on comp os ms-windows misc." Part of the problem may be the linguistic clumsiness of saying all those "dots," but I suspect that more of the reason is that precision isn't nearly as necessary because you seldom type out newsgroup names, unlike email addresses.

The entire premise of the Usenet newsgroup name scheme is that of a hierarchy. The name scheme makes figuring out how to name new groups easy and, more importantly, it maps over to a hierarchical directory (or folder) structure. On the UNIX machines that hold the newsgroups, therefore, you will find a directory called `news`. Inside that directory sit other directories corresponding to the top-level parts of the hierarchy: `alt`, `comp`, `misc`, `news`, `rec`, `sci`, and so on. These directories are abbreviations for alternate, computers, miscellaneous, news, recreation, and science, respectively.

If we continue with our example of `comp.os.ms-windows.misc` and look into the `comp` directory, we see more directories corresponding to `lang`, `os`, `sys`, and so on. Under `os` we find many directories, one for each operating system; there are `cpm`, `ms-windows`, `ms-dos`, `vms`, and gobs of other systems that you may have never even heard of. I certainly haven't heard of all of them. After we go into the `ms-windows` directory, we find the lowest level directories that correspond to the individual topics about Microsoft Windows, including `advocacy`, `announce`, `misc`, `nt`, `programmer`, `setup`, and others. Once inside those directories (feel like you're in a Russian doll again?), you find the files that hold the text of the messages (see figure 6.1).

Figure 6.1   *The Usenet hierarchy tree.*

This system may seem a tad clumsy, but remember as a user you don't need to traverse that entire directory structure. It exists to categorize and classify newsgroups and to provide a storage system that maps onto a UNIX directory structure.

Message Construction

On the surface a Usenet posting looks much like an email message. The posting includes a From: line and a Subject: line, and a fair amount of other stuff in the header. Then comes the body of the message and a signature. The header has a few new lines that you might find interesting.

```
Newsgroups: comp.os.ms-windows.misc
```

First comes the Newsgroups: line, which lists, separated by commas, all the newsgroups to which the message is posted. You can post a message to more than one group at a time by putting more than one group in the Newsgroups: line—at this point an article is *cross-posted*. If you must post an article in several groups (which is generally frowned on as a waste of bandwidth), make sure to post via the Newsgroups: line and not through individual messages. Individual messages take up more space than cross-posted articles because a machine stores only one copy of a cross-posted article along with pointers to it from different groups.

```
Follow-up-To: comp.os.ms-windows.misc
```

The next Usenet-specific line is the Follow-up-To: line, which usually contains the name of the newsgroup in which the article appears. Sometimes, however, you want to post an article in one group, but then have discussion move back to another group. In this case you put the second group in the Follow-up-To: line because whenever anyone posts a follow-up to your article, the news software makes sure that it ends up in the proper group.

```
Keywords: news, reviews, PCI, MS Office, OLE 2.0

Summary: The latest issue of a free weekly electronic newsletter.
```

Sometimes you see a Keywords: and/or Summary: line as well. Although not universal or enforced, it's often a good idea to fill in these lines for your article before you post it. That way, people who have set up their newsreaders properly can more effectively filter articles based on keywords. In addition, some newsreaders show only the header and first few lines of an article, and then let the reader decide if she wants to read that article. A few well-chosen keywords or a concise summary can help make that decision easier.

`Distribution: world`

Many articles are only relevant in specific geographic areas. You have two ways to handle this situation. First, if you're selling a car in Seattle, for instance, you can post to a specific group that goes (more or less true anyway) only to people in Seattle: `seattle.forsale`. Many of these site-specific groups exist, even down to the machine, so there's a group, `halcyon.general`, for discussion about issues affecting users of the `halcyon.com` machine.

The other method of handling this situation is to use the Distribution: line, that enables you to limit the area to which your message is distributed, even if the group encompasses all of Usenet. So if you want to post a notice about a Seattle British Car Show in `rec.autos`, you can put `seattle`, or possibly `pnw` (for Pacific Northwest) in the Distribution: line. However, you should keep one thing in mind: You should distribute many messages to the world because if the messages are not important enough to send to everyone in the world, they are often not important enough to post at all.

`Subject: NT App Note#987/29-Feb-93 posted in comp.os.ms-windows.nt.setup`

Here is a word too about the ubiquitous Subject: line. As much as it is courteous for you to provide a descriptive Subject: line in an email message, it's imperative that you do so in a Usenet posting. Most newsreaders these days show the user a list of the messages and their subjects, and if you don't provide a good Subject: line, far fewer people even notice your message.

Using Usenet

No matter what software you use to access Usenet, you must be aware of some basic concepts, tasks, and features. When the various different newsreaders are evaluated for you later in the book, I refer to these tasks and features and whether the newsreader in question does a good job of handling them for you.

Subscribing

When you first invoke a newsreader, you must subscribe to the groups you want to read. Occasionally, the newsreader automatically subscribes you to a couple basic groups, such as news.newusers.questions and news.announce.newusers. For the most part, however, the thousands of available newsgroups are in the unsubscribed category. I include a list of most of the available newsgroups in appendix D; you can flip through the appendix to see which groups you may want to read.

Generally, the first time you start up, a newsreader takes a long time because you must go through all the groups and determine to which ones you want to subscribe. The better newsreaders enable you to sort through the list at different times. In the past you had to sit for an hour or more just unsubscribing from all the groups you never read. It was a major hassle. Even now, allot plenty of time to your first newsreading session if you're doing it interactively (this rule doesn't apply to a UUCP connection, where you request only specific groups).

Reading Articles

After you subscribe to a group, the time comes to read the articles. Obviously, the first time you read, all the articles are new to you—but after that, you want to make sure that you read only previously unread articles. Most newsreaders are extremely good about keeping track of what you've read already. In the UNIX world, the .newsrc file tracks what you've read, and advanced users can edit that file manually with a UNIX text editor to subscribe or unsubscribe from several groups at once. Windows newsreaders make that task unnecessary on the whole.

You've already learned what the header for a Usenet article may look like, but many newsreaders hide most of the header from you, which is generally helpful, although a pain at times.

Discussions happen in *threads*, which are groups of related articles, generally with the same or very similar Subject: lines. Threads are important because they group both discussions that you want to read and those that you don't want to read. I will show you why that difference is a big deal later in this section.

When it comes to reading news, two basic philosophies exist. The first, which is older and not particularly popular these days, holds that you want to read 90 percent of the information in a newsgroup. To achieve this goal, the newsreader tries to show you the text of every article unless you explicitly tell it to skip that article or thread. This method may have worked better in the days when Usenet traffic was relatively sparse, but in these modern times, the traffic comes fast and thick. I liken this situation to trying to drink from a fire hose.

The second newsreader philosophy believes that you want to read only 10 percent of the articles in any given group. With the exception of moderated groups or low-volume groups where every message counts, this philosophy is far more realistic. These newsreaders usually provide a list of the unread messages in a newsgroup and then let you pick and choose which ones to read. Some newsreaders force you to read each message or thread as you pick it, whereas others make you pick a whole bunch of them at once and then read them after you've sorted through the entire newsgroup. Both of these methods have their advantages, and a good newsreader lets you do both.

Navigation

After you start reading a set of messages, you need tools for navigating them. These navigation tools were more important back in the days when character-based UNIX newsreaders were all we had because many of the Windows newsreaders replace the navigation commands with mouse actions. However, many people find the keyboard to be a better interface to reading news than a mouse anyway, so perhaps there's still room for old tools in a new world.

The most common navigation capability takes you to the next unread message, whether or not it is in the same thread as the message that preceded it. Closely related is the capability to move to the next unread message in the same thread, even if it's not next to the message you were just reading. In a well-designed newsreader, these two capabilities are closely intertwined, so the newsreader doesn't force you to know whether or not you're in a thread.

Often, these capabilities are served by a single command linked to the Spacebar, which is the largest key on the keyboard and the easiest to hit. The Spacebar thus serves as an unusual command for computers, essentially saying to the newsreader, "Do whatever makes the most sense right here." Computers hate those sort of commands, but the concept works extremely well in a newsreader where you probably want to read all of an article. The Spacebar scrolls down the page; when you hit the bottom of the article, you probably want to read the next article in the thread, so the Spacebar takes you to the next article. When you finish all the articles in that thread, you probably want to go back up and read the next thread, so the Spacebar takes you back up. Finally, after you read everything in a newsgroup, the Spacebar assumes that you want to read the next newsgroup you subscribe to and take you there. By intelligently guessing the way the user wants to read, a number of commands can all be subsumed under that one key. Too bad not all newsreaders subscribe to this concept.

You want to group discussions into threads so that you can easily read an entire one—even when it spans a fair amount of real world time. You also want to group discussions so you can ignore them more easily. Despite the fact that people should include descriptive Subject: lines in their postings, they don't always follow that rule well. If you see a long thread called "Cool Stuff," you have no idea what it's about. It may pique your curiosity, so you start reading, only to find out that it's another "my computer is better than your computer" flame war. Now you need a way to kill the entire thread and good newsreaders make that effort easy because otherwise it's a pain for you to get past the drivel to the information you want again.

An even neater feature is the capability to create a list of Subject: lines or topics about which you never want to read. This capability usually applies to anything in the header and sometimes to information in the body of the messages too. It is extremely useful for customizing your Usenet reading experience.

After you read all the messages that interest you, it's generally a good idea to mark the rest of them as read (even though you didn't) so that you don't see them again the next time you read news. Some newsreaders handle this option for you automatically, whereas others make you mark them manually as read. Sometimes, especially if you just returned from a vacation, you may want to mark everything as read without even trying to read the waiting messages. Marking everything lets you start with a clean slate and with a manageable number of messages the next day and is generally referred to as *catching up*. There's no difference between a "catch up" feature and a "mark all as read" feature, but you may see both in different programs.

Now you know all about navigating around Usenet and reading articles to your heart's content; many people never move past that point. They're called *lurkers* and, although the term has no negative connotation, it simply means people who only read and never post.

rot13

I almost forgot. You may occasionally run across articles that are completely unreadable. They may be in a newsgroup specific to a language you don't understand, but the newsreader can't help with that problem. It can, or should be able to anyway, help you with messages coded in the *rot13* format. rot13 is a simple coding scheme that assigns a number to each letter of the alphabet, starting with 1 for A and so on for every character in a message. It then adds 13 to each number and converts back into letters. The result is an utterly unreadable message, which the poster usually intended because some people may find the message offensive. If you see such a message and you are easily offended, don't read it. No one forces you to use the rot13 decoding feature that exists in most newsreaders, and if you do use that feature to read the message, you can't very well complain about the contents. I usually see the most rot13 encoded postings in joke newsgroups, usually protecting the innocent from really sick jokes.

Replying

In the course of reading Usenet news, you often see messages that aren't quite clear or that catch your interest for some reason or another. When you see such a message, you may want to send email to the poster. You could, of course, if this weren't a reasonable world, copy down the poster's email address from the header onto a little piece of paper, and when you finish reading news, use your email program to send him a message. However, that process is a bit of a pain, so most newsreaders support sending mail while you're reading news.

Use email replies whenever the rest of the group doesn't give a hoot about what you have to say to the poster. Most of us feel that our words are pearls of wisdom. But you should try to step back and think about whether your reply is best directed at the individual making the posting or the group as a whole.

People often ask questions on Usenet, saying that you should reply directly to them and that they plan to summarize to the net. Listen to what these people have to say; they only want replies via email, and because they've promised to post a summary of the replies they get, you don't need to send them mail asking for a copy personally (unless perhaps you don't stand a chance of seeing the summary in the newsgroup, and even then, ask nicely). If you ever post a question and promise a summary, live up to your promise even if you get only a couple of responses. No matter how many responses you get, format them nicely with quotation mark characters before each quoted line so that they are easy for readers to understand; messages are often confusing as to who wrote what in a summary. Never repost entire headers.

As far as what you say when you reply to postings on Usenet, read what I said about email manners earlier in this chapter. If you must carry out a flame war, do it in email; but if possible, don't do it at all.

Follow-up

Discussions are the entire point of Usenet, of course, so you eventually gather the courage to post something to a newsgroup. For most people, the easiest way to post a message is to reply to another message, an action called *following up*. A follow-up is easier for the novice because the newsreader fills in most of the lines in the header for you; the Subject:, Newsgroups:, Distribution:, and so on are generally determined by the message to which you reply.

Just as in email, you should be given the chance to quote the previous message so that readers have a chance at understanding the context of your message. Some newsreaders are picky about the proportion of quoted text to new text, and for good reason. No one wants to read a two-screen quoted letter only to see at the bottom a few words from you, "I agree with all this." Even in newsreaders that don't prevent you from overquoting, be careful and try to edit out as much of the quoted text as possible. Remember that most people have already seen that message in its original form, so you're jogging their memory more than restating the entire message. Definitely remove signatures and unnecessary previously quoted text.

Using Usenet as a method of getting a message to a specific individual is considered extremely bad form, even if you can't seem to get email to that person. Just think, everyone's discussing nuclear disarmament, and you suddenly see a message from a college friend. Your note discussing old times at Catatonic State University holds absolutely no interest for the rest of the group, and if you find yourself being flamed, suffer and don't do it again.

Posting

Although replying to a message is easier than posting a new one, if you really have something new to say, or a new question to ask, don't insert it into a different discussion thread just because it's easier to do that way. In that case, you should just post a new message, something that should be simple to do in any decent newsreader.

In general, you should avoid posting a few things. Avoid copyrighted works such as magazine articles and so on. Although it's unlikely that anyone could sue the Internet (it's a bit like boxing with a dense mist), that person might sue you for copyright infringement. Besides, posting copyrighted work is not polite—just post the complete reference to the article or whatever, along with a summary or selected quote or two if you want to pique some curiosity.

Interestingly, recipes in cookbooks are not copyrighted because they are essentially lists of instructions. However, the instructions for creating the recipe may be protected if they contain anything other than the bare bones instructions, and any preface explaining or describing the recipe is definitely protected. People often post a recipe or two from a cookbook they particularly like so that others can see if they like the recipes from that cookbook enough to buy it.

Perhaps the least obvious but most important works to avoid posting are pictures scanned in from magazines or videos digitized from TV or videotape. Most of the scanned pictures are varying degrees of erotic images, and unfortunately, most are blatant examples of copyright infringement. The magazines, *Playboy* in particular, don't look kindly on this sort of thing, and legal action may ensue. Besides, pictures suck up disk space, and the quality of a scanned image doesn't even begin to approach the high-quality photography and printing of the magazines.

In general, you should not post the headline events in the world that everyone can read about in the newspaper or possibly in ClariNet (which I talk about later in this chapter). I don't mean to imply that you can't talk about these events, but because news travels relatively slowly to all parts of the net, announcing the results of an election or a similar event is just silly. People already know about the event and if they don't, they'll figure it out from the ensuing discussion of whether the right person was elected.

Finally, never post personal email that you receive unless the sender gives you explicit permission. As with most things on the Internet, posting personal email is a legally murky area, but it's crystal-clear etiquette. People who do such things are slime.

The Newsgroup Stork

Now that you know a bit about how the messages travel from machine to machine and how the naming system works, you may wonder from where new newsgroups come. Whenever I've talked about the range of Usenet groups, I've always said something to the effect of "and if there isn't one that matches your interests, you can create one." That statement is true, if not a trivial process.

The first rule in creating new groups is that you shouldn't do so unless you are absolutely sure that no appropriate group already exists. Usually, you just haven't found the right group, and once you do, the need to create a group disappears. The Usenet structure lends itself to talking about almost any subject imaginable in an existing group. For instance, you can talk about anything Windows-related in `comp.os.ms-windows.misc`. Thus, the second rule of creating a new group is that you shouldn't create a group until the traffic in a more general group has grown unmanageable and stays that way. As a rule of thumb, you should wait six months after first thinking that you need to create a new group. One way or another, make sure that you have a Usenet old-timer on your side to help with the details and help you avoid any egregious mistakes.

After you are sure that the world really does need a group dedicated to discussion of the psychology of smelling flowers from under cork trees, for instance, you write a proposal, called a *Request for Discussion*, or *RFD*, stating what the group is called, its purpose, why no existing group serves the need, and so on. Then your job as agitator is to distribute that proposal to groups where interested parties may hang out, placing the `news.announce.newgroups` group first in the Newsgroups: line so that the moderator can correct any problems in your RFD before posting it to `news.announce.newgroups` and the others for you and setting the Follow-up-To: line so that the discussion takes place in `news.groups` rather than in any other group. You then encourage discussion of the topic for 30 days in `news.groups`, all the while collecting responses and modifying the proposal, called a *charter*, accordingly.

After 30 days, if people don't agree on your charter, you return to Go and do not collect $200 (and you start the RFD process again with a new proposal). If everyone does agree on the charter, which includes the name, purpose, and moderation status, the time has come to *Call For Votes*, or CFV, with clear and unbiased directions on how to vote. (Separate email addresses on the same machine are fine, if you can swing that.)

The CFV goes, once again, to all the interested newsgroups with `news.announce.newgroups` first in the Newsgroups: line. It lasts for between 21 and 31 days, and you must include the exact end date in the CFV. Once again, your job is to collect and tally the votes via email (and don't even think of stuffing the electronic ballot box—there's little the Usenet community hates more than a cheat). You must record each voter's email address along with the YES or NO votes for later use. You can repost the CFV during the vote to keep up awareness, but only if you don't change anything from the original CFV.

At the end of the voting period, you post the results, including the total number and the vote and email address for each of the voters, to `news.announce.newgroups` and the other interested newsgroups. Then everyone waits five days, which provides enough time to correct any mistakes or raise serious objections. You need to meet two separate goals to justify a newsgroup: a sufficient number of votes and, within that number, a sufficient number of YES votes. If you have at least 100 more YES votes (for creating the newsgroup) than NO votes, and at least two-thirds of the votes are YES votes, then the group passed.

If you don't get the required number or percentage of votes, of course, the group cannot be created. There's no shame in not having your group created, and you can try again in six months if you want and if interest seems to have increased since the original failure. If you fail more than twice, give it up and form your own mailing list. You don't need anyone's cooperation to create a mailing list.

If the vote comes out positive, someone (often the moderator of `news.announce.newgroups`), can create the group, sending out the newsgroup control message. Gradually, the group is created at different sites and propagates through much of the network. Why not the entire network? Well, nothing says a machine has to carry every Usenet group in existence, so if a system administrator decides that talking about smelling flowers is offensive, she may decide not to carry the group. None of the machines that rely on her machine for news have the group either. Nonetheless, groups focusing on technical issues enjoy relatively complete propagation, and even those discussing topics that some people find offensive enjoy wide propagation and often greater readership than the technical groups.

ClariNet

Along with all the discussion groups about computers and recreational activities and whatnot, you may see a hierarchy under *clari.*—you've found ClariNet. Unlike Usenet, ClariNet doesn't carry discussions and, in fact, I don't believe that you can post to any ClariNet groups. Rather ClariNet is dedicated to distributing commercial information, much of it the same stuff that you read in your newspaper or hear on the radio.

Also unlike Usenet, ClariNet isn't free. A site must pay a certain amount to receive the ClariNet news feed, which uses the same transport protocols and newsreaders as Usenet. Sites that receive the ClariNet feed cannot redistribute that feed on to other machines unless those machines pay for the information as well. Because of ClariNet's commercial nature, I can't predict whether you even have access to it. It's strictly up to each site.

Much of the ClariNet information comes from the press wires like UPI, along with NewsBytes computer articles, and various syndicated columnists like Dave Barry, Mike Royko, and Miss Manners. Although you can probably find much of the information in a standard newspaper, ClariNet organizes it extremely well, making reading about a single topic much easier. For instance, some groups carry local news briefs for each state, groups that carry only news about Microsoft, and groups with tantalizing names like `clari.news.goodnews`, which indeed includes only articles that are good news. Depressingly, that newsgroup sees very little traffic.

ClariNet was founded three or four years ago by Brad Templeton, who is also well known as the creator of the moderated group rec.humor.funny, which accepts only jokes that he thinks are funny (actually, someone else does the selection now). In many ways, ClariNet was an experiment because it is specifically commercial traffic flowing not only over the Internet, but via the same methods and pathways as Usenet, which is perhaps the most rabidly anti-commercial part of the Internet.

Enough on Usenet, you're ready to move next to the services that require a full connection to the Internet, FTP, Telnet, Archie, WAIS, Gopher, the World-Wide Web, and a few others.

Chapter 7

Internet Services

Throughout this book, I have walked a fine line when talking about Internet services because the level of connection varies widely, and people who can send Internet email may not be able to use FTP, for instance. The services talked about in this chapter all require a full TCP/IP connection to the Internet.

FTP Background

Despite the confusing way people occasionally refer to FTP both as a noun and a verb, most people don't have much trouble using it. FTP refers to *File Transfer Protocol* and, not surprisingly, it's only good for transferring files between machines. Nonetheless, you should keep a few salient facts in mind when using FTP.

FTP Manners

The Internet does a wonderful job of hiding geographical boundaries. You may not even realize the person with whom you correspond lives on the other side of the globe. When you're using FTP, however, you should try to keep the physical location of the remote machine in mind.

First, as with everything on the Internet, someone pays for all this traffic and, because it's probably not you directly, you should try to act like a good citizen who's being given free access to an amazing resource. You should therefore show some consideration and not use machines in Australia, say, when one in the same area of the country as you will do just fine. Because trans-oceanic traffic is expensive, many machines *mirror* others; that is, they make sure to transfer the entire contents of one machine to the other, updating the file collection on a regular, often daily basis.

Because the FTP site at `ftp.cica.indiana.edu` is popular and well kept, other sites carrying the software don't want to duplicate the effort. It's much easier to set up a mirror to `cica` so that machines in Australia and Scandinavia can all have exactly the same contents as `cica`. Mirroring not only saves work, but it enables users in those countries to access a cheaper, local site for files. Everyone wins. But only if you, as a user, utilize local sites whenever possible. You can usually tell where a site is located by looking at the two-letter country domain at the end of the address.

Sometimes, of course, the file you want exists only on a site in Finland, and nothing prevents you from getting that file if you need it. Whether or not the file is overseas, however, you also should think about the time of day when you're retrieving files. Like most things in life, other than universities during exams, more people use the Internet during their daytime hours than at night. Thus, it's generally polite to retrieve files during off hours; otherwise, you're preventing people from doing their work, and that's not polite, especially if the file you're retrieving is a massive AVI movie or something equally frivolous.

Notice that I said "their daytime hours." Because the Internet spans the globe, you have to think briefly about what time it is where you want to go. It may be 4 A.M. where you live and work, but it's the middle of the day somewhere else.

One final piece of FTP etiquette: Don't use someone else's FTP site as a temporary dumping ground for junk that you either can't store on your account or don't want to download directly.

FTP Clients

Although FTP is inherently simple to use, you may find plenty of room for FTP client software to make your life miserable. The following sections, therefore, describe several features to look for in an FTP client.

Connecting

Most of the time people use an FTP client program to log on to a remote FTP site, find a file or two, download them, and then log off. As such, a disproportionate amount of your time is spent connecting and navigating to the files you want. A good FTP client enables you to define frequently used FTP sites, along with the userid and password necessary for connecting to them. If you're especially lucky, you can define an initial directory to enter as well. This problem is minor but makes a big difference when repeated numerous times. I can't tell you how much I hate typing `ftp ftp.cica.indiana.edu` on a UNIX command line.

Navigating

After you're on, the FTP client program should make it extremely easy to move between directories. Most programs enable you to move by emulating the common Open File dialog box that you use in Windows to open and save files, which is a good start. It's helpful when the client program remembers the contents of directories; that way, if you go back to one you've already visited, you don't have to wait for it to refresh.

Listing Style

In UNIX, you can choose between several different methods of viewing files. Some show you more information, such as file size and creation date, and others show you less, to fit more on the screen. Although Windows doesn't have the problem of trying to fit multiple columns in a list (because no Windows program uses multiple column lists), not all FTP clients are good about showing you the entire filename, the file size, or the date. I think this failure is inexcusable because you need to know how large a file is before you spend an hour retrieving it, if you're connecting at a slow speed. Make sure the program you use provides this information.

Recognizing File Type and Decoding

It makes sense that an FTP client can figure out what sort of file you're retrieving much of the time by looking at the extension to the filename. If this is true, then the client can ensure it is transferring the file in the proper format and, if you're lucky, it even decodes some of the common formats you see on the Internet.

"Wait a minute," you say. "He didn't mention strange file formats before." Sorry about that; they are explained in the following sections.

ASCII Encoding

When you start exploring the wide world of FTP, you quickly discover that most files have familiar extensions to filenames, as is standard in DOS and Windows. Luckily UNIX allows long filenames, unlike DOS, so you don't have to think of eight-character names for everything. Extensions are extremely useful on the Internet because they identify the type of file at which you're looking.

In standard DOS and Windows usage, nearly every application has its own extension (.WK1, .WKS, .DOC, .WP, .DBF, .NDX, .IDX, .ZIP, and other three-letter combinations). Although in DOS and Windows, these extensions indicate the application that created the file, on the Internet, the extensions usually fall into two basic categories: those used to indicate ASCII encoding, and those used to indicate compression formats. Several others are used to mark certain types of text and graphics files.

Programs and other binary data files—files with more than just straight text in them—contain binary codes that most email programs don't understand because email programs are designed to display only text. Binary data files are data files such as word processor files, which contain formatting information or other nonprinting characters. Most programs enable you to save your files in a variety of formats, including text. If you don't save a file in some kind of text format, then it's probably a binary data file, although there are exceptions. This system isn't entirely unreasonable because computers of different types generally understand only the first 128 characters in the ASCII character set. (*ASCII* is the acronym for American Standard Code for Information Interchange.)

Still, people want to transfer files via email and other programs that cannot handle all the possible binary codes in a data file or application. Programmers therefore came up with several different ways of representing 8 bits of binary data in 7 bits of straight text. In other words, these conversion programs can take in a binary file like NOTEPAD.EXE, for instance, and convert it into a long string of numbers, letters, and punctuation marks. Another program can take that string of text and turn it back into a functioning copy of Notepad. I'll leave it to the philosophers to decide if it is the same program.

Once encoded, that file can travel through almost any email gateway and be displayed in any email program, although it's worthless until you download it to a DOS or Windows machine and decode it. The main drawback to this sort of encoding is that you always have to decode the file before you can work with it, although more and more programs decode for you automatically. In addition, because you move from an 8-bit file to a 7-bit file during the encoding process, the encoded file will be larger than the original, sometimes by up to as much as 35 percent.

After I've given you all that information so that you understand why we go through such bother, the Internet uses two main encoding formats: *uuencode*, and *atob* (read as *a to b*).

uuencode

In the UNIX world, uuencode is the most common format. You can identify a uuencoded file by its .uu extension. Uuencode is not in common usage in the Windows world, so you're unlikely to run across uuencoded Windows files very frequently. You may run across slightly different extensions on occasion; I've also seen .uud and .uue. They're all the same thing.

Most uuencoded files start with begin 644 (although other numbers are possible, depending on the file permissions of the original), followed by the filename and then rows upon rows of ASCII gibberish, each line the same length. (Actually, these lines may not all look the same length when you're viewing them under Windows, depending on your viewing application, because UNIX machines use the ASCII 10 linefeed character instead of a carriage return/linefeed, which DOS and Windows use to end a line.) All uuencoded files end with a linefeed, a space, the word end, and another linefeed.

```
begin 644Fetch Tip

M4&%T:#H;G=97AU<R%U=6YE="=')0>2YJ<&N;F%S82YG;W8A9&5C=W)L
M(6-0;F-E<G0A;5W<RUF965D+3$$N<&5A8VAN970N961U(75M;YE9&A4A;7-U

...

M(" @(" @(" @('P-*E1H97D@@9&]N)W0@<&%Y("&UE(&5N;W5W5G::"!T;R!S<&5A
F:R%F;W&@=&AE(%5N:79E<G-I='DL(&]R(&8%N>6]N92!E;92!E(2IT
```

end

atob

Frankly, I don't know a lot about the atob format, which stands for *ASCII to binary*. This format is supported by a complementary btoa convertor, which translates binary files into ASCII. It is the most efficient of the two, so atob files are slightly smaller than the equivalent uuencode file. Despite this seemingly major advantage, atob doesn't appear nearly as frequently in the UNIX world as uuencode, and it rarely appears in the Windows world. I don't even know of a Windows, or for that matter, DOS program that can even decode an atob file.

```
xbtoa Begin

!!u,+FCSu,<,$:Ozzzzzzzzzzzz!)uBh<-
35,F9)@B$j&s"z!!U@B!!!"tID750ID732zzzzzzz:g

nHZ3Zr<aDIn'8F!5[KDImo5AScC*GqNiNCbBU6F($\6Dg!:7ARfq)Ca!;,DI[6uF<PO5GB5?JAS#C(

...

)Y]!CER5-EZfI;AKXujBm+'.F(o'A/0JkO+CT/5Df0,/
AScF!+Y"UP!">MQ9]$\;:0p\<:0%>p8EU"
```

```
5->ieh-rW;\!"_]A0.[)30*b7S!(&:<+B'Bfd&6pQ0*!X5

xbtoa End N 1664 680 E b1 S 20295 R 85ec6638
```

Compression Formats

Along with the various ASCII encoded formats, you frequently see on
Internet files a number of file extensions that indicate that the files have
been compressed in some way. Almost every file available on the
Internet is compressed because disk space is at a premium everywhere.

The folks who run the Internet file sites like two things to be true about a
compression format. They want it to be as tight as possible, so as to save
the most space, and they want to ensure that the files stored in that
format will be accessible essentially forever. This requires the format of
the compressed files be made public, so that in theory any competent
programmer can write a program to expand those files should the company go out of business or otherwise disappear.

This second preference has caused some trouble over the years because
the compression market is hotly contested, and companies seldom want
to put their proprietary compression algorithms (the rules by which a file
is compressed) into the public domain where competitors can copy them.
For a while there was a project on the Internet to create a public format
based on some other public compression formats, but it never saw the
light of day. As it is, the compression format most widely available is
PKWARE's PKZIP.

UNIX Compression

UNIX has a built-in compression program called, in an uncharacteristi-
cally straightforward manner for UNIX, *compress*. Compress creates files
with the .Z extension (note the capital "Z"—it makes a difference), and
although you don't see files with that extension too often in Windows file
sites, plenty of them exist on the rest of the net (for UNIX users, of
course).

As far as I know, compress works only on a single file, but you often
want to put more than one file in an archive. In many cases, .Z files are
meant for UNIX users, so these files wouldn't be relevant to Windows
users. But, if you're itching to uncompress them, you can find DOS-level

utilities suitable for the task. Try querying an Archie server to see if someone has one published.

Don't even attempt to grab and uncompress files that have the extension .tar.Z. They represent compressed *tape archives*, which store UNIX directory structures. They will be meaningless to you as a Windows user. And since they are usually huge, don't waste bandwidth by trying to copy them to your machine.

Recently, a new format, called "gzip," has started to appear in the UNIX world. It's marked by the .z or .gz extension. I know essentially nothing about this one just yet, so if you have to expand a gzip file, try using tools on a UNIX machine or asking on the nets whether a free or shareware program can do the trick.

Self-Extracting Archives

What if you want to send a compressed file or files to a friend who you know has no compression utilities at all? Then you use a *self-extracting archive*, which is hard to describe further than its name. Compression programs can create self-extracting archives by compressing the file and then attaching a stub, or a small expansion program, to the compressed file. The self-extracting archive looks like a plain executable (.exe) to the user and if you run it, it then expands the file contained within it. Internet file sites prefer not to have many files, particularly small ones, compressed in self-extracting archives because the stubs are a waste of space for most people on the nets, who already have utilities to expand compressed files.

Unfortunately, since the extension of a self-extracting archive is identical to that of a regular application, it is difficult to tell them apart. The most obvious way to find out is to, of course, run it. But, then if it is a self-extracting archive, then it will start unpacking and creating multiple files in your *current directory*. And if you should have existing files, then they'll get mixed in. Worse, if the self-extracting archive contains a directory structure, then it will start creating directories in addition to files. (But then again, they're usually easier to delete from the Windows File Manager.)

A popular self-extracting archive program is LHA, created by the venerable Haruyasu Yoshizaki, or frequently know as just Yoshi! Yoshi's work can be found in many products meant for commercial distribution. Alas, it is DOS level only, so you'll have to drop to a DOS shell to use it.

PKZIP/PKUNZIP

The most common compression format that you'll use as a DOS or Windows user is the .ZIP format, developed and distributed by PKWARE. The two utilities, PKZIP and PKUNZIP, compress and uncompress files, as you'd expect.

Originally intended for squeezing files onto floppies for both archival and distribution, PKZIP has many more options than you'd have use for as an Internet user. For instance it can verify files on write and set the archive bits for files. Later versions can compress entire directory structures into a single archive.

For the most part, you'll use PKUNZIP for simply uncompressing files that you obtain from the Internet.

Other File Types

You may want to keep in mind a number of other issues with file types, both with formatting text files for different systems and with graphics files that you find on the Internet.

Text Files

Text files are universally indicated by the .txt extension and, after that, the main thing you have watch for is the end-of-line character.

Earlier in this chapter, I mentioned that UNIX expects the end-of-line character to be a linefeed (LF). Unless you're using a word processor or editor that can translate this linefeed into the standard end-of-line characters carriage return and linefeed (CR/LF), you're in for a big surprise. The text will look extremely long-winded, because there won't be any carriage returns. And to further confuse the issue, Macintosh prefers to end its lines with carriage returns (CR).

Because the Internet is nondenominational when it comes to computer religion (the Internet on the whole—almost every individual is rabid about his or her choice of computer platform), most communication programs are good about making sure to put any outgoing text into a format that other platforms can read. Most programs also attempt to read in text and display it correctly no matter what machine formatted it originally. Unfortunately, as hard as these programs may try, they often fail. You need to pay attention to what sort of text you send out and retrieve, either via email or FTP.

When you're sending files from Windows, the main thing to remember is to break the lines before 80 characters. "Eighty characters," you say, "how the heck am I supposed to figure out how many characters are on a line without counting them all? After all, Windows editors and word processor have superior proportionally-spaced TrueType fonts. Humph!"

Yeah, well, forget about those fonts when you're dealing with the Internet. You can't guarantee that anyone reading what you write even has those fonts, so stick to a monospaced font like Courier New. You can probably find an option in your word processor (Word for Windows has it) that enables you to Save As Text and that inserts returns at the end of each line in the process.

After your lines have hard returns at the end, you usually can send a file properly because most communications programs can handle removing the carriage returns. If you don't add these hard returns and someone tries to read your text file under DOS or UNIX, the file may or may not display correctly. There's no telling, depending on that person's indi-vidual circumstances, but you usually hear about it if you screw up. Test with something short if you're unsure whether you can send and receive text files properly.

Often, the FTP client or email program automatically strips and adds carriage returns on files coming in from the Internet. If that doesn't happen, you can run a Find and Replace in your word processor.

The other reason to view files from the Internet in a monospaced font with lines delimited by hard returns is that people on the Internet can be incredibly creative with ASCII tables and charts. Using only the standard characters you see on the keycaps on your keyboard, these people man-age to create some extremely complex tables and graphics. I can't say they are works of art, but I'm always impressed. If you wrap the lines and view in a proportionally spaced font, those ASCII tables and graphics look like textual garbage. It's the price you pay for being clever.

Graphics Files

For a long time graphics files weren't commonly posted on the Internet, except by users of a specific machine because PCs were not able to read Mac graphic file formats and vice-versa. Now, however, you can view some common formats on multiple platforms.

First among these formats is *GIF*, which stands for Graphics Interchange Format. It is a graphic file format originally created by CompuServe. GIF files almost always have the extension .gif and are popular on the Internet because the file format is internally compressed. When you open a GIF file in a program such as WinGIF or WinCIM the program expands the GIF file before displaying it.

The second type of file format you may see is *JPEG*, which stands for Joint Photographic Experts Group. JPEG files, which are generally marked by the .jpeg extension, use a different form of compression than GIF. JPEG file compression reduces the image size to as much as one-twentieth of the original size, but also reduces the quality slightly. Windows viewers abound. On the Internet, you'll find Lview, WinECJ, and WinJPEG amongst versions for virtually every graphics platform.

Telnet Usage

Because Telnet is similar to FTP in the sense that you're logging in to a remote machine, the same rules about manners apply. As long as you try to avoid bogging down the network when people want to use it for their local work, you shouldn't have to worry about it too much. When you telnet to another machine, you generally telnet into a specific program that provides information you want, and the folks making that information available may have specific restrictions on the way you can use their site. Pay attention to these restrictions because the few people who abuse a network service are the ones who ruin it for everyone else who isn't abusing it.

IRC

IRC, which stands for Internet Relay Chat, is a method of communicating with others on the Internet in real time. It was written by Jarkko Oikarinen of Finland in 1988, and has spread to 20 countries. IRC is perhaps better defined as a multiuser chat system where people gather in groups that are called *channels*, usually devoted to some specific subject (private conversations are also possible).

IRC gained a certain level of fame during the Gulf War when updates about the fighting flowed into a single channel where a huge number of people had gathered to stay up to date on the situation.

I personally have never messed with IRC much, having had some boring experiences with RELAY, a similar service on BITNET back in college. As a result, I know very little about the social customs on the IRC, and given that people often spend a lot of time on such chatting systems, there are bound to be plenty of traditions. You can find more information in the IRC tutorials posted for anonymous FTP at `cs.bu.edu` in the directory `/irc/support`.

Client programs for many different platforms exist, including WinIRC for Windows.

MUD

MUD, which stands for Multi-User Dungeon or often Multi-User Dimension, may be one of the most dangerously addictive services available on the Internet (according to a friend who weaned himself from MUDs some time back). The basic idea is somewhat like the text adventures of old, where you type in commands like "Go South," "Get knife," and so on. The differences with MUDs are that they take place in a wide variety of different realities—basically anything that someone can dream up, the characters in the dimension are actually other people and after you reach a certain level of proficiency, you can modify the dimension.

The allure of the MUDs should be obvious. Suddenly, you can become your favorite alter-ego and describe yourself in any way you want. Your alternate-reality prowess is based on your intellect and if you rise high enough, you can change your world, literally. Particularly for people who may feel powerless or put upon in the real world, the world of the MUD is an attractive escape, despite its text-environment limitations.

After the publication of an article about MUDs, the magazine *Wired* printed a letter from someone who had watched his brother fail out of an engineering degree and was watching his fiancée suffer similar academic problems as a fourth-year astrophysics student because of an addiction to MUDs. As an experiment in interactive communications and human online interactions, MUDs are extremely interesting, but you should be aware of the time they can consume from your real life.

I don't want to imply that MUDs are evil—like almost anything else they can be abused. But in other situations, they have been used in fascinating ways, such as to create an online classroom for geographically separated students.

Although MUDs are currently text-only, I'm sure that at some point rudimentary graphics will appear, followed by more realistic graphics, sound, and video, and perhaps some day even links to the virtual reality systems of tomorrow. I don't even want to speculate on what those changes may mean to society, but you may want to think about what might happen, both positive and negative.

I don't know of any MUD clients for Windows, but with the rash of WinSock-compliant software coming out these days, someone is bound to release one even as I write.

Archie

Okay, I find myself in a slight organizational bind here, but as is my wont, I'm going to confess right up front and explain why the problem exists and why I've chosen the organization herein. Right about now I need to talk about what Archie is and how you use it, but without lapsing into the technical details of what you type when you telnet to an Archie server. I want this section to contain all the background and foundation information you need, without battering you with UNIX commands or other such hoary details. If I hold off discussing Archie and Gopher and WAIS and WWW until the section that also contains the UNIX specifics, I'm afraid some readers may completely miss that information, assuming (correctly) that because they use a WinSock program they don't have to worry about UNIX commands. The problem is that splitting the information on Archie between two sections feels wrong, but I guess I just have to live with it. Thanks for listening.

Archie is a remarkable example of what happens when you apply simple technology to a difficult problem in an elegant way. Here is the problem: How do you find any given file on the nets if you don't already know where it's located? After all, in comparison with finding a single file on 2.2 million machines, the proverbial haystack looks tiny, and its cousin, the proverbial needle, sticks out like a sore thumb. In a nutshell, Archie uses normal FTP commands to get directory listings of all the files on hundreds of anonymous FTP sites around the world. It then puts these file listings into a database and provides a simple interface for searching the database. That's really all there is to Archie, and it's amazing that no one thought of it before.

You can access Archie via Telnet, via email, via command line UNIX, and via a Windows client. Later I talk about each of the basic ways to access Archie, lumping Telnet and email together, because the email interface is basically the same idea as the Telnet interface.

WAIS

Unlike almost every other resource mentioned in this book, the WAIS (or Wide Area Information Server), project had its conception in big business for big business. Here's the problem: Professionals from all walks of life, and corporate executives in particular, need tremendous amounts of information, information which is usually stored online in vast databases. But corporate executives are almost always incredibly busy people without the time, inclination, or skills to learn a complex database query language. Of course, corporate executives are not alone in this situation; many people have the same needs and limitations.

In 1991, four large companies, Apple Computer, Dow Jones & Co., Thinking Machines Corporation, and KPMG Peat Marwick joined together to create a prototype system to answer this pressing problem of information access. Apple brought its user interface design expertise, Dow Jones was involved because of its massive databases of information, Thinking Machines provided the programming and the expertise in high-end information retrieval engines, and KPMG Peat Marwick provided the information-hungry guinea pigs.

One of the initial concepts was the formation of an organizational memory—the combined set of memos, reports, guidelines, email, and whatnot—that make up the textual history of an organization. Because all of these items are primarily text and completely without structure, stuffing them into a standard relational database is like trying to fill a room with balloons: they don't fit well, they're always escaping, and you can never find anything. WAIS was designed to help with this problem.

So far I haven't said anything about how WAIS became one of the Internet's primary sources for free information and with such corporate parentage, it's in some ways surprising that it did. The important thing about the design of WAIS is that it doesn't discriminate. WAIS can incorporate data from many different sources, distribute them over various types of networks, and record whether the data is free or carries a fee. WAIS is also scalable so that it can accept an increasing number and complexity of information sources—an important feature in today's world of exponentially increasing amounts of information. The end result of these design features is that WAIS works perfectly well for serving financial reports to harried executives, but works equally well for providing science fiction book reviews to curious undergraduates.

In addition, the WAIS protocol is a standard and is freely available, as are some clients and servers. Anyone can set up her own WAIS server for anyone with a WAIS client to access. Eventually, we may see Microsoft, Lotus, and Novell duking it out over who has the best client for accessing WAIS.

Earlier in this chapter, I mentioned the problem of most people not knowing how to communicate in complex database query languages. WAIS solves that problem by implementing a sophisticated natural language input system, which is a fancy way of saying that you can talk to it in English. If you want to find more information about deforestation in the Amazon rainforest, you simply formulate your query as: "Tell me about deforestation in the Amazon rainforest." Pretty rough, eh? In its current state, WAIS does not actually examine your question for semantic content; that is, its searches are based on the useful words (ignoring "in" and "the," for instance) it finds in your question. However, nothing prevents advances in language processing from augmenting WAIS so that it has a better idea of what you mean.

In any database, you find only the items that match your search. In a very large database, however, you often find far too many items. So many, in fact, that you are equally at a loss as to what may be useful. WAIS attempts to solve this problem with *ranking* and *relevance feedback*. Ranking is just what it says. WAIS looks at each item that answers the user's question and ranks them, currently based on the proximity of words and other variables. The better the match, the higher up the document appears in your list of found items. Although by no means perfect, this basic method of ranking works well in practice.

Relevance feedback, although a fuzzier concept, also helps you refine a search. If you ask a question and WAIS returns 30 documents that match, you probably will find one or two that are almost exactly what you want. You can then refine the search by telling WAIS, in effect, that those one or two documents are "relevant" and that it should go look for other documents that are "similar" to the relevant ones. Relevance feedback is basically a computer method of pointing at something and saying, "Get me more like that."

Perhaps I can best explain relevance feedback by drawing the parallel to how you work with a reference librarian. You pose your question, the reference librarian thinks for a minute and gives you a list of some possibilities. You look at this list and then tell the librarian which items on the list are right, and the process continues. When you're using WAIS, you don't need the intermediary of the librarian; you look at the original documents yourself and point at which ones are most relevant for continuing the search.

The rise of services such as WAIS and Gopher on the Internet will by no means put librarians out of business. Rather, the opposite is true; librarians are trained in ways of searching and refining searches. We need their expertise both in setting up the information services of tomorrow, and in making sense of the frantic increase in information resources. Even more so than before, we need to eliminate the stereotype of the little old lady librarian among dusty books and replace it with an image of a person who can help us navigate through data in ways we could never do ourselves. There will always be a need for human experts.

The WAIS folks discourage the use of the term *keywords* because keywords imply that the databases are indexed and unless you type in a keyword that matches an index term, you can't find anything. In fact, keywords and Boolean queries (where you say find Rocky AND

Squirrel) were both methods of getting around the fact that, until recently, we didn't have the computer power to search the full text of the stored documents. Nor did we have the computer power to attempt natural language queries and relevance feedback. Now we do and it's a good thing.

When you put all this information together, you end up with a true electronic publishing system. This definition, pulled from a paper written by Brewster Kahle, then of Thinking Machines and now president of WAIS, Inc., is important for Internet users to keep in mind as the future becomes the present: "Electronic publishing is the distribution of textual information over electronic networks." (Kahle later mentions that the WAIS protocol does not prohibit the transmission of audio or video.)

Electronic publishing has little to do with using computer tools to create paper publications, and for those of you who know about Adobe Acrobat and Common Ground from No Hands Software, those two programs aren't directly related to electronic publishing because they both work on the metaphor of a printed page. With those programs, you create a page and then print to a file format that other platforms can read (with special readers), but never edit or reuse in any significant way. We should enjoy greater flexibility with electronic data.

So how can you use WAIS? I see two basic uses. Most of the queries WAIS gets are probably one-time shots where the user has a question and wants to see whether WAIS stores any information that can provide the answer. This use has much in common with the way reference librarians work: someone comes in, asks a question, gets an answer, and leaves.

More interesting for the future of electronic publishing is a second use: periodic information requests. As mentioned earlier, most people read specific sections of the paper and, even within those sections, are choosy about what they do and don't read. I, for instance, always read the sports section and am interested in baseball, basketball, football to a lesser extent, and hockey only if the Pittsburgh Penguins are mentioned. Even within the sports I follow more closely, baseball and basketball, I'm more interested in certain teams and players than others.

Rather than skim through the paper each Sunday to see whether anything interesting happened to the teams or players I follow, I can instead ask a question of a WAIS-based newspaper system (which is entirely possible right now, using the UPI news feed that ClariNet sells and that is currently accessible via Usenet). In fact, I may not ask just one question, but I may gradually come up with a set of questions (some specific, some abstract). Along with "What's happening with Cal Ripken and the Baltimore Orioles?" could be "Tell me about the U.S. economy."

In either case, WAIS runs my requests periodically, every day or two, and indicates which items are new in the list. Ideally, the actual searching takes place at night to minimize the load on the network and to make the search seem faster than the technology permits. Once again, this capability is entirely possible today; all that lacks for common usage is the vast quantities of information necessary to address everyone's varied interests. Although the amount of data available in WAIS is still limited (if you call 500+ sources limited), serious and important uses are already happening. For instance, a friend at Thinking Machines related a story about a friend who used WAIS to research his son's unusual medical condition and ended up knowing more than the doctor. Sounds like it's time to look for another doctor, but you get the point.

In large part due to its corporate parentage, the WAIS project has been careful to allow for information to be sold, and for the owners of the information to remain in control in terms of who can access the data and when. Although not foolproof, the fact that WAIS addresses these issues makes it easier to deal with copyright laws and information theft.

Because of the controls WAIS provides, information providers are likely to start making sources of information more widely available. With the proliferation of these information sources, it will become harder for the user to keep track of what's available. To handle that problem, WAIS incorporates a Directory of Servers, which tracks all the available information servers. Posing a question to the Directory of Servers *source* (WAIS calls sets of information sources or servers) returns a list of servers that may have information pertaining to your question. You then can easily ask the same question of those servers to reach the actual data.

Most of the data available on WAIS is public and free at the moment, and I don't expect that arrangement to change. I expect more commercial data to appear in the future, however, and in regard to that issue I want to propose two ideas. First, charges should be very low to allow and encourage access, which means that profit is made on high volume rather than high price. Given the size of the Internet, I think this approach is the way to go, rather than charging exorbitant amounts for a simple search that may not even turn up the answer to your question.

Second, I'd like to see the appearance of "information handlers" who foot the cost of putting a machine on the Internet and buying WAIS server software and then, for a percentage, allow other people to create information sources on their server. WAIS, Inc. already provides this service, and I haven't heard of any competition yet. That service allows a small publisher to make a financial newsletter, say, available to the Internet public for a small fee, but the publisher doesn't have to go to the expense of setting up and maintaining a WAIS server. This arrangement will happen more often; the question is when. Of course, as the prices of servers machines, server software, and network connections drop, the arrival of such providers will speed up.

WAIS has numerous client interfaces for numerous platforms, but you probably can use either the simple VT-100 interface via Telnet or a WinWAIS, a WinSock application.

Gopher

In direct contrast to WAIS, Gopher originated at the University of Minnesota, where it was intended to help distribute campus information to staff and students. The name is actually a two-way pun (there's probably a word for that) because Gopher was designed to enable you to "go fer" some information. Many people probably picked up on that pun, but the less well-known pun is that the University of Minnesota is colloquially known as the home of the Golden Gophers. Don't ask why. I don't know. Although one of the members of the Gopher team said that they have real, live gophers living outside of their office. I suppose it makes more sense than calling yourself the Trojans, considering that the Trojans were not only one of the most well-known groups in history that lost, but also considering that they lost the Trojan War because they fell for a really dumb trick. "Hey, there's a gigantic wooden horse outside, and all the Greeks have left. Let's bring it inside!" Not a formula for long-term survival. Now if they had formed a task force to study the Trojan Horse and report back to a committee, they wouldn't have been massacred. Who says middle management is useless?

Anyway, I digress. The point of Gopher is to make information available over the network, much in the same way that FTP does. In some respects, Gopher and FTP are competing standards for information retrieval—although I'm sure there are more FTP sites than Gopher sites. I'm equally sure that Gopher is far cooler than FTP and stands to supplant it completely at some point in the future.

Gopher has several major advantages over FTP. First, it provides a much friendlier interface than the standard command-line FTP client. Second, Gopher provides access to far more types of information resources than FTP, which only allows you to retrieve files. Gopher provides access to online phone books, online library catalogs, the text of the actual files, databases of information stored in WAIS, various email directories, Usenet news, and Archie.

Third, Gopher pulls all this information together under one interface and makes it all available from the basic menu system. If you retrieve a file via FTP and it gives you a reference to another FTP server, you as the user must connect to that site separately to retrieve any more files from there. In contrast, you connect to a single home Gopher server, and from there wend your way out into the wide world of Gopherspace without ever having to consciously disconnect from one site and connect to another (although that is what happens under the hood). Gopher servers almost always point at each other, so after browsing through one Gopher server in Europe, you may pick a menu item that brings you back to a directory on your home server. Physical location matters little in Gopherspace.

Gopher also has become popular because it uses fewer server resouces than FTP. When you connect to a Gopher server, the Gopher client software actually connects only long enough to retrieve the menu, and then it disconnects. When you select something from the menu, the client connects again very quickly, so you barely notice that you weren't actually wasting a connection on the server during that time. Administrators like using Gopher for this reason, because they don't throw as much computing power at a task such as providing files to Internet users.

The most important adjunct to Gopher is a service called *Veronica*, which stands for Very Easy Rodent Oriented Internet-wide Computer Archive, but apparently the acronym followed the name. Basically, Veronica is to Gopher what Archie is to FTP, a searching agent—hence, the punning name. You usually find a Veronica menu within an item called Other

Gopher and Information Servers, or occasionally just World. When you perform a Veronica search, you either look for Gopher directories which contain files, or you can look for everything available via Gopher, which includes the files and things like WAIS sources as well. Veronica is extremely cool and utterly indispensable for navigating Gopherspace. I used Veronica heavily while researching parts of this book.

Several Gopher clients exist for Windows: WinSock Gopher from EG&G and WinGopher from NOTIS Systems Inc. among them. You also can access Gopher via Telnet and a VT-100 interface; it's nowhere near as nice (it's slower, you can only do one thing at a time and you can't view pictures and the like online), but it works if you don't have WinSock access to the Internet.

World-Wide Web

In many ways, the World-Wide Web is the most ambitious of the major special services. The Web was started at CERN, a high-energy physics research center in Switzerland, as an academic project. It attempts to provide access to the widest range of information by linking not only documents marked up in its special *HTML* (HyperText Markup Language) format, but also additional sources of information via FTP, Gopher, and WAIS. Gateways also exist to Oracle databases and to DEC's VMS/Help systems, among others. The Web tries to suck in all sorts of data from all sorts of sources, avoiding the problems of incompatibilities by allowing a smart server and a smart client program to negotiate the format of the data. In theory, this capability to negotiate formats enables the Web to accept any type of data, including multimedia formats, once the proper translation code is added to the servers and the clients.

The theory behind the Web makes many things possible: such as linking into massive databases without needing to modify the format in which they're stored, reducing the amount of redundant or outdated information stored on the nets, and the use of intelligent agents for traversing the Web. Much of these changes haven't happened fully yet, but traffic on the Web is increasing incredibly rapidly and I anticipate the Web becoming one of the main interfaces to the massive quantities of information on the Internet. After all, with a search or two to start off right, you should be able to follow hypertext links to your heart's content until you've found the information you want.

I should probably explain *hypertext*. A term coined by Ted Nelson years ago, hypertext refers to nonlinear text. Whereas you normally read left to right, top to bottom, and beginning to end, in hypertext you follow links that take you to various different places in the document, or even to other related documents, without scanning through the entire text. Assume you're reading about wine, for instance. There's a link to information on the cork trees that produce the cork for wine bottles, so you take that link, only to see another link to the children's story about Ferdinand the Bull, who liked lying under a cork tree and smelling the flowers. That section is in turn linked to a newspaper article about the running of the bulls in Pamplona, Spain, and a hypertext jump from there takes you to a biography of Ernest Hemingway, who was a great fan of bull fighting (and of wine, to bring us full circle). This example is somewhat facetious, but I hope it gives you an idea of the flexibility a hypertext system with sufficient information in it, like the World-Wide Web, can provide.

The problem the Web faces right now is the lack of a searching agent like Archie or Veronica because the Web is so huge and spans so many services and pieces of information that it is mind-boggling to use.

You can access the Web via a terminal and a VT-100 interface, or even via email, which is really slow, but for proper usage, you must use a special browser. NCSA has thoughtfully produced WWW brousers for the three major graphical environments and have a client called Mosaic for Microsoft Windows, X Windows, and the Macintosh. One nice feature of these applications is their shared ancestry. If you learn to use Mosaic on any of these platforms, using it elsewhere is a snap.

You've just read a ton of information about the network foundations and background. If I were you, I'd take a brief break and get some fresh air before you move on to the next part, which discusses the three main ways you can access the Internet.

Part III

Connecting to the Internet

Finally, it's time to talk about how you get Internet access and what it looks like. You have three basic ways to connect to the Internet, each with pros and cons, costs and confusions. First comes email-only access, followed by terminal access, and finally, a WinSock-based connection. Don't worry about the terms and acronyms just yet, I explain them in the following chapters.

There is a fourth way of connecting to the Internet, and it's via UUCP, which stands for UNIX-To-UNIX CoPy. It is a rather archaic way of connecting, and since Windows users are taking the high road to technology, we're leaving it in the dust. Besides, there's hardly anything out there to support it since Windows and Internet access is in its infancy. (Of course, that is changing rapidly.)

I don't expect you to read each of these chapters in detail right off, although I hope the following descriptions help you to figure out which sort of connection method is best for you and thus which chapter should be first on your agenda.

Chapter 8, Email Access

At the most basic level, you can use email-only access via a commercial service, a local BBS, or a gateway from a LAN-based email package at work. This type of service is easy to find because commercial services such as CompuServe, America Online, and Delphi have local phone numbers in many locations. When I talk about the commercial services, I provide contact information so that you can find out whether there's a local number in your area.

More and more local bulletin boards also have Internet access now (sometimes via the worldwide BBS network called FidoNet), and because many boards are free, that route might be the least expensive, although potentially the least reliable as well. Finding a local BBS can be a daunting task because most communities don't have listings of them in the newspaper or anywhere. The best place to start is at your dealer or any other local computer store. These people can often point you to someone on the staff who uses bulletin boards, or they might direct you to local user groups, which often operate bulletin boards.

Another way to obtain access is through your job. As more and more businesses find themselves needing to connect to other locations, they are setting up gateways between the Internet and internal network mail packages such as cc:Mail and Microsoft Mail. This type of access is also generally free to you, but it does require that you work for an organization that provides such a service. The only way to find out about this type of connection is to ask the person who takes care of your network.

Chapter 9, Command-Line Access

This is it, the dreaded command line. I assume that because you use Windows, you're not all that interested in typing long strings of commands or remembering cryptic UNIX abbreviations that hearken back to DOS days. Nonetheless, one of the most common ways you can gain Internet access is through an account on a public access machine, usually running some form of UNIX or a custom menu system.

Finding a public access UNIX site is far more difficult than joining a commercial service, although Phil Eschallier has compiled a list of sites called the nixpub list. Check appendix D, "The nixpub List," for a copy of it, but note that it changes frequently and may be out of date by the time you read this book. To receive the latest copy of the list, send email to `mail-server@bts.com` using either `get PUB nixpub.long` or `get PUB nixpub.short` in the body of the message. Any Subject: line works. The long list is about 60K (in two parts), and the short list is about 14K—the difference lies in the amount of detail provided. The PDIAL list from Peter Kaminski, which lists only public providers that have a full connection to the Internet for Telnet and FTP, is also a good source. The PDIAL list is also in appendix B, "Newsgroup List," but if you want the latest edition, send email to `info-deli-server@netcom.com` using `Send PDIAL` in the Subject: line. What you put in the body of this message doesn't matter.

Also try calling the help desks at any local universities or colleges because some provide limited access to their machines. If you work at a university or large computer-oriented business, of course, you probably just have to ask the right person, so start with the help desk or the person who takes care of your computers. I should be honest—the hard part is not finding access, but finding affordable access preferably through a local telephone call.

If you end up with terminal access, you have little choice about using the command line and typing out every command by hand. I recommend this sort of access only if you have no choice or don't mind learning and using UNIX. If you decide to take this route, I recommend Ed Krol's *The Whole Internet Catalog and User's Guide*, which provides more complete information on this topic. Ed does a great job explaining in detail how to work with the Internet on a UNIX machine, whereas I restrict myself to talking about what you absolutely must know to get by. Besides, Ed's a great guy and he uses Eudora in real life. On the whole, you're going to be typing your fingers off.

Chapter 10, Windows Sockets (WinSock) Access

Ah, the cream of the crop. Students and staff at universities often have PCs connected to a local network. And with commercial versions of

WinSock (such as a more powerful version of the NetManage software included on the disk that comes with this book), they can connect directly to the Internet through the campus network. Most of us aren't so lucky, and even people with full network access at work or school may want to call in from home as well. To use WinSock via modem, you use either PPP (Point to Point Protocol) or the older but more common SLIP (Serial Line Internet Protocol), which an increasing number of sites offer. The disk included with this book also contains a SLIP/PPP only version of NetManage's excellent Chameleon software and WinSock interface, called Newt.

Finding a provider with SLIP access can be difficult. SLIP providers aren't as common as providers of terminal access or UUCP access, but consult the PDIAL list and check which providers in your area offer SLIP access. Long distance calls are always a possibility, and a few providers offer 800 number access for a fee.

The combination of SLIP or PPP and Newt lets you run great Windows programs that enable you to do everything on the Internet with a Windows interface. Gone are the days of the command line (well, almost), and you become familiar with programs such as Eudora for email, WS FTP , WinQVT/NET's Telnet, and WinVN for Usenet news, and a slew of other wonderful applications such as WinSock Gopher, Finger, and WAIS. If you can get a SLIP account and use it, go for it. It's the best way to surf the Internet.

Reality Check

At this point you need to think carefully about what you really want to do on the Internet because that decision will help you figure out what sort of access is right for you.

I received a call the other day from a man who had been referred to me by my Internet provider. He wanted Internet access for his business, supplying peripherals to users of Sun workstations, which run UNIX. He said that he knew a little about how to use UNIX, so I immediately started telling him about Eudora, UUCP, and SLIP. After we talked for a while, though, it became clear that he only wanted to send and receive email and that he wasn't interested in learning new stuff right now. So with a heavy heart, I recommended that he simply get an account on a

UNIX machine and use what he knew. Luckily, this particular UNIX machine does work with Eudora, so I hope that at some point he'll wean himself away from the familiar, if ugly, UNIX command-line environment to a slick Windows program.

Similarly, you must think carefully about what you want. If you only want email and the speed doesn't matter (as it did with my new acquaintance, who didn't want to wait more than an hour or two for mail to come in or go out), a commercial service or a local BBS with an Internet feed may make the most sense. Also consider the costs involved. If you want full Internet access with FTP and Telnet, and you can get a UNIX account for $240 per year flat rate, that may be a better deal than a SLIP account, which provides a nice graphical interface but which charges by the hour. I understand the concept of not having any money, so please, do only what you can afford, no matter how cool the more expensive options may seem. Credit card debt is an ugly thing.

Chapter

Email Access

The easiest way to gain limited Internet access is through one of the numerous commercial services, a local BBS with an Internet feed, or if you're lucky, through a gateway maintained by your employer that connects to your network email system. But first, the commercial services. These companies, such as CompuServe, America Online, and GEnie, provide their own fee-based services such as email, computer and non-computer discussions, file libraries, and databases of information, much like the Internet. And just to ward off this question right away, no, you cannot access files or databases on CompuServe, say, via an Internet account. Although more and more of the file archives from CompuServe are being duplicated on the Internet. The archives at `ftp.novell.com` are a good example of this.

Commercial services offer two main advantages over finding a real Internet site. First, because they have deals with the international commercial network carriers such as SprintNet and Tymnet, finding a local phone number is usually easier (although the costs are significant if you also must dial a long distance number). You pay for that easier access, however, generally with the connect-time fee for the commercial service. Second, the commercial services find it easier to offer commercial-quality information because they can charge users to access that information and then pay the information provider. Hence, you can find full-text databases of computer magazines on CompuServe, for example. But, you pay extra for any searches in those databases, with the revenue going to the publishers of those magazines. Remember, to paraphrase the Bard, "All the world's a marketing scheme."

In the past year or so, all the commercial services have added Internet email gateways. This means that you can use these services to send and receive Internet email. With a few exceptions, the commercial services are limited to email-based Internet access. Some commercial services place additional restrictions on email, such as limiting the size of the files you can receive or charging extra for Internet email (as opposed to email to other users on that service).

I discuss each of the major commercial services and mention the known features and limitations of each so that you can decide whether one of them satisfies your Internet needs. Keep in mind that rates change frequently on the online services to match with market pressures and the marketing whim of the day, so the rates mentioned in this chapter may not be accurate by the time you read this book.

Having an account on one of the commercial services can be a good way to ease into the Internet because you can send and receive email. Having the capability to send and receive email enables you to request automated information from the major Internet providers, for instance, which makes finding a local connection much easier. In addition, many of the online services provide decent graphical interfaces that are easier to use than character-based interfaces.

America Online

America Online, commonly known as AOL, has been around for only a few years but has always boasted one of the best graphical interfaces for browsing files and sending email, although the way their software handles discussions leaves much to be desired. In 1992, America Online opened their Internet gateway, and its popularity grew quickly.

Advantages

America Online doesn't charge for internal email or for email that goes in or out through their Internet gateway, which has endeared them to budget-conscious online users. In addition, America Online has reasonable monthly base rates of $9.95 for the first five hours and $3.50 per hour for each additional hour. (This service is reasonable if you plan on staying under five hours.)

America Online also makes it relatively easy to send email to a number of people at once for the same amount of connect time (which translates to cost) that you may spend to send the message to one person. This service is handy, for instance, if you write a fairly general letter to a friend and want to send it to two other friends at the same time (electronic form letters!). Just put multiple addresses in the To: and CC: boxes, and your message goes to all of them (see figure 8.1).

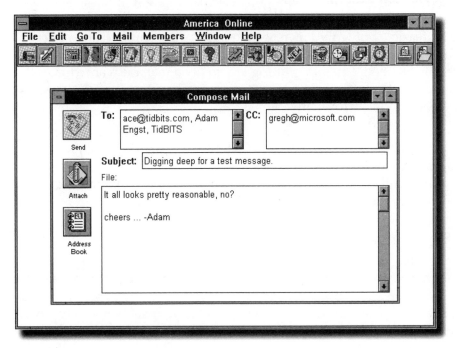

Figure 8.1   *America Online Mail window.*

Although perhaps not in final form, AOL recently opened a new section that provides access to Usenet newsgroups. The interface was simple and painfully limited, but it works. AOL mangaement also promises access to Gopherspace and WAIS sources, but as with many AOL promises, I'm not holding my breath.

Finally, AOL has a discussion area in the MCM forum about the Internet. This area is called Internet Cafe. If you use Internet email from AOL regularly, stop in and check out the discussions for the latest information on the Internet connection.

Disadvantages

If you plan to use America Online for serious Internet email, let me dissuade you somewhat. America Online limits the size of outgoing mail to the amount of text that can fit in their software's message box, or roughly 30K. Reportedly, AOL also occasionally messes up certain Internet addresses on incoming messages, making it impossible for you to reply. You can't send attached files through the gateway (it's technically feasible but would increase the traffic significantly), and America Online splits large email messages that come in from the Internet at about 15K each. This file splitting is actually a major advance for AOL because in the past they truncated incoming messages at 27K, which was a major headache for many people.

In addition, although AOL's software is fine for a message or two a day, if you anticipate joining a mailing list that can generate up to 30 messages a day (which is quite possible), America Online's interface for reading mail can quickly make your life miserable. AOL opens messages slowly and makes you confirm your actions when you delete a message or reply to a message offline.

Although I believe they have fixed most of the problems, AOL has developed a reputation for having vaguely flaky connections. As a result, Internet email sometimes arrives immediately, whereas at other times it can be delayed for up to several days. This problem isn't serious for the casual email user, but it can become frustrating quickly if you're having a conversation with someone via email or depend on your email for business reasons.

Finally, although AOL has promised faster access for many moons, they are still encumbered by the 2400 bps albatross. A fast modem doesn't help in the slightest with AOL until they enable you to dial in at the speeds that fast modems support. I hope that by the time you read this book, America Online will have finally implemented 9600 bps support for everyone, but I'm not putting any money on that bet.

Addressing

To send email from America Online to the Internet, you don't do anything special. You just type the Internet address in the To: box and fill in the Subject: box and the body of the message as you do when sending email to another AOL user.

To send email from the Internet to a user on America Online, you need to remember a few simple rules. First, you need to know the person's username. Second, type the username in lowercase letters because some email packages on the Internet are picky about upper- and lowercase. Third, remove any spaces in the name. Fourth, append an @ and the machine name and domain to the end of the address; for America Online, it's aol.com.

My username on America Online is Adam Engst. To send me email from the Internet, you address your message to adamengst@aol.com.

Connecting

You need America Online's special software to log on to the service, but America Online distributes it for free. Just call 800-827-6364 and ask them to send you the software. Alternatively, if you have a friend who already uses America Online, that person can ask America Online to send you the software, and she receives some free time online when you first log on.

BIX

BIX is one of the oldest of the commercial online services and, until it was purchased by General Videotext Corporation a year or so ago, it was the online arm of *BYTE* magazine. Because of its association with *BYTE*, BIX boasts an eclectic and technical group of subscribers.

BIX has been accessible from the Internet for quite some time, but through a relatively odd gateway that wasn't common knowledge. Recently, BIX added a direct connection to the Internet, which makes it much easier to send and receive Internet email. As an added bonus, you can even FTP files from Internet hosts and telnet into BIX from the

Internet. Other outbound services such as finger and Telnet are planned and have help information on BIX, but they didn't work when I tried them.

Advantages

BIX primarily boasts reasonable addressing schemes and an interesting and technical group of subscribers. BIX's support of FTP (and eventually other direct Internet services such as Telnet and finger) is also a major plus, and those people with local Internet access can even telnet to BIX over the Internet, saving on the costs because BIX charges less for Telnet access than for dial-in access. You can telnet into BIX by logging into an Internet machine, typing **telnet x25.bix.com**, and replying **BIX** to the Username: prompt before logging on normally.

BIX provides a great deal of Internet hand-holding in its Internet message areas (try typing **join internet** or **join ask.bix/internet**). Although getting the hang of the massively strange interface may take you some time (you reply to a message online with the Comment command, for example), for people just getting started, the hand-holding and constant advice are a great help. The Internet discussion areas on BIX are an excellent place to talk about exploring the Internet.

As it currently stands, FTP on BIX works a little oddly. Because you don't have a full UNIX-like account, BIX had to come up with a way to get the files from the remote Internet machine to your PC. The manner they chose to send these files is interesting, although occasionally confusing. Rather than storing the file on the BIX host machine and requiring an extra step to download it, they set it up so that files are automatically dumped to your PC via ZMODEM or whatever transfer protocol you normally use to download files from BIX.

I can't decide whether this system is good or bad, although I do like the way it queues up files and then downloads them when you're finished. That approach can be more efficient than sitting through each successive download, especially if you have a slow modem. Check out the following FTP session transcript to see how it works. I recommend using ZMODEM if you can; I accidentally got sucked into XMODEM, and it wasn't nearly as clean a process. Setting BIX up to use ZMODEM requires you to look in the Options area.

```
:ftp halcyon.com
```

Connected to halcyon.com.

220 halcyon FTP server (Version 2.1WU(1) Wed May 12 17:36:53 PDT 1993) ready.

Name (halcyon.com:anonymous): **<— hit Return to accept "anonymous"**

331 Guest login ok, send your complete e-mail address as password.

Password (tidbits@BIX.com): **<— hit Return to accept default password**

230-Please read the file 00-README

230- it was last modified on Thu Jan 7 23:20:24 1993 - 222 days ago

230 Guest login ok, access restrictions apply.

Remote system type is UNIX.

Using binary mode to transfer files.

Type "help download" to find out how to download files

from an Internet host computer using BIX end-to-end ftp.

BETA TEST FTP!! Questions? Bugs? Contact peabo in ask.bix/internet!

Sorry, Kermit is not supported in this version; please use X-, Y-, or

ZMODEM to download. Uploading is not supported at all yet.


```
ftp> ls
```

200 PORT command successful.

150 Opening ASCII mode data connection for /bin/ls.

total 140

-rw-r--r--	1	root	0	158	Jan 7 1993	00-README
d--x--x--x	2	root	200	512	Apr 13 08:32	bin
drwxr-xr-x	21	root	0	512	Jul 21 18:15	pub
drwxr-xr-x	19	root	0	512	Aug 9 09:32	wuarchive

```
drwxr-xr-x  2 root      0              512 Sep 18  1992 zeus

226 Transfer complete.

ftp> get 00-README

get 00-README

Starting a new queue of files to be downloaded; type "help download"

if you need assistance using BIX end-to-end ftp.

ftp> quit

Download queued files? y

Download file: 00-README

Get ready to receive using XMODEM/checksum....

[ bytes: unknown, blocks: unknown, block size 128 ]

Forgetting files previously queued.

221 Goodbye.
```

Disadvantages

BIX bothers me, I must admit. I have major trouble with their custom command-line-based interface, and I'm always fighting to end up in the proper place. For instance, to go to the section where I upload *TidBITS*, I must type **join mac.hack/tidbits**, something that I seem incapable of doing reliably. There is a graphical front end for BIX, written for Microsoft Windows, but I've not seen it to date. A graphical front end may go a long way to assuaging my complaints.

In addition, BIX has relatively high rates of $13 per month, supplemented by a connect-time charge ranging from $1 per hour for Telnet access to $9 per hour for dial-up access via SprintNet or Tymnet during weekdays. The standard non-prime time rate that you most likely pay is $3 per hour. You don't pay extra for 9600 bps access, luckily. Internet email is free until you have sent and received 10M in one month, after which BIX charges $1 for each subsequent 100K. That rate is very fair for Internet email.

If you plan to use BIX heavily, they have a 20/20 plan that costs $20.00 and provides 20 hours of connect time. This charge is in addition to your

$13.00 per month membership fee, and time over the 20 hours is charged at $1.80 per hour or $1.00 per hour if you telnet in.

Addressing

BIX does addressing right. To send email to someone on the Internet, you type his Internet email address instead of his BIX username. To send mail to me from BIX, for example, you type **MAIL: to** `ace@tidbits.com`.

Sending mail to BIX is equally easy; you just append `@bix.com` to the end of the BIX username and send it out. So my address on BIX is simply `tidbits@bix.com`.

Connecting

The sole advantage of a command-line environment is that it makes signing up for the service easy. To get an account on BIX, have your modem dial 800-695-4882 or 617-491-5410 (use 8 Data Bits, No Parity, 1 Stop Bit, Full Duplex). Press Enter a few times until you see the Login:(enter "bix") prompt and then type **bix**. At the Name? prompt, type **bix.net**. You also can telnet to BIX to sign up if you want, following the instructions in the preceding "Advantages" section.

CompuServe

Although not the cheapest of the services, CompuServe has recently put more reasonable rates into place. CompuServe has had an Internet gateway for some years. In the past year or so, they removed the file size limitation on incoming mail. CompuServe at one time refused incoming mail larger than 50K or so.

Although not specifically related to CompuServe, ZiffNet, the online-arm of the Ziff-Davis publishing company, also exists on CompuServe's machines, and thus, if you have a ZiffNet account, you have the same level of Internet access as you would if you had a CompuServe account. The main difference is that ZiffNet provides access to other information that's unavailable on CompuServe.

Advantages

Although you can use CompuServe's menu-based interface from any terminal program such as Windows Terminal, it makes my teeth hurt. There are two graphical applications that make using CompuServe's services easier and cheaper: Dvorak's NavCIS for Windows and CompuServe's own WinCIM. And even if you only anticipate using email on CompuServe, I still recommend that you get one or the other application.

NavCIS is based on Mike O'Connor's Navigator for Macintosh, and its purpose is to save users money when using CompuServe. You tell NavCIS what you want to do in terms of reading mail, sending mail, reading discussions on CompuServe, downloading files, and so on. You then tell NavCIS to log on and do everything for you. Because NavCIS works quickly by itself, it stays on for a shorter time than you normally do and saves you money. That's good! However, NavCIS was really designed for reading discussions on CompuServe, so it's clumsy for email use. Every item, mail or otherwise, is appended to a text file—your NavCIS session—which rapidly grows large and difficult to search. This is especially true for old mail that you read, but to which you haven't yet replied (see figure 8.2).

In contrast, WinCIM works much better for email because it too can transfer all mail quickly and automatically. It shows you a nice list of all your mail and enables you to sort it in several different ways. I seldom mess with the sorting, but listing mail makes much more sense than forcing the user to scroll through each message, as NavCIS does (see figure 8.4).

I often find myself receiving email that I don't have time to respond to immediately, or perhaps the message requires enough research that I don't want to respond for a day or two. In either case, it's easy to lose email in NavCIS, whereas in WinCIM you can easily see which messages need a response. WinCIM also makes it easy to save copies of outgoing messages (useful for those times when you want to say, "I didn't write that!" in a hurt tone), and you can file messages in different folders (an essential feature if you receive email about different projects).

Overall, I strongly recommend that you purchase WinCIM if you intend to use CompuServe email seriously. NavCIS is a good value only if you intend to read many of the discussion sections on CompuServe itself (possibly worthwhile, but out of the scope of this book).

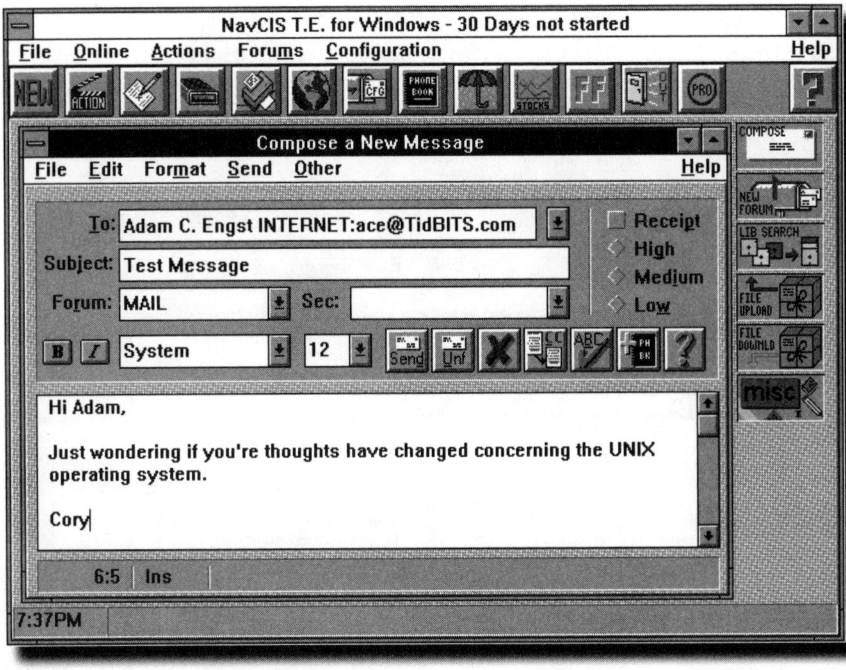

Figure 8.2 *NavCIS Session window.*

Disadvantages

I don't want to imply that CompuServe is the ideal service for Internet email, although it may sport the best combination of features. CompuServe's shortcomings fall in the areas of cost, receiving, and weird addressing formats.

Cost-wise, CompuServe no longer holds the title as the most expensive service, although it is aiming for one of the most confusing pricing structures around. CompuServe introduced a new Standard Pricing Plan, which allows unlimited access to a limited set of CompuServe services for $8.95 per month. Internet email is not included in the Standard Pricing Plan, and services that aren't included are billed at an hourly rate of $4.80 per hour for 2400 bps access or $9.60 per hour for 9600 bps access. With the monthly fee, you get a $9.00 credit toward email, which is billed at a rate of $0.15 for the first 7,500 characters and $0.05 for every 2,500 characters after the first 7,500. Confusing the issue even further, those mail charges apply to sending all mail, but only to reading email from the Internet. You don't pay for reading CompuServe email.

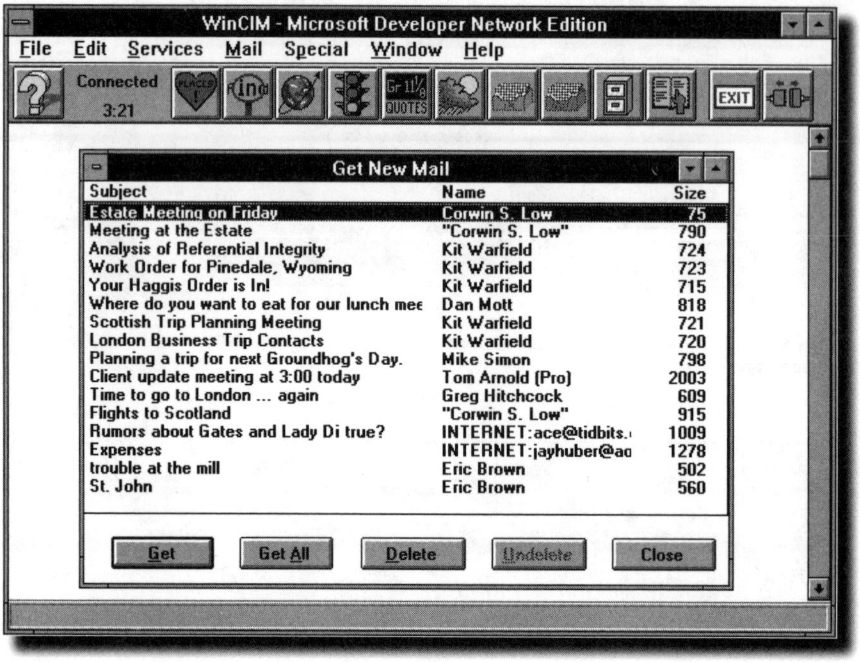

Figure 8.3   *WinCIM In Basket.*

The Alternative Pricing Plan costs only $2.50 per month and has a higher connect charge, but doesn't charge extra for Internet email. The hourly rates for the Alternative Pricing Plan are $12.80 for 2400 bps access and $22.80 for 9600 bps access. Even as I write, new pricing structures have come into play. Check with your local software supplier (or modem manufacturer) or even CompuServe for more up-to-date pricing information.

Also, CompuServe requires an irritating addressing scheme in which you must prefix >INTERNET: to the beginning of each Internet address you use. Internet addresses are enough to remember on their own without CompuServe adding its own oddities.

Addressing

You must know the magic words to add to an Internet address for CompuServe to behave properly. It's not hard—just obscure and easy to mistype. If you want to send email to my account on the Internet, ace@tidbits.com, you prefix >INTERNET: to my address, so the ungainly end result looks like >INTERNET:ace@tidbits.com. Easy enough, but people always type the address slightly wrong. It doesn't seem to make a difference whether a space lives between the colon and the start of the Internet address and spaces are verboten within an Internet address, you remember. To further complicate matters, when you receive Internet email in WinCIM or NavCIS, they politely strip the > sign from the beginning of the message. "Oh no," you think, "then replying won't work." If you thought that, then you're quite clever, but wrong, at least for WinCIM. Don't ask why, but WinCIM doesn't mind not seeing the > sign if it isn't present in a reply.

Luckily, sending email from the Internet to CompuServe poses fewer problems. You merely must follow two simple rules. First, all CompuServe addresses are pairs of octal numbers, or some such nonsense. My CompuServe address looks like 72511,306. Commas aren't allowed in Internet addresses (they usually indicate a list of addresses), so you must change the comma to a period and then add @compuserve.com. My address then becomes 72511.306@compuserve.com. Unless you have a better memory for octal numbers than I do, put CompuServe addresses in a nicknames file or address book.

Connecting

You need to purchase a CompuServe Membership Kit to access CompuServe. You can order it from mail order vendors or CompuServe. The package that I saw in a recent catalog costs only $25 and includes CIM or WinCIM, depending on the SKU. You contact CompuServe for more information at 800-848-8199. If you download WinCIM from CompuServe itself in the WinCIM Support forum, you usually get the purchase price back in connect-time credit.

Delphi

I get the impression that at one time Delphi was more popular among the online crowd. After some time in the doldrums, that popularity seems to be returning. This is due in part to Delphi's competitive pricing and full Internet access.

Advantages

Yes, you heard me right. Delphi—singularly among the commercial services—boasts full Internet access. You can telnet in and out of Delphi and access remote FTP sites to your heart's delight. Email in and out works just fine, and you can even read news there. What a deal! There's not really much point in talking about Telnet and FTP and Gopher here because I cover those subjects from the command line in the next chapter. So keep reading if you want to find out how to use the Internet tools on Delphi.

Other advantages? Hmm, because Delphi is completely connected to the Internet, email in and out should be as fast as possible. Also, like BIX, Delphi has an Internet Special Interest Group that talks about the Internet and the resources you can find on it. That's a big help for a newcomer.

Disadvantages

Delphi suffers from two problems in my estimation, and you may or may not agree with me on both. First, it appears that Delphi found it easy to add full Internet access because they run a custom menu-based system on top of DEC's VMS operating system (which is in common use on the Internet). I'm not terribly fond of VMS, having had some bad experiences with trying to use it in college, and Delphi's menu-based system is truly weird in places, especially in the file libraries. So when I log in to Delphi, I either see a custom menu system I don't much like, or an operating system that irks me. Those irritations are undoubtedly personal preference, however, and you may feel differently. Many people like VMS just fine, and many of them manage to fit into society with only a little effort.

Second, Delphi doesn't have a decent graphical interface. I can't pretend that CompuServe's menu interface is any better or worse than Delphi's; that's not the point. However, WinCIM is a perfectly reasonable graphical window into CompuServe, and Delphi is hurting in this respect.

Addressing

Like BIX, Delphi doesn't do anything strange with addressing. You can send email to an Internet user by using her Internet address rather than the Delphi address in Delphi's mail program (which is almost exactly like VMS mail for you mini buffs). If you want to send email from the Internet to someone at Delphi, simply append `@delphi.com` to the Delphi userid. So my address on Delphi looks like `adam_engst@delphi.com`.

Connecting

For information on connecting to Delphi, call 800-695-4005. Monthly rates are either $10.00 for four hours of use, with extra hours at $4.00 each, or $20.00 for 20 hours with additional hours at $1.80 each. If your account has an Internet connection, you are charged an additional $3.00 per month. Delphi often offers five hours free so that you can try out the service, so ask about the current deal when you call.

GEnie

As I started to stare into the blinding headlights of my deadline on this book, I realized that I didn't know the first thing about GEnie from first-hand experience. I've been told plenty, and I know the details of the Internet gateway, but I've never used the service. With that confession out of the way, GEnie is another large commercial service.

Advantages

The main advantage I see to GEnie is that it has a decent rate structure of $8.95 for the first four hours each month, with additional hours billed at $3.00 per hour.

Disadvantages

Addressing messages to and from GEnie isn't terrible, but it could be easier. I've heard reports that using their mail system can take some work. However, I can't comment on that subject personally.

Addressing

If you want to send email from GEnie to someone on the Internet, you must append, much like AppleLink (Apple Computer's commercial online service), @inet# to the Internet address. So my address looks like ace@tidbits.com@inet#. Because GE Information Services runs both GEnie and AppleLink, the similarity isn't surprising.

To send email from the Internet to GEnie, append @genie.geis.com to your friend's GEnie address, making it look like username@genie.geis.com. Note that apparently there is a difference between login name and user name on GEnie, and Internet email must go to the user name.

Connecting

You can get more information about GEnie by telephoning 800-638-9636.

MCI Mail

I hesitate to even mention a heavy-duty corporate, command-line-based email system like MCI Mail except for one thing: if you're clever and you can send email from another account, you can receive unlimited Internet email via MCI Mail and an 800 number for $35 per year! I know little about the system other than the fact that MCI improved its speed in the past year or so, but I gather that MCI makes its money by charging heavily for the messages you send. Let's call MCI and see what they say.

If you dial 800-444-MAIL, you wait on hold for what seems like an eternity. But, as the nice recording says, MCI Customer Support is available (or at least their recording is) 24 hours a day, seven days a week. In theory, if you wait long enough, someone will pick up the phone and tell you how to sign up for MCI Mail—or at least your friends and family.

If you're really clever, you might be able to figure out a way to download your MCI messages and convert them into a file in UNIX mailbox format so that Eudora can read them in. Then you could set Eudora so that messages appear to come from your MCI account (so that all replies go back to your MCI account). Then, even if you must call long distance to send mail with Eudora (which is easy enough to do with a number of providers), you may receive gobs of email via MCI and download it via that 800 number. But, of course, you didn't hear this suggestion from me—you figured it all out on your own.

When MCI Customer Support finally answered after ten minutes, I made the mistake of mentioning that I was writing the rate information down in a book, and I immediately got the bubonic plague treatment. Public Relations didn't answer their phone, and the supervisor only faxed me a rate sheet (the background here is that I hate fax modems and they hate me). The moral of the story is that you should never tell people you're writing a book.

Will wonders never cease? On the third try, I managed to browbeat QuickLink II and the WorldBlazer into receiving the fax, and it informed me (after six useless pages) that it costs $0.50 to send the first 500 characters of a message. The next 500 characters are an extra $0.10, each subsequent set of 1,000 characters after that (up to 10K) is also $0.10, and each set of 1,000 characters after 10K is only $0.05. Sheesh, no wonder they didn't want to tell me over the phone. All those charges come on top of the $35.00 per year for the mailbox; so if you send much mail at all via MCI, the costs add up fast.

Prodigy

Prodigy has opened an Internet gateway, but it requires special software for sending email. You can download this software, called Mail Manager DOS, form Prodigy for $4.95.

Since the costs for sending or receiving Internet email on Prodigy are quite high, I doubt that many people will rely on Prodigy for their Internet access. Each message costs $0.10 for each 6,000 character block, so a 30K file would cost $0.50. In addition, messages cannot be larger that 60K, so you cannot retrieve files via email or participate in large mailing list digests.

I don't think Prodigy wants to be available via the Internet anyway, because the Internet stands for free speech and non-commercialism. In contrast, Prodigy devotes a fifth of your screen to constant advertising and publicly censors discussions (and possibly email).

LAN Gateways

I'd like to post a large sign over this section, entitled "This space under construction!" One of the best ways to gain access to the Internet is through your employer, assuming that your employer has a local area network (LAN) attached, in some way to the Internet. These connections come in many flavors, but if we ignore the technical aspects they all boil down to either direct connections, with full access to services like FTP, Telnet, and finger or email only store-and-forward connections.

Direct connections are the soul of the .com part of the Internet. This type of connection means that your employer is shelling out somewhere from $10,000 to $30,000 per year for 24 hour, seven days per week access to the Internet from their local area network, not counting the charges for the leased telephone line. At these prices, direct connections are certainly not for everyone, or even every business, but for those lucky employees it's an untaxable benefit from their employer.

Email-only connections are typically much less expensive than direct connections, primarily because they do not require all of the complex hardware and leased lines required for the latter. Email-only connections usually store outgoing mail for some period of time (as much as a whole day, in some cases) and then dial some site that is connected directly to the Internet via modem to deliver outgoing and receive incoming mail. These types of connections are available from most of the regional Internet providors, usually under the less than obvious name "UUCP connection."

Each of these corporate answers to Internet access is much better described by the MIS person in charge of making it all work for the company. My advice is to ask that person, but bring a bribe of chocolate; they don't get away from their office much.

Command-Line Access

Welcome to 1980! In this section I take you on a fast flight through the UNIX command-line interface, glancing briefly at the commands you absolutely need to know. Why the perfunctory look? Because to a novice user, UNIX seems (to steal a quote), "nasty, brutish, and short." I know only enough UNIX to get by as a user; I never pretend to know any more than that. The UNIX I know I've picked up here and there, often seemingly by osmosis. Once or twice I've come close to being sucked in by UNIX's elegant power—elegant that is, if you're a programmer, which I'm not.

I first experienced UNIX at Cornell's Theory Center on a machine that was alternately known as tcgould or batcomputer, although everyone preferred calling it the "batcomputer." I figured out **rn** fairly quickly (due in part to its built-in help), and eventually worked my way through mail. I handled changing and listing directories, but it took me the longest time to figure out how to delete files. Eventually, I realized that I was able to FTP to my batcomputer account from an account on a different mainframe and then use FTP's aptly named **delete** command.

In the end, I tracked down a friend and asked him. "I realize everything in UNIX has to be as few letters as possible," I said, "so I've tried every possibility I can think of, including erase, delete, kill, er, de, dl, kl; you name it, I've tried it." My friend looked at me and said, "Oh, it's rm, you know, for remove."

Keep in mind that many different implementations of UNIX exist. Although I've tried to stick to the commands that should work everywhere, there's no telling whether your UNIX machine reacts in the same way as mine. Consider yourself warned; I don't go into details of different implementations or quirks when one version of a program doesn't talk to another version of the same program or anything like that. I can't believe UNIX people complain about graphical user interfaces such as Windows. Actually, I can. Operating systems are like religions, and you can't account for them.

In this chapter I mark commands that you type in **bold** within regular paragraphs and **`bold monospace`** within onscreen messages, whereas I don't mark the general names of the commands or programs in any special way because the text would become ugly fast.

Basic Commands

I assume that you understand the basics of logging into an account; the hard part is that you often must press Enter before you see the login: prompt. Minor problem, but it throws a lot of people. When you see the login: prompt, type your username, and when you see the password: prompt, type your password, which probably isn't displayed as you type it. An interesting "feature" of some UNIX flavors is that the backspace key is a valid part of your password. What this means to you (and me, since I'm a marginal typist) is that if you make a mistake while typing your password, you may as well just hit Enter a couple of times and try again, since backspace will not correct your mistake. If all goes well, you should be logged in.

But wait! Different machines provide different prompts by default, which isn't a big deal, but it means that you definitely don't see the prompt that I get on my UNIX account. Don't worry about the difference, much like DOS, the prompt is simply an environment variable, able to be set from the command line. The name of the variable is PS1, but I'll leave it to you as an exercise to figure out how to change it in the shell that you are running.

The shell you say? UNIX doesn't specify what progam will be interpreting your commands, once you've logged in. In DOS, it's almost always a program called `command.com`, but UNIX doesn't specify any one program. Rather, the system administrator will choose from a list of popular ones when she sets up your account. This choice of command interpreter will affect the way many of the commands you type work, but the commands talked about below should work in the same way on any system that you are likely to encounter.

ls

The first command that you need to know has an equivalent in every command-line interface that I've ever seen. It's the one that gives you a way to list file names and information about those files.

In UNIX, as in most command-line operating systems, you must specifically request a file list using ls, and if something in that list changes, you must request the list again to see the change. In other words, I guarantee the ls command will become ingrained into the very fabric of your fingers. As you can tell, ls stands for "list," although in true UNIX fashion, they took out half the letters to make it easier to type. (In this respect, UNIX is like French, where you seemingly don't pronounce half the letters.) A directory listing may look like the following:

```
/d/tidbits/> ls
Mail                                mail
News                                nn.help
big-dummys-guide-to-internet.hqx
```

Almost any UNIX command gains extra functionality if you use various options. I suspect this capability occurred because someone said, "But I'd like to see my directory listing in Esperanto," and an enterprising UNIX programmer said, "Hey, I can do that." So from then on, you typed **ls -e** to output the listing in Esperanto. (I'm kidding. By the way, I haven't the foggiest idea what ls-e does.) Just for fun, let's see.

```
/d/tidbits/> ls -e
ls: illegal option — e
Usage: ls [-abcdgiklmnpqrstuxABCFGLNQRSUX1] [-w cols] [-T cols]
```

```
[-I pattern]
[—all] [—escape] [—directory] [—inode] [—kilobytes]
[—literal]
[—numeric-uid-gid] [—hide-control-chars] [—reverse] [—
size]
[—width=cols] [—tabsize=cols] [—almost-all] [—ignore-
backups]
[—classify] [—file-type] [—ignore=pattern] [—
dereference]
[—quote-name] [—recursive]
[sort={none,time,size,extension}]
[—format={long,verbose,commas,across,vertical,single-
column}]
[—time={atime,access,use,ctime,status}] [—no-group]
[—help] [—version] [path...]
```

Oops, the -e option is one of the few that doesn't in some way modify the functionality of ls. What you see above is the default behavior for most UNIX commands that haven't the faintest idea what you mean, and that is to tell you all about what you *may* have meant. Despite UNIX's obtuseness, don't feel shy about trying things. After a while, you may even start to understand it.

I generally don't tell you about any of the options because you seldom need to use them (and you'd forget by the time you needed them anyway). However, ls has several important options that you may want to use at various times: **-a**, **-s**, and **-l**.

The **-a** option shows all files, including ones that start with a period and don't show up if you just use ls.

The **-s** option shows you the names of the files and also the sizes (usually in kilobytes, although sometimes in half-kilobyte blocks on older systems), which I consider essential information.

The **-l** option outputs the listing in a long format that shows all sorts of information, including privileges and dates.

In addition, you can combine the options. If, for example, you want a long directory listing showing invisible files and the file sizes, type **ls -al**. The directory listings below, slightly edited for clarity, show the different results.

```
/d/tidbits/> ls -a
.              .login        .newsrc.bak    .rnlast       nn.help
..             .mailrc       .nn            .rnsoft
```

```
.addressbook    .msgsrc        .pine-debug1  Mail
.cshrc          .mushuser      .pinerc       News
.elm            .newsrc        .profile      mail

/d/tidbits/> ls -s
total 563
    1 Mail                           1 mail
    1 News                         264 nn.help

/d/tidbits/> ls -l
total 563
drwx———    2 tidbits   users        512 Aug 13 12:36 Mail
drwxr-xr-x  2 tidbits   users        512 Jul 16 11:15 News
drwx———    2 tidbits   users        512 Aug 13 12:37 mail
-rw-r—r—    1 tidbits   users     259023 Aug 13 12:48 nn.help

/d/tidbits/> ls -al
total 737
    1 drwxr-xr-x    7 tidbits   users        512 Aug 13 12:46 .
   11 drwxr-xr-x  642 root      system     11264 Aug 13 10:31 ..
    1 -rw-r—r—      1 tidbits   users         32 Jul 16 01:36 .cshrc
    1 -rw-r—r—      1 tidbits   users        103 Jul 16 01:36 .login
    1 -rw-r—r—      1 tidbits   users         79 Jul 16 01:36 .mailrc
   70 -rw-r—r—      1 tidbits   users      71105 Aug 13 12:42 .newsrc
    1 -rw-r—r—      1 tidbits   users        198 Jul 16 01:36 .profile
    1 -rw-r—r—      1 tidbits   users         51 Jul 16 11:23 .rnlast
    8 -rw-r—r—      1 tidbits   users       7944 Jul 16 11:25 .rnsoft
    1 drwx———      2 tidbits   users        512 Aug 13 12:36 Mail
    1 drwxr-xr-x    2 tidbits   users        512 Jul 16 11:15 News
    1 drwx———      2 tidbits   users        512 Aug 13 12:37 mail
  264 -rw-r—r—      1 tidbits   users     259023 Aug 13 12:48 nn.help
```

cd

In addition to typing **ls** to see the files in a directory, you also must move between directories. You will discover that cd works almost identically in UNIX as in DOS. Typing **cd** *dirname* will move you into the directory dirname, while **cd ..** will return you to the parent directory, a generation above your current location.

```
/d/tidbits/> cd News
News> ls -l
total 120
-rw-r—r—    1 tidbits   users     108106 Aug 13 13:04 rn.help
```

```
/d/tidbits/News> cd ..
/d/tidbits> ls
Mail      News      mail      nn.help
```

As you can see, with the second command, I moved up from the News directory into my home tidbits directory.

You can travel down multiple directories with one command, if you know the entire path to the destination. To do the same thing with a single command in UNIX, you type something like **cd harddisk/applications/nisus/macros**. This command works similarly to the command in DOS, although DOS uses the backslash rather than the slash.

You may find this capability useful when you know the entire directory path; however, if you don't know the path, you must suffer with typing **cd** *dirname* to change directories, **ls -l** to list the files (so you can see where to go next), **cd** *dirname* to go into the next directory, **ls -l** to see the files, and so forth.

One final note about cd. You often may find that you want to go right to the top of the directory structure, the equivalent of **c:** on your PC. This directory is usually called the *root directory* because it's the base from which all the others spring. Yes, I know that roots aren't usually at the top, but it makes sense to say that you are going down when you delve into subdirectories, so you then must go up to get back to the top. You bounce all the way to the top by typing **cd /**, but be aware that typing this command may take you higher than you thought.

```
/d/tidbits/News> cd /
/> ls
DS200A                dev                news
DS200B                e                  news-db
DS200E                emacs.rc           opr
Mail                  etc                pcs750.bin
News                  etc.native         pub
a                     f                  scratch
archive               g                  sys
atc.boeing.com        genvmunix          tmp
b                     halcyon.com        ultrixboot
bin                   home               upgrade.hold
bos3a.delphi.com^fe,  install.profile    usr
c                     install.tmp        var
core                  lib                vmb.exe
d                     lost+found         vmunix
dec                   mail               waffle
delphi.com            mnt                wuarchive
```

As you can see, I ended up at the top of the machine's directory structure, not in the tidbits directory that I saw when I first logged in. In actuality, the directory you see when you log in to a UNIX machine (your *login directory*) is a subdirectory in a larger structure. UNIX enables you to navigate to any point in that structure to which you have been granted access.

With all the possible directories, you can get thoroughly lost quite easily. It is important to remember that typing either **cd** or **cd ~** returns you to your login directory. In my case, typing **cd** returns me to /d/tidbits from anywhere else on the system.

rm

After you know how to move between directories and display their contents, you may want to delete files. I like using rm because I'm a clean, orderly person and I get irritable when I know junk files are littering my directories, even when I can't see them (without first executing an ls command). Just type **rm** *filename*, where *filename* is the name of the file to delete and poof, the file is gone. Some UNIX systems may be set up to prompt you whether you want to delete the file; just type **y** in response to delete the file.

```
/d/tidbits> ls
Mail        News        junk.file  mail        nn.help
/d/tidbits> rm junk.file
/d/tidbits> ls
Mail     News     mail     nn.help
```

You can use rm in two other useful ways. If you want to delete several files at once, no problem. Just type **rm** *filename1 filename2 filename3*, and so on. If you want to be destructive, you can use *wildcards*, which are like one-eyed jacks in poker. If you snag a bunch of files from an FTP site, they all probably have the same extension—that is, the same last three letters after a period. To delete junk.zip, trash.zip, garbage.zip, refuse.zip, and waste.zip all at once, type **rm *.zip**. This command tells the machine to delete all files in that directory whose names end in .zip, no matter what comes before the .zip. When using *wildcards* in UNIX, keep in mind that they may not work in the same manner as in DOS. For instance, **rm *.*** will only remove all files that have a "." in them; files without a "." will be left alone. Your best guide to the differences is that UNIX is interprets what you type much more literally than DOS.

> **Caution:** Be forewarned, though, if you **rm** a file, it's toast (unlike on the PC, where you have some chance of undeleting the file). This warning is not entirely true because some systems offer a recover or undelete command, but you're on your own there.

more

Before you delete a file, you may want to see what's in it—assuming that it's a text file. In UNIX, you can use a program called "more" to display it on the screen, pausing after every screen so you can read it. UNIX's more is used almost exactly the same way as more under DOS, only with more options.

Simply type **more** *filename*, where *filename* is the name of the file you want to view and poof, the file appears on your screen. In DOS, you may be accustomed to typing **more <filename**, to redirect the input from the console to the file you wish to read. UNIX assumes that if you put a filename in the command line, you must want to read it. At the bottom of the screen, more says something to the effect of −More− (21%) to indicate that you have more to read, and you are 21 percent of the way through. At this point you have three basic controls. You press Enter to advance one line, the Spacebar to advance to the next page, or the **q** key to quit reading. Generally, you simply page all the way through the file, after which you're back at the normal UNIX prompt, whatever that may be on your system.

```
/d/tidbits> more nn.help
    Release 6.4.16                                        NN(1)

    NAME
        nn - efficient net news interface (No News is good news)

    SYNOPSIS
        nn [ options ] [ newsgroup  ¦  +folder  ¦  file ]...
        nn -g [ -r ]
        nn -a0 [ newsgroup ]...

    DESCRIPTION
        Net news is a world-wide information exchange service covering
        numerous topics in science and everyday life.  Topics are
        organized in news groups, and these groups are open for every-
        body to post articles on a subject related to the topic of the
        group.
```

```
    Nn is a 'point-and-shoot' net news interface program, or a news
—More—(0%)
```

man

Earlier in this chapter, I mentioned that rm has an option that tells it not to verify with you each file to delete. How do you find out about that option? You can try typing **help**, but there's no point because standard UNIX machines don't have a help command. UNIX programmers apparently thought that help is for weenies, so they didn't bother. However, UNIX programmers (at least the ones I know) are also lazy as all get out. They hate looking things up, and as a result, many UNIX machines have the manual online.

The UNIX manual is not the warm and fuzzy work of a professional writer, of course. In fact, the UNIX manual is one of the most user-hostile documents I've ever had the displeasure to read. It can't quite compete with IRS documentation because, as much as the IRS tries to include cute examples about Betsy's Sewing Shop, you always get the impression that they want to say "And because Betsy's Sewing Shop failed to file Form 1,463,994 `Unearned Income of Deceased Persons Temporarily Living on Other Planets,' Betsy is now doing five-to-seven for tax fraud. So don't try anything, buster!"

The online UNIX manual is commonly referred to as the "man pages," mostly because the UNIX programmers felt like stripping the last half of the word manual when creating the command. To get more information about any (well, almost any) command in UNIX, type **man** *commandname*, where *commandname* is the command you want to figure out. For instance, here's the start of the man page for rm:

```
/d/tidbits> man rm
                                                              rm(1)

    Name
        rm, rmdir - remove (unlink) files or directories

    Syntax
        rm [-f] [-r] [-i] [-] file-or-directory-name...
        rmdir directory-name...

    Description
```

```
The rm command removes the entries for one or more files
from a directory.  If there are no links to the file then
the file is destroyed.  For further information, see
ln(1).

The rmdir command removes entries for the named directo-
ries, which must be empty.  If they are not empty, the
directories remain, and rmdir displays an error message
(see EXAMPLES).

To remove a file, you must have write permission in its
directory, but you do not need read or write permission
on the file itself.  When you are using rm from a termi-
nal, and you do not have write permission on the file,
the rm command asks for con-
—More—(24%)
```

This method of invoking man assumes that you know the name of the
program with which you want help. That's often not true, and man has
an option that can possibly help in this case. To use this option, type **man
-k** *keyword* (or sometimes **apropos***). Where *keyword* is the term you
want to explore. You may find lots of junk, but you also may find a
useful command. Or, as in my case, you may find a command such as **ils**,
which looks useful but in fact hangs your account. Oh well.

```
/d/tidbits> man -k directory
basename (1)              - strip directory names from pathname
cd (1)                    - change current directory
chdir (2)                 - change working directory
chroot (1)                - change root directory for a command
chroot (2)                - change root directory
dcheck (8)                - check directory consistency
dircmp (1)                - directory comparison
dirname (1)               - deliver directory names from pathname
dtree (1L)                - display directory tree structures
getcwd (3)                - get pathname of working directory
getdirentries (2)         - get directory entries in a generic directory format
getwd (3)                 - get current working directory pathname
ils (1)                   - interactive directory browser and visual shell
mkdir (2)                 - make a directory file
mklost+found (8)          - make a lost+found directory for fsck
mknod (2)                 - make a directory or a special file
pwd (1)                   - print working directory
rmdir (2)                 - remove a directory file
scandir (3)               - scan a directory
statmon, current, backup, state (5) - statd directory and file structures
```

```
unlink (2)              - remove directory entry
uuclean (8c)            - uucp spool directory clean-up
vtree (1)               - print a visual tree of a directory structure
whois (1)               - DARPA Internet user name directory service
ypfiles (5yp)           - Yellow Pages data base and directory structure
```

Other Basic UNIX Programs

UNIX supports thousands of additional programs, and you may find that some commands exist in one flavor of UNIX (a version created by a specific company), but not in all flavors. The following are a couple of the most useful programs that I might use if I used UNIX. Remember, there are no guarantees this software is installed on your UNIX machine.

sz and rz

Rather than just looking at text files on your UNIX account, you probably want to download them to your PC. Assuming the UNIX machine you use has been set up well, you should have access to the sz program, which stands for send ZMODEM. If you haven't heard of it before, ZMODEM is a common file transfer protocol that is generally unequaled for performance and reliability. Other protocols you may run across include XMODEM, YMODEM, and Kermit. As with modems, you must match protocols on both the UNIX machine and your PC terminal emulator, so check to ensure that your emulator handles ZMODEM. Windows comes with a program called Terminal out of the box that supports XMODEM and Kermit.

Unfortunately, my UNIX-literate friend tells me that sz and rz are not common UNIX programs and, in fact, there's no telling how you can get files from your UNIX machine down to your PC. He did provide some suggestions, so if your UNIX machine doesn't have sz and rz installed, try some of these commands (matching with something your terminal emulator speaks, of course). For ZMODEM, also try typing **zm** or **zmodem**. For XMODEM, try **rz**, **xm**, or **xmodem**. It's always worth typing **kermit** to see if the froggy program exists, although Kermit is one of the slower protocols. That said, let's pretend that you have sz and rz installed.

To use sz, simply type **sz** *filename*. Most, if not all terminal emulators, recognize when the UNIX machine sends a file via ZMODEM and receives the file automatically. Most programs also either save the file in a prespecified directory or ask you where it should go. The following example file isn't big, but it illustrates the point:

```
/d/tidbits> ls
Mail          News          download.me  mail        nn.help
/d/tidbits> sz download.me
*z
### Receive (Z) download.me: 14 bytes, 0:00 elapsed, 14 cps, 0%
sz 3.24 5-16-93 finished.
```

As more alert members of our UNIX viewing audience have figured out, rz stands for receive ZMODEM. You use rz on the UNIX machine to receive a file sent from your PC. The process for receiving a file on the UNIX machine can be a little different. Not all implementations of rz under UNIX recognize that a file is coming in automatically, as most PC emulation programs do, which means that you may have to invoke rz on the UNIX machine and then go back and choose Send ZMODEM from your terminal emulator. You need not specify a filename in most cases because ZMODEM is smart enough to bring over the file. Sometimes, however, it's a good idea to give rz a filename as well, if you care about what filename you eventually want (UNIX to PC filename mappings can come out looking like Greek).

Here's what the file looks like when I ask ZTerm to send a file back to the UNIX machine. Note that I didn't type any of this information; the program did it all automatically.

```
/d/tidbits> rz
rz ready. Type "sz file ..." to your modem program
*B0100000012f4ced
### Send (Z) download.me: 14 bytes, 0:01 elapsed, 12 cps, 0%
rz 3.24 5-5-93 finished.
```

Sometimes you must pay attention to how you send files to and from the PC, but because these instructions vary from machine to machine, I can't predict what may go wrong. What you are most likely to struggle with is when to send files as binary format and when to send them as ASCII. If what you are sending is plain text, you should send it as ASCII—otherwise choose binary. I would say that you could just send everything as binary (since that simply sends every byte across, without translating anything), but UNIX and DOS differ in how they designate the end of a line of text and you *need* some translation to happen to your text files.

finger

When you want to get information about someone, you finger them. The command syntax is simple, type **finger** and then the userid; or, for a list of users logged on to a specific machine, **finger** and then the machine name preceded by an @ sign.

```
/d/tidbits> finger normg@halcyon.com
[halcyon.com]
Login name: normg                    In real life: Norm Gregory
Office: KOMO Radio, PM Star          Home phone: 206-323-6602
Directory: /d/normg                  Shell: /bin/csh
Last login Thu Aug 12 10:54 on tty20 from DS200D
Plan:

 List of Week's TV Ratings

    Prime-time ratings as compiled by the A.C. Nielsen Co. for Aug. 2-8. Top 20
 listings include the week's ranking, with rating for the week and total homes.

    An 'X' in parentheses denotes one-time-only presentation. A rating
 measures the percentage of the nation's 93.1 million TV homes. Each ratings
 point represents 931,000 households.

    1. "60 Minutes," CBS, 15.4, 14.3 million homes

    2. "20-20," ABC, 15.2, 14.2 million homes

    3. "Home Improvement," ABC, 14.8, 13.8 million homes
```

Of course, Norm has particularly good information available for fingering; most people (like me), don't have nearly as interesting stuff.

```
/d/tidbits> finger tidbits@halcyon.com
[halcyon.com]
Login name: tidbits                  In real life: Adam C. Engst
Directory: /d/tidbits                Shell: /bin/csh
Last login Wed Aug 18 16:11 on tty28 from DS200D
No Plan.
```

And, if you want to see whether a friend is logged in at a specific moment, you can check that too, via finger.

```
/d/tidbits> finger @halcyon.com
[halcyon.com]
Login      Name             TTY Idle    When          Office
breier     Breier William Schee  22      Fri 10:12
```

```
willhoek Will Parker          23 1:00 Fri 10:40
craig    Craig Suhadolnik     24 1:18 Fri 09:25
nraven   Night Raven          25      Fri 12:32
davidr   David Rogers         26   2  Fri 12:26
sharpen  Sharpened Software   27      Fri 12:43
pat      Patrick Ryan         28      Fri 12:46
andy     Andy Teh             29   3  Fri 12:44
tsparks  thomas sparks        30      Fri 12:43
```

talk

Once you know whether someone's logged in, you can talk to her online, using the talk program. I can't show you what talk looks like because I don't have anyone to talk to at this moment. When you type **talk** and a username, such as talk tidbits@halcyon.com, that user sees a message like the following one onscreen:

```
Message from Talk_Daemon@chinook at 12:59 ...
talk: connection requested by tidbits@chinook.halcyon.com.
talk: respond with:  talk tidbits@chinook.halcyon.com
```

I have no idea whether it's possible for you to talk to yourself, but I wasn't able to figure out the problem immediately, so all you see when you first invoke talk is its message telling you to hold on a minute:

```
[Waiting for your party to respond]
```

After the user answers, the screen splits into halves, and you each type in your own half. My major problems with talk are that you must be online at the same time as the other person, you never know whether you're bothering her (I usually hate when people talk to me while I'm online because I never know how to get out of what I'm doing fast enough and frankly, typing constantly and quickly is a great way to encourage Carpal Tunnel Syndrome, which can ruin your life.) If possible, the telephone works better. Although if you're talking to someone in another country, the expense probably outweighs the utility of the telephone.

irc

IRC, which stands for *Internet Relay Chat*, consists of thousands of people talking to each other in real time over the network. I mention this program here because it's sort of a massive extension to talk. I've never much enjoyed talking to strangers online because every time I've tried, the discussions seem trivial and meaningless. My ego hasn't suffered because I don't notice the same problem in real life or email, so I have chalked it up to the fact that it's hard to have meaningful conversations with complete strangers using nicknames. That said, IRC is popular, and I'm sure many people find it an excellent way to meet others and exchange ideas. Because I'm obviously not qualified to speak about it at length, I just show you the online help that I got after typing **irc** and then **/HELP**.

```
*** Help on basics
Irc is a multi-user, multi-channel chatting network.  It allows
people all over the internet to talk to one another in real-time.
Each irc user has a nickname they use.  All communication with
another user is either by nickname or by the channel that they or
you are on.  All IRCII commands begin with a / character.
Anything that does not begin with a / is assumed to be a message
that is sent to everyone on your channel.  Here is a list of
basic commands to help you get started:

        /LIST             Lists all current irc channels, number of
                          users, and topic.
        /NAMES            Shows the nicknames of all users on each
                          channel
        /JOIN <channel>   Join the named channel.  All non-commands
                          you type will now go to everyone on that
                          channel
        /MSG <nick> <msg> Sends a private message to the specified
                          person.  Only the specified nickname will
                          see this message.
        /NICK             Change your nickname
        /QUIT             Exits irc.
        /HELP <topic>     Gets help on all IRCII commands.
        /WHO <channel>    Shows who is on a given channel,
                          including nickname, user name and host,
                          and realname.
        /WHOIS <nick>     Shows the "true" indentity of someone


These commands should get you started on irc. Use the /HELP
command to find out more about things on irc, or ask question of
people... most would be happy to help you out.
```

logout

I almost forgot this step. After you finish using your UNIX account, you need to get out and hang up the modem. You can simply shut off the modem—that approach works fine, but it's not ideal. The universal command to log out under UNIX is Control-D, but it's ugly and hard to remember. Different systems use different commands; because most systems respond to **logout**, try it first, followed by **exit**, followed by **logoff**. Strange systems use **bye** or **off**, but I've never seen them outside a custom BBS interface. One of those commands should work, and if all else fails, remember that you're in control of the hangup command in your terminal emulator and the power switch on the modem.

Good luck and feel free to ask someone on your system for help. I could tell you about all sorts of other great UNIX commands that UNIX wizards use all the time and that I may have used once or twice. But in real life, assuming you don't aspire to UNIX wizardhood, you only need to know about listing files, changing directories, deleting files, reading files, and exploring other UNIX commands. UNIX has a number of other programs, such as mail, rn, nn, vi, ftp, and telnet, that you may want to use.

mail

Several UNIX programs enable you to read and reply to email—so many that I don't stand a chance at mentioning them all. Instead, I tell you about mail because it's the standard UNIX program and the only one guaranteed to be available on all UNIX machines. If you plan to use a UNIX email program exclusively, I highly recommend that you check out an alternative email program such as elm, pine, mush, or mh. There's no telling which of them your system administrator may have installed, so try typing the name on the command line, and for more information, use the man pages.

To send email from mail, type **mail**, followed by the email address of the person you want to reach. Mail then usually prompts you for the Subject: of the letter (some machines require the -s option, which makes the typed command look like `mail -s "Hi Self" ace@tidbits.com`). After that, you can type the body of the letter. Remember to press Enter at the end of each line (you're not using a full-screen editor, and you can't use the arrow keys to go back—only Delete works for editing). After you finish, press Enter once to get to a new line and then press Control-D. Some machines use two blank lines rather than Control-D, or perhaps two periods alone on a line. So, a simple mail session may look like the following:

```
/d/tidbits> mail ace@tidbits.com
Subject: Are we having fun yet?
Here's where I get to type anything I want, but since I'm talking
to myself, I can't think of anything to say. I guess that's good.

cheers ... -Adam
^d <— you don't really see this, but you do type it
Cc: tidbits@halcyon.com
```

Of course, sending mail is only half the game. You undoubtedly want to read mail too. To display the messages in your mailbox (assuming you have any), type **mail**. You should see something like the following:

```
/d/tidbits> mail
Mail version 2.18 5/19/83.  Type ? for help.
"/usr/spool/mail/tidbits": 3 messages 1 new
    1 tidbits  Fri Aug 13 10:02  17/736 "Nothing like conversations
wi"
    2 tidbits  Fri Aug 13 10:06  15/509 "Re:  Nothing like conversatio"
>N  3 tidbits  Fri Aug 13 12:09  15/484 "Are we having fun yet?"
&
```

At the & prompt, press Enter to read the first new message, which is marked by an **N** (as message 3 is marked in the preceding onscreen mail). You also can type a number corresponding to any message to read that one specifically, as in the following:

```
& 1
Message  1:
From tidbits Fri Aug 13 10:02:19 1993
Received: by halcyon.com id AA09538
  (5.65c/IDA-1.4.4 for tidbits); Fri, 13 Aug 1993 10:02:15 -0700
Date: Fri, 13 Aug 1993 10:02:15 -0700
From: "Adam C. Engst" <tidbits>
Message-Id: <199308131702.AA09538@halcyon.com>
To: tidbits@halcyon.com
Subject: Nothing like conversations with oneself
Status: RO
```

Now that I've entered the address and the Subject: line, I can type my letter. Keep in mind that the editing is minimal - backspacing only - unless you muck around a lot more and get an editor configured to work with mail. You also have to hit return at the end of each line - there isn't any word wrap by default. When you're done with the letter, you type a Control-D on a blank line to end.

There are a number of other commands that you can use to navigate between messages and work with them. The easiest way to find these commands is to use the **?** command.

```
& ?
      Mail    Commands
t <message list>                 type messages
n                                goto and type next message
e <message list>                 edit messages
f <message list>                 give head lines of messages
d <message list>                 delete messages
s <message list> file            append messages to file
u <message list>                 undelete messages
r <message list>                 reply to messages(to sender and recipients)
R <message list>                 reply to messages(to sender only)
pre <message list>               make messages go back to /usr/mail
m <user list>                    mail to specific users
q                                quit, saving unresolved messages in mbox
x                                quit, do not remove system mailbox
h                                print out active message headers
!                                shell escape
ch [directory]                   chdir to directory or home if none given
```

A <message list> consists of integers, ranges of same, or user names separated by spaces. If omitted, Mail uses the last message typed.

A <user list> consists of user names or distribution names separated by spaces. Distribution names are defined in .sendrc in your home directory.

Of these commands, you're most likely to use **n** to go on to the next message, **d** to delete one or more messages, **r** or **R** to reply to messages, **h** to display your list of messages, and **q** to quit mail.

```
& r
To: ace@tidbits.com tidbits
Subject: Re:  Are we having fun yet?
Cc: tidbits@halcyon.com
```

This is a reply to a message to myself, but once again, I'm suffering from a complete block on what to say. Nine of ten people who do this sort of thing eventually succumb to schizophrenia, so I'd better stop soon.

cheers ... -Adam
Cc: tidbits@halcyon.com

If you type **h** to redisplay your messages, you see the following:

```
& h
    1 tidbits  Fri Aug 13 10:02  17/736 "Nothing like conversations wi"
    2 tidbits  Fri Aug 13 10:06  15/509 "Re:  Nothing like conversatio"
    3 tidbits  Fri Aug 13 12:09  16/495 "Are we having fun yet?"
>N  4 tidbits  Fri Aug 13 12:26  17/581 "Re:  Are we having fun yet?"
```

Now, because talking to yourself in email is kind of sick, let's toast some of these messages, as follows:

```
& d 2 4
& h
    1 tidbits  Fri Aug 13 10:02  17/736 "Nothing like conversations
wi"
>   3 tidbits  Fri Aug 13 12:09  16/495 "Are we having fun yet?"
```

You can easily mistype when you're deleting messages (you also can just type **d** after reading a message to delete that one), but you can recover the messages by using the u command.

```
& u
& h
    1 tidbits  Fri Aug 13 10:02  17/736 "Nothing like conversations wi"
    3 tidbits  Fri Aug 13 12:09  16/495 "Are we having fun yet?"
>   4 tidbits  Fri Aug 13 12:26  17/581 "Re:  Are we having fun yet?"
```

Using the u and h commands recovered only the most recently deleted message, however, and you want all of them back. You can type **u 2** to recover the second message, but using the * wildcard to recover all of them may be easier. The * wildcard also works if you want to delete all your messages, as in the following:

```
& u *
& h
    1 tidbits  Fri Aug 13 10:02  17/736 "Nothing like conversations wi"
>   2 tidbits  Fri Aug 13 10:06  15/509 "Re:  Nothing like conversatio"
```

```
    3 tidbits  Fri Aug 13 12:09  16/495 "Are we having fun yet?"
    4 tidbits  Fri Aug 13 12:26  17/581 "Re:  Are we having fun yet?"
& d *
& h
No applicable messages
```

Finally, as you can see in the following, you can delete or recover easily a range of messages by separating the numbers with a dash rather than a space:

```
& u 1-3
& h
    1 tidbits  Fri Aug 13 10:02  17/736 "Nothing like conversations wi"
    2 tidbits  Fri Aug 13 10:06  15/509 "Re:  Nothing like conversatio"
>   3 tidbits  Fri Aug 13 12:09  16/495 "Are we having fun yet?"
```

Okay, that's enough about mail. Using mail gives me hives and frustrates me to no end. I can't recommend that you use it, but it should be available even if no other mail programs exist on your machine. There is something to be said for least common denominators, but utility is not usually among them. For novices, elm or pine are good choices because they provide full-screen interfaces that display the common commands at all times. They also enable you to select messages with the arrow keys and other seemingly obvious things like that. Remember, nothing is obvious in UNIX.

Newsreaders

Now look at two of the popular newsreaders, rn and nn. They differ primarily in philosophy: rn assumes you want to read 90 percent of the news, whereas nn assumes you want to read 10 percent of the news. Which style you prefer depends on how much time you have to read news. Both programs are powerful and complex, and both have more options than anyone should be expected to remember, much less use regularly. In keeping with the focus of this book on Windows software, I'm going give you only the briefest look at the two.

Before I discuss each program, let's talk about something they share: the .newsrc file. This file keeps track of which groups you subscribe to and which articles you've read in those groups. It also knows which groups you aren't subscribed to, which is the majority of them. Unfortunately, all of the newsreaders seem to want to subscribe you to everything when you start, which means your first session reading news is long and boring as you unsubscribe from groups that don't interest you.

You can avoid this situation. First launch either rn or nn by typing **rn** or **nn**. Then quit immediately. In rn use the **q** command; in nn use the **Q** command (case is important). The act of starting and quitting leaves you with a fresh .newsrc file that assumes you want to read all the thousands of newsgroups. If you want to avoid UNIX, download the .newsrc file to your PC; then use your favorite word processor to change all the colons (:) to exclamation points (!). Newsreaders consider any newsgroup name ending in a colon to be subscribed and any name ending in an exclamation point to be unsubscribed. Now scroll through manually and change the exclamation point back to a colon for any group that sounds interesting. You can easily subscribe and unsubscribe from groups within a newsreader as well, but dealing with thousands of them is a major pain. Next, delete the .newsrc file on the UNIX machine (don't worry—you always can have a newsreader create a new one if something goes wrong) by typing **rm .newsrc**. Then upload the edited .newsrc file and you're finished.

I should note one potential problem: You may have trouble downloading and working with the .newsrc file on your PC because filenames starting with periods on the PC are not allowed. It's not unthinkable that a communications application may refuse to create a filename starting with a period or fail to see it for uploading, although Terminal didn't bat an eyelash. If you encounter this problem, rename the file on the UNIX machine before downloading and again after uploading. In standard UNIX tradition, the rename command (which does exist) does something completely different; you need to use the mv command (which moves files) to rename a file. You can look at renaming a file as moving it from one file name to another (or you can just take my word for the fact that it works, and not twist your brain around something that unnatural). First, rename the file:

```
/d/tidbits> mv .newsrc mynewsrc
/d/tidbits> ls
Mail       News       mail       mynewsrc  nn.help   rm.help
```

Then download it:

```
/d/tidbits> sz mynewsrc
```

```
*z
### Receive (Z) mynewsrc: 71255 bytes, 0:38 elapsed, 1834 cps, 127%
sz 3.24 5-16-93 finished.
```

Edit the file on the PC (the smoke and mirrors part—I assume you know how to do a global search and replace in a word processor).

Next, upload the file to the UNIX machine:

```
/d/tidbits> rz
rz ready. Type "sz file ..." to your modem program
*B010000012f4ced
### Send (Z) mynewsrc: 71255 bytes, 1:28 elapsed, 807 cps, 56%
rz 3.24 5-5-93 finished.
```

And finally, rename the file to the name the newsreaders expect: **.newsrc**.

```
/d/tidbits> mv mynewsrc .newsrc
```

Pretty neat, eh? I provided all that detail not so much because I expect everyone to go through the entire technique, but because it's a good review of some of the UNIX commands I talked about earlier in the chapter.

rn

Now that you have a nicely edited .newsrc file, start up rn by typing **rn**. Here's what the file looks like:

```
/d/tidbits> rn
Unread news in comp.dcomm.lans.ethernet                 417 articles
Unread news in comp.lang.modula2                       1131 articles

****** 417 unread articles in comp.sys.mac.comm — read now? [ynq]
```

You immediately see the first few newsgroups to which you subscribe, and rn asks nicely if you want to read the first one. The letters in square brackets after the question indicate the question's most common answers: yes, no, and quit.

Whenever you learn a new program, determining how to look at the help file is important, even if it's not very helpful. Even though the **?** worked in mail, rn uses the h command. Type **h** and you should see something like the following (although I edited out the garbage you don't need now).

Newsgroup Selection commands:

```
y         Do this newsgroup now.
SP        Do this newsgroup, executing the default command listed in []'s.
=         Start this newsgroup, but list subjects before reading articles.
u         Unsubscribe from this newsgroup.
c         Catch up (mark all articles as read).
n         Go to the next newsgroup with unread news.
N         Go to the next newsgroup.
p         Go to the previous newsgroup with unread news.
P         Go to the previous newsgroup.
-         Go to the previously displayed newsgroup.
1         Go to the first newsgroup.
^         Go to the first newsgroup with unread news.
$         Go to the last newsgroup.
g name    Go to the named newsgroup.  Subscribe to new newsgroups this way too.
/pat      Search forward for newsgroup matching pattern.
?pat      Search backward for newsgroup matching pattern.
          (Use * and ? style patterns.  Append r to include read newsgroups.)
l pat     List unsubscribed newsgroups containing pattern.
m name    Move named newsgroup elsewhere (no name moves current newsgroup).
L         List current .newsrc.
q         Quit rn.
x         Quit, restoring .newsrc to its state at startup of trn.
^K        Edit the global KILL file.  Use commands like /pattern/j to suppress
          pattern in every newsgroup.
```

After you agree that you want to read the articles by answering yes (or actually, by typing **y**, because you don't type the entire command), rn displays the first unread message, which follows:

```
comp.dcomm.lans.ethernet #27410 (415 more)
Newsgroups: comp.dcomm.lans.ethernet,comp.dcomm.lans
From: grant@crow.csrv.uidaho.edu (Grant Lensaa)
Subject: Is there a cure for WFW?
Organization: University of Idaho
Date: Thu Aug 05 23:42:11 PDT 1993
Lines: 21


I've heard that WFW traffic is unroutable, that is to say that it cannot
be carried throughout an internetworked environment unless it is bridged
...
```

```
Netbios?  Is there anything that can be done about this?  I'm hoping that
─MORE─(94%)
```

At this point in the middle of the article, you have more possibilities, none of which are addressed in the preceding help information. You're in a different mode now, so you need different help. Type **h** to check out the more useful commands.

```
Paging commands:

SP        Display the next page.
x         Display the next page decrypted (rot13).
d         Display half a page more.
CR        Display one more line.
^R,v,^X   Restart the current article (v=verbose header, ^X=rot13).
b         Back up one page.
^L,X      Refresh the screen (X=rot13).
```

The following commands skip the rest of the current article, then behave just as if typed to the 'What next?' prompt at the end of the article:

```
n         Scan forward for next unread article.
N         Go to next article.
^N        Scan forward for next unread article with same title.
p,P,^P    Same as n,N,^N, only going backwards.
-         Go to previously displayed article.
```

Press the Spacebar to finish reading the rest of the article and poof, you're in yet another mode. Try getting help one more time, and you see yet another set of commands, as in the following:

```
Article Selection commands:

n,SP      Find next unread article (follows discussion-tree in threaded groups).
N         Go to next article.
^N        Scan forward for next unread article with same subject in date order.
p,P,^P    Same as n,N,^N, only going backwards.
_N,_P     Go to the next/previous article numerically.
-         Go to previously displayed article.
number    Go to specified article.
/pattern/modifiers
          Scan forward for article containing pattern in the subject line.
          (Use ?pat? to scan backwards; append f to scan from lines, h to scan
          whole headers, a to scan entire articles, r to scan read articles, c
          to make case-sensitive.)
```

```
/pattern/modifiers:command{:command}
          Apply one or more commands to the set of articles matching pattern.
          Use a K modifier to save entire command to the KILL file for this
          newsgroup.  Commands m and M, if first, imply an r modifier.
          Valid commands are the same as for the range command.
f,F       Submit a followup article (F = include this article).
r,R       Reply through net mail (R = include this article).
s ...     Save to file or pipe via sh.
S ...     Save via preferred shell.
w,W       Like s and S but save without the header.
C         Cancel this article, if yours.
^R,v      Restart article (v=verbose).
^X        Restart article, rot13 mode.
c         Catch up (mark all articles as read).
b         Back up one page.
^L        Refresh the screen.  You can get back to the pager with this.
X         Refresh screen in rot13 mode.
m         Mark article as still unread.
k         Kill current subject (mark articles as read).
K         Mark current subject as read, and save command in KILL file.
^K        Edit local KILL file (the one for this newsgroup).
=         List subjects of unread articles.
u         Unsubscribe from this newsgroup.
q         Quit this newsgroup for now.
Q         Quit newsgroup, staying at current newsgroup.
```

Frankly, I think you mostly use these article selection commands because you spend most of your time moving from article to article, not searching for new groups or paging within an article.

Remember that the Spacebar performs the first command listed in the square brackets. Generally, that command is the one you want to execute because rn is good at reading your mind. Initially, the end-of-article line looks like the following:

```
End of article 27410 (of 27901) — what next? [npq]
```

The default action is n, for next, which takes you to the next unread article. However, you are likely to be either very interested in the subject of the article you just read, or completely uninterested. The middle ground is less likely. If you are interested in the topic being discussed, you want to read the next article in the thread by using the **Control-N** command, generally abbreviated ^N. When you press Control-N at the end of an article, the end-of-article line looks like the following:

```
End of article 27458 (of 27901) — what next? [^Nnpq]
```

This line indicates that pressing the Spacebar enables you to read the next article in the thread, which is primarily what you want to do. If you realize that you aren't interested in a thread, of course, there's no reason to run into its uninteresting articles later on, so you can kill the entire thread temporarily by typing **k**. Use this command heavily.

After you've started reading in thread mode by using Control-N and you know to kill boring threads, you can zip through a newsgroup in no time. Because rn displays the number of unread messages left in the newsgroup at the top of each article, you can see how many articles you've killed with each successive use of k. I always find it especially gratifying when I kill an especially long and boring thread. Some people are easily amused.

As you can see in the preceding help text, you also can reply to messages by typing either the **r** or **R** command (depending on whether you want to include the text of the article in your email reply), follow up to an article by typing **f** or **F** (again, F includes the article in the followup to the newsgroup), save an article with or without its header, and quit by typing the **q** command.

It seems as though I'm glossing over parts of rn, and I am. When I use rn for real, I start it up, use Control-N on the first article to get into thread mode, and then use the Spacebar to read within a thread and k to kill boring threads. When finished with one newsgroup, rn moves on to the next. So despite rn's wads of commands, you can get along extremely well with a very few. If you do get into rn seriously, I recommend that you read over the man pages and the help carefully because some of the features—such as being able to search for articles containing specific text strings—are pretty neat, should you want to devote the time to learning how to use them effectively.

nn

Unlike rn, nn assumes that you don't want to read much of the news. Given the more than 4,000 newsgroups, many with hundreds of articles a day, this assumption is good. This assumption is also the one that most PC newsreaders make, should you move from using UNIX to a Windows reader on Usenet news.

The trick that nn uses to reduce the amount of newsgroup clutter in your life is that it forces you to select only the articles that you want to read. In contrast, rn shoves all the articles at you, one thread at a time, and asks you whether you want to read that thread. In nn, you first scroll through all the articles in the newsgroup in selection mode, and then once you've selected the articles to read, nn drops into a reading mode that looks and works much like rn. In fact, many of the commands you use with rn work in nn's reading mode as well.

Launch the program by typing **nn**, and you should see something like the following:

```
Newsgroup: comp.sys.pc.comm                          Articles: 320 of 630/2

a Duncan Coward     42  >>>Windows re-dialer?
b Lisa_R._Klein     10  Trumpet support
c Edward Vielmetti 49  >
d BEN WOLFE         30  >
e E Kaftanski       27  >>IP tunneling from NetModem/E via FastPath?
f Michael Casteel   19  >>>
g James Skee         5  Hermes 2.5???
h James Skee        23  optimizing SLIP performance
i Edward Vielmetti 13  >
j Amanda Walker     11  >


—  13:25  —  SELECT  —  help:?  — —Top 5%— —
```

The first line tells you what newsgroup you're in, how many articles are left to read of the total available, and then each detail line such as:

```
b Lisa_R._Klein     10  Trumpet support
```

provides the article ID, which you use to select that article, the name of the poster, the number of lines in the message, and the subject of the message. Alert readers may no doubt ask immediately, "But what about lines like...?"

```
c Edward Vielmetti 49  >
```

Ah, here's the beauty of nn. It groups articles in the same thread automatically, unlike rn, and it makes it clear that the articles are all in the same thread by listing only the > (greater-than) sign under the first available article. You may see multiple > signs to indicate that the article is a followup on a followup on a followup, and so on. But that's not too important. What is important is that you can easily select the articles you want to read by typing the letter to the left of the poster's name. If you want to read the entire thread under an interesting-sounding article, just type * (an asterisk) after you type the letter that corresponds to that article. Assuming that your terminal emulator and UNIX host are sufficiently advanced, you should see selected articles in reverse- or high-intensity type. And, of course, if you change your mind and want to deselect an article or a thread, typing its letter (and optionally the asterisk) removes it from your selected articles.

In the preceding example, I deleted some of the bottom articles to save space, so you'll have to take my word for it that the articles went to the letter *s*. And yet, with hundreds of available articles, you'd obviously run out of letters fast in nn's selection mode. The program circumvents this problem by providing multiple screens of article titles, each listing articles from *a* to *s* (or a higher letter, if you have more lines available in your terminal definition). Pressing either Enter or the Spacebar takes you to the next screen automatically, or you can move back and forth between screens with the < and > keys. If you want to read the messages you've marked immediately, you can type **Z**. Note that almost all commands in nn use uppercase letters because the lowercase letters are used for selecting articles.

If you select an article and the rest in the thread with a letter and an asterisk, and you use **Z** to display it immediately, your screen looks like the following:

```
Mike J. Perkins: Scripting languages for SLIP????        16 Aug 1993 14:38
   As I see more of the commercial winsock SLIPs, it occurs to me that
there is no real standard for the scripting language used in parseing
the dial-up interaction between PC and host.  In particular, the method
and the means for parseing the client IP address in the incoming stream
is certainly less than clear.  Is there any movement in this direction?
      Mike


   —
Mike J Perkins, Ph.D.                                    Univ. of Idaho
Professor                                                P.O. Box 20708
Department of Computer Science                     Moscow, Idaho 83843
   — 17:30  —comp.sys.pc.comm—  8 MORE+next  —help:?—All—
```

The line at the bottom of the message displays the time, the current newsgroup, how many more messages you've selected, the shortcut for help, and finally, the word All (which indicates that you've seen all of the article). If the article goes on for several screens, nn places a number there to indicate how far it is into the message. Some of the rn-style commands work in nn's reading mode as well, as you can tell from the reading mode help screen:

```
SCROLLING                ABSOLUTE LINE           SEARCHING
SP        1 page forw     ^      top             /RE      find regular expr.
d         1/2 page forw   gNUM   line NUM         . //     repeat last search
CR        1 line forw     $      last line
DEL       1 page back     h      header          TEXT CONVERSIONS
u         1/2 page back   H      full digest      D        decrypt article (rot13)
TAB       skip section                            c        compress spaces
GOTO ANOTHER ARTICLE
SP        next (at end of current article)       CANCEL, SUBSCRIBE, KILL
n, p      next/previous article                   C        cancel article
l         mark article for later action           U        (un)subscribe to group
k         kill subject (not permanently)          K        kill/select handling
*         select subject
                                                 QUIT / ESCAPE
SAVE                                              =        back to menu
s, o, w   save with full/short/no header         N        goto next group
:unshar :decode :patch    unpack article         X        as N, mark as read
                                                 !, ^Z     Shell escape, suspend
                                                  Q        quit nn
REPLY, POST
r         mail reply to author of article        REDRAW
m         mail (or forward article)              ^P        Repeat last message
f         post follow-up to article             ^L, ^R    Redraw screen
:post     post new article
```

If you learn how to select articles and threads, switch into reading mode, and kill nasty threads once in reading mode (by typing **k**, as in rn), you can get along fine in nn. Because you read many fewer messages, you either spend less time on the computer or you read a lot more newsgroups, your choice. Usenet is absolutely addictive though, so be careful.

vi

So far, I've avoided talking much about posting news or replying to messages because of one unpleasant fact. Although starting is easy and involves answering a few questions by pressing Enter, you then end up in a UNIX editor, probably vi, and it isn't pleasant. O'Reilly & Associates sells a book called *Learning the vi Editor* by Linda Lamb; you may want to check it out. I think I'm justified in making unpleasant comments about an editor that someone can write about for 192 pages. Put it this way: when I had to edit a special UNIX file named .login on my account, I found it was easiest to write what I wanted in a word processor (making sure I had hard returns at the end of each line), copy it, invoke vi on a new version of the file, switch to insert mode, and then paste my text in. That's awful, and I'm thoroughly embarrassed about it, but UNIX editors and I don't get along.

Here, then, are the absolutely basic commands you must know to use vi. You edit a file by typing **vi** *filename*, or you may be dumped into vi by rn or nn to edit a posting. In either case, you end up with the file listed at the bottom of the screen and a bunch of tildes (~) taking up any blank lines if the file isn't large enough to fill the screen. At this point, you're in a mode in which you can move around with the arrow keys.

```
To: noah@apple.com
Subject: Re: Q840av / AudioVision 14" Display don't work "out of
the box"
Newsgroups: comp.sys.mac.announce
In-Reply-To: <noah-170893175443@90.130.0.233>
References: <1993Aug10.175723.5878@netcon.smc.edu>
Organization: "A World of Information at your Fingertips"
Cc:
Bcc:


~
~
~
~
"/d/tidbits/.letter" 10 lines, 295 characters
```

To start inserting text at the bottom of the message, use your arrow keys to move down to the line above the first tilde. You can't move down any further (and keep in mind that you're not working on a PC—moving all the way to the right does not wrap you around to the next line).

Type **i** to enter insert mode and type your text, pressing Enter at the end of each line for safety's sake (the text may wrap, but I can't guarantee it). If you make a mistake, you can use Delete to go back and fix it, but don't try to use the arrow keys in insert mode because they don't work; they insert letters into your file instead.

Press Escape to return to the mode where your arrow keys work. At this point there are probably thousands of useful editing commands, but I'm going to tell you about only a few. Type **x** to delete the character that your cursor is on and type **dd** to delete the line you are on. If you just need to replace a single character, position your cursor over it, type **r**, and then type a single replacement character. If you make a mistake with any of these commands, undo the last change by typing **u**.

You can always go back into insert mode by positioning your cursor in the appropriate place and typing **i**. If you make a line too long, you can switch out of insert mode, move to the end using the arrow keys, switch back into insert mode, press Enter to break the line, switch out of insert mode, and then type **J** to join the line you're on with the line below it.

After you finish editing the file, if you want to save it and quit, first make sure you aren't in insert mode; then type **ZZ**. If you don't want to save the changes, instead of ZZ, type **:** (a colon) and then, at the command-line prompt that appears at the bottom of the screen, type **quit!**. This series of commands exits you without saving your changes. I use :quit! heavily.

ftp

FTP, or File Transfer Protocol, is almost trivial to use, especially in comparison with other UNIX programs. It does have a fair number of picky little options, however, and such nonsense that no one ever uses in daily life. I'm going to discuss the standard FTP commands and show you the results that come back from the FTP server.

To start, you invoke FTP and tell it where to go by typing **ftp** and the exact name of the file site. You must know the name of the site beforehand, and you must type it correctly; otherwise, FTP complains about an "unknown host." If you blow the name and end up at a blank `ftp>` prompt without connecting to a site, try typing **open** along with the correct file site name. Alternatively, you can swear at the machine, type **quit**, and try the original FTP command again. Here's what FTP looks like when you get it right:

```
/d/tidbits> ftp ftp.acns.nwu.edu
Connected to ftp.acns.nwu.edu.
220 casbah.acns.nwu.edu FTP server (SunOS 4.1) ready.
```

Next, FTP wants a login name, just as you need a login name or userid to log in to your UNIX account. Unless you're logging into your own account at another machine (at which point you use your own userid), type the name **anonymous.** Again, you must spell it correctly, or FTP asks for a password that you don't know and then spits at you about an incorrect login or some such problem. If you spell the name wrong, your backup command is **user anonymous,** which lets you start the login process again.

```
Name (ftp.acns.nwu.edu:tidbits): anonymous
331 Guest login ok, send ident as password.
```

FTP responds to a successful anonymous login by asking for your identity as a password. I've never heard of anyone checking these things in FTP logs, but it's polite to enter your full email address. Like all good passwords, it doesn't appear as you type, which isn't a big deal because your email address isn't secret. However, if you make a mistake, don't sweat it; no one really cares. Well, almost no one. Some sites check the email address you enter against the name of the machine from which you use FTP and reject attempts that don't match properly. Therefore, typos may count! Also, even if you provide a good password, sites often don't allow more than a certain number of anonymous users to log in at the same time or at the same time from the same machine (causing trouble if someone else on your machine is using the FTP site already, for instance), so it may kick you out and tell you to try again later.

```
Password: tidbits@halcyon.com  <- this didn't really appear
onscreen
230 Guest login ok, access restrictions apply.
```

Now that you've passed through the final set of locked FTP doors, you can get down to business. Simple or not, FTP suffers from the standard navigational problem of a command-line interface—you must list the directory to see where you are and what files are around; then you must change the directory, list the files to see what's around, and so on. Listing the directories is a drag. First, list the files using the same command that lists files in UNIX, **ls:**

```
ftp> ls
200 PORT command successful.
150 ASCII data connection for /bin/ls (198.137.231.1,1029) (0
bytes).
```

```
bin
dev
etc
private
pub
usr
226 ASCII Transfer complete.
34 bytes received in 0.06 seconds (0.55 Kbytes/s)
```

The preceding directories are standard UNIX directories; you get accustomed to seeing them. In general, you learn that usually you can look for stuff in the pub directory because it stands for public. Oh, how did I know they were directories? Experience. You can use the dir command to list the contents of the current directory as well, and then it is somewhat more obvious that these are directories.

Second, drop down into the next directory and again use the same command as in UNIX, **cd**, along with the name of the directory you want to enter:

```
ftp> cd pub/winarch
250 CWD command successful.
```

Okay, I cheated, I admit it. While I was online preparing this example, I switched down into the pub directory, then listed the files again, and saw the winarch directory. I didn't use that part of the transcript because I like falsifying the evidence. Specifying two or more directories is perfectly legal and an extremely good idea. Unfortunately, specifying directories requires that you know the path beforehand, which is seldom the case for me.

Now, see what's in this directory by typing **ls** again:

```
ftp> ls
200 PORT command successful.
150 ASCII data connection for /bin/ls (198.137.231.1,1037) (0
bytes).
READ.ME
winarch.zip
226 ASCII Transfer complete.
57 bytes received in 0.01 seconds (5.6 Kbytes/s)
```

Now that you can see what you want, you have to *get* it. That's all there is to it; simply type **get** and the filename. I like using Windows terminal emulators because they enable me to copy the filename, type **get** and a space at the command line, and then paste in the name. Keep in mind that the file will probably be renamed on your PC because DOS is a lot more restrictive with filenames than UNIX.

If you want to retrieve a set of files at once, type **mget** along with a list of filenames or a filename with a wildcard such as * in it. So, if you want to retrieve all the zipped files in a certain directory, type **mget *.zip**. Because I'm primarily looking at this situation from the consumer's point of view, I'll quickly mention that the complements to **get** and **mget** are **put** and **mput**. You're far less likely to **put** files than to **get** them.

```
ftp> get READ.ME
200 PORT command successful.
150 ASCII data connection for READ.ME (198.137.231.1,1038)
226 ASCII Transfer complete.
local: READ.ME remote: READ.ME
27463 bytes received in 17 seconds (16 Kbytes/s)
```

With a name like **READ.ME**, I assume that the contents are ACSII text. Because I knew the file type, I didn't need to change the file transfer mode because the default ASCII mode (see the third line, ASCII data connection for...) worked fine. However, if the poster had chosen to upload a smaller, compressed version of READ.ME (renamed to readme.zip), I would have had to issue the binary command to switch FTP into the mode where it can reliably transfer binary files such as self-extracting archives. The opposite of the binary command is the ascii command, which returns you to ASCII mode.

FTP doesn't display any feedback while it's working, although if you type **hash** before starting the transfer, FTP prints a hash mark (#) after transferring a block of data. Typing **hash** again toggles that setting off. I seldom have trouble with FTP, so I usually don't bother.

FTP then displays the specifics about the file transfer, noting that the throughput was 16K per second and it took 17 seconds to transfer. Just to compare, consider that it took me about three minutes to download this same file to the PC using ZMODEM. That's right, once you have it on your UNIX account, you next download it to your PC. See sz earlier in this chapter for information on sending the file to your PC.

I should mention that the file ends up in the current directory on your UNIX account, which is most likely your main directory. However, if you changed directories before you invoked FTP, the file ends up in that directory instead.

Having retrieved your file, you have no reason to stick around, so type **quit** to get back to the UNIX command line:

```
ftp> quit
221 Goodbye.
```

And that is that. FTP must have another 60 or 70 commands all told, but I've always been perfectly happy with the preceding subset, and I'll bet you will be happy too. To recap quickly (and in order that you can use them), here are the commands:

ftp *sitename*	connect to sitename
anonymous	not a command, but the login name
email address	not a command, but the password
ls	list the files and directories
cd *dirname*	change the directory to dirname
get *filename*	retrieve filename to your account
quit	quit out of FTP

telnet

FTP may seem simple, but Telnet is a piece of cake because it enables you to log in to another machine as though you dialed it locally. At that point, you're just using UNIX or VMS or VM/CMS or some other nasty operating system in a different place, so you don't need to know much else. The other possibility is that you telnet into a special application, such as a library card catalog or a game, and that special application has its own interface. I can't help you there, but most of the applications provide some sort of help.

Aside from the standard method of telnetting, there are two quirks: specifying a port number, which some applications require, and telnetting to an IBM mainframe running a full-screen interface. I mention these quirks later in this section, but first, I discuss the basic Telnet syntax.

Grab a hostname at random to peruse the InterNIC, or Internet Network Information Center. Several companies run this Internet service for the government, and there's good information there. The easiest way to invoke Telnet is to type **telnet** and the sitename, as in the following:

```
/d/tidbits> telnet RS.INTERNIC.NET
Trying...
Connected to RS.INTERNIC.NET.
Escape character is '^]'.
```

As you can see, this machine didn't ask for login or password information, but there's no reason it couldn't have required a special account like "guest." Usually a Telnet site tells you whether it wants you to use a special login name.

```
SunOS UNIX (rs) (ttyp1)


*****************************************************************************
* — InterNIC Registration Services Center   —
*
* For gopher, type:                   GOPHER <return>
* For wais, type:                     WAIS <search string> <return>
* For the *original* whois type:      WHOIS [search string] <return>
* For the X.500 whois DUA, type:      X500WHOIS <return>
* For registration status:           STATUS <ticket number> <return>
*
* For user assistance call (800) 444-4345 ¦ (619) 455-4600 or (703)
742-4777
* Please report system problems to ACTION@rs.internic.net
*****************************************************************************
Please be advised that the InterNIC Registration host contains INTERNET
Domains, IP Network Numbers, ASNs, and Points of Contacts ONLY. Please
refer to rfc1400.txt for details (available via anonymous ftp at
either nic.ddn.mil [/rfc/rfc1400.txt]  or ftp.rs.internic.net
[/policy/rfc1400.txt]).
Cmdinter Ver 1.3 Wed Aug 18 00:36:31 1993 EST
[vt102] InterNIC >
```

This particular site also runs a number of other programs, including a WAIS client and a Gopher client. Because you're now playing by this machine's rules, type **gopher** and see what happens:

```
[vt102] InterNIC > gopher

            Internet Gopher Information Client v1.03
```

```
            Root gopher server: rs.internic.net

 ->  1.   Information about the InterNIC/
     2.   InterNIC Information Services (General Atomics)/
     3.   InterNIC Registration Services (NSI)/
     4.   InterNIC Directory and Database Services (AT&T)/


Press ? for Help, q to Quit, u to go up a menu        Retrieving Directory..-
```

Having invoked the local Gopher client, now you're playing by the Gopher's rules. To navigate, you move the —> pointer using the up- and down-arrow keys, and either pressing Enter or the right-arrow key moves you down into a subfolder, if you can call it that.

Almost all Telnet clients provide an easy way to leave, so if you get stuck or lost, try typing commands such as **quit**, **exit**, or **logout**. You also can try **help** or **?** to see what local commands may be available.

It's distinctly time for dessert, so explore how you telnet to a specific port number by telnetting to the Cookie Server. Watch closely:

```
/d/tidbits> telnet astro.temple.edu 12345
Trying...
Connected to astro.ocis.temple.edu.
Escape character is '^]'.
"Every time I think I know where it's at, they move it."
Connection closed by foreign host.
```

That's all there is to it—you simply append the port number, which you have found in some list or the like (I've never found an easy way to figure it out) to the standard **telnet** *sitename* command.

Finally, what about full-screen IBM interfaces? Like many other things IBM has done, they don't get along well with the rest of the computing world. In fact, Telnet itself doesn't work well to an IBM mainframe running VM or MVS. For those machines, which usually identify themselves by mentioning one of their operating systems when you telnet to them, you need to use a related program, called "tn3270." Otherwise, the program works about the same as Telnet; you just type **tn3270** *sitename*. After you get in, you must use the appropriate keys to send the key sequences that the IBM mainframe expects. Figuring out which keys on your keyboard map to the IBM keys is difficult, but I recommend trying the keypad keys or the combination of Escape and a number key. Good luck; you'll need it. This is a good question for a local administrator because she should know how the local system has been set up. In any event, here's what tn3270 looks like:

```
/d/tidbits> tn3270 cornella.cit.cornell.edu
Trying...
Connected to cornella.cit.cornell.edu.
Unable to open file /etc/map3270
Unable to open file /etc/map3270
Using default key mappings.
```

I got stuck here and wasn't able to do much of anything. Oh well, I probably can't remember the password to that account any more anyway.

```
VM/XA SP ONLINE


        *******
      ***     ***                                                    ***     ***
      **       **                                                     **      **
     ***        *                                                     **      **
     **                                                               **      **
    ***                                                               **      **
    ***              ****      ** ***      ** ****      ****           **      **
    ***              **  **    ******      *******      **  **         **      **
    ***              **   **   **  **      **   **      **   **        **      **
     **              **   **   **          **   **      ********       **      **
    ***        *     **   **   **          **   **      ********       **      **
     **       **     **   **   **          **   **      **             **      **
    ***      ***     **   **   **          **   **      **   **        **      **
     *******        ****      ****         **** **      *****         ****    ****


              Cornell University Ithaca, New York

       This system is for authorized use only.  Type: CUINFO CIT ABUSE



   LOGON
                                                  RUNNING    CORNELLA
```

Now you've learned about all there is to using Telnet in the real world. Once again, if you want, you can check out the man pages for Telnet, or type **telnet** and then **help**, but you don't have to worry about most of Telnet's commands and options.

archie

Now that you've learned about Telnet, look at how you use the special services such as Archie, WAIS, Gopher, and the World-Wide Web from a UNIX command-line environment. The trick is Telnet, because in each case you must telnet to another machine that runs a character-based version of the service. First, explore Archie because it has almost no interface, although it's extremely useful for finding files available via FTP. You can telnet to a number of public Archie servers, and I've listed them in the resources list at the end of the book. Here, I pick a specific one in the U.S. to avoid burdening overseas connections.

To start, you connect to an Archie site:

```
/d/tidbits> telnet archie.sura.net
Trying...
Connected to yog-sothoth.sura.net.
Escape character is '^]'.
```

Then you log in to the Archie program by providing entering archie as the userid:

```
SunOS UNIX (yog-sothoth.sura.net)

login: archie
Last login: Wed Aug 18 01:55:47 from borris.eece.unm.
                Welcome to the ARCHIE server at SURAnet

Please report any problems to archie-admin@sura.net

PLEASE use the client software if you can. If things continue as
they are we will limit the number interactive logins.  Client
software is available on ftp.sura.net in /pub/archie/clients
```

Consider asking your system administrator to install the Archie client software on your machine so that you don't have to tie up the Archie servers around the world by logging into them. The Archie clients are more polite than a person can ever be.

```
Site update/change information should be sent to archie-
updates@bunyip.com

SURAnet is trying out a new, experimental service called qarchie.
qarchie only supports doing searches on the database.  However
queries should complete much faster using the qarchie interface.
```

To try this out, you can log into this machine as qarchie. Please
use the qarchie service unless there is a reason that you cannot.
If you cannot, please send mail to archie-admin@sura.net explaining why. Thanks.

The problem of the percentage becoming negative is a known problem which will be fixed in the future.

```
archie.ac.il              132.65.20.254    (Israel server)
archie.ans.net            147.225.1.10     (ANS server, NY (USA))
archie.au                 139.130.4.6      (Austrailian Server)
archie.doc.ic.ac.uk       146.169.11.3     (United Kingdom Server)
archie.edvz.uni-linz.ac.at 140.78.3.8      (Austrian Server)
archie.funet.fi           128.214.6.102    (Finnish Server)
archie.internic.net       198.49.45.10     (AT&T server, NY (USA))
archie.kr                 128.134.1.1      (Korean Server)
archie.kuis.kyoto-u.ac.jp 130.54.20.1      (Japanese Server)
archie.luth.se            130.240.18.4     (Sweedish Server)
archie.ncu.edu.tw         140.115.19.24    (Taiwanese server)
archie.nz                 130.195.9.4      (New Zeland server)
archie.rediris.es         130.206.1.2      (Spanish Server)
archie.rutgers.edu        128.6.18.15      (Rutgers University (USA))
archie.sogang.ac.kr       163.239.1.11     (Korean Server)
archie.sura.net           128.167.254.195  (SURAnet server MD (USA))
archie.sura.net(1526)     128.167.254.195  (SURAnet alt. MD (USA))
archie.switch.ch          130.59.1.40      (Swiss Server)
archie.th-darmstadt.de    130.83.22.60     (German Server)
archie.unipi.it           131.114.21.10    (Italian Server)
archie.univie.ac.at       131.130.1.23     (Austrian Server)
archie.unl.edu            129.93.1.14      (U. of Nebraska, Lincoln (USA))
archie.uqam.ca            132.208.250.10   (Canadian Server)
archie.wide.ad.jp         133.4.3.6        (Japanese Server)
```

Client software should be supported at all of these sites.

Telnet sites often provide a hefty chunk of information when you first
log in so that you know where you are and what's happening. In
Archie's case, the site tells you about the latest client software and all the
Archie servers around the world. If you see an Archie server nearer to
you, you should use it.

Now you can search for a file. I've stacked the deck on this search because I uploaded the file, which is a long review of the word processor
Nisus that I published in *TidBITS* and distributed separately as well.

```
archie> prog tidbits-nisus
# matches / % database searched:    3 /-24%
```

I presume that **prog** stands for "program," but it would be nice if Archie used a standard term like "find." You can type a word after **prog** or, if you know how, you can type a regular expression, which is a way of specifying patterns of text rather than specific text strings. Archie is a difficult language to master, so don't worry about it for now.

After it updates the # of matches and % of database searched for several minutes, Archie displays the matches, showing the site name, the IP number for that site, when the database at that site was last updated, and the full pathname of the file so that you know where to get it via FTP.

```
Host akiu.gw.tohoku.ac.jp   (130.34.8.9)
Last updated 02:42 31 Jul 1993

    Location: /pub/mac/doc/tidbits
       FILE       rw-r—r—       95707  Apr 16  1992    tidbits-nisus.etx

Host uceng.uc.edu   (129.137.33.1)
Last updated 02:22 29 Jul 1993

    Location: /pub/wuarchive/systems/mac/info-mac/Old/digest/tb
       FILE       r—r—r—        41244  Apr 14  1992    tidbits-nisus.etx.Z

Host knot.queensu.ca   (130.15.48.43)
Last updated 06:43 21 Jul 1993

    Location: /wuarchive/systems/mac/info-mac/Old/digest/tb
       FILE       r—r—r—        41244  Apr 14  1992    tidbits-nisus.etx.Z
```

I was fairly sure that this search string wouldn't turn up many responses. One of the major problems with Archie is its enthusiasm; when you give it a generic search string, it returns up to 1,000 hits on the database, which scroll by, out of control, for some time. Let's try to prevent this situation from happening:

```
archie> help
```

```
 Help gives you information about various topics, including all
the commands that are available and how to use them.  Telling
archie about your terminal type and size (via the "term" vari-
able) and to use the pager (via the "pager" variable) is not
necessary to use help, but provides a somewhat nicer interface.
```

```
Currently, the available help topics are:

    about    - a blurb about archie
    bugs     - known bugs and undesirable features
    bye      - same as "quit"
    email    - how to contact the archie email interface
    exit     - same as "quit"
    help     - this message
    list     - list the sites in the archie database
    mail     - mail output to a user
    nopager  - *** use 'unset pager' instead
    pager    - *** use 'set pager' instead
    prog     - search the database for a file
    quit     - exit archie
    set      - set a variable
    show     - display the value of a variable
    site     - list the files at an archive site
    term     - *** use 'set term ...' instead
    unset    - unset a variable
    whatis   - search for keyword in the software description database
```

For information on one of these topics type:

```
    help <topic>
```

A '?' at the help prompt will list the available sub-topics.

```
Help topics available:
        about    bugs     bye      email
        list     mail     nopager  pager
        prog     regex    set      show
        site     term     unset    whatis
```

I can't convey how I determined which command may be the right one to explore further, but experience (you'll get it, don't worry!) claims that commands such as set generally work for changing settings. I see a few other interesting commands in this help screen: mail, list, and whatis. More on those commands later in this section.

```
Help topic? set
```

The 'set' command allows you to set one of archie's variables. Their values affect how archie interacts with the user. Archie distinguishes between three types of variable: "boolean", which may be either set or unset, "numeric", representing an integer within a pre- determined range, and "string", whose value is a string of characters (which may or may not be restricted).

Currently, the variables that may be set are:

```
      autologout - numeric.   Number of minutes before automatic log out
      mailto     - string.    Address that output is to be mailed to
      maxhits    - numeric.   'prog' stops after this many matches
      pager      - boolean.   If set use the pager, otherwise don't
      search     - string.    How 'prog' is to search the database
      sortby     - string.    How 'prog' output is to be sorted
      status     - boolean.   Report how the search is progressing
      term       - string.    Describes your terminal
```

Each variable has a corresponding subtopic entry under 'set'.
See them for
Press return for more:
 more details. Also, see help on 'unset' and 'show'.

Subtopics available for set:
        autologout   mailto maxhits pager
        search sortby status term

Yup, that's it, you want to find out more about the maxhits variable:

'set' subtopic? **maxhits**

'maxhits' is a numeric variable whose value is the maximum number of matches you want the 'prog' command to generate.

If archie seems to be slow, or you don't want a lot of output this can be set to a small value. "maxhits" must be within the range 0 to 1000. The default value is 1000.

Example:

    set maxhits 100

'prog' will now stop after 100 matches have been found

Bingo! If you type **set maxhits 20** before you issue your prog command, Archie limits the results to 20 hits. You may not see what you want, but you should get a sense if you're on the right track.

But what about those other commands that sounded interesting? If you issue the mail command along with a userid after a prog command finishes, Archie mails the results of that search to the address you specify. This approach can be a good way to keep the list of hits for later perusal, or if you're searching for someone else, you can email him the results.

The list command isn't necessarily useful, but you may find it fun to search the list of FTP sites in Archie's database. Try typing **list win3** to see how many sites have *win3* in their names.

Finally, the whatis command accesses a human-maintained database of file descriptions and searches it for files whose descriptions contain your search string. For instance, try the following:

```
archie> whatis stuffit
sit          produce StuffIt archives for downloading to the MacIntosh
```

It took me three or four tries using whatis before I found anything that matched, and as you can see, there's not much even for a near-ubiquitous program like PKZip.

Perhaps the only real problem with command line Archie is that there's no link to an FTP client so that you can find a file and retrieve it immediately, without having to exit Archie and run FTP. The X windows version of archie, creatively named *xarchie* does have integrated FTP, and I suspect that the archie clients for Windows will soon follow suit.

WAIS

To access WAIS via a UNIX account, you once more rely on Telnet, although the interface completely changes when you arrive at the WAIS server. John Curran has written a decent VT-100 interface that provides one advantage over all of the graphical interfaces I've seen. The difference is that the VT-100 interface enables you to pick from all the sources, or information databases, about which WAIS knows. The graphical interface makes you first find the appropriate source and then start your search, which takes a bit longer the first time you use WAIS. Anyway, take a look.

```
/d/tidbits> telnet quake.think.com
Trying...
Connected to quake.think.com.
Escape character is '^]'.


SunOS UNIX (quake)
```

Accessing WAIS is a matter of telnetting to quake.think.com normally, no special port numbers or IBM mainframes here.

```
login: wais
```

You must log in to WAIS specifically; you aren't dumped in by default. No big deal, the login name is **wais**.

```
Last login: Wed Aug 18 09:47:29 from vax1.utulsa.edu
SunOS Release 4.1.1 (QUAKE) #3: Tue Jul 7 11:09:01 PDT 1992

Welcome to swais.
Please type user identifier (optional, i.e user@host):
ace@tidbits.com
```

Although you don't need a password as such for WAIS, it does ask you to identify yourself. You don't have to, but good net citizens do because they're using someone else's machine.

```
TERM = (vt100)


Starting swais (this may take a little while)...
```

Press Enter to agree that you're using a VT-100 terminal. It takes a few seconds to run the swais program that displays the sources. After swais runs, the screen should fill up as follows:

```
SWAIS                        Source Selection              Sources: 462
  #            Server                       Source                 Cost
001:  [           archie.au]  aarnet-resource-guide              Free
002:  [       munin.ub2.lu.se]  academic_email_conf              Free
003:  [wraith.cs.uow.edu.au]  acronyms                           Free
004:  [      archive.orst.edu]  aeronautics                      Free
005:  [ ftp.cs.colorado.edu]  aftp-cs-colorado-edu               Free
006:  [nostromo.oes.orst.ed]  agricultural-market-news           Free
007:  [      archive.orst.edu]  alt.drugs                        Free
```

```
008:    [      wais.oit.unc.edu]   alt.gopher                           Free
009:    [sun-wais.oit.unc.edu]     alt.sys.sun                          Free
010:    [      wais.oit.unc.edu]   alt.wais                             Free
011:    [alfred.ccs.carleton.]     amiga-slip                           Free
012:    [       munin.ub2.lu.se]   amiga_fish_contents                  Free
013:    [       maat.mct.anl.gov]  anl-gif                              Free
014:    [       maat.mct.anl.gov]  anl-misc                             Free
015:    [   coombs.anu.edu.au]     ANU-Aboriginal-Studies       $0.00/minute
016:    [   coombs.anu.edu.au]     ANU-Asian-Computing          $0.00/minute
017:    [   coombs.anu.edu.au]     ANU-Asian-Religions          $0.00/minute
018:    [          150.203.76.2]   ANU-Australian-Economics     $0.00/minute

Keywords:

<space> selects, w for keywords, arrows move, <return> searches, q quits, or ?
```

The first line shows the number of sources currently available, 462—
daunting, but you can manage. The second line is the heading for the
sources themselves, listing the number of the source (presumably out of
462, so you have a sense of how far along in the list you are), the actual
server that the source lives on (because WAIS sources can live anywhere
on the Internet and be accessible from one place) the name of the source,
and the cost, if any. I don't believe any of the sources listed currently
have prices associated with them, but it's possible that fee-based sources
may appear in the near future. At that point I assume that the WAIS
software helps you enter the information necessary for purchasing the
information you find.

After the headings come the actual entries, and you can move up and
down using the arrow keys on your keyboard. When you see a source
that interests you, highlight it by moving to it with the arrow keys and
then press the Spacebar, as the help line at the bottom of the screen
suggests. You can select more than one source at a time, and if you want
to deselect one, the Spacebar does that too. Before you get into searching
a source, take a look at the help, which accessible by typing a ?.

```
SWAIS                           Source Selection Help
Pa1


j, down arrow, ^N       Move Down one source
k, up arrow, ^P         Move Up one source
J, ^V, ^D               Move Down one screen
K, <esc> v, ^U          Move Up one screen
###                     Position to source number ##
```

```
/sss                        Search for source sss
<space>, <period>           Select current source
=                           Deselect all sources
v, <comma>                  View current source info
<ret>                       Perform search
s                           Select new sources (refresh sources list)
w                           Select new keywords
X, -                        Remove current source permanently
o                           Set and show swais options
h, ?                        Show this help display
H                           Display program history
q                           Leave this program
```

Good thing you checked the help because it provides easier and faster ways of moving around the massive number of sources available. You can use **J** or **K** to flit between screens, or if you have an idea where in the alphabet a source falls, you can attempt to hit it by guessing at the numbers around it. Also, if you know the name of the source, typing / and the first few letters of the name should take you straight to it.

If you cannot determine from the name what sort of information is stored in a database, typing **v** displays the administrative information and a description of a source.

Now go down to the Info-Mac Digest and see if you can find any information about problems with the Centris 650, because my sister's boyfriend is looking to buy one. First, highlight that source with the arrow keys and then hit the Spacebar to mark it. Then type **w** to enter the keywords.

SWAIS		Source Selection	Sources: 462
#	Server	Source	Cost
217:	[wilma.cs.brown.edu]	hyperbole-ml	Free
218:	[sol.acs.unt.edu]	hytelnet	Free
219:	[sunsite.unc.edu]	IAT-Documents	Free
220:	[next2.oit.unc.edu]	ibm.pc.FAQ	Free
221:	[ds.internic.net]	iesg	Free
222:	[ns.ripe.net]	ietf-docs	Free
223:	[ds.internic.net]	ietf	Free
224:	[borg.lib.vt.edu]	ijaema_a	Free
225:	[cicg-communication.g]	imag.fr.doc.magazines	Free
226:	[cicg-communication.g]	imag.ouvrages	Free
227:	[cicg-communication.g]	imag.rapports	Free
228:	[enuxhb.eas.asu.edu]	india-info	Free
229:	[enuxva.eas.asu.edu]	indian-classical-music	Free

```
230:   [     munin.ub2.lu.se]  inet-libraries                 Free
231:   [cmsun.cmf.nrl.navy.m]  info-afs                       Free
232: * [ cmns-moon.think.com]  info-mac                       Free
233:   [ cmns-moon.think.com]  info-nets                      Free
234:   [     quake.think.com]  INFO                           Free

Keywords: Centris 650 bugs

Enter keywords with spaces between them; <return> to search; ^C to cancel
```

An asterisk appears next to the source I marked, and I picked a few keywords that seemed as though they might turn up interesting articles from Info-Mac. After you enter the keywords, press Enter to start the search that presents this list of hits.

> I always have trouble going back and changing my keywords because my terminal seldom seems to display them well. I always have to backspace over everything and retype them. Sometimes the keywords don't display, but the cursor remains at the end of the previous set, so I backspace over the nothingness until I'm at the start of the line again. I don't know why this happens, or if it's normal, but it can be a pain at times.

```
SWAIS                              Search Results
It0
  #    Score     Source              Title                           Lines
001:  [ 858]  (cmns-moon.think)  Info-Mac Digest V11 #120:  Centris Video    60
002:  [ 842]  (cmns-moon.think)  Info-Mac Digest V11 #34:   FPUs on new Ce   54
003:  [ 810]  (cmns-moon.think)  Info-Mac Digest V11 #159:  LC520 .vs. Ce    39
004:  [ 810]  (cmns-moon.think)  Info-Mac Digest V11 #142:  [R] Power-PC     33
005:  [ 810]  (cmns-moon.think)  Info-Mac Digest V11 #137:  Hard Drive Pr    46
006:  [ 810]  (cmns-moon.think)  Info-Mac Digest V11 #90:   68040 does not   39
007:  [ 810]  (cmns-moon.think)  Info-Mac Digest V11 #66:   [*] SoftwareFP   36
008:  [ 810]  (cmns-moon.think)  Info-Mac Digest V11 #37:   Centris 610 -    41
009:  [ 762]  (cmns-moon.think)  Info-Mac Digest V11 #145:  Upgrade from     35
010:  [ 762]  (cmns-moon.think)  Info-Mac Digest V11 #133:  Centris and D    28
011:  [ 762]  (cmns-moon.think)  Info-Mac Digest V11 #121:  [*] Centris 6    30
012:  [ 762]  (cmns-moon.think)  Info-Mac Digest V11 #119:  Apple IIGS Mo    20
013:  [ 762]  (cmns-moon.think)  Info-Mac Digest V11 #118:  Centris 610 V    20
014:  [ 762]  (cmns-moon.think)  Info-Mac Digest V11 #118:  Centris 610 c    29
015:  [ 762]  (cmns-moon.think)  Info-Mac Digest V11 #107:  Monitor power    25
016:  [ 762]  (cmns-moon.think)  Info-Mac Digest V11 #98:   MacsBug on Cen   36
017:  [ 762]  (cmns-moon.think)  Info-Mac Digest V11 #85:   Apple 16" w/ C   31
```

```
018:    [ 762] (cmns-moon.think)  Info-Mac Digest V11 #79:  LC III or Cent    38
```

```
<space> selects, arrows move, w for keywords, s for sources, ? for help
```

Here you have a good number of possibilities. Unfortunately, the name and number of each Info-Mac Digest is part of the title of each entry, so you see only a small part of each actual subject article. No matter, they're easy enough to read. Notice the Score column to the left of the Source column. The higher the number in this column, the more closely the article matches your search criteria. In theory, the articles at the top of the list should be exactly what you want, and the articles further down might or might not work out.

As before, the basic commands of the Spacebar and the arrow keys are listed for your reading convenience, but I bet more useful commands are hidden in the help. A quick **?** reveals the following:

```
SWAIS                        Search Results Help            Page:   1
```

```
j, ^N           Move Down one item
k, ^P           Move Up one item
J               Move Down one screen
K               Move Up one screen
R               Show relevant documents
S               Save current item to a file
m               Mail current item to an address
##              Position to item number ##
/sss            Position to item beginning sss
<space>         Display current item
<return>             Display current item
¦               Pipe current item into a unix command
v               View current item information
r               Make current item a relevant document
s               Specify new sources to search
u               Use it; add it to the list of sources
w               Make another search with new keywords
o               Set and show swais options
h               Show this help display
H               Display program history
q               Leave this program
```

You may find many of these commands useful, especially the capability to mail information back to yourself. After you look at the results of your search, press the Spacebar to display the selected article, such as the abbreviated one that follows:

```
0029001MAC
190211
Info Mac Digest
hades@coos.dartmouth.edu (Brian Hughes)
Info-Mac Digest V11 #34:  FPUs on new Centris machines (C)

Date: Thu, 11 Feb 1993 10:21:56 -0500
From: hades@coos.dartmouth.edu (Brian Hughes)
Subject: FPUs on new Centris machines (C)

Tim Castle writes:

>There has been a lot said over the past couple of weeks about the new
>Centris machines, announced earlier in Tokyo, primarily about the
>'040LC's and their lack of FPUs. I sent a posting which passed along the
>fact (as given by an Apple system engineer) that the '040LC chips are
>not standard '040RC chips with 'failed FPUs, but chips redesigned and
>manufactured without the FPUs by Motorola.

    And this is correct. In fact it was confirmed by an Apple engineer
over on comp.sys.mac.hardware just the other day.

(END)
```

If the article spans more than one screen, page through it by pressing the Spacebar after each screen. At the end of the article, indicated by (END), the Spacebar doesn't work; to exit the pager, you must type **q**.

> **Caution:** If you type **q** anywhere else in the WAIS client, it quits instantly and you must log in again.

The fact that the VT-100 WAIS client shows you all the possible sources is both a blessing and a curse. Seeing all the possible sources and browsing through them is nice, but dealing with 462 of anything is overwhelming. Still, the VT-100 WAIS client provides access in a usable fashion, and that's what counts.

Gopher

Tunneling through gopher holes of information in a character-based environment is harder than in a graphical environment because you must go up through the levels you go down. Gopher provides access to all sorts of information and files, and it links to anonymous FTP sites and WAIS for added utility. Gopher is inherently hierarchical, like most directory structures; but unlike folders, if you dive down into several levels, you must come back out the same way. The graphical versions of Gopher don't suffer this problem because they generally provide a visual representation of the tree that you are perusing. You can jump several levels up by just clicking on the part of the tree you are interested in. Although your local UNIX machine can install the same client you see in the following, you can always telnet to a public Gopher server like this one. The effect is the same, but if you can use a local client (see what happens if you type **gopher** at the UNIX prompt), that method is preferable for everyone.

```
/d/tidbits> telnet consultant.micro.umn.edu
Trying...
Connected to hafnhaf.micro.umn.edu.
Escape character is '^]'.

AIX telnet (hafnhaf)
```

Login as "gopher" to use the gopher system.

```
IBM AIX Version 3 for RISC System/6000
(C) Copyrights by IBM and by others 1982, 1991.
login: gopher
```

By now you're probably bored stiff with my explanations of logging in to a machine via Telnet, so I'll try to avoid sounding like a broken record. Like WAIS, Gopher wants you to log in to the machine with a special username, **gopher** in this case.

```
Last unsuccessful login: Mon Aug 16 09:57:11 1993 on pts/1 from
access.telecomm.umn.edu
Last login: Wed Aug 18 12:49:00 1993 on pts/18 from gateway.cary.ibm.com
TERM = (vt100)
Erase is Ctrl-H
```

```
Kill is Ctrl-U
Interrupt is Ctrl-C
I think you're on a vt100 terminal

Press ? for Help, q to Quit, u to go up a menu        Retrieving Directory..\
```

If you're not using a VT-100 terminal, there's no telling if the client will work.

```
           Internet Gopher Information Client 2.0 p14


                Root gopher server: gopher2.tc.umn.edu

        1.  Information About Gopher/
        2.  Computer Information/
        3.  Internet file server (ftp) sites/
        4.  Fun & Games/
        5.  Libraries/
        6.  Mailing Lists/
        7.  News/
    —>  8.  Other Gopher and Information Servers/
        9.  Phone Books/
       10.  Search Gopher Titles at the University of Minnesota <?>
       11.  Search lots of places at the U of M <?>
       12.  UofM Campus Information/

Press ? for Help, q to Quit, u to go up a menu              Page: 1/1
```

After you're in the Gopher menus, move around with the arrows, press Enter to select a menu item, and type **u** to move up a level. Notice that some of the entries end with /, which indicates they are directories, and other entries end with <?>, which indicates you can perform full text searches on them.

Gopherspace is so huge these days that although it's fun to browse through the various menus at times, if you want to find anything specific, you use Veronica, which is usually located under a menu called "Other Gopher and Information Servers" or "World."

```
            Internet Gopher Information Client v1.11

           Search titles in Gopherspace using veronica

    —>  1.                                               .
        2.  FAQ:  Frequently-Asked Questions about veronica  (1993/06/24).
```

```
3.  How to compose  veronica queries (NEW June 24) READ ME!!.
4.  Search gopherspace for GOPHER DIRECTORIES  (PSINet) <?>
5.  Search gopherspace for GOPHER DIRECTORIES  (U. Pisa) <?>
6.  Search gopherspace using veronica at PSINet <?>
7.  Search gopherspace using veronica at University of Pisa <?>

Press ? for Help, q to Quit, u to go up a menu                Page: 1/1
```

I have no idea why item 1 is blank, but the important things to note in the Veronica screen are that items ending with a period are text files that you can immediately view onscreen (or, even neater, mail to yourself) and that Veronica enables you to search two types of data within Gopherspace. Items 4 and 5 enable you to search for the names of other Gopher directories only, whereas with items 6 and 7 you can search for the titles of all items in Gopherspace, including individual files. Search directories first because the search is likely to narrow more quickly and be easier to wrap your mind around.

If you select item 4, you see a pseudo dialog box into which you can type the word you want to search for. In this case, I typed **tidbits**.

```
+ — — — — —Search gopherspace for GOPHER DIRECTORIES  (PSINet) — — — — — —+
¦                                                                          ¦
¦ Words to search for   tidbits                                            ¦
¦                                                                          ¦
¦                                    [Cancel ^G] [Accept - Enter]          ¦
¦                                                                          ¦
+ — — — — — — — — — — — — — — — — — — — — — — — — — — — — — — — — — — — — — +
```
And here's what Gopher came up with:
```
                      Internet Gopher Information Client v1.11


        Search gopherspace for GOPHER DIRECTORIES  (PSINet): tidbits

  —> 1.  'Tidbits' - a Macintosh Electronic Magazine/
     2.  Tidbits/
     3.  Tidbits/
     4.  tidbits-175.etx/
     5.  tidbits-175.etx/
     6.  tidbits-175.etx/
     7.  tidbits-175.etx/
     8.  tidbits-175.etx/
     9.  Info-Mac-Tidbits/


Press ? for Help, q to Quit, u to go up a menu                Page: 1/1
```

When you see a number of items that all look the same (which is all too common because of duplication of resources on the Internet), you can check where they live with the = command. If something seems slow, it may be because that particular Gopher server is located far away.

Enough for now, you should be able to navigate through Gopherspace adequately by moving into and out of various menu levels and by using Veronica to search for specific Gopher servers and items in Gopherspace.

Oops, I almost forgot. One of Gopher's most impressive features is the way it links with Telnet to provide access to other, non-Gopher services. At the top level is an item called "Internet file server (ftp) sites," which takes you to any FTP site. Gopher is an excellent way to FTP files because, for technical reasons, it puts less of a load on a server than FTP. The major problem with using Gopher to look for and snag files is that unlike FTP, it's impossible to determine file sizes unless the server is running the latest Gopher+ extensions.

Along the same lines of linking to other services, in the Other Gopher and Information Servers directory is an item for Terminal Based Information, which uses Telnet to access a number of campus-wide information systems and the like. Selecting one of these items drops you into whatever special Telnet interface the service uses.

```
              Internet Gopher Information Client v1.11

                    Terminal Based Information

          1.  Appalachian State University <TEL>
          2.  CUline, University of Colorado,Boulder <TEL>
          3.  Columbia University - ColumbiaNet <TEL>
   —>     4.  Cornell CUINFO <TEL>
          5.  MIT TechInfo <TEL>
          6.  NYU ACF INFO system <TEL>
          7.  New Mexico State University NMSU/INFO <TEL>
          8.  North Carolina State University Happenings! <TEL>
          9.  Princeton News Network <TEL>
          10. The GC EduNET System (A K-12 education resource) <TEL>
```

```
11. U of Saskatchewan Library INFOACCESS system <TEL>
12. University of New Hampshire's VideoTex <TEL>
13. University of North Carolina at Chapel Hill INFO <TEL>

Press ? for Help, q to Quit, u to go up a menu
Page: 1/1
```

Another item in the "Other Gopher and Information Servers" directory enables you to access WAIS sources as though they were normal Gopher databases. If you find all 462 sources daunting, you may consider using Veronica to search all of Gopherspace for a topic along with the keyword **.src** to indicate that you want to find only matching WAIS sources. I don't know whether that method is foolproof, but it works for me.

Enjoy Gopherspace, but don't let it overwhelm you. If you use a local Gopher client and you find a service within Gopherspace that you particularly like, you can mark neat items with bookmarks by typing **a** when pointing at that item. At any point, typing **v** displays your bookmarks so that you can jump to them without tunneling through Gopherspace.

HYTELNET

I'm not going to explore HYTELNET in depth, but suffice it to say that it stands for *hypertelnet* and provides a poor man's Gopher interface to information resources available via Telnet or tn3270. Like Gopher, HYTELNET enables you to select items from a menu by moving the cursor to them with the up- and down-arrow keys and then using the right- and left-arrow keys to move either to the next level down, or back to the previous level. After you finally reach a description of a service, you can move to the Telnet command embedded in the description, and by selecting, it actually telnets directly to that location. Because HYTELNET works with Telnet, of course, it provides yet another interface to Archie, WAIS, Gopher, and the World-Wide Web, but once you're in, you're still using a normal Telnet interface. Here's a partial HYTELNET session that I started by typing **hytelnet**:

```
                    Welcome to HYTELNET
                       version 6.5
                     June 20, 1993

          What is HYTELNET?        <WHATIS>
          Library catalogs         <SITES1>
          Other resources          <SITES2>
          Help files for catalogs  <OP000>
          Catalog interfaces       <SYS000>
          Internet Glossary        <GLOSSARY>
          Telnet tips              <TELNET>
          Telnet/TN3270 escape keys <ESCAPE.KEY>
          Key-stroke commands      <HELP>


  ....................................................
  Up/Down arrows MOVE    Left/Right arrows SELECT    ? for HELP anytime

          m  returns here      q  quits
  ....................................................

          HYTELNET 6.5 was written by Peter Scott
          E-mail address: aa375@freenet.carleton.ca
```

On this screen I moved down to the Other Resources item and used the
right-arrow key to go into it.

```
                Other Telnet-accessible resources

        <ARC000>  Archie: Archive Server Listing Service
        <CWI000>  Campus-wide Information systems
        <FUL000>  Databases and bibliographies

        <DIS000>  Distributed File Servers (Gopher/WAIS/WWW)
        <ELB000>  Electronic books
        <FEE000>  Fee-Based Services

        <FRE000>  FREE-NETs & Community Computing Systems
        <BBS000>  General Bulletin Boards
        <HYT000>  HYTELNET On-line versions

        <NAS000>  NASA databases
        <NET000>  Network Information Services
        <DIR000>  Whois/White Pages/Directory Services

        <OTH000>  Miscellaneous resources
```

Here I just stuck with the first item, Archie servers:

```
              Archie: Archive Server Listing Service

<ARC005> Advanced Network & Services, Inc (USA)
<ARC003> Deakin File Server (Australia)
<ARC002> Finnish University and Research Network Server (Finland)
<ARC008> Hebrew University of Jerusalem (Israel)
<ARC006> Imperial College, London (England)
<ARC016> InterNIC Directory and Database Server
<ARC001> McGill School of Computer Science Server (Canada)
<ARC010> Melbourne (Australia)
<ARC012> National Central University, Chung-li, Taiwan
<ARC011> Rutgers University Archive Server (USA)
<ARC014> Sogang University (Korea)
<ARC004> SURAnet Server (USA)
<ARC013> Technische Hochschule Darmstadt (Germany)
<ARC015> University of Lulea (Sweden)
<ARC007> University of Nebraska, Lincoln (USA)
<ARC009> Victoria University, Wellington (New Zealand)
```

Again, I used the right-arrow key to go into the first Archie server listed
(that one run by Advanced Network & Services), resulting in the following screen (which I could have used to telnet to that site, but I didn't,
because you saw what that screen looks like earlier in this chapter).

```
                  Advanced Network & Services, Inc

TELNET ARCHIE.ANS.NET or 147.225.1.31
login: archie

'help' for help
Problems, comments etc. to archie-admin@ans.net

Client software is available on ftp.ans.net:/pub/archie/clients,
and documentation can be found in /pub/archie/doc on the same
machine.

Advanced Network & Services, Inc.     E-Mail: shiao@ans.net
100 Clearbrook Road                   Office: (914) 789-5340
Elmsford, NY 10523
```

There's nothing particularly wrong with HYTELNET, but it doesn't
excite me. I don't find it any easier to use than Gopher, and Gopher
provides access to the same sorts of things. I suppose your choice
depends on how you work.

World-Wide Web

The World-Wide Web (WWW) is the least structured of the special services and, like Gopher, it can link to all of the others, making the boundaries blur quickly. If you use the World-Wide Web VT-100 interface, everything blurs quickly. In my opinion a hypertext interface is almost impossible to implement well in a character-based environment. Such an interface must enable you to select a specific marker in the text to jump to a related chunk of text. With only textual markers, it's hard to keep track of where you are and where you may want to go. Let me show you what I mean. WWW is based at CERN in Switzerland, so telnet there:

```
/d/tidbits> telnet info.cern.ch
Trying...
Connected to nxoc01.cern.ch.
Escape character is '^]'.


CERN Information Service
(ttypb on nxoc01)


                                                 Overview of the Web
                     GENERAL OVERVIEW

   There is no "top" to the World-Wide Web. You can look at it from many points
   of view. If you have no other bias, here are some places to start:

   by Subject[1]          A classification by subject of interest. Incomplete
                          but easiest to use.

   by Type[2]             Looking by type of service (access protocol, etc) may
                          allow to find things if you know what you are looking
                          for.

   About WWW[3]           About the World-Wide Web global information sharing
                          project

Starting somewhere else

   To use a different default page, perhaps one representing your field of
   interest, see  "customizing your home page"[4].

What happened to CERN?

   This default default page used to be the  CERN-specific but inappropriate
```

```
for users world-wide. However, the CERN[5] and HEP[6] lists are still there!
So if you are at CERN, set your environment variable, logical name, etc.,
WWW_HOME to "http://info.cern.ch/" to get the CERN home page back!
   [End]
1-6, Up, Quit, or Help:
```

As the welcome text says, the World-Wide Web has no top. You are where you are, and you can probably go somewhere else from there. Look at the Web in terms of the services it connects to, or [2] in the preceding screen. That should show you a bit about how you move around and some of the problems the Web faces in presenting information.

```
                          Data sources classified by access protocol
             DATA SOURCES CLASSIFIED BY TYPE OF SERVICE

   See also categorization exist by subject[1] .

  World-Wide Web[2]        List of W3 servers . See also: about the WWW
                           initiative[3] .

  WAIS[4]                  Find WAIS index servers using the directory of
                           servers[5] , or lists by name[6] or domain[7] . See
                           also: about WAIS[8] .

  Network News[9]          Available directly in all www browsers. See also this
                           list of FAQs[10].

  Gopher[11]               Campus-wide information systems, etc, listed
                           geographically. See also: about Gopher[12] .

  Telnet access[13]        Hypertext  catalogues by Peter Scott. See also: list
                           by Scott Yanoff[14] . Also, Art St George's index[15]
                           (yet to be hyperized) etc.

  VAX/VMS HELP[16]         Available using the help gateway[17] to WWW.
                              Data sources classified by access protocol (44/43)

  Anonymous FTP[18]        Tom Czarnik's list of (almost) all sites. Search them
                           all with full hypertext archie gateways[19]  (or
                           telnet to ARCHIE[20] )— An index of almost everything
                           available by anonymous FTP.

  TechInfo[21]             A CWIS system from MIT. Gateway access thanks to
                           Linda Murphy/Upenn. See also more about techninfo[22]
                              .
```

```
X.500[23]                  Directory system originally for eletronic mail
                           addresses. (Slightly uneven view though gateway).

WHOIS[24]                  A simple internet phonebook system.

Other protocols           Other forms of online data[25] .
```

```
                                                              Tim BL[26]
```

```
    [End]
```

You can get into plenty, so check out Gopher because you just looked at
its VT-100 interface, and you can decide which you like better.

```
1-26, Back, Up, Quit, or Help: 11
gopher://gopher.micro.umn.edu:70/11/
Other%20Gopher%20and%20Information%20Server
Select one of:

        All the Gopher Servers in the World[1]
        Search titles in Gopherspace using veronica[2]
        Africa[3]
        Asia[4]
        Europe[5]
        International Organizations[6]
        Middle East[7]
        North America[8]
        Pacific[9]
        South America[10]
        Terminal Based Information[11]
        WAIS Based Information[12]

    [End]
```

You see the problem. Rather than being able to point and shoot with the
arrow keys, you must look and see what number to type. The numbers
change on every screen, and large screens (such as the comp hierarchy of
newsgroups, which are also available) can have hundreds of numbers
from which to choose. Checking the help displays the following:

```
WWW LineMode Browser version 1.4a (WWWLib 1.1a)    COMMANDS AVAILABLE

You are reading
 "gopher://gopher.micro.umn.edu:70/11/
Other%20Gopher%20and%20Information%20Serv"
```

```
whose address is
  gopher://gopher.micro.umn.edu:70/11/
Other%20Gopher%20and%20Information%20Servs

  List                List the references from this document.
  <number>            Select a referenced document by number (from 1 to 12).
  Recall              List visited documents.
  Recall <number>     Return to a previously visited document
                      as numbered in the recall list.
  HOme                Return to the starting document.
  Back                Move back to the last document.
  Next                Take next link from last document.
  Previous            Take previous link from last document.
  Go address          Go to document of given [relative] address
  Verbose             Switch to verbose mode.
  Help                Display this page.
  Manual              Jump to the online manual for this program
  Quit                Leave the www program.
```

It's good that Web tells us where we are, but the format isn't particularly readable in all cases. The Home, List, and Recall commands simplify navigation because Home theoretically takes you to the home page you started on, List shows you a simple list of all the possible links for the current item, and Recall (with a number) enables you to jump back to a previously visited area.

Frankly, although I think the Web is extremely cool, searching for specific bits of information—especially in its VT-100 interface—is not simple, unlike the Gopher/Veronica combination or WAIS. I'm bothered by this situation because I wholeheartedly approve of the concept of linking the text internally to other texts, but I think the Web needs some sort of agent like Veronica to start the search process. In time, it will happen, I suspect.

I talk more about a graphical interface to the Web in chapter 10, but suffice it to say that the VT-100 interface takes you into the Web and the Quit command takes you out. Where you travel while in the Web is entirely up to you.

Chapter

Windows Sockets (WinSock) Access

I've included a quote from Andrew S. Tanenbaum to illustrate a point: "Never underestimate the bandwidth of a station wagon full of tapes hurtling down the highway."

In this chapter we will talk about accessing the world wide Internet, Al Gore's "Information Superhighway," via a narrow, rocky goat trail. The goat trail I am referring to is the phone line connected to your modem which, although well maintained, is still a fairly small pipe through which to pump color images of the coffee room at Indiana State University. The Information Superhighway will be taxed to its limits in the next few years, not by university professors shipping models of the earth's climate, but by you and I using Mosaic to look at art collections in Australia. Andrew was correct in thinking that we focus on the current, coolest technology—frequently overlooking the obvious, effective, older technology. This chapter is all about using the NetManage software, Chameleon Sampler, included in the back of this book (current, sophisticated technology), to access the phone line (older, but reliable, technology), in order to connect to Internet resources (totally unpredictable technology).

Several companies have developed TCP/IP stacks (or interfaces) so that Windows will conform with the WinSock application program interface (API). By doing so, dozens of applications that are written and utilized that API can now effectively communicate on the Internet.

Think of these TCP/IP stacks as universal translators. They take information from your application, such as a Gopher client, via WinSock, and translate that into a packet of network information, headed for its destination (a Gopher server). I won't dive into the nitty gritty of *how* this works, but it's important to understand that the underlying hardware is almost irrelevant. You could be running a 2400 bps SLIP connection or an Ethernet connection and none of the network applications running above it—Telnet, FTP, mail, and ping, for example—will even care. The only thing *you'll* notice is performance.

There is so much WinSock-compatible software available that there's no way they all can be covered in detail within this book. Rather, I'll concentrate on the cream of the crop in various categories. The idea is to give you a flavor of what is possible, and what you may see, so you can make more informed decisions about what *you* might choose to use. Besides, by the time this book goes to press, there will be many more applications available.

As far as what will be discussed, Chameleon Sampler from NetManage will be discussed first as it is included with this book. Then, for those people who must use a modem and SLIP to connect, different implementations of SLIP will be discussed. After covering low-level software, email programs, Usenet newsreaders, FTP clients, and utility applications such as NCSA Telnet, Archie, and Finger are covered. Next up are Gopher clients, the WAIS and World-Wide Web clients, and then a couple of commercial WinSock stacks from Distinct and InterCon are explored.

With those preliminaries out of the way, let's look at Chameleon Sampler.

Chameleon Sampler

NetManage's Chameleon Sampler has a special version of NetManage's excellent TCP/IP software stack for the Windows desktop, Newt, which has been limited to SLIP and PPP interfaces only.

TCP/IP is a protocol definition for computer networks. In human terms, we would call it a language and, like language, you must use one that is understood by the person you are addressing in order to communicate. On the Internet, the common language is TCP/IP. Your computer will have to speak TCP/IP to communicate with any of the resources there.

If you will be accessing the Internet from a large company with a dedicated connection, you must purchase a full-blown commercial version of Chameleon 4.0. The commercial version of Chameleon includes over two dozen applications *and* support for network interfaces such as Ethernet or Token Ring. If this is the case, you should talk to your systems administrator about configuration and setup. In some ways, setup for a network card and local area network is much more complicated than anything you may see setting up SLIP or PPP.

Because those of you with system administrators can ask for help, I'm going to concentrate on details of interest to the individual who has no local system administrator, and must rely solely on this book and the administrator at some public provider. Therefore, I'm not going to talk about many of the issues specific to dedicated Token Ring or Ethernet connections. Frankly, there's not much that I could add to the installation instructions that come with the commercial package. With version 4.0, NetManage has made installation fairly straightforward.

I realize that there's a Catch-22 problem here, but one of the better sources I've seen for NetManage configuration tips, and help with WinSock in general, is the Usenet newsgroup `alt.winsock`. If you have access to Usenet news *before* you get Chameleon up and running, you might try that avenue.

Newt Questions

Now, let's go over the questions you need to ask to configure Newt on your own. First, of course, comes the connection method, via local area network or via SLIP. If you're using the software on the Sampler diskette to attach via phone lines, this choice is made: either SLIP or PPP. If you're connecting via a network, most of the same rules apply (but again, your system administrator knows the details). Second, find out whether you are supposed to enter a static IP address manually, or if it is assigned dynamically when you call your host machine each time.

If your address is assigned manually, you need to find out what your static IP address number will be. It will be four numbers, separated by periods, and should look something like mine, which is 192.135.191.128. If you connect manually, you also need a gateway address number in the same format. You may need this gateway address with dynamic addressing, but perhaps not. Depending on the configuration of your site, you also may need to find out your network class and subnet mask, and your system administrator should know what to tell you here. No matter what, you need to know the name and number address of one or more *domain name servers*, which are machines that translate between names that you enter—such as ftp.tidbits.com—and the numeric IP addresses that the machines all speak. Finally, although you don't need it to configure Chameleon, now is a good time to ask your system administrator for the address of your NNTP (Net News Transport Protocol) news server.

Here's the summary:

Connection method: SLIP, PPP, Token Ring, Ethernet

Addressing style: Static, Dynamic

IP Address (if static): Something like 192.135.191.128

Gateway Address (if necessary): Something like 192.135.191.253

Network class (if static and necessary): A, B, or C

Subnet Mask (if Static and necessary): 255.255.255.0 for a class C address, subnetted at 8 bits

Nameservers: Something like nwnexus.wa.com - 192.135.191.1

NNTP news server: Something like nwfocus.wa.com

I realize this information is a bit much to swallow at once, but that's why I go over how to configure Newt in the following section, so you can see where each piece of information goes.

SLIP vs. PPP

An increasing number of people who don't work at a large business or university want access to the Internet, and an increasing number of Internet providers are springing up to meet that demand. Because individuals seldom have the level of connectivity enjoyed by those in business or education, they must make do with slower connections and, until recently, with uglier ones as well. That has changed with the availability of SLIP (Serial Line Internet Protocol, and sometimes indicated as SL/IP) and PPP (Point to Point Protocol) accounts that are available to anyone. Although distinctly slower (because they work with modems rather than dedicated networks), SLIP and PPP provide decent performance in normal situations and, more importantly, they provide access to some extremely cool software.

What's the difference between SLIP and PPP, and should you care? The answer to the first part of the question seems to be that PPP is SLIP done right. Apparently, SLIP literally was designed on the back of an envelope and implemented in an afternoon. PPP, in contrast, was designed more carefully and is far more flexible, so it supports multiple protocols (such as Novell's IPX and TCP/IP) at the same time and over the same connection. The capability to support multiple protocols is neat because you can use TCP/IP programs while dialed into an Novell server. However (and this fact is probably a testament to SLIP's simplicity), SLIP is more prevalent, in terms of both support and available accounts.

As far as whether or not you should care, my impression is that at the moment it doesn't make much difference. My opinion may change in the next year or so; PPP may become more pervasive, based upon its technical superiority. For the moment, however, SLIP seems to be the way to go.

SLIP in the world of Windows these days means a WinSock TCP/IP stack that supports SLIP as one of its interfaces. There are several of these available now, including Peter Tattam's excellent Trumpet WinSock in the shareware arena, and Distinct, FTP Software, InterCon, and of course NetManage, all in the commercial arena (except for readers of this book, who get it free).

Getting an Account

When it comes time for you to get a SLIP account, the details are up to you, in terms of what company you work with and the like. You can find a list of companies that provide SLIP services in Peter Kaminski's PDIAL list, in appendix C, "PDIAL List." However, once you decide on a provider, you must get certain information in order to configure your SLIP program. Some of the necessary information comes from setting up Newt, as discussed previously, so you should combine the information for Newt with the information for SLIP. For convenience, they are listed as follows:

Phone number: What number do you call to connect to your server?

Login name: What is the SLIP account login name? This name can be different from your userid or machine name.

Password: What password should you provide when logging in?

MTU: What is the maximum transmission unit size? (I've heard 1006 batted around commonly.)

Header Compression: Should you use RFC 1144 TCP Header Compression? (Don't worry about what it does; just ask.)

Login Procedure: What should you expect to receive from your host machine, and how should your machine respond when logging in? This should be *exactly* described; you will be having a really stupid machine interpret it all.

And from the Newt configuration:

What is your **IP address** in number form (such as 192.135.191.128)?

What is your **default gateway address** in number form?

What are the **numeric addresses** of one or more **name servers?**

What is the name and number address of your **NNTP** (Net News Transport Protocol) server?

 # Newt

Newt is the name of the WinSock TCP/IP stack that ships with the NetManage application suite. The version that comes with this book is limited to SLIP and PPP for its network interface. I've used the commercial version to support Ethernet and Token Ring local area networks with great success.

Installation and Setup

Network software typically is not the easiest thing to install on your PC, requiring the intervention of a systems manager, or network-savvy user. Well, in this case, I've appointed *you* network manager, systems consultant, and overall network seer. Take a deep breath, and exhale slooowly. The reason you won't have any problems with this network installation is that we've made the network exceedingly simple by using SLIP, or PPP.

To install Newt on your system, place the floppy disk containing an installable Newt in your a: or b: drive, and from the Windows Program Manager, bring up the Run dialog box from the File menu. You then type **a:\setup**, or **b:\setup**, depending on where your 3.5-inch floppy disk drive is located.

This dialog box will ask whether you want to install into the default directory c:\netmanag, and will then proceed to copy and expand the files from the distribution disk onto your hard disk. Once this process is finished, you'll be ready to configure Newt.

Configuring Newt seems a little awkward because there is no Newt application. You need to start the Custom application and enter the configuration values there (see figure 10.1). Once Custom is set up, Newt will automatically launch every time you launch Custom.

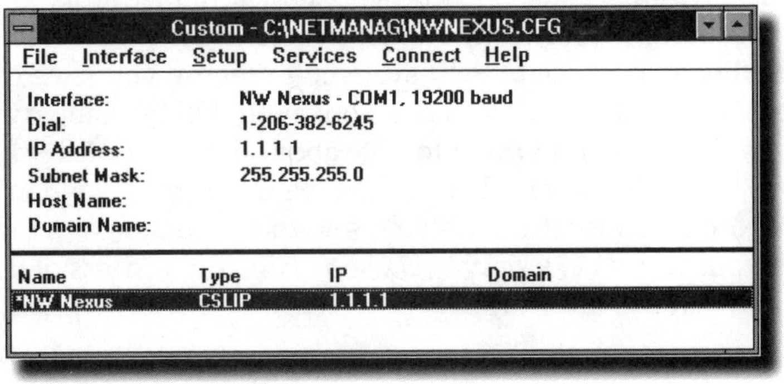

Figure 10.1   Custom main window.

If you're slightly nervous about IP terminology and want to get started right away, I suggest you take a peek at appendix F, "Special Internet Access Offer." I've provided a configuration specifically tailored for the Northwest Nexus provider in Seattle which includes all the parameters you need except those for your modem. However, if you want to dive into IP or don't want to make long distance calls from, say, Florida to Washington to reach Northwest Nexus, then continue reading.

The first item on the agenda is to add a network interface. You may choose any name you like, but the interface type must match the network that you plan to use: SLIP, CSLIP (compressed SLIP), or PPP. Only after you have defined an interface can you configure other parameters. Parameters that I know need to be set for SLIP and PPP will be listed and explained, less critical parameters (such as SNMP setup) will be addressed as an exercise.

IP Address

Your IP address is what uniquely identifies your computer from all the other computers on the Internet (it will be one of about four billion different valid IP addresses). As you may guess, it is critical that this piece of information be correct, or no one will know where to send information to you. There are essentially two ways of setting this information. (Well actually three, but the third doesn't apply to SLIP or PPP so I'm leaving it out.)

userformat

Dynamic addressing is a term used by system administrators to describe a method of sending your computer an IP address as part of the login sequence when you attach to their system. If you use your free time on Northwest Nexus, included with this book, you will be using dynamic addressing. The important thing to note about dynamic addressing is that it really doesn't matter what you set the IP address to when you configure Newt, because this will be reset when you attach to the server. I have set mine to 1.1.1.1, only because the default address of 0.0.0.0 is the only one that *will not* work.

Static, or manual, addressing is where the system manager assigns you an IP address and you use that address forever (or until the systems change). To set this, you choose IP Address from the Setup menu and type in the address that your system administrator gave you (see figure 10.2).

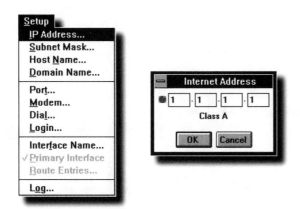

Figure 10.2   *Custom IP Address setting.*

Manual addressing typically would be used in a local area network environment, or in a situation where there are few dial-up clients.

Subnet Mask

Subnet masks are a way for the computer to determine the extent of your local area network. If I give the computer an address like 129.101.100.20, the first thing it needs to know is whether that address is local or somewhere out on the Internet. The explanation of how that happens involves fiddling with ones and zeros, doing something called exclusive ORs, and essentially coming up with a "Yes, it's local," or a "No, it's not." For SLIP and PPP, this parameter usually is not used at all, because you are setting up a local area network of only two nodes: your own, and the SLIP or PPP host. In cases where you may need to choose a valid subnet mask, you have no choice but to seek the advice of you system administrator.

Hostname

In most cases, a host name is not required for SLIP or PPP users. If you are attaching using a manual or static IP address, however, your system administrator may need to assigned a host name to that address. Simply choose Host Name from the Setup menu, and type in what was given to you (see figure 10.3).

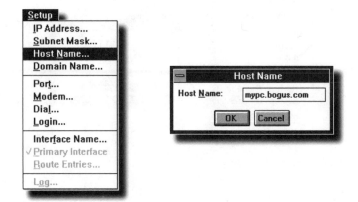

Figure 10.3   *Custom Host Name setting.*

Domain Name

You can think of a domain name as a text equivalent to the netmask, except that the domain name is used in a SLIP or PPP context. The domain name is the part of an Internet address that uniquely identifies the organization to which an address belongs. Most Internet addresses will look something like machine.organization.type. In this case, *Machine* would be the name of a particular computer, such as migraine (a machine I named for the way it made me feel). *Organization* would be the company, school, or other Internet entity name, such as Microsoft. The last part of the address, which I call *type*, would be a designator that indicates what kind of organization this is. In Microsoft's case it would be *com*, for commercial. So, if we assembled this fictitious address, we would have migraine.microsoft.com; the *domain name* here would be microsoft.com.

When you ask your PC to contact a machine with the name "piggy," it automatically will append whatever domain name you have chosen to the address given. If, on the other hand, you give it a complete name, such as piggy.microsoft.com, it will correctly interpret this as non-local and resolve the address via a domain name server lookup. Here again, ask your system administrator what the correct domain name is for you and set this under Domain Name in the Setup menu.

Default Gateway

This is another item that is more than likely moot, due to the fact that you will probably establish a SLIP or PPP connection. This parameter is used to tell your PC where to send information if the IP address fails the "is this local" test of the netmask. If, in fact, you must set a netmask, you may also need to set a default gateway (according to information provided to you along with the netmask). This should be in the form of an IP address and the machine associated with that address probably will not be a computer at all, but rather a router. This item can be found under the Services menu, and is called Default Gateway.

Domain Servers

This is a critical configuration parameter that must be supplied by the system administrator. When you type in the address of some machine on the Internet, the computer must map this onto an IP address in order to start communicating with it. This is done by asking a computer that knows such things: namely, the domain server. To avoid a "chicken and egg" problem, the address for the domain server must be expressed as an IP address. This item can be set from the Services menu by selecting Domain Servers.

Communication Parameters

Up to now, we've talked about true network issues. Everything having to do with serial ports, modems, and phone numbers will be discussed in their own section. The actual communication parameters settings are extremely dependent on your own computer hardware and modem, but these items will be described as generally as possible.

Port

Your PC will have either a serial port attached to a modem, or an internal modem disguising itself as a serial port. Standard PC architecture allows for 4 serial ports, called COM1 through COM4, and you need to know to which one your modem is attached. In addition to which COM port, you will need to get values for *baud rate* (speed), number of data bits, number of stop bits, parity and flow control and enter them into the Port Settings dialog box. The baud rate is associated with your modem, and the other parameters are associated with the service provider's machine: usually no-parity, 8 data bits, 1 stop bit (see figure 10.4).

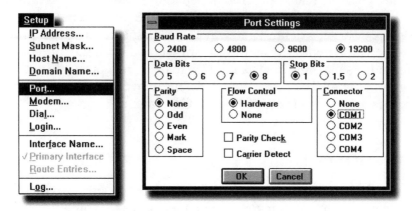

Figure 10.4 *Custom Port Settings.*

Modem

Hayes did the world a favor many years ago by producing modems so rugged and reliable that almost anyone who bought a modem bought a Hayes. What this has done for us is establish a *de facto* standard for modem command languages. When you bring up the modem configuration screen from the Setup menu, it gives you three basic modem types from which to choose: Hayes, Telebit, and Multitech. My suggestions are simple: If you have one of the three types, choose that type; if you have *anything* else, choose Hayes. If you don't have one of the three listed, it's likely that your modem manufacturer has implemented the Hayes command set (or a reasonable facsimile of it), and the Hayes setup sequences will work fine.

Dial

This item is fairly straightforward. In the Dial dialog box, type in the phone number that you need to dial in order to connect to your service provider. All of the other settings are optional, but you may wish to bump the default time-out to 45 seconds or so if your modem, service provider, and/or telephone company takes a long time to make the connection. Choose Redial, if you struggle with busy signals or other annoying characteristics found with some service providers. Oh, and be sure to check the box for Signal When Connected. That way, you'll get a beep when you connect and are ready to access the Internet.

Login

userformat

Filling in the information for the Login dialog box does nothing but supply variable information to the scripting language. In the scripting language, rather than typing your username and password all over the slip.ini file, you type **$u** for username and **$p** for password.

slip.ini

The slip.ini file contains a description of the login interactions for several service providers, including the one I use: Northwest Nexus. The format of these entries is similar to that of your win.ini or system.ini file. It includes an identifying section for the interface, followed by two entries: a script defining the interaction with the host; and the interface type: SLIP, CSLIP or PPP.

The scripting language itself is best described in the file netmanag.wri, in a section entitled SLIP Scripting. The format essentially is send-expect, send-expect, but there are special macros that accept the incoming IP address (-i), and send characters such as carriage-return ($r). If you need to create a new script for a provider that is not listed in the slip.ini that we've shipped, please read the documentation carefully. I've done this myself, with excellent results. One last note regarding the scripting language and dynamic IP addresses: When I was building the script for Northwest Nexus, I needed to be able to skip past the first IP address and pick up the second on a single line. The macro needed to do this ($-) is documented in the NetManage Gopher server under the support directory, and it is documented in later release documentation from NetManage.

Basic Usage

Once the configuration is complete, using the Custom application is simplicity itself. Simply double-click on the Custom icon in the Chameleon group of the Program Manager. If you have everything configured correctly, Custom will automatically launch Newt, which is a cute green Chameleon as a minimized icon.

Once you've established the actual SLIP or PPP connection, you simply leave Custom running, and your other WinSock applications will (or should) correctly interact with the WinSock stack. One major difference between using Newt on a local area network and using Newt with SLIP or PPP is that on a LAN, you simply open the selected WinSock application, and Newt will start automatically. I really like this feature, but it's not available in Newt's serial interface.

If there isn't a time-out for non-activity set on your service provider, it's easy to forget that you have a SLIP connection running, and to start wondering why nobody is calling you. Keep in mind that closing all applications that are *using* the SLIP connection does not kill the connection and hang up of the phone. Of course, if you have children, a spouse, or a roommate, ignore this warning—you will not forget.

I find that occasionally I want to know whether the newest and coolest WinSock application I have found is actually *doing* something while it sits there telling me it's "retrieving." If you double-click Newt, you will see that there are some ways you can influence the WinSock stack directly. Primarily, I am interested in seeing whether there is any actual information being passed from the host to my own computer, so I choose Interface, from the Statistics menu. This enables me to see how many packets of data are flowing in and out of my PC (see figure 10.5).

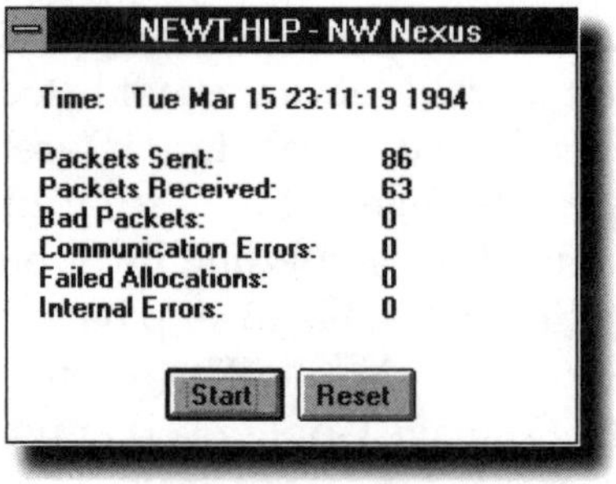

Figure 10.5   *Newt statistics.*

Another interesting aspect of the Newt screen is that if you are using dynamic addressing, this is the only place where it will reflect your current correct IP address. The IP address that you see on the Custom screen will always be the one that you typed in, not the one that was picked up from the server. Personally, I'd like to see this changed to reflect the current correct IP address.

Overall Evaluation

Newt is the very best of the SLIP implementations that I've used. Since I've had only good experiences with Newt, I was overjoyed when NetManage allowed Hayden Books to distribute this SLIP-only version with the book. The only feature that I would encourage NetManage to explore in a future revision would be richer scripting language for interacting with the service provider. No two services offer up IP address or logins in exactly the same way, and a more full-featured scripting language would certainly improve their overall connectivity.

Trumpet

Peter Tattam's WinSock is getting attention as the only available shareware WinSock (during a time when there is a lot of attention focused on Windows TCP/IP). It is mentioned here both for the sake of completeness and because it's another WinSock implementation that you can look at without running down to the store with your checkbook.

When doing the research for this book, I used Trumpet with nearly all of the applications described herein, and was satisfied with its performance. Configuring and using Trumpet is relatively painless, and the accompanying documentation is clear if you look in the right places for SLIP configuration.

One thing to remember about its documentation is that it also describes how to set up Trumpet to use directly connected networks via something called *packet drivers*. Since you probably will connect to the Internet via modem, this won't apply to you at all. Simply concentrate on the sections that talk about SLIP and you should be fine.

The critical item to remember here is that you should fill in any old IP address on the configuration screen to do dynamic addressing, as we've described for Northwest Nexus in other parts of this book. When you run your connection script, it will replace whatever IP address you've typed.

I struggle with Trumpet only in the area of reliability. Sometimes, I would be running some application and have the entire system freeze from time to time. From what I've seen posted in alt.winsock, it is unusual but not unheard of. On the plus side, Peter seems to have done a great job of making his WinSock compatible with the API. This means that all your WinSock-compliant software will work.

Distinct TCP/IP

Distinct's WinSock implementation has some interesting and unique features. One thing that bothers me about most WinSock implementations is the two-step process for starting up an application. First, you must start up an application that lets you dial, and then initialize the WinSock; only then can you start the application that you wanted to run in the first place. Distinct's application suite automatically dials and initializes WinSock when opened.

Distinct includes a program called Network Monitor, which at first glance would appear to yield the same information as you can get from Newt statistic. Further investigation, however, reveals something called "Capture" in the Options menu (see figure 10.6). Capture saves traces of all network information and writes it to disk. Now, while I don't recommend this for the faint of heart, it has tremendous potential for discovering exactly what may be wrong with your interaction with some network resource, given the right interpreter.

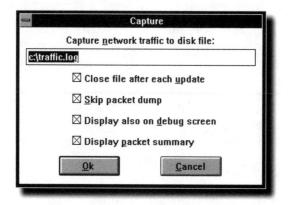

Figure 10.6   *Distinct Network Monitor.*

Installing Distinct's TCP/IP stack—or the "runtime," as they call it—is not as straightforward as some. If you pay attention, however, and dot all your "i"s and cross all your "t"s, you should get a clean install.

A final compliment for Distinct is their connection scripting language. Compared to most of the scripting languages out there for interacting with a host, Distinct has created a thing of beauty. I'm confident that there are no service providers out there that would have difficulty in communicating with Distinct.

You can order Distinct's package from:

Distinct Corporation
P.O. Box 3410
Saratoga, California 95070
Marketing email: mktg@distinct.com
Sales: 408-741-0781

InterCon TCP/Connect II

I cannot talk about InterCon with much authority, since the TCP/IP stack will not handle dynamic addressing—which is essential for connecting to Northwest Nexus, my service provider. However, InterCon *does* support RARP and BootP for resolving IP addresses dynamically and, of course, manual addressing.

Even though I'm unable to describe InterCon's WinSock in any depth, when commercial packages are covered at the end of this chapter InterCon's excellent application suite will be discussed. (You can run all of the applications on another WinSock—such is the beauty of having standardized APIs.)

InterCon's TCP/Connect can be purchased from InterCon at:

InterCon Systems Corporation
950 Herndon Parkway
Herndon, Virginia 22070
Email comment@intercon.com
Phone: 703-709-9890

Email Programs

Considering that email is the ubiquitous application on the Internet, you should use the best email program available; otherwise, you slowly (or quickly) go stark raving mad. I've looked at many email programs in my time, and although a number of them are becoming more and more impressive, not many compete with Steve Dorner's freeware Eudora. Currently at version 1.4, Eudora does most everything right. Again, I don't want to imply that other programs aren't good, only that none I've seen compare completely with Eudora.

Eudora

Steve Dorner first wrote Eudora while working at the University of Illinois. Because of its academic heritage, Eudora was made freely available on the Internet and, because of its clean interface and full feature set, it rapidly became the email application of choice. In July, 1992, Steve left the University of Illinois and went to work for a company called QUALCOMM, where he continued to enhance Eudora. Because Steve and QUALCOMM wanted to give something back to the education community and taxpayers who made Eudora possible, and because free software is the best advertising for commercial software, Eudora has remained freeware (at least through version 1.4.)

QUALCOMM's commercial version of Eudora, version 2.0, provides everything in the freeware version with some additioanl features, most notably the capability to filter messages into specific mailboxes based on the sender, or the subject line, or what not. It's an extremely useful feature.

To answer the question everyone always asks, Steve says that he named his Post Office Protocol program "Eudora," after Eudora Welty, the author of a short story he had read called, "Why I Live at the P.O."

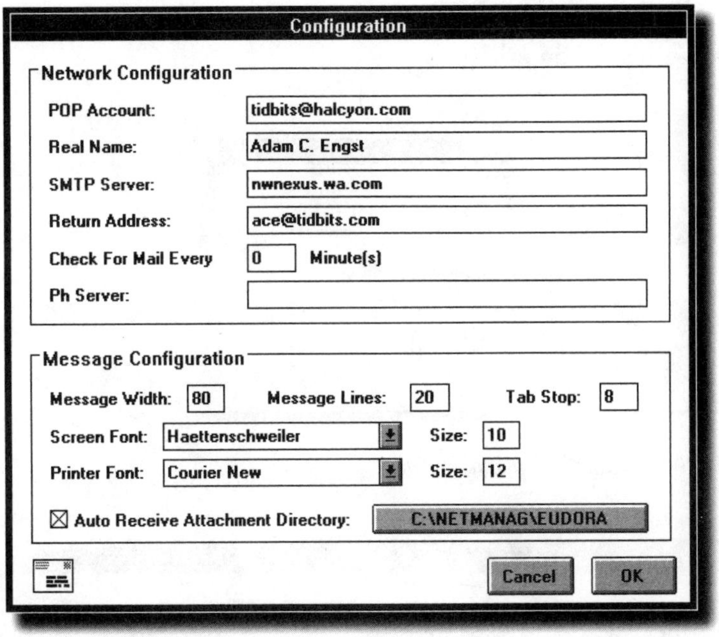

Figure 10.7   Eudora Configuration.

Installation and Setup

Although powerful, Eudora has a surprisingly simple setup that you perform in two large dialog boxes. First, from the Special menu, choose Configuration (see figure 10.7).

Despite all the fields you can fill in, only the first few are at all important. The POP Account: field holds the full address of your POP account. The best place to find out what to put here is your system administrator. The next field, Real Name:, should be obvious. Return Address: should be set to whatever address accepts mail for you.

For most people, that's all there is to the setup process. You may choose to look at the POP server for mail every two minutes, as I do (I keep a phone near me at all times, too; it's a communications thing), by setting the Check for Mail Every: field to 2. Click on the OK button to close the Configuration dialog box.

The remainder of Eudora's configuration happens in the Special menu as well (see figures 10.8 and 10.9).

Figure 10.8   *Eudora's Special menu.*

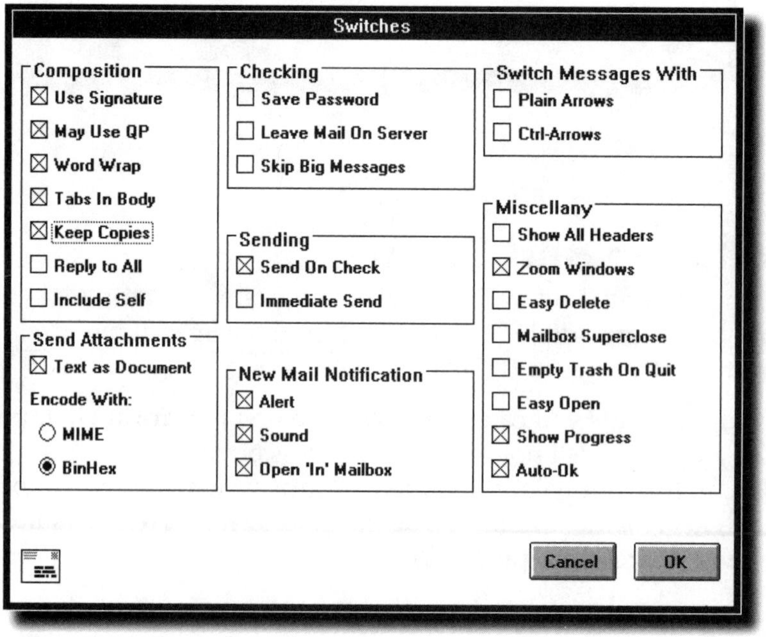

Figure 10.9   *Eudora Switches dialog box.*

You may think that this many checkboxes in a single dialog box may seem like overkill, but these options enable you to configure Eudora quickly and easily in order to handle many different situations. I, for instance, keep copies of all the messages I send—although many people don't go to that trouble—so I check Keep Copies. Similarly, people have different preferences in terms of how they want to be notified of new mail, and Eudora's Switches cover all the bases. After you set the Switches you want, click on the OK button to save your preferences.

Basic Usage

Most of the time, you're most likely to use Eudora simply to create new messages, read incoming mail, reply to messages, and the like. Creating a message is the first thing to do. From the Message menu, choose New Message or, if you're like most people, press Control-N.

Eudora opens a new window with three parts: a row of switch icons at the top—so that you can toggle items such as signatures on a per message basis; an area for the header; and the message area. Tabbing takes you from one header item to another, and finally to the Message window (see figure 10.10). With Eudora you can add to a Recipients menu (from the Special menu), and the people you add as Recipients show up in a hierarchical New Message To menu under the Message menu. Selecting someone from that hierarchical menu opens a new message with the To: line already filled in (the From: line is always filled in for you).

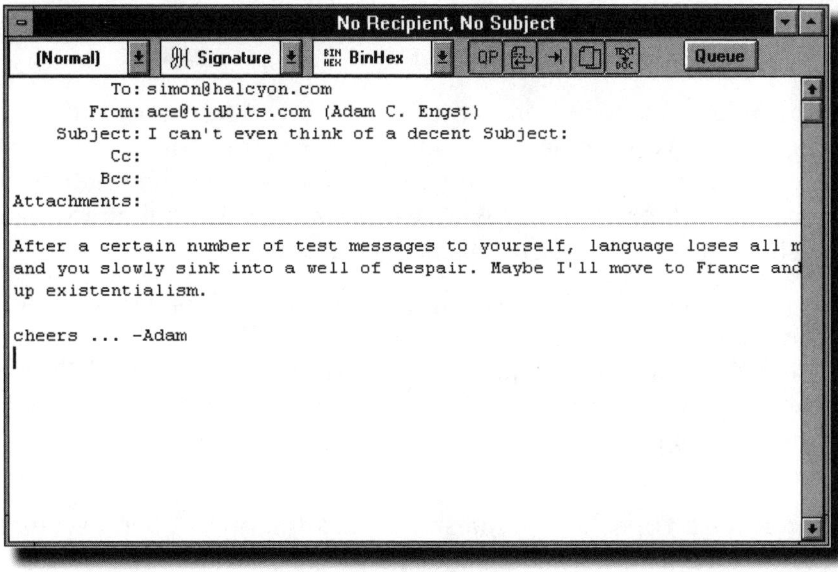

Figure 10.10   Creating new mail in Eudora.

Eudora has a good text entry environment, and wraps paragraphs as you write and edit (which is not true of all email programs, so don't laugh). In fact, Eudora can do some neat things with text, as evidenced by the commands in the Edit menu (see figure 10.11).

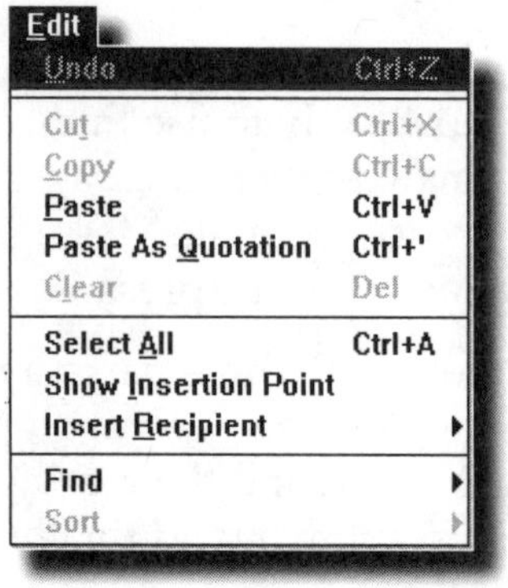

Edit	
Undo	Ctrl+Z
Cut	Ctrl+X
Copy	Ctrl+C
Paste	Ctrl+V
Paste As Quotation	Ctrl+'
Clear	Del
Select All	Ctrl+A
Show Insertion Point	
Insert Recipient	▶
Find	▶
Sort	▶

Figure 10.11   Eudora's Edit menu.

I especially like Eudora's Insert Recipient and Paste as Quotation capabilities. I often want to send to a friend an email address for which I have a shortcut, and it's nice to be able to simply Insert Recipient in the text where I'm typing. Paste as Quotation is also useful when you're pulling several messages together in one reply.

Clicking on the Queue button in the New Mail window queues the message for delivery (remember I unchecked the Immediate Send switch when configuring Eudora). If you work on a network rather than via a SLIP dial-up, as I do, you may want to send all of your mail immediately, at which point that Queue button changes to Send.

Because I also have the Send On Check switch turned on, if I go to the File menu and select Check Mail (making sure my SLIP connection is active or will connect automatically), Eudora connects to my POP server to receive any waiting mail, and then sends any queued mail. If I only want to send mail, I can choose Send Queued Messages, also from the File menu.

If the In Box isn't open already (a switch makes it open when new mail arrives), open it from the Message menu by choosing In Box.

Eudora's mailboxes (they all look like the one in figure 10.12, and you can have any number of them) provide a clean display of your mail. The window contains a toolbar and a main window.

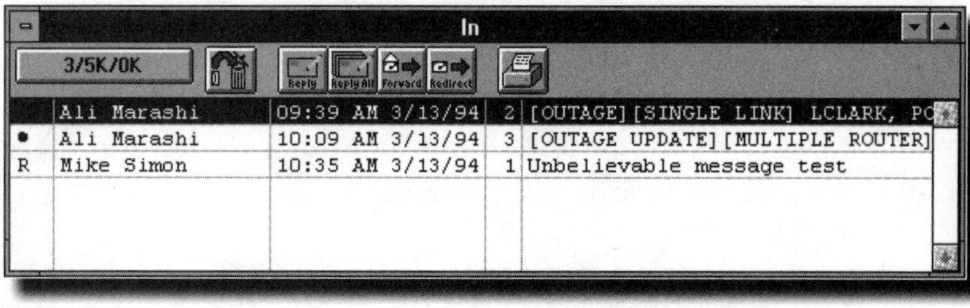

	Ali Marashi	09:39 AM 3/13/94	2	[OUTAGE][SINGLE LINK] LCLARK, PC
•	Ali Marashi	10:09 AM 3/13/94	3	[OUTAGE UPDATE][MULTIPLE ROUTER]
R	Mike Simon	10:35 AM 3/13/94	1	Unbelievable message test

Figure 10.12   Mail waiting for you in Eudora's In Box.

The toolbar enables you to Reply, Forward, and Trash—whereas the main body indicates a set of messages. On the left side is an indicator that shows the number of messages in the mailbox, the amount of space on disk it takes up, and the amount of space that is wasted (which you can recover by choosing Compact Mailboxes from the Special menu).

In the main window, a status and priority column to the left of the window displays various characters which indicate the messages you haven't read, which ones you have replied to, forwarded, redirected. If you are in your Out Box, the various characters indicate which messages have been sent. Some programs mark deleted messages in this way as well, but Eudora copies deleted messages to a Trash mailbox available under the Mailbox menu. The next column is the name of the sender, followed by the time and date, the number of lines in the message, and the subject of the message.

Double-clicking on any message will open the Message window (see figure 10.13).

The Eudora Message window is a simple display window with the Subject at the top and a Priority pop-up menu that you can use to mark messages for your own reference. You can select and find text in the window, but you cannot change it. Again, my only complaint about the way Eudora handles incoming messages is that it cannot display more than approximately 30K of text in a window, so it truncates longer messages into two or more pieces, which is irritating at times. However, Eudora can save multiple selected messages to a single file, removing the header information in the process, so that the files appear to have been intact before being saved.

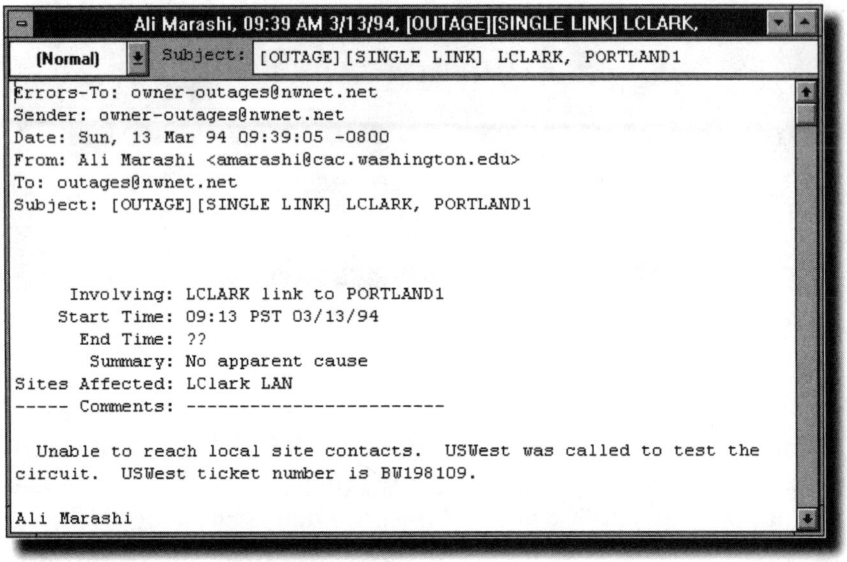

Figure 10.13   Eudora's Message window.

With a message open, you can click on the toolbar to Reply, Forward, Redirect, or Delete the current message. Or, you can use the features found in the Message menu (see figure 10.14).

Figure 10.14   Eudora's Message menu.

Most of the items in the Message menu are self-explanatory, but Redirect is an interesting and useful command. When you forward a message to someone via Eudora, your address becomes the Reply-To address. However, if you want the original sender's address to remain as the Reply-To address, you use Redirect. That way, when the person you're redirecting mail to receives the message and replies, that reply goes to the original sender, not back to you.

Eudora's Special Features

Steve Dorner appears to pay attention to both form and function. In addition to an excellent feature set, he has graced this application with interesting features such as buttons labeled "Trash Them," rather than that standard affirmation "OK." Touches like these make Eudora more interesting to use than most applications, because the personal touches are occasionally surprising.

Eudora can sort mailboxes according to status, priority (which you set), sender, date, and subject, which is a helpful feature for anyone who receives a significant amount of mail.

Using Eudora's Transfer menu, you can instantly move one or more messages to any of your mailboxes, and you can create any number of them. Eudora mailboxes are in the same format as the UNIX mail mailboxes, so you can download a UNIX mailbox and read it with Eudora.

If you create multiple settings files, different people can use the same copy of Eudora to send and receive their personal email. This setup is handy if a number of people all share the same computer, but don't want to share the same email account ("Hey, no poking about in my email!").

Overall Evaluation

Although perhaps not perfect, you must have Eudora. Aside from the 30K limitation on messages, I can say almost nothing negative about Eudora. However, any such faults are easily outweighed by Eudora's capabilities—some relatively unusual—such as queuing up mail and sending it all at once, which is essential for anyone using SLIP.

Administrative Details

Eudora 1.4 is free and comes courtesy of the University of Illinois and QUALCOMM. I'll make the latest version available at `ftp.halcyon.com`, should you want to check periodically to make sure you're running the latest and greatest.

Version 2.0 is commercial, and you can get more information from QUALCOMM via email at `eudora-sales@qualcomm.com`.

Other WinSock Email Programs

Although I like Eudora, you should try other mail programs. Some of them, like Eudora, originally were programmed at a university and thus are free. I'm sure I've missed a few, but discussed below are the ones I know about and which work without any unusual software on the host (I'm assuming that POP is relatively widespread, because without it you cannot use even Eudora). I'll try to post most of these programs on `ftp.halcyon.com`, but some of them may have distribution restrictions, and you'll have to find those at the original sites.

NetManage's Email

One of the applications that installs with the NetManage WinSock stack is their own email package. I've featured Eudora here, as it is the one that I use myself, and it's an excellent package. I have to say, however, that I'm thinking about switching to NetManage's email. I swap email packages more reluctantly than I swap dentists, but I'm impressed enough to consider it. The NetManage product offers rule-based mail filtering (like the commercial version of Eudora) and an excellent set of mail handling utilities. For those of us who receive email by the megabyte, a variety of ways to handle mail—both as it comes in and after the fact—are a boon.

NetManage's package has another advantage for you: You already have it and it's installed. The only customization necessary should be under the Network->Mail Server item of the Settings menu, where you must select a mail host and mail gateway (see figure 10.15).

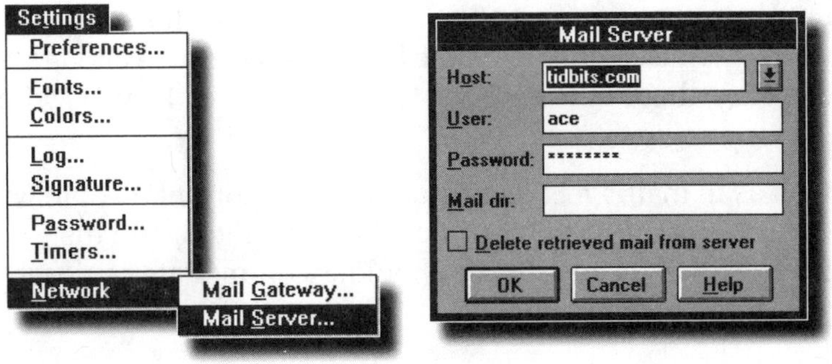

Figure 10.15   *NetManage email customization.*

WinQVT/NET Mail

We will see more about WinQVT/NET later in this chapter, when Usenet newsreaders, Telnet and FTP, are discussed. What the folks at QPC Software have done is integrate Telnet FTP, Usenet news, Mail, and a UNIX-style line printer demon into one integrated package. For some, this will be attractive since configuration happens only once, and it offers essentially one-stop-shopping for the most basic Internet access.

In describing the QVT mail package, basic is a useful term. For the casual mail user, this may be a plus, as there are very few options. And to do simple mail retrieving and delivery, it works fine. The first screen you'll see in WinQVT is encouragingly simple—three menu items: File, Send Mail, and Setup. "Setup," I thought, "that will be where I configure all the nice things that I like to do with my mail." Actually, clicking on the Setup pull-down enables you to set up fonts and printer characteristics—not exactly what I expected.

Don't be overly influenced by my lack of enthusiasm for WinQVT/NET. Other parts of their integrated package will be discussed later in this chapter. They are solid well-done Windows applications that are fairly bare-bones—compared to some of the non-integrated packages.

Usenet Newsreaders

At one time in my life, choice of newsreaders was a religious quest. I was working in a job that required me to keep current in some areas best covered in Usenet newsgroups. Spending one or two hours each day wading through the chaff in even the best newsgroups is enough to make you picky about newsreaders. It's enough to make you switch jobs too, but that's another story.

Here, much as in mail, I feel that flexibility is important. People will find a way of wading through newsgroups that suits them, and the newsreader that you choose to use should accommodate as closely as possible the way that you work.

WinVN

My current favorite newsreader is WinVN. It seems clear from first glance that Mark Riordan et al. has concentrated on function and flexibility, rather than on cool default color schemes and shortcut buttons. The paradigm, which we will see repeated in every newsreader described here, is to present the user with an initial list of groups from which to select a group to read from and be presented with a list of current articles from that group. Although all the newsreaders that I've seen for Windows do this in similar ways, WinVN is a bit more flexible regarding setup and presentation.

Installation and Setup

Create a Program Group and Program Item for WinVM using the methods outlined in your Windows documentation. (You probably do this all the time when you download applications to your PC.)

At this point, you are ready to run WinVN. As always, you must first start the WinSock interface by running NetManage's Custom (or whatever WinSock interface you may be using), then double-click on the WinVN icon you just installed. This brings up the WinVN News Server Configuration screen (see figure 10.16).

The critical item to change on this screen is the NNTP (News) edit box. This should be set to the name of the NNTP server, as given to you by your system administrator. In the case of Northwest Nexus, this would be nwfocus.wa.com. In most cases, you will not wish to change the TCP port that WinVN uses; it will default to the standard port for NNTP. Last of all, you should fill in the name of a machine that can forward SMTP mail for you. You learn more about this below in the section on POP, but this enables you to send mail and forward news articles from within the WinVN program. You may wish to select SMTP as the mail transport type, or MAPI if that's what you use, but I haven't tested the MAPI interface, so you're on your own there. Click on the OK button, and WinVN will ask if you would like to get the latest group list from the server. Since this is your first time on, you do need to retrieve the group list, but read the warning at that bottom; it *will* be time consuming.

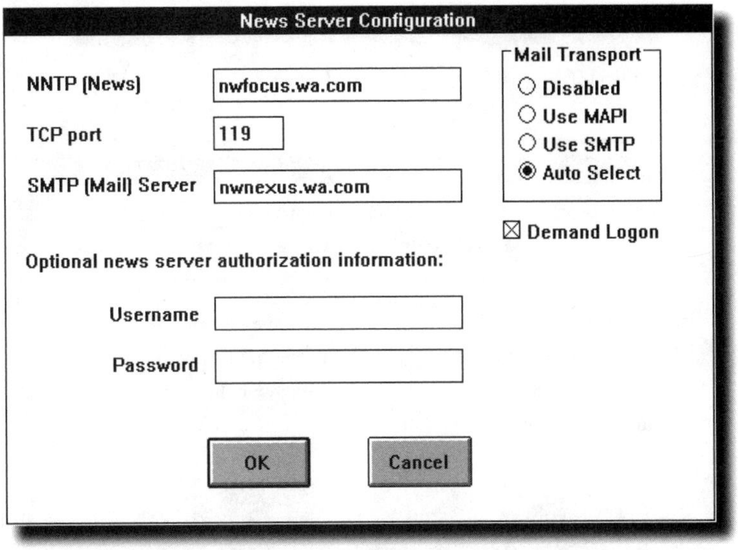

Figure 10.16   *WinVN News Server configuration screen.*

Once the entire list of 4,500 or so groups has been retrieved, you have the option of selecting to which of them you would like to subscribe. You do this by scrolling to the group, holding down the Control key, and clicking on each group in which you are interested. Once this process is finished, click on OK to complete the group selection.

Choose Configure Personal Info from the Config menu. The information required here is self-explanatory; however, it is extremely necessary if you wish your news postings to make sense to the rest of the world (see figure 10.17).

Next, you need to make some choices about how WinVN looks and interacts with you. You do this in the Configure Miscellaneous Options dialog box accessed from the Config menu (see figure 10.18).

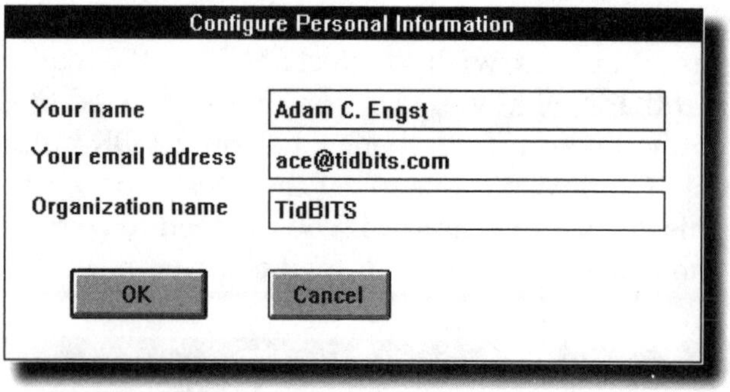

Configure Personal Information

Your name	Adam C. Engst
Your email address	ace@tidbits.com
Organization name	TidBITS

OK   Cancel

Figure 10.17   *WinVN Configure Personal Info.*

Configure Miscellaneous Options

Check for new groups on startup
○ Yes   ○ No   ◉ Ask

Article Fetch Limit
Ask if more than 300 articles

☒ New window for each group   ☒ Append saved articles
☐ New window for each article   ☒ Full-name 'from' in group window
☒ Compute threads   ☒ Show unsubscribed groups
☒ Confirm batch operations

OK   Cancel

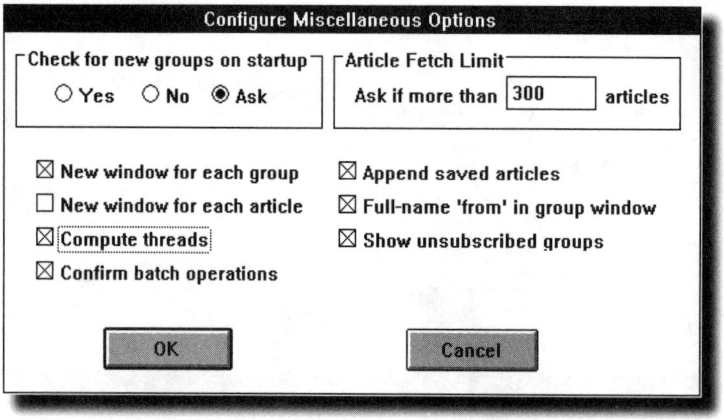

Figure 10.18   *WinVN Configure Miscellaneous Options.*

The non-default option that you certainly will wish to choose is Compute threads. This enables you to view all of the postings to a particular subject as a group, rather than intermixed with all of the other postings in chronological order. This is one of the single most important features of any newsreader for anyone who is more than a casual Usenet addict; yet, it's missing from many implementations.

Basic Usage

By double-clicking on any of the groups in the main window, you can retrieve the subject lines of all the current articles in that group in a new window (see figures 10.19 and 10.20).

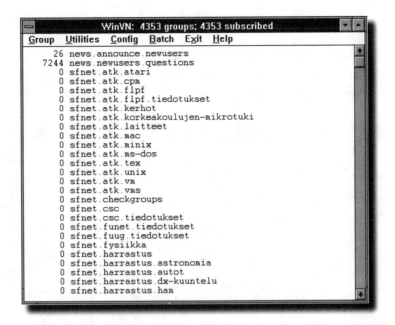

Figure 10.19   *WinVN main window.*

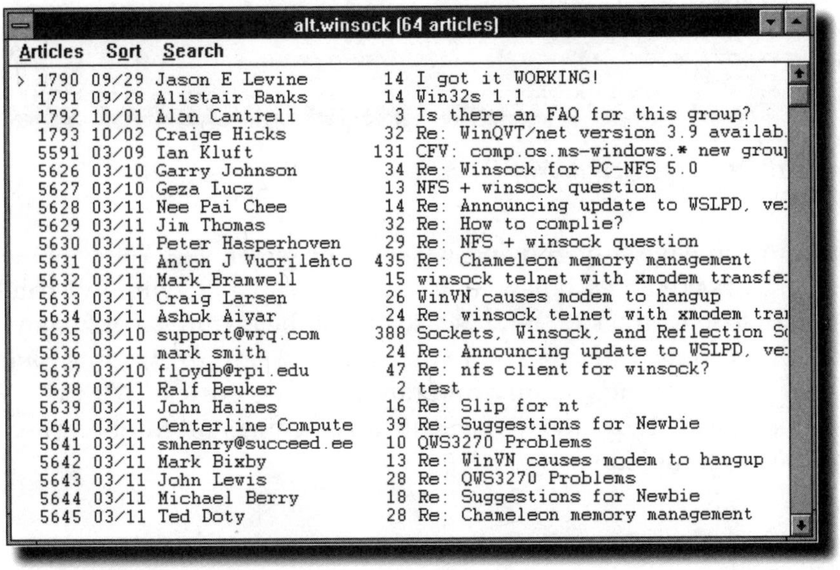

Figure 10.20   *WinVN Group window.*

Threads are identified by white space to the right of the article, with only the first posting in the thread listing the actual subject line, and each subsequent follow-up showing no subject at all. By double-clicking on any of the subject lines, you may retrieve the article associated with it, in a new window (see figure 10.21).

```
┌─────────────────────────────────────────────────────────────────┐
│ ─        Re: Sonics / Suns / Spurs ??? [47 lines]        ▼ ▲    │
├─────────────────────────────────────────────────────────────────┤
│ File   Search   View   Respond                                   │
├─────────────────────────────────────────────────────────────────┤
│ Path: nwnexus!cyber2.cyberstore.ca!math.ohio-state.edu!howland.reston.ans │
│ From: 1200-cu@garnet.berkeley.edu (mARK wITTEMAN)                 │
│ Newsgroups: rec.sport.basketball.pro                             │
│ Subject: Re: Sonics / Suns / Spurs ???                          │
│ Date: 11 Mar 1994 03:22:17 GMT                                  │
│ Organization: University of California, Berkeley                 │
│ Lines: 36                                                        │
│ Message-ID: <2loo59$51s@agate.berkeley.edu>                     │
│ References: <1994Mar9.122330.6171@news.weeg.uiowa.edu> <21nfk8INNc84@dns1 │
│ NNTP-Posting-Host: garnet.berkeley.edu                          │
│                                                                  │
│ In article <2lof5nINNbs3@owl.csrv.uidaho.edu>,                  │
│ LONG PETER WILLIAM <long923@cs.uidaho.edu> wrote:               │
│ >Excess (Excess@nmsu.edu) wrote:                                │
│ >                                                                │
│ >                                                                │
│ >: The way Jazz, Spurs and Houston are playing right now....the Midwest │
│ >: teams seems to have better chances than slumping Suns, and injury-pro │
│ >: GSW, and as usual dumb -:) Portland.                          │
│ >: You could have waited at least till the end of this week to check if │
│ >: Seattle beats SA and Rockets because they may be the only team to sto │
│ >: any midwest finalist.                                         │
│ >                                                                │
│ >Those midwest teams, damn!  Are they hot!  Especially those Jazz...   Th │
│ >so hot, they forgot all about those dumb-ass Blazers, and didn't even n │
│ >how badly they got diced/sliced (Malone - 14 pts, 0-0 FT, Stockton - wa │
│ >the court?) by such a dumb team.  Stay honest, punk...         │
│                                                                  │
│ Dumb Blazers?  Keep in mind you're talking about a team that has won 10 d │
└─────────────────────────────────────────────────────────────────┘
```

Figure 10.21   *A retrieved WinVN article.*

Okay, do you have enough windows on your screen yet? The way that WinVN works (with each new item creating a separate window), can be a bit hard to keep track of, but it's also one of the features that I enjoy. I frequently will read through more than one newsgroup at a time *while* sending mail to friends, family, and random news posters. With WinVN, this is possible without too much context switching and fumbling about with the Program Manager.

Special Features

WinVN does threading, which I wouldn't consider to be a "special feature" except that many of the other readers do not. Threading enables me to read all of a subject that piques my interest, and totally skip ones that do not (searching endlessly through the subject lines looking for "Re: Re: Re: Heating your home with the Intel baseboard heater.").

I also like the mail features of WinVN. It seems that I'm always finding some article in Usenet news that I would like to pass on to someone, and a decent email interface is the easiest, most convenient way to accomplish this. The fact that WinVN also includes a simple interface for sending original mail is a bonus when I only have a quick note to jot off.

Administrative Details

WinVN, currently at version 0.90.3, is in the public domain. According to the `readme.txt` file, the primary distribution site is `titan.ksc.nasa.gov`, in the directory `/pub/win3/winvn`. Whenever possible, it's a good idea to go to the source for this sort of program, to ensure that you're getting the newest and best. Thanks to Mark Riordan and the crew listed in the `help/about` file for an excellent newsreader!

NEWT News

The folks at NetManage have been including a newsreader with their standard TCP/IP suite for the last couple of versions, and I've been using it occasionally for as long as they've been supplying it. If you have the commercial package, you may be able to live with NEWT News for a while.

Installation and Setup

If you've installed the commercial version of Chameleon, NEWT News is already on your disk and almost ready to run. To read news, you need only supply the name of your NNTP server.

Start NEWT News by double-clicking on the icon, and then choosing Connect (see figure 10.22).

Enter the NNTP server name supplied by your systems administrator for News Server Name. Then, go and get some coffee and maybe even pop some corn, because now, one by one, NEWT News is going to retrieve the list of newsgroups, all 4,500 of them. This can take about five minutes on a 14,400 baud modem, and significantly longer on anything slower.

Once this list is compiled, you are faced with a tedious task. From the list of all newsgroups, you must now choose which ones you would like to read, by selecting them from the scrollable list and then clicking on the "+" Subscribe icon to add them to the subscribed list. Having finished this process, closing the Groups window returns you to the News main window—ready to select a group (see figure 10.23).

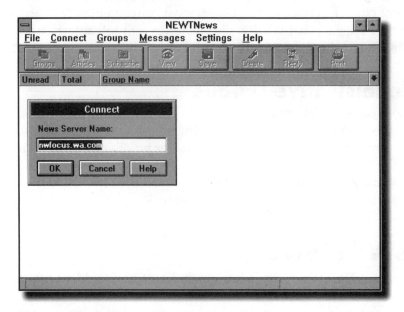

Figure 10.22 *NEWT Connect dialog box.*

Basic Usage

Double-clicking on a group name retrieves a list of the current articles available in that group. The articles list has three columns of information: Flags, From, and Subject. The flags column shows some status information about the article in question; for instance, once you've read that article, the flags column will have an "R" in it (see figure 10.24). The From and Subject columns are self-explanatory.

Double-clicking on an article opens up a new window that displays the article. If you invoke the Smart Buttons from the Settings menu, the most commonly-used operations are also accessible via large, well-labeled buttons across the top. For instance, when reading an article you may read the next article by clicking on the Next button, or reverse the process with the Previous button (see figure 10.25).

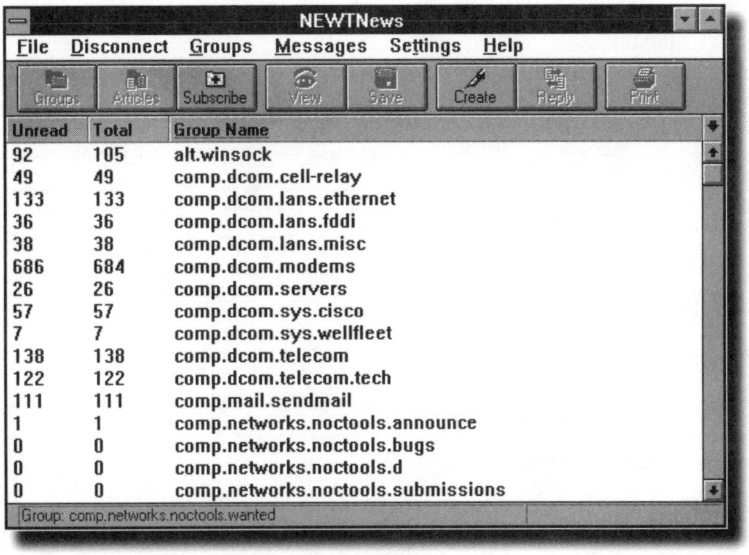

Figure 10.23 NEWT News main window.

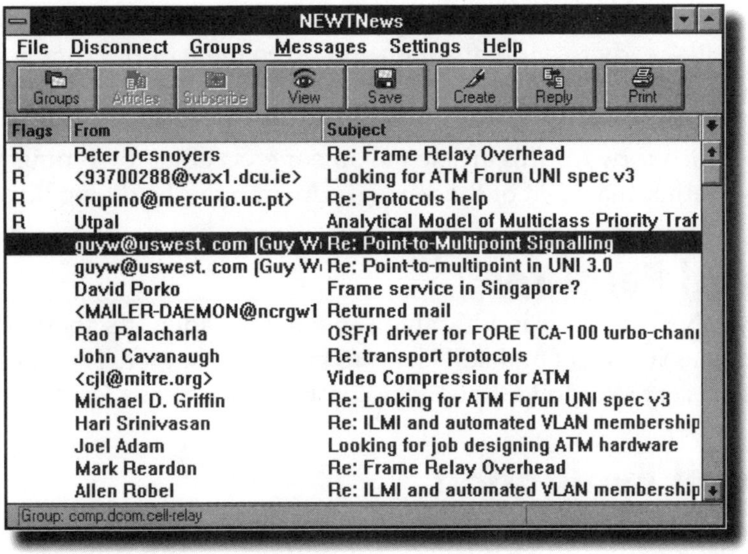

Figure 10.24 NEWT News articles.

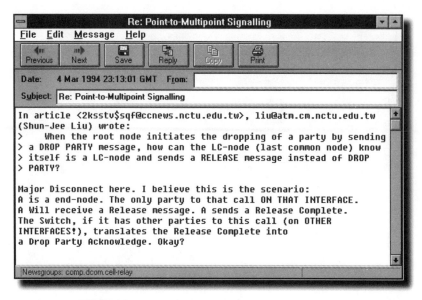

Figure 10.25   NEWT News postings.

Clicking on the Reply button brings up a new window with the quoted article in it—ready to annotate and send off to the world. From here you can add additional newsgroups to post your reply to by adding them to the To dialog box in the upper right. Although it's not instantly clear, you may also forward this article to someone via email by typing their address, rather than that of the newsgroup, into the To dialog box.

Special Features

Although NEWT News is a highly usable newsreader, it's about as utilitarian as it can get and still claim to be a newsreader. The interface is clean, and very Windows-standards compliant. Also, it's learned easily.

Overall Evaluation

NEWT News is a training wheels-type newsreader. If you have purchased the commercial NetManage Chameleon package, you should use it for a while, before scraping your knees with a more fully-featured threading package. For an advanced news user, the lack of threading is the only unforgivable feature. NetManage informs us they will be including threading in a forthcoming software release.

Administrative Details

NEWT News is a part of the Chameleon package from NetManage. As far as I know, there is no other way to obtain NEWT News, or any other single piece of Chameleon, aside from the TCP/IP stack itself.

WinQVT/NET News

WinQVT/NET offers a Usenet newsreader among the list of applications in its integrated repertoire. WinQVT/NET's newsreader is in the tradition of xrn, from the world of UNIX and X Windows, and has an upper pane for both lists of newsgroups and article subjects, and a lower pane for actually viewing articles. In this way, they have opted for an opposite viewpoint from that of WinVN.

Installation and Setup

Install WinQVT/NET by uncompressing the .zip file into a directory on your hard disk. Create a Program Group, and a Program Item for the application, wnqvtwsk.exe. Once this is done, start WinQVT/NET and configure it by selecting News from the Setup menu (see figure 10.26).

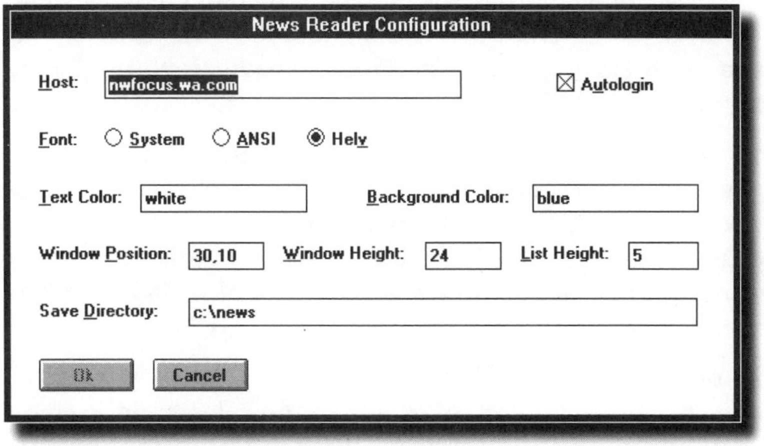

News Reader Configuration	
Host: nwfocus.wa.com	☒ Autologin
Font: ○ System ○ ANSI ◉ Helv	
Text Color: white	Background Color: blue
Window Position: 30,10 Window Height: 24	List Height: 5
Save Directory: c:\news	
Ok Cancel	

Figure 10.26   *WinQVT/NET News configuration.*

The only critical item of information to be changed is Host, which must be set to your own NNTP server name. Once this is set, you may click on the News button from the button bar to open the actual news application. From here, pull down the Newsgroups menu and select Subscribe.

Basic Usage

Once you've selected the list of newsgroups you wish to read, the only thing you can do with this newsreader is read news. No bells and whistles—just click on the group you would like to read. The groups list will be replaced by the articles list, and you are ready to read articles. There really are no other options. You can choose articles, read them, and post your own articles, all by clicking on one of the buttons labeled Read or Followup.

The newsreader in WinQVT/NET is simple and effective, but certainly not very full-featured. The lack of threading and integrated mail makes it an unlikely candidate for anyone but a raw beginner looking for the simplest possible interface.

FTP Programs

Ranking in popularity after email and perhaps even before news, FTP is one of the base applications that ties the Internet together. Despite its relative simplicity—even from a command line—FTP works far better when you can use a graphical application to navigate through remote directories and files.

I'm going to gloss over the programs that let you set your PC up as an FTP server because, although they're neat, they require a direct and constant connection to be significantly useful. Percentage-wise, almost no one sets up a PC as an FTP server relative to the number of people who retrieve files via FTP. If you do want to retrieve files via FTP, read on for a description of the FTP server features of Win/QVT.

As in the previous sections, there are a number of FTP clients available. They range from the simplest, most non-graphical version, included in the WinQVT/NET package, to the excellent WNFTP.

NetManage FTP

NetManage's FTP was the first graphical FTP I used on the PC, having learned to live with a command line version on UNIX machines for my early Internet life. That version was almost identical to the one that ships with this book. It is now my second favorite—right behind the commercial version that ships with NetManage 4.0.

The basic idea behind all of the graphical FTP programs is that they should show you a current picture of the file structure on the remote machine, along with a picture of your local machine, and enable you to move files from one environment to the other as quickly and intuitively as possible.

Basic Usage

If you've accomplished the standard install from the NetManage floppy, you already have FTP installed. When first launched, FTP lists the contents of the local current working directory, which is probably c:\netmanag (the default NetManage install directory). The user interface is divided into three vertical sections from left to right: local management, operations, and remote management (see figure 10.27).

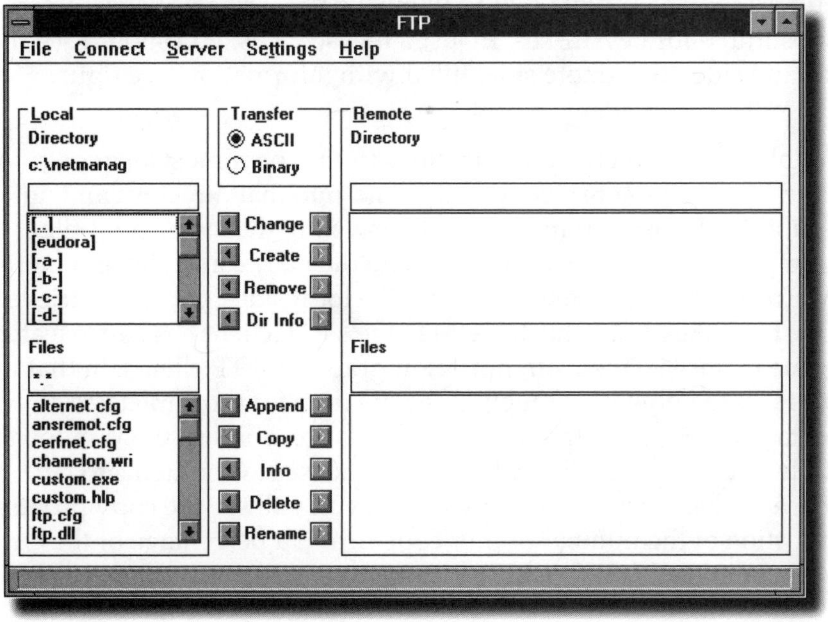

Figure 10.27 *NetManage FTP window.*

Upon closer scrutiny, you'll be reminded of Windows' Common Open dialog boxes. You should be able to navigate throughout volumes on both your local machine and attached remote machine with relative ease.

The center column of this application is a list of actions, with arrows on each side. As you may expect, clicking on the arrow pointing left performs that operation on the item selected in the adjoining window. For example, by typing the name for a new directory into the dialog box above the local directory listing, and clicking on the Create arrow which points at the local side, you can create a new directory on your local machine.

I'll give another example of this type of operation in a minute. But first, let's talk about connecting to remote machines. The act of connecting is fairly simple; click on the Connect menu item, and you'll be asked to supply a host name, a username for that host, and a password. To connect to the anonymous FTP server at `halcyon.com`, for instance, use `ftp.halcyon.com` as the host, `anonymous` as the user name and your mail address as the password (something along the lines of `yourID@halcyon.com`). Note that with most password edit boxes, asterisks are substituted for keystrokes. In just a few seconds, you should see the right-hand side, the remote side, filled with information (see figure 10.28).

By double-clicking on the pub directory (found on almost all anonymous FTP sites) on the remote side, you descend into that directory and automatically see the list of remote files displayed in the lower right file window. Clicking on one of those remote file names and clicking on the Copy arrow pointing at *your* machine (the local side), you can retrieve that file from the remote host. NetManage's FTP client has a nice feature here, one that is lacking from most non-graphical FTP clients, in that it enables you to know how much of the file transfer is complete as a percentage of the entire transfer. If, for instance, you use the Windows multiple select feature (Control-Click) to choose several items to be copied, and then click on the copy arrow, you will see the copy process as a function of the number of files copied, and a percentage of the entire transfer completed (see figure 10.29).

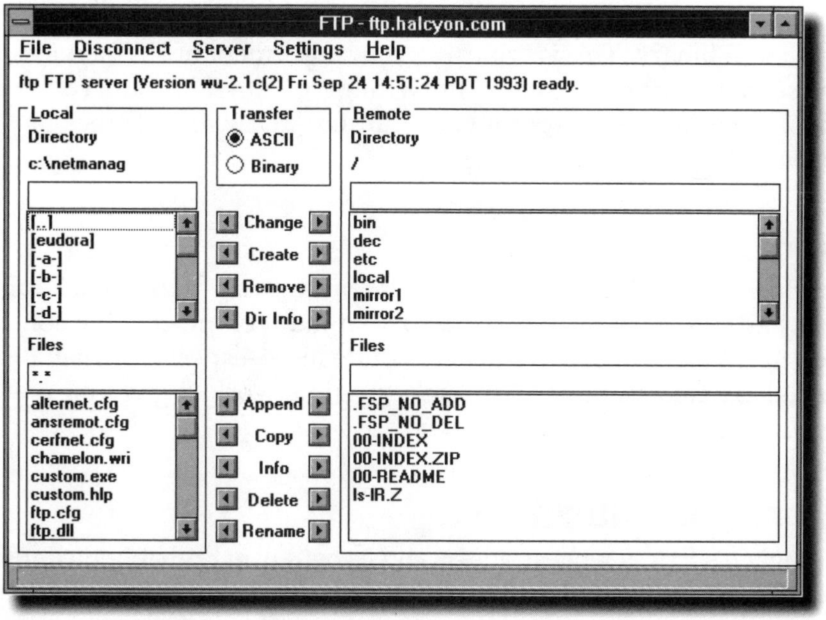

Figure 10.28 *NetManage FTP connect.*

Figure 10.29 *NetManage FTP transfer.*

The only remaining part of the interface that isn't intuitive for new FTP users is the little Transfer box in the center column of the FTP window, on top. The choices here are Binary or ASCII. The rule of thumb here is that if you plan to load the file into Notepad directly and read it (like readme, or better yet, readme.txt files), choose ASCII. If the file is stored on a UNIX machine remotely (which is *very* likely), choosing ASCII will do some essential conversions for you and make it easier to deal with on the local machine. If it's anything else, such as a .zip file, for instance, then choose Binary. This is critical to your enjoyment of FTP services, because transferring a file using the wrong format will produce unusable results, requiring you to repeat your transfers and wasting precious bandwidth.

Special Features

I like the layout of NetManage's FTP. It appears very intuitive (simple is good), and clear (clear is also good). The amount of information conveyed during an actual file transfer is quite nice—especially when I'm attached via modem rather than high-speed network. It gives me a way to predict how long a transfer will take.

Overall Evaluation

NetManage's FTP is well-designed and easy to use. Probably the indication is the number of public domain FTP clients that mimic the interface almost exactly. I'm not sure who came up with the design first, but for now it seems to be the way things are done, with one notable exception (which I'll mention briefly, later in this section).

Administrative Details

I'm quite pleased that NetManage's FTP client is so full-featured. You benefit immensely because it's included with this book. With FTP in hand, you can retrieve any of the other packages I've mentioned here which are publicly available. And, a product as easy to learn and use as NetManage's FTP will make that process enjoyable. Here again, the commercial version of this client is slightly better, adding a View File feature to their file manipulation options, among a few other niceties.

Other FTP Programs

There actually are quite a few FTP programs available from FTP sites (Hmm, I see a problem here—unless you already have an FTP client...), but they fall into two basic categories: clients that look almost identical to NetManage's FTP, and clients that mimic the UNIX command line FTP.

WS FTP

WS FTP by John A. Junod, is one of the graphical, "looks like NetManage's" variety. It's so much like NetManage's, in fact, that I'll talk about its special features rather than redescribe the interface.

There are two features of WS FTP that are great ideas: user definable viewers and a debugging window. User definable viewers means that you can associate file types (such as .txt) with specific viewers (such as Windows Notepad). Having associations means that you don't need to download files to your disk and then switch applications to view them. Both are real time-savers.

The debug window will become more and more useful as FTP host sites put textual information into their login screens. A typical graphical FTP client offers the user a terse version of the information presented by the FTP server—mostly file and directory names. However, many sites put detailed messages into their login sequence to convey information critical to users of that site. The Debug Window, besides being an excellent debugging tool for problems with remote connections, can capture these login messages into a scrollable window for your perusal (see figure 10.30).

```
┌─ ──────────────────── Debug Window ──────────────────── ▼ ▲
 Commands  Options  Log  Exit                              About ▲
  WS_FTP Written by John A. Junod                                 ▲
  Modifications by Santanu Lahiri
  Connected to 129.79.26.27 port 21                              ▒
  220-
  220-    You have reached ftp.cica.indiana.edu [129.79.26.27].  All
  220-    anonymous ftp transactions are logged. If you find this
  220-    policy unacceptable, terminate your connection NOW.
  220-
  220 cica FTP server [Version wu-2.1c(7) Wed Feb 16 15:49:20 EST 1994] ready.
  USER anonymous
  331 Guest login ok, send your complete e-mail address as password.
  PASS xxxxxx
  230-**
  230-** You have reached ftp.cica.indiana.edu [129.79.26.27] at
  230-** the Center for Innovative Computer Applications [CICA] at
  230-** Indiana University in Bloomington, Indiana USA.
  230-**
  230-** To request our help file e-mail:  ftp@cica.indiana.edu      ▼
```

Figure 10.30   *WS FTP's Debug Window.*

WinQVT/NET FTP

The FTP client that launches from WinQVT/NET is an example of the non-graphical UNIX-mimicking FTP clients. Probably the only difference that you will see between this client and running FTP from a UNIX command prompt, is that most of the common commands are available from pull-down menus. (If you aren't into menus, or your mouse hand is busy holding the *Internet Starter Kit for Windows,* you can also issue all the commands that you would use on the UNIX command line version.) I suppose there's nothing wrong with this interface, but it seems like a waste of a perfectly good graphical environment.

Telnet and Friends

Okay, I admit it; I've run into a completely ambiguous group of software that isn't really related in any way. I'm talking about programs such as Telnet, Archie, Finger, and Talk. They do a variety of things, but most of them are one-trick ponies, so I've decided to lump them all together here, under "Telnet and Friends." This title sounds like a nerdy Saturday morning cartoon show.

NetManage Telnet

Telnet is merely a way of connecting a local text window to a remote machine. The interaction that happens from there is determined by the ingenuity of the applications programmers on that remote site. NetManage has provided a great tool to connect to that site.

Basic Usage

Operating NetManage's Telnet (and every other Telnet that I've seen) is a matter of deciding what machine you wish to attach to, and telling it to attach. The thing to remember is, once the connection is made, you are playing by the rules of the remote machine (see figure 10.31).

By clicking on Connect and choosing `archie.sura.net` as the host, you connect to the Archie server at sura.net. You then log in as user "archie" and read the text they display for further information on how to run the Archie server.

```
┌─────────────────────────────────────────────────────────────┐
│ ─           Telnet - archie.sura.net              ▼ ▲       │
│ File   Edit   Disconnect   Settings   Script   Network   Help│
│    archie.kr                128.134.1.1      (Korean Server)  ▲
│    archie.kuis.kyoto-u.ac.jp 130.54.20.1     (Japanese Server)│
│    archie.luth.se           130.240.18.4     (Swedish Server) │
│    archie.ncu.edu.tw        140.115.19.24    (Taiwanese server)│
│    archie.nz                130.195.9.4      (New Zealand server)│
│    archie.rediris.es        130.206.1.2      (Spanish Server) │
│    archie.rutgers.edu       128.6.18.15      (Rutgers University (USA))│
│    archie.sogang.ac.kr      163.239.1.11     (Korean Server)  │
│    archie.sura.net          128.167.254.195  (SURAnet server MD (USA))│
│    archie.sura.net(1526)    128.167.254.195  (SURAnet alt. MD (USA))│
│    archie.switch.ch         130.59.1.40      (Swiss Server)   │
│    archie.th-darmstadt.de   130.83.22.60     (German Server)  │
│    archie.unipi.it          131.114.21.10    (Italian Server) │
│    archie.univie.ac.at      131.130.1.23     (Austrian Server)│
│    archie.unl.edu           129.93.1.14      (U. of Nebraska, Lincoln (USA))│
│    archie.uqam.ca           132.208.250.10   (Canadian Server)│
│    archie.wide.ad.jp        133.4.3.6        (Japanese Server)│
│                                                              │
│ Client software should be supported at all of these sites.   │
│                                                              │
│ archie>                                                    ▼ │
│ ◀                                                          ▶ │
│ ┌─────┐                                                      │
│ │Ready│                       │VT100│        │       │24, 9││
└─────────────────────────────────────────────────────────────┘
```

Figure 10.31 *NetManage Telnet to* `archie.sura.net`*.*

Overall Evaluation

Telnet is an essential part of your Internet toolkit, since a great number of services available on the Internet are not offered as graphical client/server applications. Library databases constitute probably the best example of this, but the list is surprisingly long and includes many useful information services.

Administrative Details

NetManage's Telnet is part of the package that you got with the book, and the installation procedure will have installed it correctly. There are other Telnet programs available on the Internet. But since one text window is much like another, there's no pressing need for you to go find the coolest and best. For completeness, you may try the Terminal button on WinQVT/NET, to look at another way of accomplishing Telnet.

TN3270

TN3270 is a version of Telnet that enables you to connect to IBM mainframes—emulating an IBM block mode terminal. If you can avoid

TN3270 and still accomplish what you need on the Internet, do so. IBM 3270 type terminals are what I learned to use in college and they hold a special fascination for me, but then, so do teletypes.

Running TN3270 is exactly the same as running normal Telnet, so you shouldn't have any problems there. It's after you connect that things may seem a little strange.

Unlike most other terminal types, block mode terminals only send characters to the host when a special attention key is pressed. This attention key is typically the Enter key (the one on the keypad, which is different from the Enter key on the main keyboard, and which has a different function). A standard IBM 3279-A has 24 function keys, and some applications will use all 24 of them, making for lots of Alt-F6 sorts of key mappings. Probably the most important thing to know about interacting with a 3270-type terminal is that there is a key called Clear. This key is mapped to the Esc key on your PC keyboard, so you should hit that Esc whenever you see **MORE...** in the status line of the TN3270 window. This is IBM's way of telling you there's more information ready to scroll onto the screen. TN3270 is thoughtfully holding it for you— allowing you to read page by page.

WS Archie

For some reason, archie programs have been slow in migrating to the Windows environment. In fact, the one that I'm about to describe was released almost too late to make it into my hands for description in this book. In some cases, like this, the thing is well worth the wait and I'm glad to be able to talk about a full-featured Archie client here.

Basic Usage

Install WS Archie as you have many of the programs in this chapter, by creating a directory for it, unzipping ws_archie.zip into that directory and creating an item for it in the Windows Program Manager. Once you have accomplished this, there is a bit of file editing to be done, and you are ready to go. Next, in Notepad, or your favorite text editor, open up the file wsarchie.ini. Now you will need to change the values in the [FTP] section to reflect your own information. It will more than likely look like this:

```
[FTP]
Comman=c:\winsock\ws ftp\ws    ftp    %h:%d/%f
FtpUserName=anonymous
FtpPasswork=ace@halcyon.com
ftpDirectory=c:\temp
```

Now the question that you may be asking at this point is, "If this is Archie, why is the .ini file talking about FTP?" The answer to that question is that any good Archie client will optionally enable you to retrieve the file that you've just found. For this particular archie, I would suggest that you retrieve the companion program WS FTP, and put the path to it into the Command= entry in wsarchie.ini. This will enable you to use the option to fetch the file you've selected from the list.

Now you can save the wsarchie.ini file and open the application. The first time you run WS Archie, you will want to enter a relevant server in the Archie Server drop-down list box. By clicking on the down arrow, you can choose from the list of available servers—keeping in mind that servers on the same continent are going to work faster for you than ones that are a satellite-link away. The Search For box seems pretty self-explanatory: it's the item for which you are looking. the radio buttons are the right can use some explanation, however.

Selecting one of the radio button options tells Archie how you would like to match your text with items Archie finds on FTP servers. For instance, you can have Archie find "cow" in Moscow, cow, and scowl—but not Cowabunga or Cow-list in a case sensitive search (see figure 10.32). You can use F1 to get an explanation of all the other Search types.

Once an item is found, you may be able to retrieve it from the site listed. If you've set up WS FTP in the wsarchie.ini file as I have, you retrieve the file simply by highlighting it in the files list box and selecting Retrieve from the File Menu. I like this feature a lot, because it completes the circle for me. When I go looking for a file on the Internet, using Archie, it's not usually becuase I just need to know where to find it. It's because I want the file, and this feature of WS Archie makes the retrieval easy.

Special Features

Below the Hosts, Directories, and Files listboxes, WS Archie displays all of the detailed information regarding the currently selected file. This is nice when I'm wondering "how big is this file, or when was it stuffed out into this archive?"

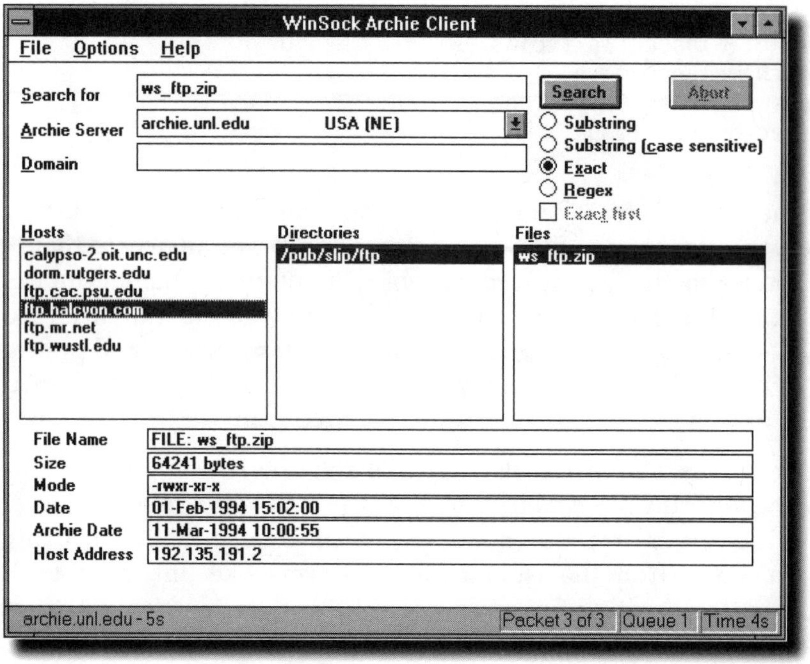

Figure 10.32   Archie's main window screen.

Also, you can set up defaults for all the settings in the main screen by selecting User Preferences from the Options menu.

Overall Evaluation

When combined with WS FTP, this Archie client is among the best that I've seen. It does all the mundane things that an Archie should do—like enabling me to choose a particular server to query, and to set the query type. The addition of automatically FTPing the file is a nice touch that I've enjoyed in X Windows versions. The only feature that may be missing from this Archie would be a way to set the "niceness" of my query. Niceness is a way of indicating to the Archie server how much priority to give this query. Low priority queries take longer to return results than high priority ones. It's possible that David Woakes, the author, simply assumed (correctly) that, given the choice, everyone would choose the highest priority.

Administrative Details

This WS Archie is still pretty early in the post-development stage (Alpha version 0.1), but I've seen no problems at all with it so far. It's a bit hard to find. It will be available at `ftp.halcyon.com` in the directory **/pub/slip/wsarchie**. Congratulations to David Woakes, the author on the first really great Archie for Windows. According to the files that come with WS Archie, it's freely distributable and can be used without charge at your own risk.

Finger

Finger, as its name may imply, is a very personal sort of information tool. Fingering someone is an attempt to find out information about the individual based upon information that you do have: such as their userid and domain name (or IP address). This is all accomplished by a Finger server, fingerd, usually (but not always) on a UNIX platform. The Finger server program will, based on a request from some client, look up various information about an particular login name, and return that to the requester. This information usually includes, but isn't limited to, the real name of the person, when they last logged in, whether they are currently logged in, and the contents of a file called ".plan".

More interesting to most people is the Finger client itself, which enables you to finger other people. I find Finger useful for accessing certain types of information over the Internet. People put all sorts of neat things in their .plan files, ranging from the Neilsen ratings for the last week's television shows to the latest reports of earthquake activity and back to current baseball scores.

Installation and Setup

Installing Finger 3.1 by Lee Murach is as simple as unzipping `finger31.zip` onto an area of your hard disk, and creating a program item for Windows. You'll notice that `finger31.zip` unpacks a lot of filename.c and source code-type things, but you don't really need them to run Finger. If you aren't interested in WinSock C source code, you can delete everything except `finger.exe`.

Basic Usage

Operating Finger is simplicity itself. Open the application by double-clicking on the program item that you created during installation, and select Host from the Host menu. Finger then enables you to type in a host name and a username to finger (see figure 10.33).

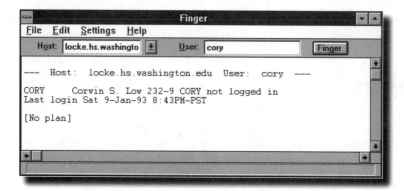

Figure 10.33   Finger host and username.

Keep in mind that there's nothing limiting what can be kept in a .plan file, so if you are interested in what America is watching on the television these days, try fingering normg at the host halcyon.com.

Special Features

The only other thing that you can do with Finger is to leave the username field blank, and (in some cases, not all) get a listing of everyone on the host whom you've named.

Overall Evaluation

I like Finger a lot. It's small, sweet, and to the point. And as long as people continue to store useful bits of information in .plan files, Finger remains an essential part of your WinSock software kit.

I haven't run into any problems with Finger, other than a lack of response from some sites. But that isn't Finger's fault. Finger is considered by some system administrators to be a security risk. It certainly gives people more information than they may have had without access to Finger. For that reason, and possibly because of system load effects, you will find machines that do not respond to your Finger requests.

Administrative Details

I found `finger31.zip` at the WinSock archive site `sunsite.unc.edu`, in the directory `/pub/micro/pc-stuff/ms-windows/WinSock/apps`, and though it comes with several versions of his readme file, Lee says nothing about the legal status of either the program executable, or the source code.

Gopher

The University of Minnesota's Gopher system lends itself to graphical interfaces. Because Gopher is inherently a list-based system, it maps perfectly to separate windows of lists between which you can switch back and forth, clicking on interesting items to explore deeper in Gopherspace.

WSGopher

WSGopher is a complete Gopher client, developed by EG&G of Idaho, Inc., with a Windows-standard interface. I've spent enough time in Idaho Falls to know there's not much to distract programmers from their tasks there in the wintertime, so I'm not surprised at the excellent job they've done in WSGopher.

Installation

As with most of the applications in this section, installing WSGopher is a matter of extracting the files from the .zip file, `wsg-09g.zip`, and creating a program item for Windows. In the case of WSGopher, be careful to fill in the "Working Directory" with the directory where `wsgopher.exe` and `wsgopher.ini` reside.

Basic Usage

A graphical Gopher client is fairly intuitive by nature. But there are a few concepts that make using Gopher a lot clearer. The main concept is that Gopher servers are a collection of files, other Gopher servers, and other information links.

It's important to know that a primary function of Gopher servers is to reference to other sources of information. The goal is to make this reference transparent.

To demonstrate this behavior, and to show nearly everything you need to know about using WSGopher, open the application and type Alt-E to open the Bookmark Editor window. This window shows you about all of the Gopher servers specifically mentioned in the wsgopher.ini file, and enables you to attach to one by selecting it from the list and clicking on the Fetch button (see figure 10.34).

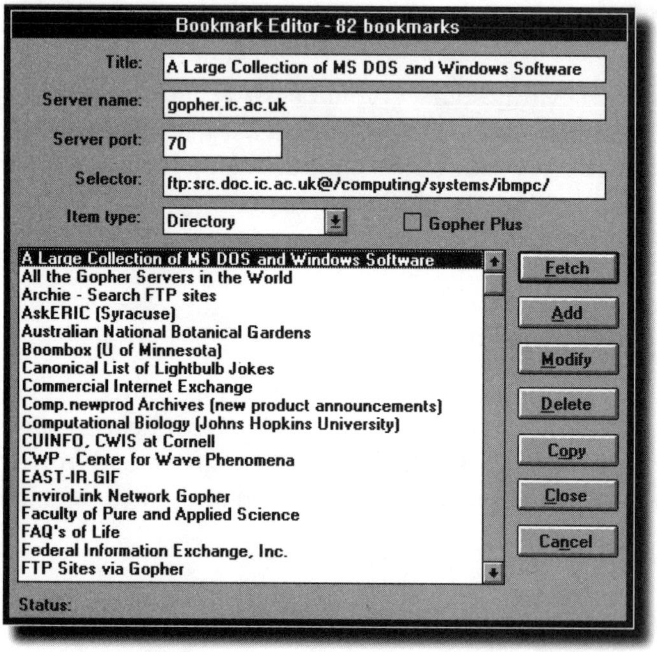

Figure 10.34   The WSGopher Bookmark Editor window.

If I choose the list item, "All the Gopher servers in the world," a list of items starts appearing on your WSGopher mail window and does what it advertises: lists all the Gopher servers in the world. This is a bit daunting, to say the least. However, WSGopher presents you with a list of nothing but other Gopher servers, and no end of documents. Double-clicking on any of these items will present you with the main screen from that server.

The last important note about WSGopher is an explanation of icon use. Some are obvious like the yellow file folder icon, which denotes a collection of documents or other folders. I may have chosen a different icon for local folders than other Gopher server links—but I guess that transparency is part of the concept. Other icons you will find on the screen are the readable document icon, the standard paper with lines and a corner folded, and the generic binary icon (covered with ones and zeros).

Special Features

WSGopher accommodates searches of Gopherspace via both Archie and Veronica, making this a quite versatile way to explore the Internet file spaces.

If you find a treasure trove in Gopherspace, you probably want to ensure you can find your way back at some future time. WSGopher has made that easy, by implementing a common Gopher feature called "Bookmarks." By typing Alt-S, you can save the current window as a bookmark, and return to it at any time by bringing up the Edit Bookmarks from the Bookmarks menu and selecting it from the list. The Recent menu shows you any of the last several Gopher servers which you have looked at and enables you to reattach by selecting it, without having saved it as a bookmark.

Overall Evaluation

WNGopher is as good as I've seen, including some commercial versions such as WinGopher from NOTIS Systems, Inc., and NetManage's from the Chameleon 4.0 distribution. I'm not a heavy Gopher user, but for my needs, WNGopher is more than sufficient.

Administrative Details

EG&G is a government contractor, doing mostly DOE work at the Idaho Nuclear Engineering Labs. The copyright notice included with WNGopher makes it clear that it is freely distributable and protected by U.S. copyright laws. Aside from that, distribution is achieved from two main points:

`boombox.micro.umn.edu`
in the directory `pub/gopher/Windows`

`sunsite.unc.edu`
in the directory `pub/micro/pc-stuff/windows/WinSock/apps`

WinGopher

WinGopher, from NOTIS Systems, is a commercial Gopher client, and compares favorably with WSGopher. The general operation and presentation are very similar to WSGopher, except that its bookmarks do not appear to be supported. And, it isn't immediately clear how to choose a Gopher server manually—which is something that I do a lot.

World-Wide Web

World Wide Web is a hypertext information browser that supports styled text, images, and sounds. There is virtually no limit to the types of information that can be presented from a WWW server. If your computer can present it, you probably can put it into a WWW server. The real problem that we are seeing on the Internet with WWW servers is that images and sounds and (for goodness sake) movies are huge, and chew up tons of bandwidth. For readers of this book who are attached to the Internet through modems, this can be a real problem. If you have less than a 9600 bps modem, I would suggest that WWW clients, such as NCSA's Mosaic, and Cello, probably are not something you will enjoy—unless you are someone who follows the movement of glaciers.

NCSA Mosaic for Windows

Mosaic for Windows, from the National Center for Supercomputing Applications (NCSA), is a nearly identical to the versions for the Macintosh and X Windows. That's one of the nice things about graphical user interfaces—they can look and behave the same across multiple platforms and operating systems. Mosaic installs simply by expanding the .zip file `wmos20a2.zip`, into a directory on your hard disk, and then editing `mosaic.ini`. You should change three entries in `mosaic.ini`: `e-mail=`; `SMTP_Server=`; and `NNTP_Server=`. Change to reflect the correct values for your mail server, news server, and email address, and then copy `mosaic.ini` to your windows directory. You can edit it via Notepad.

Once this is accomplished, open the application `mosaic.exe`, and you should see the NCSA Mosaic "Home Page," which is an excellent starting point for exploring the world of WWW servers. Speaking of starting points, if you pull down the menu with that name, you will find more information sources than you are likely to exhaust in a year or two of trying.

Mosaic is fun, intuitive, and quite addicting. Remember to move your mouse cursor across the face of the document you are reading and watch for changes in the cursor type. These changes indicate that a hypertext link is available. If you'd like to examine more information about a subject, simply click on this area.

Navigating through the WWW servers is an interesting and occasionally rewarding experience. WWW servers are beginning to crop up everywhere on the Internet, providing access to art collections in Australia and course descriptions in Utah. I fully expect Mosaic to be a model from which multimedia applications are delivered to homes thoughout the world in the years to come. You can get a glimpse of it this afternoon.

You can get NCSA's mosaic for Windows, version 2.0 from the WinSock archive at `sunsite.unc.edu`, in the directory `pub/micro/pc-stuff/windows/WinSock/apps`.

Cello

Cello is another WWW information browser, and to me appears very similar to Mosaic. There are differences in the pull-down menus, but the basic idea of presenting multimedia hyperlinks to information servers is the same. You can install Cello by extracting the file `cello.zip` to an area of your hard disk and installing it as a program item in your Program Manager. Double-clicking on Cello will open up the application and present the equivalent of the Mosaic Home Page.

One major difference that I can see from Mosaic is that Cello doesn't seem to be able to connect to WWW sites manually. This seems like an unreasonable shortcoming to me, because I need to connect to WWW servers at some of the strangest sites. Some of my friends have their own Home Pages and their sites are not publicly available (see figure 10.35).

NetManage 4.0

Throughout this book, I have talked about the software that comes packaged with this book: the Chameleon Sampler, version 3.11 from

NetManage. Chameleon 4.0, the current full-blown commercial package from NetManage, is a complete set of Internet utilities incorporating all of the best from the Sampler and a *lot* more.

Figure 10.35   *Cello's start-up screen.*

A quick count of icons in the installed Chameleon 4.0 tells me that there are 17 clients available. Wow! I'm not even sure what to do with all of them—NewtPROFS, for instance. I have this vague recollection that PROFS is an IBM-based email/office automation system, but I have no idea where I would attempt to verify that this is, indeed, a snazzy implementation. For the most part, though, the clients in the commercial Chameleon are pertinent and very much a part of my Internet tool suite.

One overall observation about the tools in Chameleon 4.0, as opposed to the 3.11 tools, is that NetManage has gone to great lengths to maintain the same general look and feel, while adding some really useful improvements. The most noticeable and powerful of these is the scripting language, which is available now for automating your Telnet sessions. I've not had much time for fiddling with this yet, but early indications are that it is an extremely useful addition to the standard Telnet and TN3270 applications.

Email

So far, NetManage's email application is the only one that would make me consider giving up Eudora. It's a fairly typical mailer with all the usual mail editing and forwarding capabilities (see figure 10.36). But, it does one thing that the free Eudora currently does not do: auto-filter incoming mail.

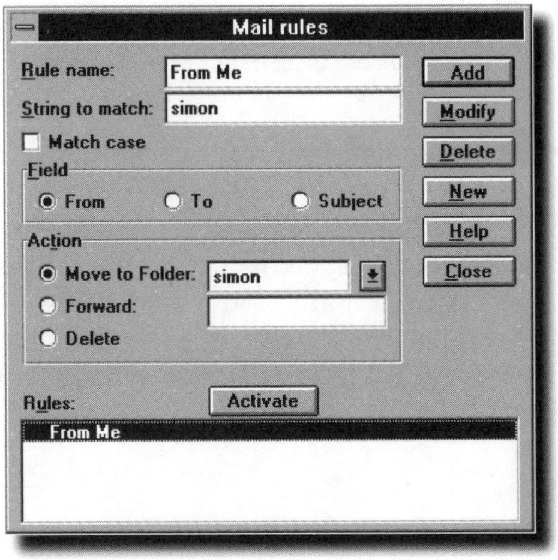

Figure 10.36   *Chameleon's Mail rules.*

By selecting Rules from the Services menu, you can choose to take actions on mail, based upon values in the From, To, or Subject headers of incoming mail. For instance, I like to have all my mail from myself (it's a bad habit you catch from testing mail programs) stuffed into a folder called "Schitzo". I can simply click on From, filter on my mail address as the string, and tell it which folder to stuff. This saves me from seeing all those messages from myself intermixed with useful mail. I'm sure that there are other, more generally useful things that can be done with this feature, but I'm happy just to not have to read my test mail every time I look through my current list.

Another nice feature is the idea of multiple mailboxes and passwords. If you login as Postmaster, the Mailboxes item from the Services menu enables you to create mailboxes for all of the mail accounts that you use and password protect each of them (see figure 10.37).

Figure 10.37   Chameleon Mail Services/Mailboxes screen.

If several people use the same machine for their Internet mail, this feature keeps mail folders and messages private. A separate mail utilities program also is included for such tasks as compacting mail folders, generating mailboxes from message files, and generally administrating your email files. There are not many options available in Mail Utilities, and it is hard to determine why they were not simply included as a menu on the mail program itself, but it's nice to have that utility in some form.

News

I covered NEWT News in depth earlier in this chapter, in the section on newsreaders, so I won't bore you with more details. For completeness' sake, I'll say that NEWT News is a reasonably complete newsreader with only one flaw: no threading. I can forgive almost anything in a newsreader, but threading is important to me.

FTP

As with NEWT News, Chameleon's FTP program already has been covered in some depth, but I will describe some of the features of the commercial product that aren't part of the Sampler version.

On the main screen, there's only one major difference—and it's a really nice feature. In the files section there's an item called View that enables you to view a document directly, rather than first transferring it across, switching to Notepad, and reading the new file. Here you must be careful about the file transfer type. Make sure it is ASCII so that translations from UNIX text (unless the remote site is DOS or NT) can occur. Viewing is particularly nice when you come across a read.me.this.instant.or.die.a.horrible.death file. You can easily comply, without worrying about translating that (perfectly legal) UNIX file name into something you can fit on your PC (see figure 10.38).

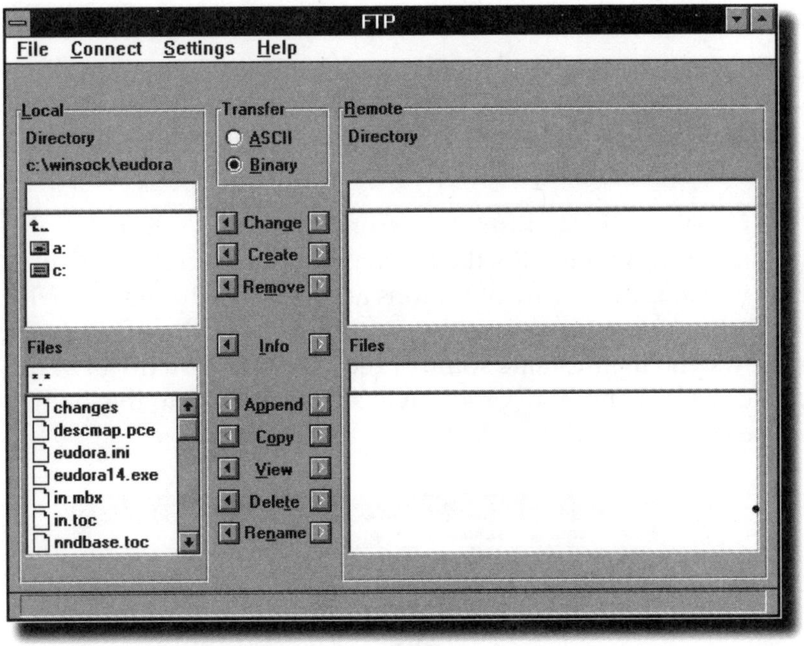

Figure 10.38 *Chameleon FTP 4.0 main screen.*

Other new features include a Diagnose Connection feature that will invoke Ping, pointing at the remote FTP machine to tell you whether it's still alive. This can be important when you're wondering whether your modem is really that slow or the server in Finland has just exploded in flames.

Telnet

The Telnet client included in the 4.0 release has a large number of differences from the one that comes with the Sampler. I won't try to identify all of them, but I will describe some of the more interesting ones.

Probably the most powerful of the new features is the addition of a scripting language to their Telnet clients (including TN3270 and TN5250). This allows the user to automate interaction with remote Telnet servers with tremendous flexibility. Along with the new capability comes a script development environment, with debugging features. This is not something everyone will need, but it certainly adds flexibility and function to something as basic as Telnet.

Under the File menu, you will find more printing and session capture options. You can now capture a Telnet session to disk, or spool it to a local printer (which can be handy if you happen to be writing a book about the Internet and trying to capture text from a command).

Last in my list of coolest differences from the Sampler disk on Telnet is under the Settings menu. It's the Button Pad Configuration feature. It enables you to create a row of buttons across the bottom of your Telnet screen that, when pressed, issue some command or character string. This allows you to automate some of the tasks that you do all of the time, such as **ls -l** and **mailx root </etc/services** (I like to live on the edge) (see figure 10.39).

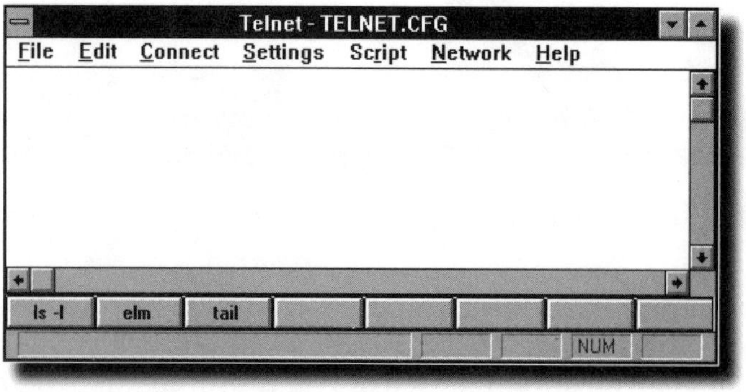

![Telnet - TELNET.CFG window with menu items File, Edit, Connect, Settings, Script, Network, Help and buttons labeled ls -l, elm, tail]

Figure 10.39   *Chameleon 4.0 Telnet with buttons.*

Finger and Whois

For personal information about persons on the Internet, Chameleon includes Finger and Whois clients. The Finger client is fairly vanilla, with a place for entering hostname, username, and a scrollable window for the incoming finger data. The only unusual feature that I noticed was a

Verbose setting, in the Settings menu. Without this checked, a hostname query without a username attached will produce a single line of information on each person currently logged in on that machine. If you *do* check Verbose, that same query will give all finger information on each of these same people.

Whois looks almost identical in form and function to the user and, in fact, accepts the same query data, but it accesses a different server database. There really are no configuration options for a Whois client, but you can fiddle with fonts and colors (as with all of NetManage's products).

For both Whois and Finger, graphical interfaces may at first glance seem overkill, but a scrollable feedback window is extremely nice in both applications (since the amount of information coming back from, say, fingering "help" at stanford.edu is not easily read as it scrolls by).

Overall Evaluation

The 4.0 version of Chameleon is a mature, well thought-out suite of TCP/IP products. I've used 4.0 for a couple of months now, both on a local area network, and as a SLIP account. I've been quite pleased with the changes from 3.11. Two of the applications that I use most, mail and news, could be absolutely the best there are with very little more work. And even then, my problems with them are strictly personal and qualitative—they are not failings of the product.

NetManage is supporting the business community better than most with the addition of TN5250 and NewtPROFS, both applications for IBM mainframe/minicomputers. This attitude is also reflected, to some degree, in NetManage's attention to providing network managers with tools they need to keep their networks working. More evidence of this can be found in their Simple Network Management Protocol implementation. All you really need to know is that if you're working on a corporate LAN and need to get this software approved by your system management staff, they'll be impressed that Newt provides them with SNMP management information.

Administrative Details

Chameleon 4.0 is available to people who have purchased this book at substantial discounts, via a coupon in the back of the book. In fact, this is such a good deal, it's worth buying the book even if all you want is an inexpensive copy of Chameleon. Tell all your friends!

TCP/Connect II

A Macintosh version with exactly the same name has an excellent reputation on that platform. Although their TCP/IP stack could not be made to work with text-based dynamic addressing, I was able to load the software and look at the suite of clients that InterCon ships.

The list of available clients and services that the installation program presents is impressive. I usually install everything available, and then eliminate whatever I decide I don't want, but in the case of TCP/Connect I was fearful that my measly 200 megabyte hard disk simply couldn't deal with everything, and so left out some of the less interesting stuff.

Email

The email program from InterCon is a typical POP mail client. Among the nice features they have included are MIME support for sending binary files via email, autoforwarding to send all mail you receive to another address, and the capability to define distribution lists, enabling you to send mail to your frequent standard groups.

MIME support is a given these days for mailers that send Internet mail. The capability to send binary files has quickly grown from a nice feature into something that mail users demand. Some mail programs that support Internet mail via a gateway, rather than directly, have neglected to implement this rapidly growing standard and cannot send binary files to anyone unless the other site is using exactly the same mail package. Needless to say, I'm happy to see that InterCon is on the ball here.

The autoforwarding feature seems interesting, but more useful if you have a computer that is continuously connected, rather than a typical SLIP on-again off-again connection. Speaking of permanent connections, they also implement straight SMTP mail, just like most UNIX hosts, but this would only be useful if you had a permanent IP address and a continuous connection to receive and transfer mail twenty-four hours a day.

Mail distribution groups are great for people like me who need to send mail to set groups of people all the time. For instance, I'm constantly looking for people who understand my peculiar sense of humor. When I find one, I include him on my list of people to whom to send witty comments and quips. I've had offers of money and other considerations to remove people from this list, so you can see that I take lists very seriously.

News

InterCon's NNTP newsreader is on a par with most of the other Windows-based newsreaders I've seen. Once you've set it up to talk to your NNTP host, you need to subscribe to whatever newsgroups you would like to read, and then go about your Usenet news reading. One area that most NNTP newsreaders typically fall short in is the process of subscribing to newsgroups, but not so with InterCon.

InterCon has chosen to present the newsgroups hierarchically. They present you with the top level of categories, and then let you narrow the scope a bit before diving into the group names themselves.

This enables you to subscribe to groups in which you are interested, while bypassing things such as `alt.technology.goes.boink.boink.boink`. If you consider the fact that there are approximately 4,500 newsgroups available from which to choose, anything that allows you to divide things up and make some logical sense out of it all is worth a lot.

News reading with the InterCon reader is a matter of double-clicking on the group that you would like to read and choosing the article to read in the same fashion. Posting and follows are accomplished by selecting the appropriate item from the Posting menu.

This newsreader, as with many others, suffers from a lack of support for threads or integrated email. I can live without these features, but it makes me cranky.

FTP

This FTP client gives me a serious sense of *deja vu*, because it looks and behaves almost exactly like the one from NetManage. The screen is divided in the same way, and the files and directories are in the same places; I actually have to look twice to see which one I've started.

The one special feature that I noticed with this client is that you may select Command Entry from the Window menu and issue FTP commands directly. I'm not talking only normal, UNIX command-line FTP commands, but the actual low-level commands that FTP uses to communicate with the server. This looks like about as much fun as hitting myself on the head with a hammer, but more painful.

Telnet

One interesting feature that I noticed about Telnet that comes with the InterCon package is that it's not called Telnet, but VT320. Okay, I know what a VT320 is. It's a terminal that Digital Equipment Corporation delivered, designed as a follow-on to the ubiquitous VT52, VT100, and VT220, which defined the standards for text-based ASCII terminals in the '70s and '80s. I guess that I can understand naming your Telnet application after the latest and best in a long line of terminals, but it's a bit confusing for the uninitiated.

Something that's been added in this area, which I haven't had the time or inclination to test, is the idea of a Telnet redirector. What this does, supposedly, is replace the serial communications driver (COMM.DRV) with one of InterCon's design that enables you to use "any Windows communications program as a terminal emulator for the Telnet protocol." I can see where this would be very attractive to anyone who has a lot of time invested in learning a communications package.

Overall Evaluation

I really like a lot of the ideas in InterCon's package, but since it doesn't support grabbing IP addresses in the way I need, it's hard for me to be too enthusiastic. I'm intrigued by the remote protocol support for programs such as rsh, rexec, and rcp, which would enable me to initiate programs in a remote UNIX host from the safety and security of Windows.

It's easy to see that InterCon has a tremendously creative bunch of programmers putting together their TCP/IP suite—and they are headed in the direction in which I want to go—but it may be a little while before I can make effective use of all the cool ideas they've come up with.

One last note about TCP/Connect II: I love the manual! I hate manuals and rarely ever read them, even when circumstances would indicate that I really should. When I finally gave up on figuring out the scripting problem with my service provider, I decided to read the manual and got a big surprise. It's clear, well written, and to the point. They even include some appendices on Internet information sources. Their list of Internet mail gateways is the most comprehensive I've seen.

Administrative Details

For more information, contact InterCon electronically at `sales@intercon.com` or at:

InterCon Systems Corporation
950 Herndon Pkwy., Ste. 420
Herndon, VA 22070
703-709-5500
703-709-5555 (fax)

Distinct TCP/IP

When Distinct's WinSock interface was discussed earlier in this chapter, I mentioned that it did something no other WinSock that I have access to will do: It dials automatically when you invoke one of their applications. Distinct also is doing some other interesting things that I should mention, because they have potential for making the Distinct WinSock very popular.

Distinct is currently selling software development kits for both Microsoft C++ and Microsoft Visual Basic programmers, to assist in producing new applications for their implementation of WinSock. I realize that other companies also are actively pursuing this, but the easiest to get and least expensive that I've seen is the one from Distinct. What this could mean, coupled with the clean invocation of SLIP when an application runs, is that you may be seeing many applications distributed using the Distinct run-time.

Email

There is no email client packaged with Distinct's TCP/IP. I did, however, load up Eudora and emailed for awhile with that on top of Distinct's WinSock. The only problem I encountered was that normal WinSock applications such as Eudora don't automatically invoke the Distinct WinSock SLIP dialer. This is relatively easy to overcome, by starting up something such as Ping, and pinging, say, the POP server (actually, it's not important what you ping, just that the SLIP connection is made).

News

Here again, no Usenet newsreader is shipped with the Distinct TCP/IP package. But WinVN, an NNTP-based newsreader discussed earlier in this chapter, worked just fine (albeit with the same caveats as email). The Distinct WinSock would appear to be well-implemented from this perspective. The test always lies in seeing what breaks with *other peoples'* programs, not your own.

 # FTP

Distinct does ship a FTP client with their product, and it comes with a refreshingly different interface. Distinct chose to represent the directories on each side of the local/remote connection as trees, much as we've all been taught to think of directories in DOS and UNIX. I like the idea of this, but they could take it a bit further. Once I've started navigating down some pathway, I frequently decide to turn tail and run the other way, back several levels at least. If Distinct maintained all the tree information, rather than just one level, I could choose to move back to anywhere that I've already seen, and start again (see figure 10.40).

Lest I sound negative here, I hasten to add that I truly like the simple, clean interface that the folks at Distinct have come up with, and I applaud their originality. The Quick Menu buttons across the top are certainly clear and, well, quick. Of all the FTP clients that I've seen, this is the one I'd feel most comfortable handing to an executive, or a five-year-old, to figure out.

Distinct FTP [crow.csrv.uidaho.edu - ASCII]

Action   Options   Help

Get   Put   Ren   Del   Mkdir   Print   Help

Drive: C: C:\WINDOWS\DISTINCT
No files selected   Settings

DISTINCT

BOOTP.EXE	D-INFO.HLP	DTCPIP.DRV
BOOTP.HLP	DATABILI.DLN	DTCPIP.HLP
CISCO.DLN	DATABILI.HUP	FINGER.EXE
CONFIG.EXE	DEFAULT.TEL	FTP-CLNT.EXE
CONFIG.HLP	DISTINCT.DLL	FTP-CLNT.HLP

Host: crow.csrv.uidaho.   /users/simon
No files selected   Settings

simon
—.elm
—.tin
— Mail
— mail

.cshrc	818	Jan 5 1993
.forward	18	Mar 3 14:03
.gopherrc	0	Jun 10 1993
.login	377	Jan 5 1993
.msgsrc	2	Mar 14 17:04
.newsrc	51507	Mar 14 17:16

Figure 10.40   Distinct's FTP screen.

Telnet

Distinct's Telnet is similar in design and function to the FTP client, in that it uses similar-looking Quick Menu buttons. I find the addition of an FTP Quick Menu button especially handy when I'm logged into halcyon.com, doing some UNIX-y Internet thing, and end up with a file that I would be much happier handling on my PC. By simply clicking the FTP Quick Menu button, I can start up FTP, ready to attach to halcyon.com.

The other interesting feature on the Quick Menu set for Telnet is the Monitor button. By pressing the Monitor Quick Menu button, you can bring up the network monitor application (discussed above, in the section on "Distinct's WinSock"). I like their network monitor for diagnostic reasons. I also like this easy access from Telnet (see figure 10.41).

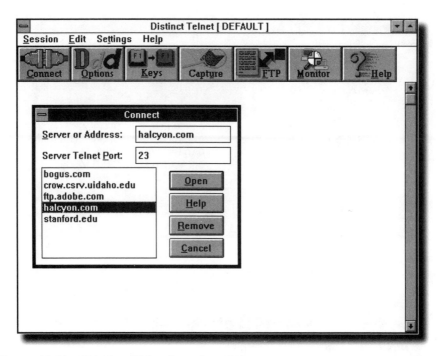

Figure 10.41   *Distinct Telnet's main window.*

From what I can tell, Distinct's terminal emulation appears flawless. I use many applications in UNIX that (inadvertently) test the capabilities of a terminal emulator pretty severely, and had no problems whatsoever. It tells the UNIX box that it's a VT100, and carries it off well.

Overall Evaluation

I'm impressed with Distinct's WinSock more than with their other applications. Not that their applications are substandard, but it's pretty evident that they have concentrated on providing an excellent TCP/IP basis, and that applications take second priority. Some evidence of this lies in the fact that their application suite lacks items such as email and newsreaders.

Rather than view this as a problem, I applaud this choice. I would much rather have a truly great WinSock connecting me to the network, and have to go looking for mail and newsreaders, than have 30 clients shipped with a WinSock that interacts poorly with the rest of my programs, or doesn't work correctly with standard WinSock applications.

The applications that do ship on the Distinct disks are simple, solid, and quite functional. I've described some fairly interesting bells and whistles on other products, but there's not all that much I want to do with Telnet. I want to connect to a remote computer, run some commands, and then return to my nice homey Windows. Distinct's Telnet does that very nicely.

Administrative details

For more details, contact Distinct Corporation at:

Distinct Corporation
12901 Saratoga Avenue
P.O. Box 3410
Saratoga, CA 95070-1410
408-741-0781
408-741-0795 (fax)

Part IV

Appendices

I certainly hope that you have enough of a life that you don't pore through the following appendices in great detail, absorbing every molecule of information. I don't intend you to do that; instead, I recommend that you flip through them more or less at random until you see a section that looks interesting. The appendices are all straight lists of information, and although you may want to explore a certain section in detail, I included them as pointers, as launch pads to get you started.

Appendix A, Internet Resources

Perhaps the hardest part for an Internet novice is finding interesting mailing lists and Gopher sites. It's not actually difficult, but it can take some effort to achieve the proper mindset. This resource list, although making no pretensions on completeness, should help you get started. After you have explored some of the resources mentioned here, you will undoubtedly happen on others that either didn't exist at the time of publication or that are not mentioned. That's good. The bulk of this list was ably compiled by Ken Stuart, and thanks are due to him for his efforts.

Appendix B, Newsgroup List

Appendix B is a long list of many of the thousands of newsgroups that currently exist on Usenet. It comes by way of the editors, Gene Spafford and David Lawrence, and is regularly posted in various groups on Usenet. So many newsgroups are available that it can be overwhelming. I hope this list helps you figure out which few newsgroups you want to read. I especially recommend checking out the descriptions of some of the alternate groups.

Appendix C, PDIAL List

Peter Kaminski's PDIAL list, although not guaranteed to be up to date or accurate, is the best source in which to find a local provider with full Internet access. I recommend finding the latest changes with a provider by sending email to the information addresses if you already have email access in some fashion, or by giving them a call if you don't have email access just yet.

Appendix D, The nixpub List

Phil Eschallier's nixpub list is another valuable resource when you're looking for a local provider. The major difference between the PDIAL list and the nixpub list is that not all machines on the nixpub list offer full Internet access—you may be limited to email only, for instance. Still, the nixpub list is an invaluable guide to the smaller providers.

Appendix E, Glossary

Appendix E provides you with a list of common words and their definitions. If you're ever troubled by a vocabulary question—at least, regarding the Internet—check here.

Appendix F, Special Internet Access Offer

Last, but certainly not least, appendix F provides details about our special Internet access offer. A brief description of Northwest Nexus (the access provider) and of the connecting procedure is included.

Appendix

Internet Resources

Ken Stuart and I compiled this appendix (you can contact us kps1@cornell.edu and ace@tidbits.com, respectively). Compiling this information was nearly an impossible task. I was trying to finish writing this book early, and there was no way I could humanly do it without help. Luckily, I was able to draft the skillful assistance of Ken Stuart, who pored through the massive lists of raw material I had gathered, combed the List of Lists, and generally spent some time surfing the Internet for interesting resources.

We never intended that this list be complete or even moderately exhaustive because that too is an impossible task. The Internet is so vast and moves so quickly that to attempt a comprehensive directory is an act of hubris worthy of a lightning bolt from Zeus. Instead, we've selected a number of different resources and categorized them in some rough ways so that you can browse through and see whether anything catches your interest. Our categories made sense to us, but they certainly aren't approved by the Library of Congress. They are intentionally broad to ensure that you can scan them quickly without worrying about looking in the right place.

To give you an idea of the immensity of the resources available, I counted almost 800 Gopher servers alone in a folder called "All the Gopher Servers in the World." That number is more than we could conceivably explore because the information would have changed by the time we finished.

Don't worry if you don't see anything in here that interests you—that probably only means that we didn't happen across the mailing list or Gopher site that fits your interests. Rather, use this list as a springboard to the Internet. As you spend more time on the Internet—participating in mailing lists and newsgroups, browsing Gopherspace, or searching WAIS—you will come across more resources. Just make a note of them and investigate when you have some time. Spread the word to others who share your interests so that they too can explore what you've found.

Also, we've included a section called Internet Meta-Resources, which are resources much like this one that point to resources on specific topics. Of them, the InterNIC Gopher server at is.internic.net and Scott Yanoff's Special Internet Connections list are among the most useful. We recommend that you check them out soon because they provide pointers to many other resources.

The resources we have listed in this appendix fall into several major categories: WAIS servers that you can search using WAIS software, newsgroups that have FAQ (Frequently Asked Questions) postings at a specific FTP site, mailing lists, Gopher servers, and Telnet sites.

WAIS Sources

Unfortunately, there don't seem to be any Windows clients for WAIS. Glance back to chapter 9, "Terminal Access," for instructions on how to telnet into quake.think.com (hint: login as **wais**), and search WAIS sources.

FAQs and FTP Sites

Way back when, I talked briefly about the concept of the Frequently Asked Question (FAQ), and I said that many newsgroups on Usenet had created lists of these questions along with the answers. We decided not to include newsgroups in this resource section specifically because Gene Spafford and David Lawrence gave me permission to reprint their massive list of newsgroups, complete with short descriptions. You'll find that information in appendix B, "Newsgroup List."

Nonetheless, because these FAQs are extremely useful, we decided to list a bunch of them in this section so that you can find out answers to the common questions raised in these newsgroups. And because we use the newsgroup name in listing the FAQ files, you can use these categories to learn a bit more about the newsgroups listed as well. Although you can read the newsgroup in question for a month or so and wait until the FAQ list goes by (they're usually posted on a regular basis), it's probably more efficient for you to retrieve a specific file via FTP from `rtfm.mit.edu` in the directory /pub/usenet/*name.of.group* (where you replace *name.of.group* with the name of the group you want to research).

The /pub/usenet directory on `rtfm.mit.edu` is so large that FTP clients will slow down considerably when you're retrieving it for the first time. Thus, I recommend that you either browse it with Gopher instead or enter the specific directory you want to visit into the FTP directory dialog box so that you don't have to see the list of all the groups when you want only one.

We also included a few FTP sites that have interesting files. For them, just use Gopher or FTP to connect and retrieve files as you want. Of course, the best ways to find additional FTP sites that contain interesting files are to use either Veronica within Gopher or Archie to search FTP sites. Either method should turn up plenty of sites for you to peruse.

When we include a pointer to a file or files on an FTP site other than the one that holds the FAQ files, we provide a brief description, the name of the site, and the directory in which the file(s) are stored.

Mailing Lists

Mailing lists are often the hardest to find of all the resources. Therefore, we've included a number of interesting lists. We chose a specific format to convey a great deal of information in a small space, so pay attention. The item in the first column is the *list name*. That's also the userid to which you send submissions. The second column is the *userid of the address* to which you send subscription requests and other administrative requests. The item in the third column is the *nodename* for both the previous two columns. The fourth column, if present, is a brief *description* of the list if it's not apparent from the list name. Here's an example:

```
tidbits    listserv    ricevm1.rice.edu    Weekly electronic
                                            newsletter
```

To subscribe to the TidBITS list, you combine column two and column three and send email to `listserv@ricevm1.rice.edu` (and follow the rules laid out in chapter 5 for subscribing to LISTSERV-based lists: namely, type the line **SUBSCRIBE TIDBITS** *your full name* on the first line of the message). To submit a posting, you combine column one and column three and send it to `tidbits@ricevm1.rice.edu`.

Here's a slightly different example:

```
ultralight-flight    ultralight-flight-request    ms.uky.edu
```

Here, the userid to which you send subscription requests is a UNIX mailing list, as indicated by the `-request` at the end of it. There are no special rules for UNIX mailing lists, so you just combine column two and three and send email to `ultralight-flight-request@ms.uky.edu` with a request for subscription to sign up, and then you submit postings to the combination of column one and column three, or `ultralight-flight@ms.uky.edu`.

By now you are certainly asking, "How can I tell what sorts of things are discussed on any given list?" The best way to find out that information is to subscribe and watch the postings for a day or so. If the postings don't meet your expectations, sign off from the list (to sign off, type the **SIGNOFF** *listname* command for LISTSERV-based lists or send email to the -`request` address for other lists). There are some automated methods of reading the charter for a list, but frankly, they aren't consistent. Even if you can find them, there's no guarantee that the discussions will interest you. They may be too technical or not technical enough, or perhaps the list has started talking about a side topic that doesn't excite you.

Telnet Sites

Telnet resources require you to use a Telnet client, but after that you have to play by the rules of the service you're connecting to. I can't help you there, although following the rules shouldn't be a problem because most Telnet-based services are simple. We haven't provide too many of these resources, in part because they are the ugliest to use and the least Windows-like.

For the services we do mention, we provide a description of the site, the name of the site you telnet to, and the login name and password if any exist.

Gopher Servers

Gopher servers are a bit more problematic than the other resources listed here. The problem is that you can access Gopher servers in three ways: directly by using the Other Gopher Resources item in Gopher, by searching with Veronica, or by browsing manually through Gopherspace. This last technique is the least efficient, and we don't recommend it when you are trying to find anything specific. Veronica searches are accurate and useful, but may return more than you want to peruse. The first method is the most trouble because you have to type in the name of the Gopher server manually. This method is the most accurate, however. We leave it to you to decide which you want to use, but we recommend a combination of direct access and Veronica.

In most cases we've provided the address of the Gopher server (and the Port Number unless it is the default, 70) in question so that you can travel there directly. On occasion we left the address worded in terms of a Veronica search. After all, you must do some of this exploration on your own, and Veronica leads you down the most interesting paths.

Now, on to the resources!

Air and Space; Astronomy and Astrophysics

WAIS Sources

```
nrao-fits.src
eros-data-center.src
stsci-preprint-db.src
sci.astro.hubble.src
```

FAQ Files and FTP Sites

```
sci.space
sci.space.new
sci.space.shuttle
rec.aviation.answers
rec.aviation.simulators
alt.sci.planetary
sci.astro
sci.astro.fits
```

Mailing Lists

aircraft	listserv	grearn.bitnet
airline	listserv	cunyvm.cuny.edu
aviation	listserv	mc.lcs.mit.edu

aviation-theory	listserv	mc.lcs.mit.edu	
flight-sim	flight-sim-request	grove.iup.edu	
isss	listserv	jhuvm.hcf.jhu.edu	International Student Space Simulations
space	listserv	andrew.cmu.edu	
ultralight-flight	ultralight-flight-request	ms.uky.edu	

Anthropology and Archaeology

WAIS Sources

```
ANU-Aboriginal-Studies.src
ANU-Thai-Yunnan.src
ANU-Coombspapers-Index.src
archaeological_computing.src
```

Mailing Lists

aia-l	listserv	brynmawr.edu	American Institute of Archaeology
ancien-l	listserv	ulkyvm.louisville.edu	
anthro-l	listserv	ubvm.bitnet	
arch-l	listserv	dgogwdg1.bitnet	
classics	listserv	uwavm.u.washington.edu	

ethnohis	listserv	nic.surfnet.nl	Ethnology and history
humbio-l	humbio-request	acc.fau.edu	All aspects of human biology
indknow	listserv	uwavm.u. washington.edu	Indigenous knowledge
marine-l	listserv	uoguelph.ca	
museum-l	listserv	unmvm.bitnet	
natchat	listserv	tamvm1.tamu.edu	Lives and cultures of any of the world's indigenous peoples

Automotive

FAQ Files and FTP Sites

rec.motorcycles
rec.motorcycles.dirt
rec.motorcycles.harley
rec.motorcycles.racing
rec.audio.car

Mailing Lists

autox	autox-request	autox.team.net	
ev	listserv	sjsuvm1.sjsu.edu	Electric vehicles
honda	listserv	mscrc.sunysb.edu	

| moto.chassis | moto.chassis-request | oce.orst.edu | Theory and practice of motorcycle chassis design and construction |
| vintagevw @rocky.er. usgs.gov | robert@whiplash. er.usgs.gov | | Vintage Volkswagens |

Biology and Environment

WAIS Sources

```
biology-journal-contents.src
Cell_Lines.src
IUBio-fly-clones.src
bionic-genbank-software.src
Oligos.src
online-mendelian-inheritance-in-man.src
Salk-Genome-Center.src
IUBio-INFO.src
bionic-directory-of-servers.src
the-scientist.src
NOAA_National_Environmental_Referral_Service.src
great-lakes-factsheets.src
```

FAQ Files and FTP Sites

sci.bio (includes "A Biologist's Guide to Internet Resources")
```
bionet.announce
bionet.general
bionet.info-theory
sci.environment
talk.environment
```

Mailing Lists

aqua-l	listserv	vm.uoguelph.ca	Aquaculture
bee-l	listserv	albnyvm1.bitnet	
bio-naut	listserv	irlearn.bitnet	
biosph-l	listserv	ubvm.bitnet	
biotech	listserv	umdc.bitnet	
camel-l	listserv	sakfu00.bitnet	
cbt-general	cbt-general-request	virginia.edu	Circadian rhythms
consbio	listserv	uwavm.u.washington.edu	
cvnet	listserv	yorkvm1.bitnet	Color and vision research
deepsea	listserv	uvvm.uvic.ca	
dinosaur	dinosaur-request	donald.wichitaks.ncr.com	
envbeh-l	listserv	graf.poly.edu	Environmental behavior
envst-l	listserv	brownvm.bitnet	Environmental studies programs
forens-l	listserv	acc.fau.edu	Forensic studies of all types
humbio-l	humbio-request	acc.fau.edu	All aspect of human biology
lactacid	listserv	searn.sunet.se	Biology and uses of lactic acid bacteria

marine-l	listserv	uoguelph.ca	
orgche-l	listserv	rpicicge.bitnet	
socinsct	listserv	albany.bitnet	Social insect biology
vetinfo	listserv	ucdcvdls.bitnet	

Gopher Servers

Not Just Cows

Use Veronica via Gopher to search for the term *cows*. From the returned choices, choose "Not Just Cows" for extensive information on agricultural resources

EcoGopher at the University of Virginia

`ecosys.drdr.`
`virginia.edu`

EnviroGopher at CMU

`envirolink.hss.`
`cmu.edu`

GreenGopher at University of Virginia

`ecosys.drdr.`
`Virginia.EDU`

Bedford Institute of Oceanography (Canada)

`biome.bio.`
`dfo.ca`

Global Biological Information Servers

`weeds.mgh.`
`harvard.edu`

Business, Economics, and Jobs

FAQ Files and FTP Sites

```
misc.invest
misc.jobs.contract
misc.jobs.misc
misc.jobs.offered
misc.jobs.offered.entry
misc.jobs.resumes
misc.consumers
alt.business.multi-level
misc.legal
```

Mailing Lists

ajbs-l	listserv	pucc.princeton.edu	
apogees	listserv	fraix11.bitnet	
e-europe	listserv	pucc.princeton.edu	
economy	listserv	tecmtyvm.mty. itesm.mx	Economy and economic problems of less developed countries
fedjobs	listserv	dartcms1. dartmouth.edu	
fedtax-l	listserv	shsu.bitnet	
ioob-l	listserv	uga.bitnet	Industrial/ organizational psychology and organization behavior
market-l	listserv	ucf1vm.cc.ucf.edu	
mba-l	listserv	marist.bitnet	

oil-gas	listserv	pavnet.nshor. ncoast.org	
quality	listserv	pucc.princeton.edu	Total Quality Management (TQM) in manufacturing and service industries
space- investors	space- investors- request	cs.cmu.edu	
trdev-l	listserv	psuvm.psu.edu	Information on the training and the development of human resources

Gopher Servers

Online Career Information Center (job listings)	ns.oar.net port 7000

Cultures, Social Groups, and Lifestyles

FAQ Files and FTP Sites

```
misc.kids
soc.college
soc.culture.african.american
soc.culture.asian.american
soc.culture.caribbean
soc.culture.china
soc.culture.esperanto
```

```
soc.culture.esperanto.news.answers
soc.culture.europe
soc.culture.french
soc.culture.german
soc.culture.greek
soc.culture.hongkong
soc.culture.indian
soc.culture.iranian
soc.culture.italian
soc.culture.japan
soc.culture.jewish
soc.culture.latin-america
soc.culture.lebanon
soc.culture.magyar
soc.culture.mexican
soc.culture.netherlands
soc.culture.taiwan
soc.culture.turkish
soc.feminism
soc.net-people
soc.penpals
alt.hackers
alt.homosexual
alt.co-ops
alt.computer.consultants
```

Mailing Lists

africa-l	listserv	brufmg.bitnet	
balt-l	listserv	ubvm.cc.buffalo.edu	
bisexu-l	listserv	brownvm.brown.edu	
bubba-l	listserv	knuth.mtsu.edu	
e-hug	listserv	dartcms1.bitnet	Electronic Hebrew users newsletter
femisa	listserv	mach1.wlu.ca	
gaynet	gaynet-request	athena.mit.edu	
gay-libn	listserv	vm.usc.edu	

hungary	listserv	ucsbvm.bitnet	
india-l	listserv	utarlvm1.bitnet	
inmylife	listserv	wkuvx1.bitnet	Beatles era popular culture
j-food-l	listserv	jpnknu10.bitnet	Japanese food and culture
kidsnet	listserv	vms.cis.pitt.edu	For the use of children and teachers in grades K-12
latino-l	listserv	amherst.edu	
mail-men@usl.com	mail-men-request@attunix.att.com		men's issues
mail.yiddish	dave@lsuc.on.ca		
masonic	ptrei@asgard.bbn.com		
mexico-l	listserv	tecmtyvm.mty.itesm.mx	
misg-l	listserv	psuvm.psu.edu	Malaysian affairs
natchat	listserv	tamvm1.tamu.edu	Lives and cultures of any of the world's indigenous peoples
native-l	listserv	tamvm1.tamu.edu	
norwaves	listserv	nki.no	Weekly news from Norway
pacific	listserv	brufpb.bitnet	Peoples of Pacific Ocean and Islands
pakistan	listserv	asuvm.inre.asu.edu	
pcorps-l	listserv	cmuvm.csv.cmich.edu	Peace Corps

poland-l	listserv	ubvms.bitnet	
russia	listserv	indycms.iupui.edu	Russia and her neighbors
sca	sca-request	mc.lcs.mit.edu	Society for Creative Anachronism
scouts-l	listserv	tcubvm.bitnet	
sovnet-l	listserv	indycms.bitnet	
tibet-l	listserv	ucs.indiana.bitnet	
ukraine	listserv	indycms.iupui.edu	
un	listserv	indycms.iupui.edu	
urbanites	listserv	psyche.mit.edu	
wisenet	listserv	uicvm.uic.edu	Women in science, mathematics, or engineering
wmst-l	listserv	umdd.umd.edu	Women's studies issues

Games (Board and Electronic)

FAQ Files and FTP Sites

```
alt.games.tiddlywinks
rec.gambling
rec.games.board
rec.games.bridge
rec.games.chess
rec.games.corewar
rec.games.design
rec.games.diplomacy
rec.games.empire
rec.games.frp.announce
rec.games.go
```

```
rec.games.int-fiction
rec.games.misc
rec.games.moria
rec.games.mud.announce
rec.games.mud.diku
rec.games.mud.misc
rec.games.netrek
rec.games.pbm
rec.games.pinball
rec.games.video
rec.games.video.arcade
rec.games.video.classic
rec.games.video.misc
rec.games.video.nintendo
rec.games.video.sega
```

Mailing Lists

adnd-l	listserv	utarlvm1.bitnet	Advanced Dungeons & Dragons
dark-sun	listserv	le.ac.uk	
chess-l	listserv	grearn.bitnet	
consim-l	listserv	vm.ucs.ualberta.ca	Wargames
dipl-l	listserv	mitvma.mit.edu	Diplomacy
shadowrn	listserv	hearn.bitnet	
shogi-l	listserv	technion.bitnet	
snes	listserv	spcvxa.spc.edu	Super Nintendo Entertainment System
traveller	traveller-request		engrg.uwo.ca

Gopher Servers

Pointers to Telnet-based interactive games	itsa.ucsf.edu

Government, Politics, and Activism

WAIS Sources

```
US Congress Phone-Fax WAIS.src
gsa-cfda.src (Catalog of Federal Domestic Assistance)
World factbook.src
Omni-Cultural-Academic Resource.src
US-Budget-1993.src
US-Gov-Programs.src
ota.src (Office of Technology Assessment)
```

FAQ Files and FTP Sites

```
talk.politics.drugs
talk.politics.misc
talk.politics.space
alt.society.civil-liberty
alt.politics.homosexuality
alt.politics.libertarian
alt.anarchism
alt.activism
```

Addresses and phone numbers of members of Congress	`nifty.andrew.cmu.edu`	/pub/QRD/qrd/ info/GOVT/con- gress-103
Resumes of cabinet members	`nifty.andrew.cmu.edu`	/pub/QRD/qrd/ info/GOVT/cabinet
Government Accounting Office reports	`cu.nih.gov`	/GAO-REPORTS

Mailing Lists

amnesty	listserv	vms.cis.pitt.edu	
animal-rights	listserv	cs.odu.edu	
canada-l	listserv	vm1.mcgill.ca	
ec	listserv	vm.cc.metu.edu.tr	European Community
govdoc-l	listserv	psuvm.bitnet	
green	listserv	indycms.iupui.edu	
greenorg	listserv	indycms.bitnet	
hr-l	listserv	vms.cis.pitt.edu	Human rights issues
libernet	listserv	dartmouth.edu	For libertarians
mideur-l	listserv	ubvm.bitnet	Middle European politics
politics	listserv	ucf1vm.cc.ucf.edu	Serious discussion of politics
un	listserv	indycms.iupui.edu	
y-rights	listserv	sjuvm.bitnet	Rights of kids and teenagers

Telnet Sites

FedWorld Government BBS	fedworld.doc.gov

Miscellaneous

President Clinton's email address	president@whitehouse.gov
Vice President Gore's email address	vice.president@whitehouse.gov

Gopher Servers

Other government documents	sunsite.unc.edu	
The Freedom of Information Act	eryx.syr.edu	Other Gopher and Information Service/North America/USA/General/ EGIS

Health Issues

Mailing Lists

addict-l	listserv	kentvm.kent.edu	
aidsnews	listserv	rutvm1.bitnet	
alcohol	listserv	lmuacad.bitnet	
amalgam	listserv	vm.gmd.de	
autism	listserv	sjuvm.bitnet	
c+health	listserv	iubvm.ucs. indiana.edu	Computers and Health
deafblnd	listserv	ukcc.uky.edu	
diabetic	listserv	pccvm.bitnet	
drugabus	listserv	umab.bitnet	
fit-l	listserv	etsuadmn.bitnet	Wellness, exercise, and diet
granola	listserv	vtvm2.cc.vt.edu	
healthre	listserv	ukcc.uky.edu	U.S. health reform
l-hcap	listserv	ndsuvm1.bitnet	Technology for the handicapped

lymenet-l	listserv	lehigh.edu	
minhlth	listserv	dawn.hampshire.edu	Issues of minority health
nrsing-l	listserv	nic.umass.edu	
pharm	pharm-request	dmu.ac.uk	
safety	listserv	uvmvm.bitnet	Environmental, health, and safety issues
smoke-free	listserv	ra.msstate.edu	For people recovering from addiction to cigarettes
stroke-l	listserv	ukcc.uky.edu	
stut-hlp	listserv	bgu.edu	For people who stutter and their families
wmn-hlth	listserv	uwavm.u.washington.edu	Women's health issues
RSI-East	listserv	sjuvm.stjohns.edu	Carpal Tunnel Syndrome and other typing-related injuries

Gopher Servers

CAMIS (Center for Advanced Medical Informatics at Stanford)	camis.stanford.edu

Hobbies, House, and Home

WAIS Sources

```
recipes.src
homebrew.src
```

FAQ Files and FTP Sites

```
alt.aquaria
alt.magic
alt.radio.scanner
rec.backcountry
rec.bicycles.misc
rec.boats.paddle
rec.climbing
rec.crafts.brewing
rec.crafts.textiles
rec.org.sca
rec.pets
rec.pets.birds
rec.pets.cats
rec.pets.dogs
rec.photo
rec.puzzles
rec.puzzles.crosswords
rec.pyrotechnics
rec.radio.amateur.antenna
rec.radio.amateur.digital.misc
rec.radio.amateur.equipment
rec.radio.amateur.homebrew
rec.radio.amateur.misc
rec.radio.amateur.packet
rec.radio.amateur.policy
rec.radio.amateur.space
rec.radio.cb
rec.radio.info
rec.radio.noncomm
rec.radio.shortwave
```

```
rec.radio.swap
rec.roller-coaster
rec.scouting
rec.scuba
rec.skate
rec.skydiving
rec.guns
rec.models.railroad
rec.models.rc
rec.arts.bonsai
rec.aquaria
alt.sewing
alt.locksmithing
misc.consumers.house
rec.food.cooking
rec.food.recipes
rec.food.veg
rec.woodworking
alt.bonsai
alt.drumcorps
rec.arts.marching.drumcorps
rec.arts.comics.info
```

Recipes via FTP	`gatekeeper.dec.com`	/pub/recipes

Mailing Lists

aquarium	listserv	`emuvm1.cc.emory.edu`
birdeast	listserv	`arizvm1.bitnet`
birdchat	listserv	`arizvm1.bitnet`
birdcntr	listserv	`arizvm1.bitnet`
birdwest	listserv	`arizvm1.bitnet`
bicycles	bicycles-request	`bbn.com`
bonsai	listserv	`cms.cc.wayne.edu`
bread	bread-digest-request	`cykick.infores.com`

canine-l	listserv	psuvm.bitnet	
cards	cards request	tanstaafl. uchicago.edu	
clocks	listserv	suvm.syr.edu	
coins@rocky. er.usgs.gov	robert@ whiplash.er. usgs.gov		
comics-l	listserv	unlvm.unl.edu	
cube-lovers	cube-lovers-request	ai.ai.mit.edu	Rubik's Cube
dollh-l	listserv	ferris.bitnet	
equine-l	listserv	psuvm.bitnet	
firearms	firearms-request	cs.cmu.edu	
gardens	listserv	ukcc.uky.edu	
golden	listserv	hobbes.ucsd.edu	Golden retriever enthusiasts
hamlicen	listserv	vmd.cso.uiuc.edu	Licensing matters of ham radio
homebrew	homebrew-request	%hpfcmr@hplabs. hp.com	
hunting	listserv	tamvm1.tamu.edu	
info-hams	listserv	wsmr-simtel20. army.mil	
jugglen	listserv	indycms.iupui.edu	
martial-arts	martial-arts-request	dragon.cso. uiuc.edu	
mount-l	listserv	trmetu.bitnet	Mountaineers
orchids	listserv	scu.bitnet	
origami-l	origami-l-request	nstn.ns.ca	
photo-l	listserv	buacca.bitnet	

pinhole	pinhole-request	mintir.fidonet.org	
postcard	listserv	idbsu.bitnet	
quilt	listserv	cornell.edu	
railroad	listserv	cunyvm.cuny.edu	
roots-l	listserv	vm1.nodak.edu	Genealogical research
sca	sca-request	mc.lcs.mit.edu	Society for Creative Anachronism
scouts-l	listserv	tcubvm.bitnet	
scuba-l	listserv	browvm.bitnet	
stamps	listserv	cunyvm.cuny.edu	
tandem	listserv	hobbes.ucsd.edu	Tandem bicycle enthusiasts
woodwork	listserv	ipfwvm.bitnet	

Humanities and History

WAIS Sources

ANU-French Database.src
ANU-Pacific-Manuscripts.src

FAQ Files and FTP Sites

sci.classics
soc.history

Archive of classical Latin texts and commentaries	ftp.u.washington.edu	public/classics/texts or public/classics/commentaries

Rome Reborn: The Vatican Library and Renaissance Culture, an exhibit at the Library of Congress	seq1.loc.gov	/pub/vatican.exhibit

Mailing Lists

albion-l	listserv	ucsbvm.bitnet	
ansaxnet	u47c2@wvnvm.wvnet.edu		
c18-l	listserv	psuvm.bitnet	18th century
camelot	camelot-request	castle.ed.ac.uk	
classics	listserv	uwavm.u.washington.edu	
contex-l	listserv	uottawa.bitnet	Ancient texts
elenchus	listserv	acadvm1.uottawa.ca	Christian thought and literature in late antiquity
emedch-l	listserv	uscvm.bitnet	Chinese history in the 3rd through 6th centuries A.D.
espora-l	listserv	ukanvm.bitnet	Spanish and Portuguese historical studies
hislaw-l	listserv	ulkyvm.louisville.edu	History of the law
histec-l	listserv	ukanvm.bitnet	History of evangelical Christianity
holocaus	listserv	uicvm.uic.edu	

hopos-l	listserv	ukcc.uky.edu	History of philosophy of science
humanist	listserv	utorepas.bitnet	Application of computers to scholarship in the humanities
indology	listserv	liverpool.ac.uk	Classical India
ioudaios	listserv	yorkvm1.bitnet	First-century Judaism
marine-l	listserv	uoguelph.ca	
mediev-l	listserv	ukanvm.cc.ukans.edu	Middle ages
milhst-l	listserv	ukanvm.cc.ukans.edu	Military history
nat-1492	listserv	tamvm1.tamu.edu	Effects of the voyage of Christopher Columbus to the New World of the Americas in 1492
ortrad-l	listserv	mizzou1.missouri.edu	Oral tradition studies
prezhist	listserv	kasey.umkc.edu	Presidential history forum
renais-l	listserv	ulkyvm.louisville.edu	
rushist	listserv	vm.usc.edu	History of Russia 1462-1917
sharp-l	listserv	iubvm.ucs.indiana.edu	Society for the History of Authorship, Reading, and Publishing
shothc-l	listserv	sivm.bitnet	Society for History of Technology

```
victoria      listserv      iubvm.bitnet
wwii-l        listserv      ubvm.cc.buffalo.edu
```

Telnet Sites

HNSOURCE: Central Information Server for Historians	hnsource.cc.ukans.edu	login: history
Institute of Historical Research Information Server	clus1.ulcc.ac.uk	login: ihr-uk password: ihr-uk

Miscellaneous

The National Endowment for Humanities can be contacted via email for publications or grant applications	nehopa@gwuvm.gwu.edu

Literature, Fiction, and Writing

WAIS Sources

```
Science-Fiction-Series-Gide.src
sf-reviews.src
proj-gutenberg.src
poetry.src
POETRY-index.src
```

FAQ Files and FTP Sites

```
alt.fan.tolkien
rec.arts.books
rec.arts.books.tolkien
rec.arts.prose
rec.arts.sf.written
misc.writers
misc.writing
alt.fan.dave_barry
alt.fan.douglas-adams
alt.quotations
```

Mailing Lists

amlit-l	listserv	umcvmb.missouri.edu	American literature
chaucer	listserv	siucvmb.siu.edu	
copyediting-l	listserv	cornell.edu	
crewrt-l	listserv	umcvmb.missouri.edu	Creative writing
dorothyl	listserv	kentvm.kent.edu	Mystery genre
e-poetry	listserv	ubvm.cc.buffalo.edu	
fiction	listserv	psuvm.psu.edu	
fwake-l	listserv	irlearn.bitnet	
journet	listserv	qucdn.queensu.ca	For journalists and journalism educators
litera-l	listserv	tecmtyvm.mty.itesm.mx	Literature and related topics
mendele	listserv	yalevm.ycc.yale.edu	Yiddish literature and language
milton-l	milton-request	urvax.urich.edu	Life and work of John Milton
modbrits	listserv	kentvm.kent.edu	Modern British and Irish literature

poet@scruz. ucsc.edu	tcbowden@clovis. felton.ca.us		
rra-l	listserv	kentvm.kent. edu	Romance Readers Anonymous
russian	listserv	asuacad. bitnet	
scrnwrit	listserv	tamvm1.bitnet	Screen writing for film and TV
sf-lovers	listserv	rutgers.edu	
shaksper	listserv	utoronto. bitnet	
sharp-l	listserv	iubvm.ucs. indiana.edu	Society for the History of Authorship, Reading, and Publishing
superguy	listserv	ucf1vm.bitnet	Strange, serialized, humorous, superhero fiction
tolkien	listserv	jhuvm.bitnet	
twain-l	listserv	vm1.yorku.ca	
vampyres	listserv	guvm.bitnet	
welsh-l	listserv	irlearn.ucd.ie	

Linguistics and Languages

WAIS Sources

```
ANU-Asian-Computing.src
ANU-Pacific-Linguistics.src
```

FAQ Files and FTP Sites

```
sci.lang
```

Mailing Lists

classics	listserv	uwavm.u. washington.edu	
esper-l	listserv	trearn.bitnet	Esperanto
gaelic-l	listserv	irlearn.bitnet	
indology	listserv	liverpool.ac. uk	Classical India
lantra-l	listserv	finhutc.bitnet	Translation and interpretation of natural languages
latin-l	listserv	psuvm.psu.edu	
linguist	listserv	uniwa.uwa.oz.au	
mail.yiddish	dave@lsuc.on. ca		
mendele	listserv	yalevm.ycc. yale.edu	Yiddish literature and language
nat-lang	listserv	tamvm1.tamu. edu	Languages of any of the world's indigenous peoples
nihongo	listserv	mitvma.mit. edu	Japanese language
russian	listserv	asuacad.bitnet	
slart-l	listserv	cunyvm.cuny. edu	Second language acquisition, research, and teaching
welsh-l	listserv	irlearn.ucd.ie	

Macintosh

WAIS Sources

```
merit-archive-mac.src
mac.FAQ.src
macintosh-tidbits.src
macintosh-news.src
tcl-talk.src
comp.sys.mac.programmer.src
```

FAQ Files and FTP Sites

```
alt.aldus.pagemaker
comp.sys.mac.advocacy
comp.sys.mac.apps
comp.sys.mac.comm
comp.sys.mac.games
comp.sys.mac.hardware
comp.sys.mac.misc
comp.sys.mac.programmer
comp.sys.mac.scitech
comp.sys.mac.system
comp.sys.mac.wanted
```

QuicKeys FTP site	`gaea.kgs.ukans.edu`	/quickeys
Frontier FTP site	`gaea.kgs.ukans.edu`	/frontier
Applescript FTP site	`gaea.kgs.ukans.edu`	/applescript
Nisus FTP site	`gaea.kgs.ukans.edu`	/nisus
Info-Mac Archive Site	`sumex-aim.stanford.edu`	/info-mac
Mac.Archive	`mac.archive.umich.edu`	
Macintosh Mirror Site	`wuarchive.wustl.edu`	/mirrors
Apple's FTP Site	`ftp.apple.com`	/dts
Macintosh FTP Site List	`sumex-aim.stanford.edu`	/info-mac/ comm/info

Mailing Lists

macscrpt	listserv	dartcms1. dartmouth.edu	Scripting with AppleScript and Frontier
hypercrd	listserv	purccvm.bitnet	
info-mac	listserv	ricevml. rice.edu	
macprog	listserv	wuvmd.wustl.edu	
mac-security	mac-security- request	eclectic.com	
modlshop	listserv	vma.cc.nd.edu	
pagemakr	listserv	indycms.iupui. edu	
quickeys	listserv	gaea.kgs. ukans.edu	
nisus	listserv	gaea.kgs. ukans.edu	
tidbits	listserv	ricevm1.rice. edu	Weekly electronic newsletter
photshop	listserv	ecnuxa.bitnet	
word-mac	listserv	alsvid.une. edu.au	
macpb-1	listserv	yalevm.ycc. yale.edu	PowerBooks
dtp-1	listserv	antigone.uu. holonet.net	Desktop publishing
mac040	mac040- request	rascal.ics. utexas.edu	68040 (accel- erator) users
kanjitalk	kanjitalk- request	crl.go.jp	
mac-1	listserv	yalevm.ycc.	

		yale.edu	
cap-l	listserv	yalevm.bitnet	Columbia Appletalk Protocol
direct-l	listserv	uafsysb. bitnet	Macromedia Director
macappli	listserv	dartcms1. bitnet	News and usage tips about applications
machrdwr	listserv	dartcms1. bitnet	Macintosh hardware
macmail	listserv	utoronto. bitnet	Mac Mail
macnet-l	listserv	yalevm.bitnet	Macintosh networking issues
macprog	listserv	wuvmd.bitnet	Macintosh programming
macsystm	listserv	dartcms1. bitnet	Advice about Macintosh systems
mt3270-l	listserv	brownvm. bitnet	Macintosh tn3270 betatest
qm-l	listserv	yalevm.bitnet	QuickMail (CE software) users
tincan-l	listserv	yalevm.bitnet	Macintosh terminal emulator issues
4d	4d-request	mit.edu	
info-prograph	info- prograph- request	grove.iup.edu	

Gopher Servers

Apple Computer Higher Education Gopher server	`info.hed.apple.com`

Microsoft Windows

FAQ Files and FTP Sites

```
comp.os.ms-windows.advocacy
comp.os.ms-windows.announce
comp.os.ms-windows.apps
comp.os.ms-windows.misc
comp.os.ms-windows.nt.misc
comp.os.ms-windows.nt.setup
comp.os.ms-windows.programmer.misc
comp.os.ms-windows.programmer.tools
comp.os.ms-windows.programmer.win32
comp.os.ms-windows.setup
```

Windows software and device drivers	`ftp.cica.indiana.edu`	/pub/pc/win3
DOS and Windows software	`wsmr-simtel20.army.mil`	pd1:<msdos>
Windows Archives	`wuarchive.wustl.edu`	/mirrors/win3
Microsoft Developer Support	`ftp.uu.net`	/vendors/microsoft
Windows Archives and FAQs	`sonygate.sony.com`	/pub/comp.binaries.ms-windows

Mailing Lists

`access-l`	`listerv`	`indycms.bitnet`	Microsoft Access
`foxpro-l`	`fileserv`	`polarbear.rankin-inlet.nt.ca`	Foxpro

msmail-l	listserv	yalevm.bitnet	MS-MAIL
win3-l	listserv	uicvm	Windows in general
word-pc	mailserv	ufobi1.uni-forst.gwdg.de	Microsoft Word for Windows

Gopher Servers

Microsoft Windows	gopher.usmacs.maine.edu
HSS PC CLC Microsoft Windows (by section)	mercury.cc.umr.edu
Microsoft Windows	muspin.gsfc.nasa.gov
Microsoft Windows	gauss.math.stthomas.edu
Microsoft Windows	malia.tamu.edu
Microsoft Windows Software	info-server.lanl.gov
Microsoft Word for Windows (RS/6000s and PCs)	ns3.CC.Lehigh.edu
Windows Software	nfo.asu.edu
advocacy: Microsoft Windows	ccsun42.csie.nctu.edu.tw
Microsoft Windows Version 3 Forum	newshost.cca.vu.nl
Einfuehrung in Microsoft Word fuer Windows 2.0	olymp.wu-wien.ac.at
European Microsoft Windows NT Academic Centre ftp area	gopher.ed.ac.uk

Microsoft Excel for Windows 4.0 (taulukkolaskenta ym., englanninkielinen)	`gopher.hut.fi`
Microsoft Windows	`gopher.ictp.trieste.it`

Music and Dance

WAIS Sources

```
Sheet_Music_Index.src
rec.music.early.src
music-surveys.src
MuTeX.src
IAT-Documents.src
lyrics.src
BGRASS-L.src
```

FAQ Files and FTP Sites

```
alt.guitar.tab
alt.rock-n-roll
alt.rock-n-roll.hard
alt.rock-n-roll.metal
rec.music.a-cappella
rec.music.bluenote
rec.music.classical
rec.music.classical.performing
rec.music.compose
rec.music.dylan
rec.music.folk
rec.music.funky
rec.music.industrial
rec.music.info
rec.music.makers
rec.music.makers.bass
rec.music.makers.guitar
```

```
rec.music.makers.guitar.tablature
rec.music.makers.percussion
rec.music.makers.synth
rec.music.misc
rec.music.newage
rec.music.phish
rec.music.reggae
rec.music.synth
alt.music.a-cappella
alt.music.alternative
alt.music.enya
alt.music.progressive
alt.music.rush
alt.music.ska
alt.music.tmbg
comp.music
```

Mailing Lists

78-1	listserv	cornell.edu	Music and recordings of the pre-LP era
allmusic	listserv	auvm.bitnet	
bgrass-1	listserv	ukcc.uky.edu	
blues-1	listserv	brownvm.bitnet	
brass	brass-request	geomag.gly.fsu.edu	
classm-1	listserv	brownvm.brown.edu	
dance-1	listserv	hearn.bitnet	Folk dancing
ballroom	ballroom-request	athena.mit.edu	
dead-heads	listserv	virginia.edu	
dj-1	listserv	ndsuvm1.bitnet	Campus dj's
earlym-1	listserv	aearn.edvz. uni-linz.ac.at	Early music
emusic-1	listserv	auvm.bitnet	Electronic music
filmus-1	listserv	ubvm.ucs. indiana.edu	Film music

folk_music	listserv	nysernet.org	
jpop	jpop-request	ferkel.ucsb.edu	Japanese popular music
kissarmy	listserv	wkuvx1.bitnet	
opera-l	listserv	brfapesp.bitnet	
piporg-l	listserv	albany.edu	Pipe organs
rmusic-l	listserv	gitvm1.bitnet	Music industry
savoynet	savoynet-request	cescc.bridgewater.edu	Gilbert and/or Sullivan
u2	grace@delphi.com		
undercover	listserv	snowhite.cis.uoguelph.ca	Rolling Stones
vw5earn	listserv	awiwuw11.bitnet	Early music

Pictures, Graphics, and Visual Arts

FAQ Files and FTP Sites

```
alt.binaries.pictures.d
alt.binaries.pictures.fine-art.d
alt.binaries.pictures.fine-art.digitized
alt.binaries.pictures.fine-art.graphics
alt.binaries.pictures.fractals
alt.binaries.pictures.utilities
alt.binaries.pictures.misc
comp.fonts
comp.graphics
alt.graphics.pixutils
```

Smithsonian Institute photo archives	photo1.si.edu or sunsite.unc.edu	/pub/multimedia/pictures/smithsonian

Mailing Lists

artcrit	listserv	yorkvm1.bitnet	
art-support	listserv	newcastle.ac.uk	
clayart	listserv	ukcc.bitnet	
image-l	listserv	trearn.bitnet	Image processing and related issues

Gopher Servers

French architectural images	gopher.hs.jhu.edu	GrabBag/Images/French.Architecture
Other architectural images	libra.arch.umich.edu	

Publications

WAIS Sources

```
London-Free-Press-Regional-Index.src
factsheet-five.src
```

FAQ Files and FTP Sites

Books in HyperCard format	sumex-aim.stanford.edu	/info-mac/info/nms
InterText (fiction)	network.ucsd.edu	/pub/intertext
The PowerderKeg Magazine	epas.utoronto.edu	
Other online magazines	ftp.eff.org	

Mailing Lists

`prog-pubs`	`prog-pubs-request`	`fuggles.acc.virginia.edu`	Progressive and/or alternative publications and other media
`sharp-l`	`listserv`	`iubvm.ucs.indiana.edu`	Society for the History of Authorship, Reading, and Publishing
`vidpro-l`	`listserv`	`uxa.ecn.bgu.edu`	Video production and operations

Telnet Sites

LOCIS: Library of Congress Information System	`locis.loc.gov`

Gopher Sites

Books Online via the Internet Wiretap	`wiretap.spies.com`	Internet Wiretap/ Wiretap Online Library/Classics
The Electronic Newsstand	`gopher.netsys.com` port 2100	
Electronic Books	`chico.rice.edu`	/Information by Subject Area
OCF Online Library	`ocf.berkeley.edu` (Gopher +)	
O'Reilly & Associates Online Catalog	`gopher.ora.com`	

Religion and Philosophy

WAIS Sources

```
ANU-ZenBuddhism-Calendar.src
ANU-Asian-Religions.src
bible.src
Book_of_Mormon.src
Quran.src
```

FAQ Files and FTP Sites

```
soc.religion.quaker
alt.atheism
alt.atheism.moderated
alt.pagan
soc.religion.bahai
```

The Electric Mystic's Guide	`panda1.uottawa.ca`	/pub/religion
Scrolls from the Dead Sea: The Ancient Library of Qumran and Modern Scholarship, an Exhibit at the Library of Congress	`seq1.loc.gov`	/pub/deadsea. scrolls.exhibit

Mailing Lists

`baltuva`	`listserv`	`vm1.mcgill.ca`	
`baptist`	`listserv`	`ukcc.uky.edu`	
`belief-l`	`listserv`	`brownvm.bitnet`	
`buddha-l`	`listserv`	`ulkyvm.louisville.edu`	
`christia`	`listserv`	`finhutc.bitnet`	
`eochr`	`listserv`	`queensu.ca`	Eastern Orthodox Christian

islam-l	listserv	ulkyvm.louisville.edu	
ivcf-l	listserv	ubmv.bitnet	Intervarsity Christian Fellowship
ministry-l	listserv	gacvax1.bitnet	
nt-greek	listserv	virginia.edu	Greek New Testament
obj-rel	listserv	emuvm1.cc.emory.edu	Discussions about religion and the nature of the universe
orthodox	listserv	indycms.iupui.edu	
ot-hebrew	ot-hebrew-request	virginia.edu	Hebrew Old Testament
pagan	listserv	drycas.club.cc.cmu.edu	
philrelsoc	listserv	hampvms.bitnet	Philosophy, religion, and society magazine for intense debate
shaker	listserv	ukcc.uky.edu	
theology	u16481@uicvm.bitnet		

Gopher Servers

The Vulgate Bible	ccat.sas.upenn.edu	After connecting, choose "Search all CCAT menus..." on the term *vulgate* to receive a search prompt for the Vulgate itself.

Sciences, Math, and Engineering

FAQ Files and FTP Sites

```
sci.geo.geology
sci.geo.meteorology
sci.image.processing
sci.math
sci.math.num-analysis
sci.med
sci.med.occupational
sci.misc
sci.physics
alt.sci.physics.new-theories
rec.video.satellite
sci.answers
sci.aquaria
sci.comp-aided
sci.cryonics
sci.crypt
sci.electronics
sci.fractals
sci.skeptic
comp.speech
comp.robotics
comp.software-eng
comp.compression
comp.compression.research
```

Mailing Lists

chminf-l	listserv	iubvm.bitnet
circuits-l	listserv	uwplatt.edu
cybsys-l	listserv	bingvaxu.cc. binghamton.edu
fusion	listserv	zorch.sf-bay.org
geograph	listserv	finhutc.bitnet

idforum	listserv	yorkvm1.bitnet	Industrial design
ilas-net	listserv	technion.technion.ac.il	International Linear Algebra Society
mech-l	listserv	utarlvm1.bitnet	
opt-proc	listserv	taunivm.bitnet	Holography
optics	listserv	toe.towson.edu	
physics	listserv	marist.bitnet	
polymerp	listserv	rutvm1.bitnet	
quake-l	listserv	vm1.nodak.edu	
samath	listserv	saksu00.bitnet	Mathematics issues
seism-l	listserv	bingvma.bitnet	
textiles	listserv	trearn.bitnet	

Gopher Servers

GeoGopher (Geological Sciences)	dillon.geo.ep.utexas.edu

Shopping

Telnet Sites

MarketBase Online Catalog of Goods and Services	MB.COM	login: mb

Gopher Servers

On-line Bookstore	nstn.ns.ca	/Other Gophers in Nova Scotia/Roswell Electronic Computer Bookstore

Sports and Exercise

FAQ Files and FTP Sites

```
rec.running
rec.sport.disc
rec.sport.fencing
rec.sport.football.misc
rec.sport.football.pro
rec.sport.hockey
rec.sport.misc
rec.sport.pro-wrestling
rec.sport.tennis
rec.sport.volleyball
alt.sport.pool
```

Mailing Lists

cricket	listserv	vm1.nodak.edu	
drs	listserv	dartcms1.dartmouth.edu	Dead Runners Society
golf-l	listserv	ubvm.cc.buffalo.edu	
gymn	owner-gymn	athena.mit.edu	All aspects of the sport of gymnastics
hockey-l	listserv	maine.maine.edu	College hockey
jays	jays-request	hivnet.ubc.ca	Toronto Blue Jays baseball team
lacros-l	listserv	villvm.bitnet	Men's lacrosse
pbp-l	listserv	etsuadmn.etsu.edu	Play-by-play sportscasters for all sports
sportpsy	listserv	templevm.bitnet	Exercise and sports psychology

statlg-l	listserv	sbccvm.bitnet	Baseball stats
swim-l	listserv	uafsysb.uark.edu	
weights	weights-request	mickey.disney.com	
yacht-l	listserv	grearn.bitnet	
t-and-f	cmahler	nic.gac.edu	Track and field

Telnet Sites

NBA schedules	culine.colorado.edu 859
NHL schedules	culine.colorado.edu 860
MLB schedules	culine.colorado.edu 862
NFL schedules	culine.colorado.edu 863

Travel

FAQ Files and FTP Sites

```
rec.travel
rec.travel.air
```

| Travel Info such as travelogues, guides, FAQs | ccu.umanitoba.ca | /pub/rec-travel |

Mailing Lists

| hospex | listserv | plearn.bitnet | Hosting foreign visitors |
| hospex-l | listserv | plearn.bitnet | Hospitality exchange |

| travel-advisories | travel-advisories-request | stolaf.edu | U.S. State Department travel advisories |
| travel-l | listserv | trearn.bitnet | Discussion of tourism |

Miscellaneous

Travel by Modem   For information, email to `travel@delphi.com`

TV, Movies, and Theatre

FAQ Files and FTP Sites

```
alt.tv.mst3k
alt.tv.mwc
alt.tv.northern-exp
alt.tv.prisoner
alt.tv.red-dwarf
alt.tv.ren-n-stimpy
alt.tv.seinfeld
alt.tv.simpsons
alt.tv.tiny-toon
rec.arts.sf.movies
rec.arts.sf.reviews
rec.arts.startrek.current
rec.arts.startrek.fandom
rec.arts.startrek.info
rec.arts.startrek.misc
rec.arts.startrek.tech
rec.arts.movies
rec.arts.tv
rec.arts.tv.soaps
alt.fan.letterman
alt.fan.ren-and-stimpy
alt.cult-movies
alt.cult-movies.rocky-horror
rec.arts.theatre
```

Mailing Lists

90210	90210-request	ferkel.ucsb.edu	
disc-l	listserv	sendit.nodak.edu	Discovery Channel
film-l	listserv	vmtecmex.bitnet	
melrose-place	melrose-place-request	ferkel.ucsb.edu	
mst3k	rsk@gynko.circ.upenn.edu		Mystery Science Theater 3000
sf-lovers	listserv	rutgers.edu	
stagecraft	stagecraft-request	jaguar.cs.utah.edu	
strek-l	listserv	pccvm.bitnet	
trek-review-l	listserv	cornell.edu	
tv-l	listserv	trearn.bitnet	

Hard to Classify

WAIS Sources

weather.src

FAQ Files and FTP Sites

talk.bizarre
alt.folklore.urban

Navy News Service   nctamslant.navy.mil

| High Weirdness By Email | | nexus.yorku.ca | /pub/Internet-info/high-weirdness |

Mailing Lists

janitor	listserv	ukanvm.cc.ukans.edu	Discussion of any topic of interest to those engaged in the cleaning of public buildings
meh2o-l	listserv	taunivm.tau.ac.il	Information and research related to water in the middle east
nerdnosh@scruz.ucsc.edu	tcbowden@clovis.felton.ca.us		Virtual campfire gathering of storytellers
oracle	oracle-request	iuvax.cs.indiana.edu	The Usenet Oracle is available to answer all your questions. For assistance, send mail to oracle@iuvax.cs.indiana.edu by typing the word **help** in the subject line.
psi-l	listserv	rpiecs.bitnet	ESP, out-of-body experiences, dream experiments, and altered states of consciousness

skeptic	listserv	yorkvm1.bitnet	
transit	listserv	gitvm1.bitnet	Issues related to public transit
weird-l	listserv	brownvm.bitnet	All manner of weirdness
wx-talk	listserv	uiucvmd.bitnet	Discussing weather-related phenomena
wxspot	listserv	uiucvmd.bitnet	Severe storm spotter issues
giggles	listserv	vtvm1.cc.vt.edu	Forum for jokes, stories, and anecdotes
tftd-l	listserv	tamvm1.bitnet	Thought for the Day

Gopher Servers

ASCII Cows: do a Veronica search on the terms "cows" and you'll find this amusing collection of cows drawn with standard keyboard characters.			
AskERIC Educational Gopher	ericir.syr.edu		
Armadillo, the Texas Gopher	chico.rice.edu Port 1170		
Whole Earth 'Lectronic Magazine	The WELL's Gopherspace	gopher. well.sf. ca.us	
Electronic Frontier Foundation	gopher.eff.org		Includes a collection of electronic magazines.

Internet Meta-Resources

WAIS Sources

`Directory-of-Servers.src`

FAQ Files and FTP Sites

Scott Yanoff's List of Special Internet Services (Highly recommended!)	`csd4.csd.uwm.edu`	/pub/inet.services.txt
Internet and Computer Mediated Communication	`ftp.rpi.edu`	/pub/communications
Campus-Wide Information Systems	`ftp.oit.unc.edu`	pub/docs/about-the-net/cwis/cwis-l
The Incomplete Guide to the Internet	`ftp.ncsa.uiuc.edu`	/Education/ Education_Resources
A guide to the Internet from the Electronic Frontier Foundation	`ftp.eff.org. stanford.edu`	/pub/Publications/ Big-Dummy/Other-versions/bigd-win.zip
A Cruise of the Internet (requires color)	`nic.merit.edu`	/resources/cruise.dos

Mailing Lists

`net-happenings`	`listserv`	`is.internic.net`	Things that happen on the Net

tow	listserv	vm1.nodak.edu	The Online World
nettrain	listserv	ubvm.cc.buffalo.edu	Network Trainers List
edupage	listserv	bitnic.educom.edu	Twice-weekly newsletter on information technology. Back issues of Edupage are available by WAIS, Gopher, and anonymous ftp from educom.edu.
Bits & Bytes Online	jmachado@ pacs.pha.pa.us		Miscellaneous electronic news. Type **SUB SCRIBE** in the subject header and your email address in the body of the message.

Telnet Sites

archie.ans.net	(ANS server, NY (USA))
archie.au	(Austrailian Server)
archie.doc.ic.ac.uk	(United Kingdom Server)
archie.edvz.uni-linz.ac.at	(Austrian Server)
archie.funet.fi	(Finnish Server)
archie.internic.net	(AT&T server, NY (USA))
archie.kr	(Korean Server)
archie.kuis.kyoto-u.ac.jp	(Japanese Server)
archie.luth.se	(Swedish Server)

archie.ncu.edu.tw	(Taiwanese server)
archie.nz	(New Zealand server)
archie.rediris.es	(Spanish Server)
archie.rutgers.edu	(Rutgers University (USA))
archie.sogang.ac.kr	(Korean Server)
archie.sura.net	(SURAnet server MD (USA))
archie.sura.net (1526)	(SURAnet alt. MD (USA))
archie.switch.ch	(Swiss Server)
archie.th-darmstadt.de	(German Server)
archie.unipi.it	(Italian Server)
archie.univie.ac.at	(Austrian Server)
archie.unl.edu	(U. of Nebraska, Lincoln (USA))
archie.uqam.ca	(Canadian Server)
archie.wide.ad.jp	(Japanese Server)

Gopher Servers

InterNIC Information Services (Highly recommended!)	is.internic.net	This is an official site for Internet information.
Merit/NSFNET Information Services (Internet Info)	nic.merit.edu	

Miscellaneous

If you can't use FTP, you can still retrieve FTPable files via email	ftpmail.decwrl.dec.com	Type **help** in the first line of the message.

Books

Whole Earth Online Almanac by Don Rittner (a massive directory of resources online, including the Internet)	Brady Books, $32.95	ISBN 1-56686-090-3
Directory to the Internet by Eric Braun	Fawcett Columbine	ISBN 0-449-908-984
!%@::A Directory of Electronic Mail Addressing & Networks by Donnalyn Frey and Rick Adams	O'Reilly & Associates, $24.95	ISBN 1-56592-031-7

Appendix

Newsgroup List

The following list of newsgroups was taken from several periodic postings to the news.lists newsgroup on Usenet. Gene Spafford first created the list and acted as the original editor until May, 1993, and David Lawrence now edits the list. Keep in mind that this list is not exhaustive, and it was probably out of date the day after I pulled it off Usenet. Nevertheless, browsing through this list can give you a good idea of what newsgroups you might want to read. When you're forced to choose from thousands of possibilities, this list can be a big help. And if reading lists doesn't excite you, at least check out the descriptions of the alt groups. Some of the puns are punishable by death. Okay, I'll stop now.

Currently Active Usenet Newsgroups

The following is a list of currently active USENET newsgroups as of February 1, 1994. This list does not include the gatewayed Internet newsgroups (see below). The groups distributed worldwide are divided into seven broad classifications: news, soc, talk, misc, sci, comp, and rec. Each of these classifications is organized into groups and subgroups according to topic.

Table B.1   USENET Newsgroup Classifications

Abbreviation	Description
comp	Topics of interest to both computer professionals and hobbyists, including topics in computer science, software source code, and information on hardware and software systems.
sci	Discussions marked by special and usually practical knowledge, relating to research in or application of the established sciences.
misc	Groups addressing themes not easily classified under any of the other headings or which incorporate themes from multiple categories.
soc	Groups primarily addressing social issues and socializing.
talk	Groups largely debate-oriented and tending to feature long discussions without resolution and without appreciable amounts of generally useful information.
news	Groups concerned with the news network and software themselves.
rec	Groups oriented towards the arts, hobbies, and recreational activities.

These "world" newsgroups are (usually) circulated around the entire USENET — this implies world-wide distribution. Not all groups actually enjoy such wide distribution, however. Some sites take only a selected subset of the more "technical" groups, and controversial "noise" groups are often not carried by many sites (these groups are often under the talk and soc classifications). Many sites do not carry some or all of the comp.binaries groups.

There are groups in other subcategories, but they are local—to institutions, to geographic regions, and so forth—and they are not listed here. Note that these distribution categories can be used to restrict the propagation of news articles. The current distributions are listed in table B.2.

Table B.2 Distribution Categories

Keyword	*Distribution*
world	Worldwide distribution (default)
can	Limited (mostly) to Canada
eunet	Limited (mostly) to European sites in EUNet
na	Limited (mostly) to North America
usa	Limited (mostly) to the United States

Other regional and local distribution categories may be available at your site. Most U.S. states have distribution categories named after the two letter abbreviation for that state or category (that is, ga for Georgia, nj for New Jersey). Use an appropriate distribution category if your article is not likely to be of interest to USENET readers worldwide.

Please notify me of any errors or changes to the information in this article.

David Lawrence
tale@uunet.uu.net

Some groups are moderated or are monitored mailing lists. They can be posted to only if you mail submissions to the coordinator (provided in a companion posting). Some selected sites provide automatic remailing to the moderator in support of B2.11, C news, and INN—posting to one of these groups automatically mails the article for the poster. Some of the moderated groups are gatewayed to USENET from the Internet and appear as newsgroups to facilitate distribution and posting from the Usenet. Some of these gatewayed Internet newsgroups are listed in the following tables, and the rest appear in a companion posting that lists alternative newsgroup hierarchies. Other of the "world" groups are bidirectionally gatewayed with Internet mailing lists; items submitted from the Internet side to the digest are split up and submitted to the USENET group, while articles submitted on the USENET side are bundled up and submitted to the mailing list. A complete list of moderated newsgroups, submission addresses, and moderators is given in a companion posting.

The "world" groups in table B.3 have been gatewayed with the listed Internet lists. Some of them may still not be gatewayed due to broken software and/or gateways; such groups are marked with an asterisk (*) in the table. Contact me if you know of their current status. Also note that the group `comp.lang.forth` is gatewayed with the Bitnet discussion list `umforth@weizmann.bitnet`, `comp.lang.apl` is gatewayed with `APL-L` at the `unb.ca` node, and `rec.railroad` is run from `railroad@queens.bitnet`. Some of these lists are gated one-way into Usenet groups; those groups have been marked with a greater-than (>) symbol in the table.

If you are reading this article from a site not on the Usenet, you may subscribe to Internet lists by writing to the request address. You form such an address by putting `-request` before the @ symbol, as in `unix-emacs-request@vm.tcs.tulane.edu`. Typing this address gets your message directly to the list maintainer instead of broadcasting it to all the readers of the list.

Also note that moderators of Usenet groups may not be in charge of the corresponding mailing list or gateway. For example, the moderator of `comp.sources.unix` does not have anything to do with the unix-sources mailing list; you should address matters concerning the mailing list to `unix-sources-request@brl.mil`.

Table B.3   World Groups

Usenet Group	Internet List
comp.databases.ingres	info-ingres@math.ams.com
comp.dcom.modems	info-modems@wsmr-simtel20.army.mil
comp.dcom.telecom	telecom@eecs.nwu.edu
comp.emacs	unix-emacs@bbn.com
comp.graphics.gnuplot	info-gnuplot@dartmouth.edu
*comp.lang.ada	info-ada@ajpo.sei.cmu.edu
comp.lang.c	info-c@brl.mil
>comp.lang.c++	info-g++@prep.ai.mit.edu

Usenet Group	Internet List
>comp.lang.c++	help-g++@prep.ai.mit.edu
comp.lang.modula2	info-m2@ucf1vm.bitnet
*comp.lang.pascal	info-pascal@brl.mil
*comp.lang.prolog	prolog@score.stanford.edu
comp.mail.mh	mh-users@ics.uci.edu
comp.os.cpm	info-cpm@wsmr-simtel20.army.mil
comp.os.minix	info-minix@udel.edu
comp.os.vms	info-vax@sri.com
comp.protocols.kerberos	kerberos@athena.mit.edu
comp.protocols.tcp-ip	tcp-ip@nic.ddn.mil
comp.society.privacy	comp-privacy@pica.army.mil
comp.sources.misc	unix-sources@brl.mil
comp.sources.unix	unix-sources@brl.mil
comp.specification.z	zforum@comlab.ox.ac.uk
comp.sys.apollo	apollo@umix.cc.umich.edu
comp.sys.apple2	info-apple@apple.com
comp.sys.atari.8bit	info-atari8-request@naucse.cse.nau.edu
comp.sys.atari.st	info-atari16-request@naucse.cse.nau.edu
comp.sys.misc	info-micro@wsmr-simtel20.army.mil
comp.sys.prime	info-prime@blx-a.prime.com
comp.sys.tahoe	info-tahoe@csd1.milw.wisc.edu
comp.sys.xerox	info-1100@tut.cis.ohio-state.edu
*comp.terminals	info-terms@mc.lcs.mit.edu
>comp.text.tex	texhax@cs.washington.edu
>comp.text.tex	info-tex@shsu.edu
comp.unix.questions	info-unix@brl.mil
comp.unix.internals	unix-wizards@brl.mil

continues

Usenet Group	Internet List
comp.windows.interviews	interviews@interviews.stanford.edu
comp.windows.x	xpert@expo.lcs.mit.edu
*rec.arts.sf.misc	sf-lovers@rutgers.edu
rec.food.recipes	recipes@rigel.dfrt.nasa.gov
rec.games.diplomacy	dipl-l@mitvma.mit.edu
rec.radio.amateur.misc	info-hams@ucsd.edu
rec.radio.amateur.packet	packet-radio@ucsd.edu
rec.radio.amateur.policy	ham-policy@ucsd.edu
rec.radio.broacasting	journal@airwaves.chi.il.us
rec.radio.info	radio-info@ucsd.edu
rec.radio.shortwave	swl-l@cuvma.columbia.edu
rec.music.funky	funky-music@hyper.lap.upenn.edu
rec.music.gdead	dead-flames@virginia.edu
rec.music.phish	phish@virginia.edu
rec.music.makers.synth	synth-l@auvm.auvm.edu
rec.sport.disc	ultimate-list@doe.carleton.ca
rec.video	videotech@wsmr-simtel20.army.mil
*sci.astro	sky-fans@xx.lcs.mit.edu
sci.astro.fits	fitsbits@nrao.edu
sci.physics	physics@unix.sri.com
sci.physics.fusion	fusion@zorch.sf-bay.org
sci.space	space@isu.isunet.edu
soc.roots	roots-l@vm1.nodak.edu

Newsgroup	Description
comp.admin.policy	Discussions of site administration policies.
comp.ai	Artificial intelligence discussions.
comp.ai.fuzzy	Fuzzy set theory, aka fuzzy logic.

Newsgroup	Description
`comp.ai.genetic`	Genetic algorithms in computing.
`comp.ai.jair.announce`	Announcements & abstracts of the Journal of AI Research. (Moderated)
`comp.ai.jair.papers`	Papers published by the Journal of AI Research. (Moderated)
`comp.ai.nat-lang`	Natural language processing by computers.
`comp.ai.neural-nets`	All aspects of neural networks.
`comp.ai.nlang-know-rep`	Natural Language and Knowledge Representation. (Moderated)
`comp.ai.philosophy`	Philosophical aspects of Artificial Intelligence.
`comp.ai.shells`	Artificial intelligence applied to shells.
`comp.answers`	Repository for periodic USENET articles. (Moderated)
`comp.apps.spreadsheets`	Spreadsheets on various platforms.
`comp.arch`	Computer architecture.
`comp.arch.bus.vmebus`	Hardware and software for VMEbus Systems.
`comp.arch.storage`	Storage system issues, both hardware and software.
`comp.archives`	Descriptions of public access archives. (Moderated)
`comp.archives.admin`	Issues relating to computer archive administration.
`comp.archives.msdos.announce`	Announcements about MS-DOS archives. (Moderated)
`comp.archives.msdos.d`	Discussion of materials available in MS-DOS archives.
`comp.bbs.misc`	All aspects of computer bulletin board systems.

continues

Newsgroup	Description
comp.bbs.waffle	The Waffle BBS and USENET system on all platforms.
comp.benchmarks	Discussion of benchmarking techniques and results.
comp.binaries.acorn	Binary-only postings for Acorn machines. (Moderated)
comp.binaries.amiga	Encoded public domain programs in binary. (Moderated)
comp.binaries.apple2	Binary-only postings for the Apple II computer.
comp.binaries.atari.st	Binary-only postings for the Atari ST. (Moderated)
comp.binaries.cbm	For the transfer of 8-bit Commodore binaries. (Moderated)
comp.binaries.ibm.pc	Binary-only postings for IBM PC/MS-DOS. (Moderated)
comp.binaries.ibm.pc.d	Discussions about IBM/PC binary postings.
comp.binaries.ibm.pc.wanted	Requests for IBM PC and compatible programs.
comp.binaries.mac	Encoded Macintosh programs in binary. (Moderated)
comp.binaries.ms-windows	Binary programs for Microsoft Windows. (Moderated)
comp.binaries.os2	Binaries for use under the OS/2 ABI. (Moderated)
comp.bugs.2bsd	Reports of UNIX* version 2BSD related bugs.
comp.bugs.4bsd	Reports of UNIX version 4BSD related bugs.
comp.bugs.4bsd.ucb-fixes	Bug reports/fixes for BSD Unix. (Moderated)

Newsgroup	Description
comp.bugs.misc	General UNIX bug reports and fixes (incl V7, uucp)
comp.bugs.sys5	Reports of USG (System III, V, etc.) bugs.
comp.cad.cadence	Users of Cadence Design Systems products.
comp.cad.compass	Compass Design Automation EDA tools.
comp.cad.pro-engineer	Parametric Technology's Pro/Engineer design package.
comp.cad.synthesis	Research and production in the field of logic synthesis.
comp.client-server	Topics relating to client/server technology.
comp.cog-eng	Cognitive engineering.
comp.compilers	Compiler construction, theory, etc. (Moderated)
comp.compression	Data compression algorithms and theory.
comp.compression.research	Discussions about data compression research. (Moderated)
comp.databases	Database and data management issues and theory.
comp.databases.informix	Informix database management software discussions.
comp.databases.ingres	Issues relating to INGRES products.
comp.databases.ms-access	MS Windows' relational database system, Access.
comp.databases.object	Object-oriented paradigms in database systems.
comp.databases.oracle	The SQL database products of the Oracle Corporation.

continues

Newsgroup	Description
comp.databases.paradox	Borland's database for DOS & MS Windows.
comp.databases.pick	Pick-like, post-relational, database systems.
comp.databases.rdb	The relational database engine RDB from DEC.
comp.databases.sybase	Implementations of the SQL Server.
comp.databases.theory	Discussing advances in database technology.
comp.databases.xbase.fox	Fox Software's xBase system and compatibles.
comp.databases.xbase.misc	Discussion of xBase (dBASE-like) products.
comp.dcom.cell-relay	Forum for discussion of Cell Relay-based products.
comp.dcom.fax	Fax hardware, software, and protocols.
comp.dcom.isdn	The Integrated Services Digital Network (ISDN).
comp.dcom.lans.ethernet	Discussions of the Ethernet/IEEE 802.3 protocols.
comp.dcom.lans.fddi	Discussions of the FDDI protocol suite.
comp.dcom.lans.misc	Local area network hardware and software.
comp.dcom.lans.token-ring	Installing and using token ring networks.
comp.dcom.modems	Data communications hardware and software.
comp.dcom.servers	Selecting and operating data communications servers.
comp.dcom.sys.cisco	Info on Cisco routers and bridges.
comp.dcom.sys.wellfleet	Wellfleet bridge & router systems hardware & software.

Newsgroup	Description
comp.dcom.telecom	Telecommunications digest. (Moderated)
comp.dcom.telecom.tech	Discussion of technical aspects of telephony.
comp.doc	Archived public-domain documentation. (Moderated)
comp.doc.techreports	Lists of technical reports. (Moderated)
comp.dsp	Digital Signal Processing using computers.
comp.edu	Computer science education.
comp.emacs	EMACS editors of different flavors.
comp.fonts	Typefonts — design, conversion, use, etc.
comp.graphics	Computer graphics, art, animation, image processing.
comp.graphics.algorithms	Algorithms used in producing computer graphics.
comp.graphics.animation	Technical aspects of computer animation.
comp.graphics.avs	The Application Visualization System.
comp.graphics.data-explorer	IBM's Visualization Data Explorer, aka DX.
comp.graphics.explorer	The Explorer Modular Visualization Environment (MVE).
comp.graphics.gnuplot	The GNUPLOT interactive function plotter.
comp.graphics.opengl	The OpenGL 3D application programming interface.
comp.graphics.research	Highly technical computer graphics discussion. (Moderated)

continues

Newsgroup	*Description*
comp.graphics.visualization	Info on scientific visualization.
comp.groupware	Software and hardware for shared interactive environments.
comp.human-factors	Issues related to human-computer interaction (HCI).
comp.infosystems	Any discussion about information systems.
comp.infosystems.announce	Announcements of internet information services. (Moderated)
comp.infosystems.gis	All aspects of Geographic Information Systems.
comp.infosystems.gopher	Discussion of the Gopher information service.
comp.infosystems.wais	The Z39.50-based WAIS full-text search system.
comp.infosystems.www	The World Wide Web information system.
comp.internet.library	Discussing electronic libraries. (Moderated)
comp.ivideodisc	Interactive videodiscs — uses, potential, etc.
comp.lang.ada	Discussion about Ada*.
comp.lang.apl	Discussion about APL.
comp.lang.basic.misc	Other dialects and aspects of BASIC.
comp.lang.basic.visual	Microsoft Visual Basic & App Basic; Windows & DOS.
comp.lang.c	Discussion about C.
comp.lang.c++	The object-oriented C++ language.
comp.lang.clos	Common Lisp Object System discussions.
comp.lang.dylan	For discussion of the Dylan language.

Newsgroup	Description
comp.lang.eiffel	The object-oriented Eiffel language.
comp.lang.forth	Discussion about Forth.
comp.lang.fortran	Discussion about FORTRAN.
comp.lang.functional	Discussion about functional languages.
comp.lang.hermes	The Hermes language for distributed applications.
comp.lang.idl-pvwave	IDL and PV-Wave language discussions.
comp.lang.lisp	Discussion about LISP.
comp.lang.lisp.mcl	Discussing Apple's Macintosh Common Lisp.
comp.lang.logo	The Logo teaching and learning language.
comp.lang.misc	Different computer languages not specifically listed.
comp.lang.ml	ML languages including Standard ML, CAML, Lazy ML, etc. (Moderated)
comp.lang.modula2	Discussion about Modula-2.
comp.lang.modula3	Discussion about the Modula-3 language.
comp.lang.oberon	The Oberon language and system.
comp.lang.objective-c	The Objective-C language and environment.
comp.lang.pascal	Discussion about Pascal.
comp.lang.perl	Discussion of Larry Wall's Perl system.
comp.lang.pop	Pop11 and the Plug user group.
comp.lang.postscript	The PostScript Page Description Language.

continues

Newsgroup	Description
comp.lang.prolog	Discussion about PROLOG.
comp.lang.sather	The object-oriented computer language Sather.
comp.lang.scheme	The Scheme Programming language.
comp.lang.sigplan	Info & announcements from ACM SIGPLAN. (Moderated)
comp.lang.smalltalk	Discussion about Smalltalk 80.
comp.lang.tcl	The TCL programming language and related tools.
comp.lang.verilog	Discussing Verilog and PLI.
comp.lang.vhdl	VHSIC Hardware Description Language, IEEE 1076/87.
comp.laser-printers	Laser printers, hardware & software. (Moderated)
comp.lsi	Large scale integrated circuits.
comp.lsi.testing	Testing of electronic circuits.
comp.mail.elm	Discussion and fixes for the ELM mail system.
comp.mail.headers	Gatewayed from the Internet header-people list.
comp.mail.maps	Various maps, including UUCP maps. (Moderated)
comp.mail.mh	The UCI version of the Rand Message Handling system.
comp.mail.mime	Multipurpose Internet Mail Extensions of RFC 1341.
comp.mail.misc	General discussions about computer mail.
comp.mail.mush	The Mail User's Shell (MUSH).
comp.mail.sendmail	Configuring and using the BSD sendmail agent.

Newsgroup	Description
comp.mail.uucp	Mail in the uucp network environment.
comp.misc	General topics about computers not covered elsewhere.
comp.multimedia	Interactive multimedia technologies of all kinds.
comp.newprod	Announcements of new products of interest. (Moderated)
comp.object	Object-oriented programming and languages.
comp.object.logic	Integrating object-oriented and logic programming.
comp.org.acm	Topics about the Association for Computing Machinery.
comp.org.decus	Digital Equipment Computer Users' Society newsgroup.
comp.org.eff.news	News from the Electronic Frontier Foundation. (Moderated)
comp.org.eff.talk	Discussion of EFF goals, strategies, etc.
comp.org.fidonet	FidoNews digest, official news of FidoNet Assoc. (Moderated)
comp.org.ieee	Issues and announcements about the IEEE & its members.
comp.org.issnnet	The International Student Society for Neural Networks.
comp.org.lisp-users	Association of Lisp Users related discussions.
comp.org.sug	Talk about/for the The Sun User's Group.
comp.org.usenix	USENIX Association events and announcements.

continues

Newsgroup	Description
comp.org.usenix.roomshare	Finding lodging during Usenix conferences.
comp.os.386bsd.announce	Announcements relating to the 386bsd operating system. (Moderated)
comp.os.386bsd.apps	Applications which run under 386bsd.
comp.os.386bsd.bugs	Bugs and fixes for the 386bsd OS and its clients.
comp.os.386bsd.development	Working on 386bsd internals.
comp.os.386bsd.misc	General aspects of 386bsd not covered by other groups.
comp.os.386bsd.questions	General questions about 386bsd.
comp.os.coherent	Discussion and support of the Coherent operating system.
comp.os.cpm	Discussion about the CP/M operating system.
comp.os.geos	The GEOS operating system by GeoWorks for PC clones.
comp.os.linux.admin	Installing and administering Linux systems.
comp.os.linux.announce	Announcements important to the Linux community. (Moderated)
comp.os.linux:development	Ongoing work on the Linux operating system.
comp.os.linux.help	Questions and advice about Linux.
comp.os.linux.misc	Linux-specific topics not covered by other groups.
comp.os.lynx	Discussion of LynxOS and Lynx Real-Time Systems.
comp.os.mach	The MACH OS from CMU & other places.
comp.os.minix	Discussion of Tanenbaum's MINIX system.

Newsgroup	Description
comp.os.misc	General OS-oriented discussion not carried elsewhere.
comp.os.ms-windows.advocacy	Speculation and debate about Microsoft Windows.
comp.os.ms-windows.announce	Announcements relating to Windows. (Moderated)
comp.os.ms-windows.apps	Applications in the Windows environment.
comp.os.ms-windows.misc	General discussions about Windows issues.
comp.os.ms-windows.nt.misc	General discussion about Windows NT.
comp.os.ms-windows.nt.setup	Configuring Windows NT systems.
comp.os.ms-windows.programmer.misc	Programming Microsoft Windows.
comp.os.ms-windows.programmer.tools	Development tools in Windows.
comp.os.ms-windows.programmer.win32	32-bit Windows programming interfaces.
comp.os.ms-windows.setup	Installing and configuring Microsoft Windows.
comp.os.msdos.apps	Discussion of applications that run under MS-DOS.
comp.os.msdos.desqview	QuarterDeck's Desqview and related products.
comp.os.msdos.mail-news	Administering mail & network news systems under MS-DOS.
comp.os.msdos.misc	Miscellaneous topics about MS-DOS machines.
comp.os.msdos.pcgeos	GeoWorks PC/GEOS and PC/GEOS-based packages.
comp.os.msdos.programmer	Programming MS-DOS machines.

continues

Newsgroup	Description
comp.os.msdos.programmer.turbovision	Borland's text application libraries.
comp.os.os2.advocacy	Supporting and flaming OS/2.
comp.os.os2.announce	Notable news and announcements related to OS/2. (Moderated)
comp.os.os2.apps	Discussions of applications under OS/2.
comp.os.os2.beta	All aspects of beta releases of OS/2 systems software.
comp.os.os2.bugs	OS/2 system bug reports, fixes and work-arounds.
comp.os.os2.misc	Miscellaneous topics about the OS/2 system.
comp.os.os2.multimedia	Multimedia on OS/2 systems.
comp.os.os2.networking	Networking in OS/2 environments.
comp.os.os2.programmer.misc	Programming OS/2 machines.
comp.os.os2.programmer.porting	Porting software to OS/2 machines.
comp.os.os2.setup	Installing and configuring OS/2 systems.
comp.os.os2.ver1x	All aspects of OS/2 versions 1.0 through 1.3.
comp.os.os9	Discussions about the os9 operating system.
comp.os.qnx	Using and developing under the QNX operating system.
comp.os.research	Operating systems and related areas. (Moderated)
comp.os.vms	DEC's VAX* line of computers & VMS.
comp.os.vxworks	The VxWorks real-time operating system.

Newsgroup	Description
`comp.os.xinu`	The XINU operating system from Purdue (D. Comer).
`comp.parallel`	Massively parallel hardware/ software. (Moderated)
`comp.parallel.pvm`	The PVM system of multi-computer parallelization.
`comp.patents`	Discussing patents of computer technology. (Moderated)
`comp.periphs`	Peripheral devices.
`comp.periphs.scsi`	Discussion of SCSI-based peripheral devices.
`comp.programming`	Programming issues that transcend languages and OSs.
`comp.programming.literate`	Literate programs and programming tools.
`comp.protocols.appletalk`	Applebus hardware & software.
`comp.protocols.dicom`	Digital Imaging and Communications in Medicine.
`comp.protocols.ibm`	Networking with IBM mainframes.
`comp.protocols.iso`	The ISO protocol stack.
`comp.protocols.kerberos`	The Kerberos authentication server.
`comp.protocols.kermit`	Info about the Kermit package. (Moderated)
`comp.protocols.misc`	Various forms and types of protocol.
`comp.protocols.nfs`	Discussion about the Network File System protocol.
`comp.protocols.ppp`	Discussion of the Internet Point to Point Protocol.
`comp.protocols.tcp-ip`	TCP and IP network protocols.
`comp.protocols.tcp-ip.ibmpc`	TCP/IP for IBM(-like) personal computers.

continues

Newsgroup	Description
comp.publish.cdrom.hardware	Hardware used in publishing with CD-ROM.
comp.publish.cdrom.multimedia	Software for multimedia authoring & publishing.
comp.publish.cdrom.software	Software used in publishing with CD-ROM.
comp.realtime	Issues related to real-time computing.
comp.research.japan	The nature of research in Japan. (Moderated)
comp.risks	Risks to the public from computers & users. (Moderated)
comp.robotics	All aspects of robots and their applications.
comp.security.misc	Security issues of computers and networks.
comp.security.unix	Discussion of Unix security.
comp.simulation	Simulation methods, problems, uses. (Moderated)
comp.society	The impact of technology on society. (Moderated)
comp.society.cu-digest	The Computer Underground Digest. (Moderated)
comp.society.development	Computer technology in developing countries.
comp.society.folklore	Computer folklore & culture, past & present. (Moderated)
comp.society.futures	Events in technology affecting future computing.
comp.society.privacy	Effects of technology on privacy. (Moderated)
comp.soft-sys.khoros	The Khoros X11 visualization system.

Newsgroup	Description
`comp.soft-sys.matlab`	The MathWorks calculation and visualization package.
`comp.soft-sys.sas`	The SAS statistics package.
`comp.soft-sys.shazam`	The SHAZAM econometrics computer program.
`comp.soft-sys.spss`	The SPSS statistics package.
`comp.soft-sys.wavefront`	Wavefront software products, problems, etc.
`comp.software-eng`	Software Engineering and related topics.
`comp.software.licensing`	Software licensing technology.
`comp.software.testing`	All aspects of testing computer systems.
`comp.sources.3b1`	Source code-only postings for the AT&T 3b1. (Moderated)
`comp.sources.acorn`	Source code-only postings for the Acorn. (Moderated)
`comp.sources.amiga`	Source code-only postings for the Amiga. (Moderated)
`comp.sources.apple2`	Source code and discussion for the Apple2. (Moderated)
`comp.sources.atari.st`	Source code-only postings for the Atari ST. (Moderated)
`comp.sources.bugs`	Bug reports, fixes, discussion for posted sources.
`comp.sources.d`	For any discussion of source postings.
`comp.sources.games`	Postings of recreational software. (Moderated)
`comp.sources.games.bugs`	Bug reports and fixes for posted game software.

continues

Newsgroup	Description
comp.sources.hp48	Programs for the HP48 and HP28 calculators. (Moderated)
comp.sources.mac	Software for the Apple Macintosh. (Moderated)
comp.sources.misc	Posting of software. (Moderated)
comp.sources.postscript	Source code for programs written in PostScript. (Moderated)
comp.sources.reviewed	Source code evaluated by peer review. (Moderated)
comp.sources.sun	Software for Sun workstations. (Moderated)
comp.sources.testers	Finding people to test software.
comp.sources.unix	Postings of complete, UNIX-oriented sources. (Moderated)
comp.sources.wanted	Requests for software and fixes.
comp.sources.x	Software for the X windows system. (Moderated)
comp.specification	Languages and methodologies for formal specification.
comp.specification.z	Discussion about the formal specification notation Z.
comp.speech	Research & applications in speech science & technology.
comp.std.c	Discussion about C language standards.
comp.std.c++	Discussion about C++ language, library, standards.
comp.std.internat	Discussion about international standards.
comp.std.lisp	User group (ALU) supported standards. (Moderated)
comp.std.misc	Discussion about various standards.

Newsgroup	Description
comp.std.mumps	Discussion for the X11.1 committee on Mumps. (Moderated)
comp.std.unix	Discussion for the P1003 committee on UNIX. (Moderated)
comp.std.wireless	Examining standards for wireless network technology. (Moderated)
comp.sw.components	Software components and related technology.
comp.sys.3b1	Discussion and support of AT&T 7300/3B1/UnixPC.
comp.sys.acorn	Discussion on Acorn and ARM-based computers.
comp.sys.acorn.advocacy	Why Acorn computers and pro-grams are better.
comp.sys.acorn.announce	Announcements for Acorn and ARM users. (Moderated)
comp.sys.acorn.tech	Software and hardware aspects of Acorn and ARM products.
comp.sys.alliant	Info and discussion about Alliant computers.
comp.sys.amiga.advocacy	Why an Amiga is better than XYZ.
comp.sys.amiga.announce	Announcements about the Amiga. (Moderated)
comp.sys.amiga.applications	Miscellaneous applications.
comp.sys.amiga.audio	Music, MIDI, speech synthesis, other sounds.
comp.sys.amiga.datacomm	Methods of getting bytes in and out.
comp.sys.amiga.emulations	Various hardware & software emulators.
comp.sys.amiga.games	Discussion of games for the Com-modore Amiga.
comp.sys.amiga.graphics	Charts, graphs, pictures, etc.

continues

Newsgroup	*Description*
comp.sys.amiga.hardware	Amiga computer hardware, Q&A, reviews, etc.
comp.sys.amiga.introduction	Group for newcomers to Amigas.
comp.sys.amiga.marketplace	Where to find it, prices, etc.
comp.sys.amiga.misc	Discussions not falling in another Amiga group.
comp.sys.amiga.multimedia	Animations, video, & multimedia.
comp.sys.amiga.programmer	Developers & hobbyists discuss code.
comp.sys.amiga.reviews	Reviews of Amiga software, hardware. (Moderated)
comp.sys.apollo	Apollo computer systems.
comp.sys.apple2	Discussion about Apple II micros.
comp.sys.apple2.comm	Apple II data communications.
comp.sys.apple2.gno	The AppleIIgs GNO multitasking environment.
comp.sys.apple2.marketplace	Buying, selling and trading Apple II equipment.
comp.sys.apple2.programmer	Programming on the Apple II.
comp.sys.apple2.usergroups	All about Apple II user groups.
comp.sys.atari.8bit	Discussion about 8-bit Atari micros.
comp.sys.atari.advocacy	Attacking and defending Atari computers.
comp.sys.atari.st	Discussion about 16-bit Atari micros.
comp.sys.atari.st.tech	Technical discussions of Atari ST hard/software.
comp.sys.att	Discussions about AT&T microcomputers.
comp.sys.cbm	Discussion about Commodore micros.
comp.sys.concurrent	The Concurrent/Masscomp line of computers. (Moderated)

Newsgroup	Description
`comp.sys.convex`	Convex computer systems hardware and software.
`comp.sys.dec`	Discussions about DEC computer systems.
`comp.sys.dec.micro`	DEC Micros (Rainbow, Professional 350/380).
`comp.sys.encore`	Encore's MultiMax computers.
`comp.sys.harris`	Harris computer systems, especially real-time systems.
`comp.sys.hp`	Discussion about Hewlett-Packard equipment.
`comp.sys.hp.apps`	Discussion of software and apps on all HP platforms.
`comp.sys.hp.hardware`	Discussion of Hewlett-Packard system hardware.
`comp.sys.hp.hpux`	Issues pertaining to HP-UX & 9000 series computers.
`comp.sys.hp.misc`	Issues not covered in any other comp.sys.hp.* group.
`comp.sys.hp.mpe`	Issues pertaining to MPE & 3000 series computers.
`comp.sys.hp48`	Hewlett-Packard's HP48 and HP28 calculators.
`comp.sys.ibm.pc.demos`	Demonstration programs which showcase programmer skill.
`comp.sys.ibm.pc.digest`	The IBM PC, PC-XT, and PC-AT. (Moderated)
`comp.sys.ibm.pc.games.action`	Arcade-style games on PCs.
`comp.sys.ibm.pc.games.adventure`	Adventure (non-rpg) games on PCs.
`comp.sys.ibm.pc.games.announce`	Announcements for all PC gamers. (Moderated)

continues

Newsgroup	Description
`comp.sys.ibm.pc.games.flight-sim`	Flight simulators on PCs.
`comp.sys.ibm.pc.games.misc`	Games not covered by other PC groups.
`comp.sys.ibm.pc.games.rpg`	Role-playing games on the PC.
`comp.sys.ibm.pc.games.strategic`	Strategy/planning games on PCs.
`comp.sys.ibm.pc.hardware`	XT/AT/EISA hardware, any vendor.
`comp.sys.ibm.pc.hardware.cd-rom`	CD-ROM drives and interfaces for the PC.
`comp.sys.ibm.pc.hardware.chips`	Processor, cache, memory chips, etc.
`comp.sys.ibm.pc.hardware.comm`	Modems & communication cards for the PC.
`comp.sys.ibm.pc.hardware.misc`	Miscellaneous PC hardware topics.
`comp.sys.ibm.pc.hardware.networking`	Network hardware & equipment for the PC.
`comp.sys.ibm.pc.hardware.storage`	Hard drives & other PC storage devices.
`comp.sys.ibm.pc.hardware.systems`	Whole IBM PC computer & clone systems.
`comp.sys.ibm.pc.hardware.video`	Video cards & monitors for the PC.
`comp.sys.ibm.pc.misc`	Discussion about IBM personal computers.
`comp.sys.ibm.pc.rt`	Topics related to IBM's RT computer.
`comp.sys.ibm.pc.soundcard`	Hardware and software aspects of PC sound cards.
`comp.sys.ibm.ps2.hardware`	Microchannel hardware, any vendor.

Newsgroup	Description
comp.sys.intel	Discussions about Intel systems and parts.
comp.sys.isis	The ISIS distributed system from Cornell.
comp.sys.laptops	Laptop (portable) computers.
comp.sys.m6809	Discussion about 6809's.
comp.sys.m68k	Discussion about 68k's.
comp.sys.m68k.pc	Discussion about 68k-based PCs. (Moderated)
comp.sys.m88k	Discussion about 88k-based computers.
comp.sys.mac.advocacy	The Macintosh computer family compared to others.
comp.sys.mac.announce	Important notices for Macintosh users. (Moderated)
comp.sys.mac.apps	Discussions of Macintosh applications.
comp.sys.mac.comm	Discussion of Macintosh communications.
comp.sys.mac.databases	Database systems for the Apple Macintosh.
comp.sys.mac.digest	Apple Macintosh: info & uses, but no programs. (Moderated)
comp.sys.mac.games	Discussions of games on the Macintosh.
comp.sys.mac.graphics	Macintosh graphics: paint, draw, 3D, CAD, animation.
comp.sys.mac.hardware	Macintosh hardware issues & discussions.
comp.sys.mac.hypercard	The Macintosh Hypercard: info & uses.
comp.sys.mac.misc	General discussions about the Apple Macintosh.

continues

Newsgroup	*Description*
comp.sys.mac.oop.macapp3	Version 3 of the MacApp object-oriented system.
comp.sys.mac.oop.misc	Object-oriented programming issues on the Mac.
comp.sys.mac.oop.tcl	Symantec's THINK Class Library for object programming.
comp.sys.mac.portables	Discussion particular to laptop Macintoshes.
comp.sys.mac.programmer	Discussion by people programming the Apple Macintosh.
comp.sys.mac.scitech	Using the Macintosh in scientific & technological work.
comp.sys.mac.system	Discussions of Macintosh system software.
comp.sys.mac.wanted	Postings of "I want XYZ for my Mac."
comp.sys.mentor	Mentor Graphics products & the Silicon Compiler System.
comp.sys.mips	Systems based on MIPS chips.
comp.sys.misc	Discussion about computers of all kinds.
comp.sys.ncr	Discussion about NCR computers.
comp.sys.newton.announce	Newton information posts. (Moderated)
comp.sys.newton.misc	Miscellaneous discussion about Newton systems.
comp.sys.newton.programmer	Discussion of Newton software development.
comp.sys.next.advocacy	The NeXT religion.
comp.sys.next.announce	Announcements related to the NeXT computer system. (Moderated)
comp.sys.next.bugs	Discussion and solutions for known NeXT bugs.

Newsgroup	Description
comp.sys.next.hardware	Discussing the physical aspects of NeXT computers.
comp.sys.next.marketplace	NeXT hardware, software and jobs.
comp.sys.next.misc	General discussion about the NeXT computer system.
comp.sys.next.programmer	NeXT-related programming issues.
comp.sys.next.software	Function, use and availability of NeXT programs.
comp.sys.next.sysadmin	Discussions related to NeXT system administration.
comp.sys.novell	Discussion of Novell Netware products.
comp.sys.nsc.32k	National Semiconductor 32000 series chips.
comp.sys.palmtops	Super-powered calculators in the palm of your hand.
comp.sys.pen	Interacting with computers through pen gestures.
comp.sys.powerpc	General PowerPC Discussion.
comp.sys.prime	Prime Computer products.
comp.sys.proteon	Proteon gateway products.
comp.sys.psion	Discussion about PSION Personal Computers & Organizers.
comp.sys.pyramid	Pyramid 90x computers.
comp.sys.ridge	Ridge 32 computers and ROS.
comp.sys.sequent	Sequent systems (Balance and Symmetry).
comp.sys.sgi.admin	System administration on Silicon Graphics's Irises.
comp.sys.sgi.announce	Announcements for the SGI community. (Moderated)
comp.sys.sgi.apps	Applications which run on the Iris.

continues

Newsgroup	Description
comp.sys.sgi.bugs	Bugs found in the IRIX operating system.
comp.sys.sgi.graphics	Graphics packages and issues on SGI machines.
comp.sys.sgi.hardware	Base systems and peripherals for Iris computers.
comp.sys.sgi.misc	General discussion about Silicon Graphics' machines.
comp.sys.sinclair	Sinclair computers, eg. the ZX81, Spectrum and QL.
comp.sys.stratus	Stratus products, incl. System/88, CPS-32, VOS and FTX.
comp.sys.sun.admin	Sun system administration issues and questions.
comp.sys.sun.announce	Sun announcements and Sunergy mailings. (Moderated)
comp.sys.sun.apps	Software applications for Sun computer systems.
comp.sys.sun.hardware	Sun Microsystems hardware.
comp.sys.sun.misc	Miscellaneous discussions about Sun products.
comp.sys.sun.wanted	People looking for Sun products and support.
comp.sys.tahoe	CCI 6/32, Harris HCX/7, & Sperry 7000 computers.
comp.sys.tandy	Discussion about Tandy computers: new & old.
comp.sys.ti	Discussion about Texas Instruments.
comp.sys.transputer	The Transputer computer and OCCAM language.
comp.sys.unisys	Sperry, Burroughs, Convergent and Unisys* systems.

Newsgroup	Description
`comp.sys.xerox`	Xerox 1100 workstations and protocols.
`comp.sys.zenith.z100`	The Zenith Z-100 (Heath H-100) family of computers.
`comp.terminals`	All sorts of terminals.
`comp.text`	Text processing issues and methods.
`comp.text.desktop`	Technology & techniques of desktop publishing.
`comp.text.frame`	Desktop publishing with FrameMaker.
`comp.text.interleaf`	Applications and use of Interleaf software.
`comp.text.sgml`	ISO 8879 SGML, structured documents, markup languages.
`comp.text.tex`	Discussion about the TeX and LaTeX systems & macros.
`comp.theory.info-retrieval`	Information Retrieval topics. (Moderated)
`comp.unix.admin`	Administering a Unix-based system.
`comp.unix.advocacy`	Arguments for and against Unix and Unix versions.
`comp.unix.aix`	IBM's version of UNIX.
`comp.unix.amiga`	Minix, SYSV4 and other *nix on an Amiga.
`comp.unix.aux`	The version of UNIX for Apple Macintosh II computers.
`comp.unix.bsd`	Discussion of Berkeley Software Distribution UNIX.
`comp.unix.dos-under-unix`	MS-DOS running under UNIX by whatever means.

continues

Newsgroup	Description
`comp.unix.internals`	Discussions on hacking UNIX internals.
`comp.unix.large`	UNIX on mainframes and in large networks.
`comp.unix.misc`	Various topics that don't fit other groups.
`comp.unix.osf.misc`	Various aspects of Open Software Foundation products.
`comp.unix.osf.osf1`	The Open Software Foundation's OSF/1.
`comp.unix.pc-clone.16bit`	UNIX on 286 architectures.
`comp.unix.pc-clone.32bit`	UNIX on 386 and 486 architectures.
`comp.unix.programmer`	Q&A for people programming under Unix.
`comp.unix.questions`	UNIX neophytes group.
`comp.unix.shell`	Using and programming the Unix shell.
`comp.unix.sys3`	System III UNIX discussions.
`comp.unix.sys5.misc`	Versions of System V which predate Release 3.
`comp.unix.sys5.r3`	Discussing System V Release 3.
`comp.unix.sys5.r4`	Discussing System V Release 4.
`comp.unix.ultrix`	Discussions about DEC's Ultrix.
`comp.unix.unixware`	Discussion about Novell's UnixWare products.
`comp.unix.user-friendly`	Discussion of UNIX user-friendliness.
`comp.unix.wizards`	For only true Unix wizards. (Moderated)
`comp.unix.xenix.misc`	General discussions regarding XENIX (except SCO).
`comp.unix.xenix.sco`	XENIX versions from the Santa Cruz Operation.

Newsgroup	Description
`comp.virus`	Computer viruses & security. (Moderated)
`comp.windows.garnet`	The Garnet user interface development environment.
`comp.windows.interviews`	The InterViews object-oriented windowing system.
`comp.windows.misc`	Various issues about windowing systems.
`comp.windows.news`	Sun Microsystems' NeWS window system.
`comp.windows.open-look`	Discussion about the Open Look GUI.
`comp.windows.suit`	The SUIT user-interface toolkit.
`comp.windows.x`	Discussion about the X Window System.
`comp.windows.x.apps`	Getting and using, not programming, applications for X.
`comp.windows.x.i386unix`	The XFree86 window system and others.
`comp.windows.x.intrinsics`	Discussion of the X toolkit.
`comp.windows.x.pex`	The PHIGS extension of the X Window System.
`misc.activism.progressive`	Information for Progressive activists. (Moderated)
`misc.answers`	Repository for periodic USENET articles. (Moderated)
`misc.books.technical`	Discussion of books about technical topics.
`misc.consumers`	Consumer interests, product reviews, etc.
`misc.consumers.house`	Discussion about owning and maintaining a house.

continues

Newsgroup	Description
misc.education	Discussion of the educational system.
misc.education.language.english	Teaching English to speakers of other languages.
misc.emerg-services	Forum for paramedics & other first responders.
misc.entrepreneurs	Discussion on operating a business.
misc.fitness	Physical fitness, exercise, body-building, etc.
misc.forsale	Short, tasteful postings about items for sale.
misc.forsale.computers.d	Discussion of misc.forsale.computers.*.
misc.forsale.computers.mac	Apple Macintosh related computer items.
misc.forsale.computers.other	Selling miscellaneous computer stuff.
misc.forsale.computers.pc-clone	IBM PC related computer items.
misc.forsale.computers.workstation	Workstation related computer items.
misc.handicap	Items of interest for/about the handicapped. (Moderated)
misc.headlines	Current interest: drug testing, terrorism, etc.
misc.health.alternative	Alternative, complementary and holistic health care.
misc.health.diabetes	Discussion of diabetes management in day to day life.
misc.int-property	Discussion of intellectual property rights.
misc.invest	Investments and the handling of money.

Newsgroup	Description
misc.invest.canada	Investing in Canadian financial markets.
misc.invest.funds	Sharing info about bond, stock, real estate funds.
misc.invest.real-estate	Property investments.
misc.invest.stocks	Forum for sharing info about stocks and options.
misc.invest.technical	Analyzing market trends with technical methods.
misc.jobs.contract	Discussions about contract labor.
misc.jobs.misc	Discussion about employment, workplaces, careers.
misc.jobs.offered	Announcements of positions available.
misc.jobs.offered.entry	Job listings only for entry-level positions.
misc.jobs.resumes	Postings of resumes and "situation wanted" articles.
misc.kids	Children, their behavior and activities.
misc.kids.computer	The use of computers by children.
misc.kids.vacation	Discussion on all forms of family-oriented vacationing.
misc.legal	Legalities and the ethics of law.
misc.legal.computing	Discussing the legal climate of the computing world.
misc.legal.moderated	All aspects of law. (Moderated)
misc.misc	Various discussions not fitting in any other group.
misc.news.east-europe.rferl	Radio Free Europe/Radio Liberty Daily Report. (Moderated)
misc.news.southasia	News from Bangladesh, India, Nepal, etc. (Moderated)

continues

Newsgroup	*Description*
misc.rural	Devoted to issues concerning rural living.
misc.taxes	Tax laws and advice.
misc.test	For testing of network software. Very boring.
misc.wanted	Requests for things that are needed (NOT software).
misc.writing	Discussion of writing in all of its forms.
news.admin.misc	General topics of network news administration.
news.admin.policy	Policy issues of USENET.
news.admin.technical	Technical aspects of maintaining network news. (Moderated)
news.announce.conferences	Calls for papers and conference announcements. (Moderated)
news.announce.important	General announcements of interest to all. (Moderated)
news.announce.newgroups	Calls for newgroups & announcements of same. (Moderated)
news.announce.newusers	Explanatory postings for new users. (Moderated)
news.answers	Repository for periodic USENET articles. (Moderated)
news.config	Postings of system down times and interruptions.
news.future	The future technology of network news systems.
news.groups	Discussions and lists of newsgroups.
news.lists	News-related statistics and lists. (Moderated)
news.lists.ps-maps	Maps relating to USENET traffic flows. (Moderated)

Newsgroup	*Description*
news.misc	Discussions of USENET itself.
news.newsites	Postings of new site announcements.
news.newusers.questions	Q & A for users new to the Usenet.
news.software.anu-news	VMS B-news software from Australian National Univ.
news.software.b	Discussion about B-news-compatible software.
news.software.nn	Discussion about the "nn" news reader package.
news.software.notes	Notesfile software from the Univ. of Illinois.
news.software.readers	Discussion of software used to read network news.
rec.answers	Repository for periodic USENET articles. (Moderated)
rec.antiques	Discussing antiques and vintage items.
rec.aquaria	Keeping fish and aquaria as a hobby.
rec.arts.animation	Discussion of various kinds of animation.
rec.arts.anime	Japanese animation fan discussion.
rec.arts.anime.info	Announcements about Japanese animation. (Moderated)
rec.arts.anime.marketplace	Things for sale in the Japanese animation world.
rec.arts.anime.stories	All about Japanese comic fanzines. (Moderated)
rec.arts.bodyart	Tattoos and body decoration discussions.
rec.arts.bonsai	Dwarfish trees and shrubbery.

continues

Newsgroup	Description
rec.arts.books	Books of all genres, and the publishing industry.
rec.arts.books.tolkien	The works of J.R.R. Tolkien.
rec.arts.cinema	Discussion of the art of cinema. (Moderated)
rec.arts.comics.info	Reviews, convention information and other comics news. (Moderated)
rec.arts.comics.marketplace	The exchange of comics and comic related items.
rec.arts.comics.misc	Comic books, graphic novels, sequential art.
rec.arts.comics.strips	Discussion of short-form comics.
rec.arts.comics.xbooks	The Mutant Universe of Marvel Comics.
rec.arts.dance	Any aspects of dance not covered in another newsgroup.
rec.arts.disney	Discussion of any Disney-related subjects.
rec.arts.drwho	Discussion about Dr. Who.
rec.arts.erotica	Erotic fiction and verse. (Moderated)
rec.arts.fine	Fine arts & artists.
rec.arts.int-fiction	Discussions about interactive fiction.
rec.arts.manga	All aspects of the Japanese storytelling art form.
rec.arts.marching.drumcorps	Drum and bugle corps.
rec.arts.marching.misc	Marching-related performance activities.
rec.arts.misc	Discussions about the arts not in other groups.
rec.arts.movies	Discussions of movies and movie making.

Newsgroup	Description
`rec.arts.movies.reviews`	Reviews of movies. (Moderated)
`rec.arts.poems`	For the posting of poems.
`rec.arts.prose`	Short works of prose fiction and followup discussion.
`rec.arts.sf.announce`	Major announcements of the SF world. (Moderated)
`rec.arts.sf.fandom`	Discussions of SF fan activities.
`rec.arts.sf.marketplace`	Personal for sale notices of SF materials.
`rec.arts.sf.misc`	Science fiction lovers' newsgroup.
`rec.arts.sf.movies`	Discussing SF motion pictures.
`rec.arts.sf.reviews`	Reviews of science fiction/fantasy/ horror works. (Moderated)
`rec.arts.sf.science`	Real and speculative aspects of SF science.
`rec.arts.sf.starwars`	Discussion of the Star Wars universe.
`rec.arts.sf.tv`	Discussing general television SF.
`rec.arts.sf.written`	Discussion of written science fiction and fantasy.
`rec.arts.startrek.current`	New Star Trek shows, movies and books.
`rec.arts.startrek.fandom`	Star Trek conventions and memorabilia.
`rec.arts.startrek.info`	Information about the universe of Star Trek. (Moderated)
`rec.arts.startrek.misc`	General discussions of Star Trek.
`rec.arts.startrek.reviews`	Reviews of Star Trek books, episodes, films, &c. (Moderated)
`rec.arts.startrek.tech`	Star Trek's depiction of future technologies.

continues

Newsgroup	Description
rec.arts.theatre	Discussion of all aspects of stage work & theatre.
rec.arts.tv	The boob tube, its history, and past and current shows.
rec.arts.tv.soaps	Postings about soap operas.
rec.arts.tv.uk	Discussions of telly shows from the UK.
rec.arts.wobegon	"A Prairie Home Companion" radio show discussion.
rec.audio	High fidelity audio.
rec.audio.car	Discussions of automobile audio systems.
rec.audio.high-end	High-end audio systems. (Moderated)
rec.audio.pro	Professional audio recording and studio engineering.
rec.autos	Automobiles, automotive products and laws.
rec.autos.antique	Discussing all aspects of automobiles over 25 years old.
rec.autos.driving	Driving automobiles.
rec.autos.marketplace	Buy/Sell/Trade automobiles, parts, tools, accessories.
rec.autos.misc	Miscellaneous discussion about automobiles.
rec.autos.rod-n-custom	High performance automobiles.
rec.autos.simulators	Discussion of automotive simulators.
rec.autos.sport	Discussion of organized, legal auto competitions.
rec.autos.tech	Technical aspects of automobiles, et. al.
rec.autos.vw	Issues pertaining to Volkswagen products.

Newsgroup	*Description*
`rec.aviation.announce`	Events of interest to the aviation community. (Moderated)
`rec.aviation.answers`	Frequently asked questions about aviation. (Moderated)
`rec.aviation.homebuilt`	Selecting, designing, building, and restoring aircraft.
`rec.aviation.ifr`	Flying under Instrument Flight Rules.
`rec.aviation.military`	Military aircraft of the past, present and future.
`rec.aviation.misc`	Miscellaneous topics in aviation.
`rec.aviation.owning`	Information on owning airplanes.
`rec.aviation.piloting`	General discussion for aviators.
`rec.aviation.products`	Reviews and discussion of products useful to pilots.
`rec.aviation.simulators`	Flight simulation on all levels.
`rec.aviation.soaring`	All aspects of sailplanes and hang-gliders.
`rec.aviation.stories`	Anecdotes of flight experiences. (Moderated)
`rec.aviation.student`	Learning to fly.
`rec.backcountry`	Activities in the Great Outdoors.
`rec.bicycles.marketplace`	Buying, selling & reviewing items for cycling.
`rec.bicycles.misc`	General discussion of bicycling.
`rec.bicycles.racing`	Bicycle racing techniques, rules and results.
`rec.bicycles.rides`	Discussions of tours and training or commuting routes.
`rec.bicycles.soc`	Societal issues of bicycling.
`rec.bicycles.tech`	Cycling product design, construction, maintenance, etc.

continues

Newsgroup	Description
rec.birds	Hobbyists interested in bird watching.
rec.boats	Hobbyists interested in boating.
rec.boats.paddle	Talk about any boats with oars, paddles, etc.
rec.climbing	Climbing techniques, competition announcements, etc.
rec.collecting	Discussion among collectors of many things.
rec.collecting.cards	Collecting all sorts of sport and non-sport cards.
rec.collecting.stamps	Discussion of all things related to philately.
rec.crafts.brewing	The art of making beers and meads.
rec.crafts.metalworking	All aspects of working with metal.
rec.crafts.misc	Handiwork arts not covered elsewhere.
rec.crafts.quilting	All about quilts and other quilted items.
rec.crafts.textiles	Sewing, weaving, knitting and other fiber arts.
rec.crafts.winemaking	The tasteful art of making wine.
rec.equestrian	Discussion of things equestrian.
rec.folk-dancing	Folk dances, dancers, and dancing.
rec.food.cooking	Food, cooking, cookbooks, and recipes.
rec.food.drink	Wines and spirits.
rec.food.historic	The history of food making arts.
rec.food.recipes	Recipes for interesting food and drink. (Moderated)
rec.food.restaurants	Discussion of dining out.
rec.food.sourdough	Making and baking with sourdough.

Newsgroup	*Description*
rec.food.veg	Vegetarians.
rec.gambling	Articles on games of chance & betting.
rec.games.abstract	Perfect information, pure strategy games.
rec.games.backgammon	Discussion of the game of backgammon.
rec.games.board	Discussion and hints on board games.
rec.games.board.ce	The Cosmic Encounter board game.
rec.games.bolo	The networked strategy war game Bolo.
rec.games.bridge	Hobbyists interested in bridge.
rec.games.chess	Chess & computer chess.
rec.games.chinese-chess	Discussion of the game of Chinese chess, Xiangqi.
rec.games.corewar	The Core War computer challenge.
rec.games.design	Discussion of game design related issues.
rec.games.diplomacy	The conquest game Diplomacy.
rec.games.empire	Discussion and hints about Empire.
rec.games.frp.advocacy	Flames and rebuttals about various role-playing systems.
rec.games.frp.announce	Announcements of happenings in the role-playing world. (Moderated)
rec.games.frp.archives	Archivable fantasy stories and other projects. (Moderated)
rec.games.frp.cyber	Discussions of cyberpunk related roleplaying games.
rec.games.frp.dnd	Fantasy role-playing with TSR's Dungeons and Dragons.
rec.games.frp.live-action	Live-action roleplaying games.

continues

Newsgroup	Description
rec.games.frp.marketplace	Role-playing game materials wanted and for sale.
rec.games.frp.misc	General discussions of role-playing games.
rec.games.go	Discussion about Go.
rec.games.hack	Discussion, hints, etc. about the Hack game.
rec.games.int-fiction	All aspects of interactive fiction games.
rec.games.mecha	Giant robot games.
rec.games.miniatures	Tabletop wargaming.
rec.games.misc	Games and computer games.
rec.games.moria	Comments, hints, and info about the Moria game.
rec.games.mud.admin	Administrative issues of multiuser dungeons.
rec.games.mud.announce	Informational articles about multiuser dungeons. (Moderated)
rec.games.mud.diku	All about DikuMuds.
rec.games.mud.lp	Discussions of the LPMUD computer role playing game.
rec.games.mud.misc	Various aspects of multiuser computer games.
rec.games.mud.tiny	Discussion about Tiny muds, like MUSH, MUSE and MOO.
rec.games.netrek	Discussion of the X window system game Netrek (XtrekII).
rec.games.pbm	Discussion about Play by Mail games.
rec.games.pinball	Discussing pinball-related issues.
rec.games.programmer	Discussion of adventure game programming.
rec.games.rogue	Discussion and hints about Rogue.

Newsgroup	Description
rec.games.roguelike.angband	The computer game Angband.
rec.games.roguelike.announce	Major info about rogue-styled games. (Moderated)
rec.games.roguelike.misc	Rogue-style dungeon games without other groups.
rec.games.trivia	Discussion about trivia.
rec.games.video.3do	Discussion of 3DO video game systems.
rec.games.video.advocacy	Debate on merits of various video game systems.
rec.games.video.arcade	Discussions about coin-operated video games.
rec.games.video.arcade.collecting	Collecting, converting, repairing etc.
rec.games.video.atari	Discussion of Atari's video game systems.
rec.games.video.classic	Older home video entertainment systems.
rec.games.video.marketplace	Home video game stuff for sale or trade.
rec.games.video.misc	General discussion about home video games.
rec.games.video.nintendo	All Nintendo video game systems and software.
rec.games.video.sega	All Sega video game systems and software.
rec.games.xtank.play	Strategy and tactics for the distributed game Xtank.
rec.games.xtank.programmer	Coding the Xtank game and its robots.
rec.gardens	Gardening, methods and results.
rec.guns	Discussions about firearms. (Moderated)

continues

Newsgroup	Description
rec.heraldry	Discussion of coats of arms.
rec.humor	Jokes and the like. May be somewhat offensive.
rec.humor.d	Discussions on the content of rec.humor articles.
rec.humor.funny	Jokes that are funny (in the moderator's opinion). (Moderated)
rec.humor.oracle	Sagacious advice from the USENET Oracle. (Moderated)
rec.humor.oracle.d	Comments about the USENET Oracle's comments.
rec.hunting	Discussions about hunting. (Moderated)
rec.juggling	Juggling techniques, equipment and events.
rec.kites	Talk about kites and kiting.
rec.mag	Magazine summaries, tables of contents, etc.
rec.martial-arts	Discussion of the various martial art forms.
rec.misc	General topics about recreational/participant sports.
rec.models.railroad	Model railroads of all scales.
rec.models.rc	Radio-controlled models for hobbyists.
rec.models.rockets	Model rockets for hobbyists.
rec.models.scale	Construction of models.
rec.motorcycles	Motorcycles and related products and laws.
rec.motorcycles.dirt	Riding motorcycles and ATVs off-road.
rec.motorcycles.harley	All aspects of Harley Davidson motorcycles.

Newsgroup	Description
rec.motorcycles.racing	Discussion of all aspects of racing motorcycles.
rec.music.a-cappella	Vocal music without instrumental accompaniment.
rec.music.afro-latin	Music with Afro-Latin, African and Latin influences.
rec.music.beatles	Postings about the Fab Four & their music.
rec.music.bluenote	Discussion of jazz, blues, and related types of music.
rec.music.cd	CDs — availability and other discussions.
rec.music.celtic	Traditional and modern music with a Celtic flavor.
rec.music.christian	Christian music, both contemporary and traditional.
rec.music.classical	Discussion about classical music.
rec.music.classical.guitar	Classical music performed on guitar.
rec.music.classical.performing	Performing classical (including early) music.
rec.music.compose	Creating musical and lyrical works.
rec.music.country.western	C&W music, performers, performances, etc.
rec.music.dementia	Discussion of comedy and novelty music.
rec.music.dylan	Discussion of Bob's works & music.
rec.music.early	Discussion of pre-classical European music.
rec.music.folk	Folks discussing folk music of various sorts.
rec.music.funky	Funk, rap, hip-hop, house, soul, r&b and related.

continues

Newsgroup	Description
rec.music.gaffa	Discussion of Kate Bush & other alternative music. (Moderated)
rec.music.gdead	A group for (Grateful) Dead-heads.
rec.music.indian.classical	Hindustani and Carnatic Indian classical music.
rec.music.indian.misc	Discussing Indian music in general.
rec.music.industrial	Discussion of all industrial-related music styles.
rec.music.info	News and announcements on musical topics. (Moderated)
rec.music.makers	For performers and their discussions.
rec.music.makers.bass	Upright bass and bass guitar techniques and equipment.
rec.music.makers.guitar	Electric and acoustic guitar techniques and equipment.
rec.music.makers.guitar.acoustic	Discussion of acoustic guitar playing.
rec.music.makers.guitar.tablature	Guitar tablature/chords.
rec.music.makers.marketplace	Buying & selling used music-making equipment.
rec.music.makers.percussion	Drum & other percussion techniques & equipment.
rec.music.makers.synth	Synthesizers and computer music.
rec.music.marketplace	Records, tapes, and CDs: wanted, for sale, etc.
rec.music.misc	Music lovers' group.
rec.music.newage	"New Age" music discussions.
rec.music.phish	Discussing the musical group Phish.
rec.music.reggae	Roots, Rockers, Dancehall Reggae.
rec.music.reviews	Reviews of music of all genres and mediums. (Moderated)

Newsgroup	Description
`rec.music.video`	Discussion of music videos and music video software.
`rec.nude`	Hobbyists interested in naturist/ nudist activities.
`rec.org.mensa`	Talking with members of the high IQ society Mensa.
`rec.org.sca`	Society for Creative Anachronism.
`rec.outdoors.fishing`	All aspects of sport and commercial fishing.
`rec.parks.theme`	Entertainment theme parks.
`rec.pets`	Pets, pet care, and household animals in general.
`rec.pets.birds`	The culture and care of indoor birds.
`rec.pets.cats`	Discussion about domestic cats.
`rec.pets.dogs`	Any and all subjects relating to dogs as pets.
`rec.pets.herp`	Reptiles, amphibians and other exotic vivarium pets.
`rec.photo`	Hobbyists interested in photography.
`rec.puzzles`	Puzzles, problems, and quizzes.
`rec.puzzles.crosswords`	Making and playing gridded word puzzles.
`rec.pyrotechnics`	Fireworks, rocketry, safety, & other topics.
`rec.radio.amateur.antenna`	Antennas: theory, techniques and construction.
`rec.radio.amateur.digital. misc`	Packet radio and other digital radio modes.
`rec.radio.amateur.equipment`	All about production amateur radio hardware.

continues

Newsgroup	Description
rec.radio.amateur.homebrew	Amateur radio construction and experimentation.
rec.radio.amateur.misc	Amateur radio practices, contests, events, rules, etc.
rec.radio.amateur.policy	Radio use & regulation policy.
rec.radio.amateur.space	Amateur radio transmissions through space.
rec.radio.broadcasting	Discussion of global domestic broadcast radio. (Moderated)
rec.radio.cb	Citizen-band radio.
rec.radio.info	Informational postings related to radio. (Moderated)
rec.radio.noncomm	Topics relating to noncommercial radio.
rec.radio.scanner	"Utility" broadcasting traffic above 30 MHz.
rec.radio.shortwave	Shortwave radio enthusiasts.
rec.radio.swap	Offers to trade and swap radio equipment.
rec.railroad	For fans of real trains, ferroequinologists.
rec.roller-coaster	Roller coasters and other amusement park rides.
rec.running	Running for enjoyment, sport, exercise, etc.
rec.scouting	Scouting youth organizations worldwide.
rec.scuba	Hobbyists interested in SCUBA diving.
rec.skate	Ice skating and roller skating.
rec.skiing	Hobbyists interested in snow skiing.
rec.skydiving	Hobbyists interested in skydiving.

Newsgroup	Description
`rec.sport.baseball`	Discussion about baseball.
`rec.sport.baseball.college`	Baseball on the collegiate level.
`rec.sport.baseball.fantasy`	Rotisserie (fantasy) baseball play.
`rec.sport.basketball.college`	Hoops on the collegiate level.
`rec.sport.basketball.misc`	Discussion about basketball.
`rec.sport.basketball.pro`	Talk of professional basketball.
`rec.sport.cricket`	Discussion about the sport of cricket.
`rec.sport.cricket.scores`	Scores from cricket matches around the globe. (Moderated)
`rec.sport.disc`	Discussion of flying disc based sports.
`rec.sport.fencing`	All aspects of swordplay.
`rec.sport.football.australian`	Discussion of Australian (Rules) Football.
`rec.sport.football.canadian`	All about Canadian rules football.
`rec.sport.football.college`	US-style college football.
`rec.sport.football.fantasy`	Rotisserie (fantasy) football play.
`rec.sport.football.misc`	Discussion about American-style football.
`rec.sport.football.pro`	US-style professional football.
`rec.sport.golf`	Discussion about all aspects of golfing.
`rec.sport.hockey`	Discussion about ice hockey.
`rec.sport.hockey.field`	Discussion of the sport of field hockey.
`rec.sport.misc`	Spectator sports.
`rec.sport.olympics`	All aspects of the Olympic Games.
`rec.sport.paintball`	Discussing all aspects of the survival game paintball.

continues

Newsgroup	Description
rec.sport.pro-wrestling	Discussion about professional wrestling.
rec.sport.rowing	Crew for competition or fitness.
rec.sport.rugby	Discussion about the game of rugby.
rec.sport.soccer	Discussion about soccer (Association Football).
rec.sport.swimming	Training for and competing in swimming events.
rec.sport.table-tennis	Things related to table tennis (aka Ping Pong).
rec.sport.tennis	Things related to the sport of tennis.
rec.sport.triathlon	Discussing all aspects of multi-event sports.
rec.sport.volleyball	Discussion about volleyball.
rec.sport.waterski	Waterskiing and other boat-towed activities.
rec.toys.lego	Discussion of Lego, Duplo (and compatible) toys.
rec.toys.misc	Discussion of toys that lack a specific newsgroup.
rec.travel	Traveling all over the world.
rec.travel.air	Airline travel around the world.
rec.travel.marketplace	Tickets and accommodations wanted and for sale.
rec.video	Video and video components.
rec.video.cable-tv	Technical and regulatory issues of cable television.
rec.video.production	Making professional quality video productions.
rec.video.releases	Pre-recorded video releases on laserdisc and videotape.

Newsgroup	Description
rec.video.satellite	Getting shows via satellite.
rec.windsurfing	Riding the waves as a hobby.
rec.woodworking	Hobbyists interested in woodworking.
sci.aeronautics	The science of aeronautics & related technology. (Moderated)
sci.aeronautics.airliners	Airliner technology. (Moderated)
sci.agriculture	Farming, agriculture and related topics.
sci.answers	Repository for periodic USENET articles. (Moderated)
sci.anthropology	All aspects of studying humankind.
sci.anthropology.paleo	Evolution of man and other primates.
sci.aquaria	Only scientifically-oriented postings about aquaria.
sci.archaeology	Studying antiquities of the world.
sci.astro	Astronomy discussions and information.
sci.astro.fits	Issues related to the Flexible Image Transport System.
sci.astro.hubble	Processing Hubble Space Telescope data. (Moderated)
sci.astro.planetarium	Discussion of planetariums.
sci.bio	Biology and related sciences.
sci.bio.ecology	Ecological research.
sci.bio.ethology	Animal behavior and behavioral ecology.
sci.bio.evolution	Discussions of evolutionary biology. (Moderated)
sci.bio.herp	Biology of amphibians and reptiles.
sci.chem	Chemistry and related sciences.

continues

Newsgroup	*Description*
sci.chem.organomet	Organometallic chemistry.
sci.classics	Studying classical history, languages, art and more.
sci.cognitive	Perception, memory, judgement and reasoning.
sci.comp-aided	The use of computers as tools in scientific research.
sci.cryonics	Theory and practice of biostasis, suspended animation.
sci.crypt	Different methods of data en/decryption.
sci.data.formats	Modelling, storage and retrieval of scientific data.
sci.econ	The science of economics.
sci.econ.research	Research in all fields of economics. (Moderated)
sci.edu	The science of education.
sci.electronics	Circuits, theory, electrons and discussions.
sci.energy	Discussions about energy, science & technology.
sci.energy.hydrogen	All about hydrogen as an alternative fuel.
sci.engr	Technical discussions about engineering tasks.
sci.engr.advanced-tv	HDTV/DATV standards, formats, equipment, practices.
sci.engr.biomed	Discussing the field of biomedical engineering.
sci.engr.chem	All aspects of chemical engineering.
sci.engr.civil	Topics related to civil engineering.
sci.engr.control	The engineering of control systems.

Newsgroup	Description
`sci.engr.lighting`	Light, vision & color in architecture, media, etc.
`sci.engr.manufacturing`	Manufacturing technology.
`sci.engr.mech`	The field of mechanical engineering.
`sci.environment`	Discussions about the environment and ecology.
`sci.fractals`	Objects of non-integral dimension and other chaos.
`sci.geo.fluids`	Discussion of geophysical fluid dynamics.
`sci.geo.geology`	Discussion of solid earth sciences.
`sci.geo.meteorology`	Discussion of meteorology and related topics.
`sci.image.processing`	Scientific image processing and analysis.
`sci.lang`	Natural languages, communication, etc.
`sci.lang.japan`	The Japanese language, both spoken and written.
`sci.life-extension`	Slowing, stopping or reversing the ageing process.
`sci.logic`	Logic — math, philosophy & computational aspects.
`sci.materials`	All aspects of materials engineering.
`sci.math`	Mathematical discussions and pursuits.
`sci.math.research`	Discussion of current mathematical research. (Moderated)
`sci.math.symbolic`	Symbolic algebra discussion.
`sci.med`	Medicine and its related products and regulations.

continues

Newsgroup	Description
sci.med.aids	AIDS: treatment, pathology/biology of HIV, prevention. (Moderated)
sci.med.dentistry	Dentally related topics; all about teeth.
sci.med.nursing	Nursing questions and discussion.
sci.med.nutrition	Physiological impacts of diet.
sci.med.occupational	Preventing, detecting & treating occupational injuries.
sci.med.pharmacy	The teaching and practice of pharmacy.
sci.med.physics	Issues of physics in medical testing/care.
sci.med.psychobiology	Dialog and news in psychiatry and psychobiology.
sci.med.telemedicine	Clinical consulting through computer networks.
sci.military	Discussion about science & the military. (Moderated)
sci.misc	Short-lived discussions on subjects in the sciences.
sci.nanotech	Self-reproducing molecular-scale machines. (Moderated)
sci.nonlinear	Chaotic systems and other nonlinear scientific study.
sci.op-research	Research, teaching & application of operations research.
sci.optics	Discussion relating to the science of optics.
sci.philosophy.tech	Technical philosophy: math, science, logic, etc.
sci.physics	Physical laws, properties, etc.
sci.physics.accelerators	Particle accelerators and the physics of beams.

Newsgroup	Description
sci.physics.fusion	Info on fusion, esp. "cold" fusion.
sci.physics.particle	Particle physics discussions.
sci.physics.research	Current physics research. (Moderated)
sci.polymers	All aspects of polymer science.
sci.psychology	Topics related to psychology.
sci.psychology.digest	PSYCOLOQUY: Refereed Psychology Journal and Newsletter. (Moderated)
sci.research	Research methods, funding, ethics, and whatever.
sci.research.careers	Issues relevant to careers in scientific research.
sci.skeptic	Skeptics discussing pseudo-science.
sci.space	Space, space programs, space related research, etc.
sci.space.news	Announcements of space-related news items. (Moderated)
sci.space.policy	Discussions about space policy.
sci.space.science	Space and planetary science and related technical work. (Moderated)
sci.space.shuttle	The space shuttle and the STS program.
sci.space.tech	Technical and general issues related to space flight. (Moderated)
sci.stat.consult	Statistical consulting.
sci.stat.edu	Statistics education.
sci.stat.math	Statistics from a strictly mathematical viewpoint.
sci.systems	The theory and application of systems science.
sci.techniques.microscopy	The field of microscopy.

continues

Newsgroup	Description
sci.techniques.xtallography	The field of crystallography.
sci.virtual-worlds	Virtual Reality - technology and culture. (Moderated)
sci.virtual-worlds.apps	Current and future uses of virtual-worlds technology. (Moderated)
soc.answers	Repository for periodic USENET articles. (Moderated)
soc.bi	Discussions of bisexuality.
soc.college	College, college activities, campus life, etc.
soc.college.grad	General issues related to graduate schools.
soc.college.gradinfo	Information about graduate schools.
soc.college.org.aiesec	The Int'l Assoc. of Business and Commerce Students.
soc.college.teaching-asst	Issues affecting collegiate teaching assistants.
soc.couples	Discussions for couples (c.f. soc.singles).
soc.couples.intercultural	Inter-cultural and inter-racial relationships.
soc.culture.afghanistan	Discussion of the Afghan society.
soc.culture.african	Discussions about Africa & things African.
soc.culture.african.american	Discussions about Afro-American issues.
soc.culture.arabic	Technological & cultural issues, *not* politics.
soc.culture.argentina	All about life in Argentina.
soc.culture.asean	Countries of the Assoc. of SE Asian Nations.

Newsgroup	Description
soc.culture.asian.american	Issues & discussion about Asian-Americans.
soc.culture.australian	Australian culture and society.
soc.culture.austria	Austria and its people.
soc.culture.baltics	People of the Baltic states.
soc.culture.bangladesh	Issues & discussion about Bangladesh.
soc.culture.bosna-herzgvna	The independent state of Bosnia and Herzegovina.
soc.culture.brazil	Talking about the people and country of Brazil.
soc.culture.british	Issues about Britain & those of British descent.
soc.culture.bulgaria	Discussing Bulgarian society.
soc.culture.burma	Politics, culture, news, discussion about Burma.
soc.culture.canada	Discussions of Canada and its people.
soc.culture.caribbean	Life in the Caribbean.
soc.culture.celtic	Irish, Scottish, Breton, Cornish, Manx & Welsh.
soc.culture.chile	All about Chile and its people.
soc.culture.china	About China and Chinese culture.
soc.culture.croatia	The lives of people of Croatia.
soc.culture.czecho-slovak	Bohemian, Slovak, Moravian and Silesian life.
soc.culture.europe	Discussing all aspects of all European society.
soc.culture.filipino	Group about the Filipino culture.
soc.culture.french	French culture, history, and related discussions.

continues

Newsgroup	Description
soc.culture.german	Discussions about German culture and history.
soc.culture.greek	Group about Greeks.
soc.culture.hongkong	Discussions pertaining to Hong Kong.
soc.culture.indian	Group for discussion about India & things Indian.
soc.culture.indian.info	Info group for soc.culture.indian, etc. (Moderated)
soc.culture.indian.telugu	The culture of the Telugu people of India.
soc.culture.indonesia	All about the Indonesian nation.
soc.culture.iranian	Discussions about Iran and things Iranian/Persian.
soc.culture.israel	Israel and Israelis.
soc.culture.italian	The Italian people and their culture.
soc.culture.japan	Everything Japanese, except the Japanese language.
soc.culture.jewish	Jewish culture & religion. (c.f. talk.politics.mideast)
soc.culture.korean	Discussions about Korea & things Korean.
soc.culture.laos	Cultural and Social Aspects of Laos.
soc.culture.latin-america	Topics about Latin-America.
soc.culture.lebanon	Discussion about things Lebanese.
soc.culture.maghreb	North African society and culture.
soc.culture.magyar	The Hungarian people & their culture.
soc.culture.malaysia	All about Malaysian society.
soc.culture.mexican	Discussion of Mexico's society.
soc.culture.misc	Group for discussion about other cultures.

Newsgroup	Description
soc.culture.native	Aboriginal people around the world.
soc.culture.nepal	Discussion of people and things in & from Nepal.
soc.culture.netherlands	People from the Netherlands and Belgium.
soc.culture.new-zealand	Discussion of topics related to New Zealand.
soc.culture.nordic	Discussion about culture up north.
soc.culture.pakistan	Topics of discussion about Pakistan.
soc.culture.palestine	Palestinian people, culture and politics.
soc.culture.peru	All about the people of Peru.
soc.culture.polish	Polish culture, Polish past, and Polish politics.
soc.culture.portuguese	Discussion of the people of Portugal.
soc.culture.romanian	Discussion of Romanian and Moldavian people.
soc.culture.scientists	Cultural issues about scientists & scientific projects.
soc.culture.singapore	The past, present and future of Singapore.
soc.culture.soviet	Topics relating to Russian or Soviet culture.
soc.culture.spain	Spain and the Spanish.
soc.culture.sri-lanka	Things & people from Sri Lanka.
soc.culture.taiwan	Discussion about things Taiwanese.
soc.culture.tamil	Tamil language, history and culture.
soc.culture.thai	Thai people and their culture.
soc.culture.turkish	Discussion about things Turkish.

continues

Newsgroup	Description
soc.culture.ukrainian	The lives and times of the Ukrainian people.
soc.culture.uruguay	Discussions of Uruguay for those at home and abroad.
soc.culture.usa	The culture of the United States of America.
soc.culture.venezuela	Discussion of topics related to Venezuela.
soc.culture.vietnamese	Issues and discussions of Vietnamese culture.
soc.culture.yugoslavia	Discussions of Yugoslavia and its people.
soc.feminism	Discussion of feminism & feminist issues. (Moderated)
soc.history	Discussions of things historical.
soc.libraries.talk	Discussing all aspects of libraries.
soc.men	Issues related to men, their problems & relationships.
soc.misc	Socially-oriented topics not in other groups.
soc.motss	Issues pertaining to homosexuality.
soc.net-people	Announcements, requests, etc. about people on the net.
soc.penpals	In search of net.friendships.
soc.politics	Political problems, systems, solutions. (Moderated)
soc.politics.arms-d	Arms discussion digest. (Moderated)
soc.religion.bahai	Discussion of the Baha'i Faith. (Moderated)
soc.religion.christian	Christianity and related topics. (Moderated)

Newsgroup	Description
`soc.religion.christian.bible-study`	Examining the Holy Bible. (Moderated)
`soc.religion.eastern`	Discussions of Eastern religions. (Moderated)
`soc.religion.islam`	Discussions of the Islamic faith. (Moderated)
`soc.religion.quaker`	The Religious Society of Friends.
`soc.religion.shamanism`	Discussion of the full range of shamanic experience. (Moderated)
`soc.rights.human`	Human rights & activism (e.g., Amnesty International).
`soc.roots`	Discussing genealogy and genealogical matters.
`soc.singles`	Newsgroup for single people, their activities, etc.
`soc.veterans`	Social issues relating to military veterans.
`soc.women`	Issues related to women, their problems & relationships.
`talk.abortion`	All sorts of discussions and arguments on abortion.
`talk.answers`	Repository for periodic USENET articles. (Moderated)
`talk.bizarre`	The unusual, bizarre, curious, and often stupid.
`talk.environment`	Discussion on the state of the environment & what to do.
`talk.origins`	Evolution versus creationism (sometimes hot!).
`talk.philosophy.misc`	Philosophical musings on all topics.
`talk.politics.animals`	The use and/or abuse of animals.

continues

Newsgroup	Description
talk.politics.china	Discussion of political issues related to China.
talk.politics.crypto	The relation between cryptography and government.
talk.politics.drugs	The politics of drug issues.
talk.politics.guns	The politics of firearm ownership and (mis)use.
talk.politics.medicine	The politics and ethics involved with health care.
talk.politics.mideast	Discussion & debate over Middle Eastern events.
talk.politics.misc	Political discussions and ravings of all kinds.
talk.politics.soviet	Discussion of Soviet politics, domestic and foreign.
talk.politics.space	Non-technical issues affecting space exploration.
talk.politics.theory	Theory of politics and political systems.
talk.politics.tibet	The politics of Tibet and the Tibetan people.
talk.rape	Discussions on stopping rape; not to be crossposted.
talk.religion.misc	Religious, ethical, & moral implications.
talk.religion.newage	Esoteric and minority religions & philosophies.
talk.rumors	For the posting of rumors.

Introduction to the Alternative Hierarchies

The Usenet software allows the support and transport of hierarchies of newsgroups not part of the "traditional" Usenet through use of the distribution mechanism. These hierarchies of groups are available to sites wanting to support them and able to find a feed. In general, the entire network does not carry these groups because of their volume, restricted spheres of interest, or a different set of administrative rules and concerns.

In general, it is a bad idea to forward these newsgroups to your neighbors without asking them first; they should only be received at a site by choice. Not only is this generally accepted net etiquette, it helps to preserve the freedom to do and say as the posters please in these newsgroups, as the only people who get them are those who asked to get them. This freedom is more restricted in the Usenet as a whole because every mainstream posting and every mainstream newsgroup name must be acceptable to a much wider audience than is present in these hierarchies. Because of the sheer size of the mainstream Usenet, extra-long or controversial postings are more likely to cause problems when posted to the Usenet; however, these alternative hierarchies exist precisely to support those kinds of postings (if germane to the hierarchy).

Usually, you have no restriction on getting these groups as long as you have the capacity to receive, store, and forward the groups; software after B 2.11 news is required to make the distribution mechanism work properly for these groups. You learn how to join each distribution in the following sections.

Note that the uunet service carries all of these hierarchies. Contact uunet-request@uunet.uu.net for subscription details.

Also note that the lists in this article are totally unofficial and possibly incomplete or inaccurate. I try to keep the lists up to date but make no guarantee that any of the information contained corresponds with the named groups in any significant way. You should mail corrections and comments to the reply address listed earlier in this appendix.

alt

The alt collection of newsgroups is distributed by a collection of sites that choose to carry the groups. Many Usenet sites do not receive these groups. Following is a recent list of many active alt newsgroups.

Newsgroup	*Description*
alt.1d	One-dimensional imaging, and the thinking behind it.
alt.2600	The magazine or the game system. You decide.
alt.3d	Three-dimensional imaging.
alt.abortion.inequity	Paternal obligations of failing to abort unwanted child.
alt.activism	Activities for activists.
alt.activism.d	A place to discuss issues in alt.activism.
alt.activism.death-penalty	For people opposed to capital punishment.
alt.adjective.noun.verb.verb.verb	The penultimate alt group.
alt.adoption	For those involved with or contemplating adoption.
alt.aeffle.und.pferdle	German cartoon characters das Aeffle und das Pferdle.
alt.agriculture.misc	All about cultivating the soil and raising animals.
alt.aldus.pagemaker	Don't use expensive user support, come here instead.
alt.alien.visitors	Space Aliens on Earth! Abduction! Government Coverup!
alt.amateur-comp	Discussion and input for Amateur Computerist Newsletter.
alt.amazon-women.admirers	Worshiping women you have to look up to.

Newsgroup	*Description*
`alt.angst`	Anxiety in the modern world.
`alt.animals.lampreys`	They're eel-like, and they suck.
`alt.animation.warner-bros`	Discussions about Warner Brothers cartoons.
`alt.answers`	As if anyone on alt has the answers. (Moderated)
`alt.appalachian`	Appalachian region awareness, events, and culture.
`alt.aquaria`	The aquarium and related as a hobby.
`alt.archery`	Robin Hood had the right idea.
`alt.architecture`	Building design/construction and related topics.
`alt.architecture.alternative`	Non-traditional building designs.
`alt.architecture.int-design`	Interior design and decorating.
`alt.artcom`	Artistic Community, arts & communication.
`alt.arts.nomad`	Shifting, searching, belonging, place, identity, power?
`alt.ascii-art`	Pictures composed of ASCII characters.
`alt.asian-movies`	Movies from Hong Kong, Taiwan and the Chinese mainland.
`alt.astrology`	Twinkle, twinkle, little planet.
`alt.atari-jaguar.discussion`	As opposed to simply alt.atari.jaguar.
`alt.atari.2600`	The Atari 2600 game system, not 2600 Magazine.
`alt.atheism`	Godless heathens.
`alt.atheism.moderated`	Focused Godless heathens. (Moderated)

continues

Newsgroup	Description
`alt.autos.antique`	Discussion of all facets of older automobiles.
`alt.autos.camaro.firebird`	A couple of American sports cars.
`alt.autos.rod-n-custom`	Vehicles with modified engines and/or appearance.
`alt.backrubs`	Lower...to the right...aaaah!
`alt.banjo`	Someone's in the kitchen with Dinah.
`alt.barney.dinosaur.die.die.die`	"There's enough hatred of Barney for everyone!"
`alt.basement.graveyard`	Another side of the do-it-yourself movement.
`alt.bbs`	Computer BBS systems & software.
`alt.bbs.ads`	Ads for various computer BBS's.
`alt.bbs.allsysop`	SysOp concerns of ALL networks and technologies.
`alt.bbs.first-class`	The First Class Mac GUI BBS.
`alt.bbs.internet`	BBSs that are hooked up to the Internet.
`alt.bbs.lists`	Postings of regional BBS listings.
`alt.bbs.majorbbs`	The MajorBBS by Galacticomm, Inc.
`alt.bbs.metal`	The METAL Telecommunications Environment.
`alt.bbs.pcboard`	Technical support for the PCBoard BBS.
`alt.bbs.pcbuucp`	The commerical PCBoard gateway, PCB-UUCP.
`alt.bbs.unixbbs`	UnixBBS, from Nervous XTC.
`alt.bbs.uupcb`	PCB? I used to do that in the Sixties, man!
`alt.bbs.wildcat`	WILDCAT! BBS from Mustang Software, Inc.

Newsgroup	Description
alt.beer	Good for what ales ya.
alt.best.of.internet	It was a time of sorrow, it was a time of joy.
alt.bigfoot	Dr. Scholl's gone native.
alt.binaries.clip-art	Distribution of DOS, Mac and Unix clipart.
alt.binaries.multimedia	Sound, text and graphics data rolled in one.
alt.binaries.pictures	Additional volume in the form of huge image files.
alt.binaries.pictures.ascii	Pictures composed of ASCII characters.
alt.binaries.pictures.cartoons	Images from animated cartoons.
alt.binaries.pictures.d	Discussions about picture postings.
alt.binaries.pictures.erotica	Gigabytes of copyright violations.
alt.binaries.pictures.erotica.blondes	Copyright violations featuring blondes.
alt.binaries.pictures.erotica.d	Discussing erotic copyright violations.
alt.binaries.pictures.erotica.female	Copyright violations featuring females.
alt.binaries.pictures.erotica.male	Copyright violations featuring males.
alt.binaries.pictures.erotica.orientals	Copyright violations featuring Asians.
alt.binaries.pictures.fine-art.d	Discussion of the fine-art binaries. (Moderated)
alt.binaries.pictures.fine-art.digitized	Art from conventional media. (Moderated)
alt.binaries.pictures.fine-art.graphics	Art created on computers. (Moderated)

continues

Newsgroup	Description
`alt.binaries.pictures.fractals`	Cheaper just to send the program parameters.
`alt.binaries.pictures.furry`	Original funny animal art.
`alt.binaries.pictures.misc`	Have we saturated the network yet?
`alt.binaries.pictures.supermodels`	Yet more copyright violations.
`alt.binaries.pictures.tasteless`	Eccchh, that last one was *sick*.
`alt.binaries.pictures.utilities`	Posting of pictures-related utilities.
`alt.binaries.sounds.d`	Sounding off.
`alt.binaries.sounds.midi`	MIDI binaries.
`alt.binaries.sounds.misc`	Digitized audio adventures.
`alt.binaries.sounds.mods`	MODs and related sound formats.
`alt.binaries.sounds.movies`	Sounds from copyrighted movies.
`alt.binaries.sounds.music`	Music samples in MOD/669 format.
`alt.binaries.sounds.tv`	Sounds from copyrighted television shows.
`alt.binaries.sounds.utilities`	Sound utilities.
`alt.birthright`	Birthright Party propaganda.
`alt.bitterness`	No matter what it's for, you know how it'll turn out.
`alt.bogus.group`	A paradox for its readers.
`alt.bonehead.joel-furr`	Like alt.fan.joel-furr, for real admirers.
`alt.books.anne-rice`	The Vampire Thermostat.
`alt.books.deryni`	Katherine Kurtz's books, especially the Deryni series.
`alt.books.isaac-asimov`	Fans of the late SF/science author Isaac Asimov.

Newsgroup	Description
alt.books.m-lackey	Discussion of author Mercedes Lackey and her books.
alt.books.reviews	"If you want to know how it turns out, read it!"
alt.books.technical	Discussion of technical books.
alt.boomerang	The angular throwing club, not the Eddie Murphy flick.
alt.brain	Busboys Recovering After Intense Noogies.
alt.brother-jed	The born-again minister touring US campuses.
alt.buddha.short.fat.guy	Religion. And not religion. Both. Neither.
alt.business.misc	All aspects of commerce.
alt.business.multi-level	Multi-level (network) marketing businesses.
alt.cad	Computer Aided Design.
alt.cad.autocad	CAD as practiced by customers of Autodesk.
alt.california	The state and the state of mind.
alt.callahans	Callahan's bar for puns and fellow-ship.
alt.captain.sarcastic	For the captain's minions.
alt.cascade	Art or litter—you decide.
alt.cd-rom	Discussions of optical storage media.
alt.censorship	Discussion about restricting speech/press.
alt.cereal	Breakfast cereals and their (m)ilk.
alt.cesium	College Educated Students in Universal Mainland.
alt.child-support	Raising children in a split family.

continues

Newsgroup	Description
alt.chinchilla	The nature of chinchilla farming in America Today.
alt.chinese.text	Postings in Chinese; Chinese language software.
alt.chinese.text.big5	Posting in Chinese[BIG 5].
alt.christnet	Gathering place for Christian ministers and users.
alt.christnet.bible	Bible discussion and research.
alt.christnet.christianlife	Discussing how to live what we believe.
alt.christnet.comp.dcom.telecom	Proselytizing in the name of Edison.
alt.christnet.dinosaur.barney	Barney as seen by Christians.
alt.christnet.ethics	The scriptural foundation of Christian ethics.
alt.christnet.evangelical	Proselytizing for Christ.
alt.christnet.hypocrisy	"Vengeance is mine!" sayeth jfurr.
alt.christnet.philosophy	Philosophical implications of Christianity.
alt.christnet.second-coming.real-soon-now	It could happen.
alt.christnet.sex	Some of them still do that, you know.
alt.christnet.theology	The distinctives of God of Christian theology.
alt.clearing.technology	Traumatic Incident Reduction and Clearing.
alt.co-ops	Discussion about co-operatives.
alt.cobol	Relationship between programming and stone axes.
alt.collecting.autographs	WOW! You got Pete Rose's? What about Kibo's?

Newsgroup	Description
`alt.college.college-bowl`	Discussions of the College Bowl competition.
`alt.college.food`	Dining halls, cafeterias, mystery meat, and more.
`alt.college.us`	Is that "us" as in "U. S.", or do you just mean y'all?
`alt.comedy.british`	Discussion of British comedy in a variety of media.
`alt.comedy.firesgn-thtre`	Firesign Theatre in all its flaming glory.
`alt.comedy.vaudeville`	Vaudeville and its descendants.
`alt.comics.alternative`	You could try a book without pictures, for example.
`alt.comics.batman`	Marketing mania.
`alt.comics.elfquest`	W & R Pini's ElfQuest series.
`alt.comics.lnh`	Interactive net.madness in the superhero genre.
`alt.comics.superman`	No one knows it is also alt.clark.kent.
`alt.comp.acad-freedom.news`	Academic freedom issues related to computers. (Moderated)
`alt.comp.acad-freedom.talk`	Academic freedom issues related to computers.
`alt.comp.databases.xbase.clipper`	The Clipper database language.
`alt.comp.fsp`	A file transport protocol.
`alt.comp.hardware.homebuilt`	Designing devious devices in the den.
`alt.computer.consultants`	Geeks on Patrol.
`alt.config`	Alternative subnet discussions and connectivity.
`alt.consciousness`	Discussions on the study of the human consciousness.

continues

Newsgroup	Description
alt.conspiracy	Be paranoid — they're out to get you.
alt.conspiracy.jfk	The Kennedy assassination.
alt.consumers.free-stuff	Free offers and how to take advantage of them.
alt.cows.moo.moo.moo	Like cows would cluck or something.
alt.crackers	Snack food in little bits or big bytes.
alt.cult-movies	Movies with a cult following.
alt.cult-movies.rocky-horror	Virgin! Virgin! Virgin! Virgin!
alt.culture.alaska	Is this where the ice weasels come from?
alt.culture.austrian	You'll find more Austrians in soc.culture.austria.
alt.culture.electric-midget	They make great salad shooters.
alt.culture.hawaii	Ua Mau Ke Ea O Ka 'Aina I Ka Pono.
alt.culture.indonesia	Indonesian culture, news, etc.
alt.culture.internet	The culture(s) of the Internet.
alt.culture.karnataka	Culture and language of the Indian state of Karnataka.
alt.culture.kerala	People of Keralite origin and the Malayalam language.
alt.culture.ny-upstate	New York State, above Westchester.
alt.culture.oregon	Discussion about the state of Oregon.
alt.culture.tuva	Topics related to the Republic of Tuva, South Siberia.
alt.culture.us.asian-indian	Asian Indians in the US and Canada.
alt.culture.us.southwest	Basking in the sun of the US's lower left.

Newsgroup	*Description*
alt.culture.usenet	A self-referential oxymoron.
alt.current-events.bosnia	The strife of Bosnia-Herzegovina.
alt.current-events.clinton.whitewater	The Clinton Whitewater Scandle.
alt.current-events.la-quake	When I'm with you, I feel the earth move, baby.
alt.current-events.russia	Current happenings in Russia.
alt.current-events.ukraine	Current and fast paced Ukrainian events.
alt.current-events.usa	misc.headlines wasn't good enough for some.
alt.cyberpunk	High-tech low-life.
alt.cyberpunk.chatsubo	Literary virtual reality in a cyberpunk hangout.
alt.cyberpunk.movement	A little laxative might help.
alt.cyberpunk.tech	Cyberspace and Cyberpunk technology.
alt.cyberspace	Cyberspace and how it should work.
alt.dads-rights	Rights of fathers trying to win custody in court.
alt.dcom.telecom	Discussion of telecommunications technology.
alt.dear.whitehouse	When Hints from Heloise aren't enough.
alt.decathena	Digital's DECathena product. (Moderated)
alt.desert-storm	Continuing proof that alt groups never die.
alt.destroy.the.earth	Please leave the light on when you leave.
alt.dev.null	The ultimate in moderated newsgroups. (Moderated)

continues

Newsgroup	*Description*
alt.devilbunnies	Probably better left undescribed.
alt.discordia	All hail Eris, etc.
alt.discrimination	Quotas, affirmative action, bigotry, persecution.
alt.divination	Divination techniques (e.g., I Ching, Tarot, runes).
alt.dragons-inn	Breathing fire tends to make one very thirsty.
alt.dreams	What do they mean?
alt.dreams.lucid	What do they *really* mean?
alt.drugs	Recreational pharmaceuticals and related flames.
alt.drugs.caffeine	All about the world's most-used stimulant drug.
alt.drunken.bastards	Peeing in the potted plants.
alt.drwho.creative	Original fiction based on the Doctor Who series.
alt.education.disabled	Education for people with physical/mental disabilities.
alt.education.distance	Learning from teachers who are far away.
alt.emulators.ibmpc.apple2	Making your paperweight behave like another.
alt.emusic	Ethnic, exotic, electronic, elaborate, etc., music.
alt.ensign.wesley.die.die.die	We just can't get enough of him.
alt.evil	Tales from the dark side.
alt.exotic-music	Exotic music discussions.
alt.fan.addams	They're creepy and they're kooky, the Addams Family.
alt.fan.addams.wednesday	She's deadpan and she's homicidal.

Newsgroup	Description
`alt.fan.asprin`	I'm fond of buffered analgesics. Robert Lynn Asprin, too.
`alt.fan.bill-gates`	Fans of the original micro-softie.
`alt.fan.blues-brothers`	Anything you ever wanted to know about the Blues Brothers
`alt.fan.british-accent`	"Oooh, he just sounds soooo cool! [Giggle!]"
`alt.fan.ceiling`	Overused in movie fight scenes around the world.
`alt.fan.chris-elliott`	Get a Life, you Letterman flunky.
`alt.fan.clarence.thomas`	Probably not the one you're thinking of.
`alt.fan.conan-obrien`	Late Night with a big red pompadour.
`alt.fan.dan-quayle`	For discussion of the US Vice President.
`alt.fan.dave_barry`	Electronic fan club for humorist Dave Barry.
`alt.fan.david-bowie`	The man who fell to earth.
`alt.fan.david-lawrence`	All about cricket.
`alt.fan.devo`	Funny hats do not a band make.
`alt.fan.disney.afternoon`	Disney Afternoon characters & shows.
`alt.fan.don-n-mike`	Two radio guys.
`alt.fan.douglas-adams`	Author of "The Meaning of Liff", & other fine works.
`alt.fan.dragons`	People love automobiles at Pennsic.
`alt.fan.dune`	Herbert's drinking buddies.
`alt.fan.eddings`	The works of writer David Eddings.
`alt.fan.fabio`	A hunk of pecs.
`alt.fan.frank-zappa`	Is that a Sears poncho?

continues

Newsgroup	Description
alt.fan.furry	Fans of funny animals, a la Steve Gallacci's book.
alt.fan.g-gordon-liddy	Crime does pay, or we wouldn't have so much of it.
alt.fan.goons	Careful Neddy, it's that dastardly Moriarty again.
alt.fan.greaseman	Fans of Doug Tracht, the DJ.
alt.fan.holmes	Elementary, my dear Watson. Like he ever said that.
alt.fan.howard-stern	Fans of the abrasive radio & TV personality.
alt.fan.james-bond	On his Majesty's Secret Service (& secret linen too).
alt.fan.jen-coolest	Gosh, isn't she just wonderful?
alt.fan.jimmy-buffett	A white sports coat and a pink crustacean.
alt.fan.joel-furr	What an amazing dorkwad.
alt.fan.john-palmer	With an army of lawyers from a Michigan warren.
alt.fan.karla-homolka	Why are there so few hot, exhibitionist, S&M women?
alt.fan.laurie.anderson	Will it be a music concert or a lecture this time?
alt.fan.lemurs	Little critters with BIG eyes.
alt.fan.letterman	One of the top 10 reasons to get the alt groups.
alt.fan.lightbulbs	A hardware problem.
alt.fan.madonna	Nice #!#$, eh... And how about that puppy?
alt.fan.mike-jittlov	Electronic fan club for animator Mike Jittlov.
alt.fan.monty-python	Electronic fan club for those wacky Brits.

Newsgroup	Description
alt.fan.mst3k	I thought people hated jerks who talked in theatres.
alt.fan.noam-chomsky	Noam Chomsky's writings and opinions.
alt.fan.oingo-boingo	Have you ever played ping pong in Pago Pago?
alt.fan.pern	Anne McCaffery's s-f oeuvre.
alt.fan.piers-anthony	For fans of the s-f author Piers Anthony.
alt.fan.pratchett	For fans of Terry Pratchett, s-f humor writer.
alt.fan.q	Omnipotent being from either Star Trek or James Bond.
alt.fan.ren-and-stimpy	For folks who couldn't find alt.tv.ren-n-stimpy
alt.fan.robert-jordan	The Wheel of Time and other Robert Jordan works.
alt.fan.ronald-reagan	Jellybeans and all.
alt.fan.rush-limbaugh	Derogation of others for fun and profit.
alt.fan.shostakovich	Fans of the music of Shostakovich.
alt.fan.spinal-tap	Down on the sex farm.
alt.fan.surak	That wild and crazy Vulcan.
alt.fan.tanya-harding	Violent drama in the figure skating arena.
alt.fan.ted.thearp.dough.dough.dough	EMS Spokesman for 1993.
alt.fan.tolkien	Mortal Men doomed to die.
alt.fan.tom-robbins	31 flavours for readers.
alt.fan.u2	The Irish rock band U2.
alt.fan.vladimir.zhirinovsky	Who says World War III is a bad thing?

continues

Newsgroup	*Description*
`alt.fan.warlord`	The War Lord of the West Preservation Fan Club.
`alt.fan.wedge`	Standing by, red 2.
`alt.fan.wodehouse`	Discussion of the works of humour author P.G. Wodehouse.
`alt.fan.woody-allen`	The diminutive neurotic.
`alt.fandom.cons`	Announcements of conventions (SciFi and others).
`alt.fashion`	All facets of the fasion industry discussed.
`alt.fax`	Like comp.dcom.fax, only different.
`alt.feminism`	Like soc.feminism, only different.
`alt.fishing`	Fishing as a hobby and sport.
`alt.flame`	Alternative, literate, pithy, succinct screaming.
`alt.flame.landlord`	Flaming and ploting against the evil landlord.
`alt.flame.parents`	Flaming those that bred and/or raised you.
`alt.flame.roommate`	Putting the pig on a spit.
`alt.flame.spelling`	USENET's favourite fallacious argoomint.
`alt.folklore.college`	Collegiate humor.
`alt.folklore.computers`	Stories & anecdotes about computers (some true!).
`alt.folklore.ghost-stories`	Boo!
`alt.folklore.herbs`	Discussion of all aspects of herbs and their uses.
`alt.folklore.info`	Current urban legends and other folklore. (Moderated)
`alt.folklore.military`	Military-oriented 'urban legends' and folklore.

Newsgroup	*Description*
alt.folklore.science	The folklore of science, not the science of folklore.
alt.folklore.urban	Urban legends, a la Jan Harold Brunvand.
alt.food.cocacola	An American Classic. Buy our nostalgic art.
alt.food.fat-free	Quest for thinness.
alt.food.mcdonalds	Carl Sagan's favourite burger place.
alt.freaks	Rick James, we love you!
alt.galactic-guide	Hitch Hiker's Guide to the Known Galaxy Project.
alt.games.air-warrior	The multi-player air-combat game Air Warrior.
alt.games.doom	A really popular PC game.
alt.games.frp.dnd-util	Computer utilities for Dungeons and Dragons.
alt.games.frp.live-action	Discussion of all forms of live-action gaming.
alt.games.frp.tekumel	Empire of the Petal Throne FRPG by M. A. R. Barker.
alt.games.gb	The Galactic Bloodshed conquest game.
alt.games.lynx	The Atari Lynx.
alt.games.mk	Struggling in Mortal Kombat!
alt.games.mornington.cresent	You can't get there from here.
alt.games.mtrek	Multi-Trek, a multi-user Star Trek-like game.
alt.games.netrek.paradise	Discussion of the paradise version of netrek.
alt.games.sf2	The video game Street Fighter 2.
alt.games.torg	Gateway for TORG mailing list.

continues

Newsgroup	*Description*
alt.games.vga-planets	Discussion of Tim Wisseman's VGA Planets.
alt.games.video.classic	Video games from before the mid-1980s.
alt.games.whitewolf	Discussion of WhiteWolf's line of gothic/horror RPGs.
alt.games.xpilot	Discussion on all aspects of the X11 game Xpilot.
alt.gathering.rainbow	For discussing the annual Rainbow Gathering.
alt.geek	To fulfill an observed need.
alt.genealogy	Like soc.roots, only different.
alt.gonzalas.jaimi. escalante.hese.hese.hese	Thermodynamics. Really.
alt.good.morning	Would you like coffee with that?
alt.good.news	A place for some news that's good news.
alt.gopher	Discussion of the gopher information service.
alt.gothic	The gothic movement: things mournful and dark.
alt.gourmand	Recipes & cooking info. (Moderated)
alt.grad-student.tenured	Making a career of never getting a career.
alt.graphics.pixutils	Discussion of pixmap utilities.
alt.great-lakes	Discussions of the Great Lakes and adjacent places.
alt.guitar	You axed for it, you got it.
alt.guitar.bass	Bass guitars.
alt.guitar.tab	Discussions about guitar tablature music.

Newsgroup	Description
`alt.hackers`	Descriptions of projects currently under development. (Moderated)
`alt.hangover`	I am never drinking again.
`alt.hemp`	It's about knot-tying with rope. Knot!
`alt.hi.are.you.cute`	Are there a lot of pathetic people on the net or what?
`alt.hindu`	The Hindu religion. (Moderated)
`alt.history.living`	A forum for discussing the hobby of living history.
`alt.history.what-if`	What would the net have been like without this group?
`alt.homosexual`	Same as alt.sex.homosexual.
`alt.horror`	The horror genre.
`alt.horror.cthulhu`	Campus Crusade for Cthulhu, Ctulhu, Ctulu, and the rest.
`alt.horror.werewolves`	They were wolves, now they're something to be wary of.
`alt.hotrod`	High speed automobiles. (Moderated)
`alt.human-brain`	They're made of meat.
`alt.humor.best-of-usenet`	What the moderator thinks is funniest. (Moderated)
`alt.humor.best-of-usenet.d`	Why everyone else doesn't think it's funny.
`alt.hypertext`	Discussion of hypertext — uses, transport, etc.
`alt.hypnosis`	When you awaken, you will forget about this newsgroup.
`alt.illuminati`	See alt.cabal. Fnord.
`alt.image.medical`	Medical image exchange discussions.

continues

Newsgroup	*Description*
alt.india.progressive	Progressive politics in the Indian sub-continent. (Moderated)
alt.individualism	Philosophies where individual rights are paramount.
alt.infertility	Discussion of infertility causes and treatments.
alt.internet.access.wanted	"Oh. OK, how about just an MX record for now?"
alt.internet.services	Not available in the uucp world, even via email.
alt.internet.talk-radio	Carl Malamud's Internet Talk Radio program.
alt.irc	Internet Relay Chat material.
alt.irc.announce	Announcements about Internet Relay Chat (IRC). (Moderated)
alt.irc.hottub	Discussion of the IRC channel #hottub.
alt.irc.ircii	The IRC II client programme.
alt.irc.questions	How-to questions for IRC (International Relay Chat).
alt.japanese.text	Postings in Japanese; Japanese language software.
alt.journalism	Shop talk by journalists and journalism students.
alt.journalism.criticism	I write, therefore I'm biased.
alt.kalbo	Bald guys of the world, unite!
alt.ketchup	Whak* Whak* ...shake... Whak* Damn, all over my tie.
alt.kids-talk	A place for the pre-college set on the net.
alt.kill.the.whales	And fulfill the prophecy of Star Trek IV!
alt.lang.asm	Assembly languages of various flavors.

Newsgroup	Description
`alt.lang.basic`	The Language That Would Not Die.
`alt.law-enforcement`	No, ossifer, there's nothing illegal going on in alt.
`alt.lefthanders`	How gauche.
`alt.lemmings`	Rodents with a death wish.
`alt.life.afterlife`	The warm light at end of the tunnel is a locomotive.
`alt.life.sucks`	For the optimists among us.
`alt.locksmithing`	You locked your keys in *where?*
`alt.lucid-emacs.bug`	Bug reports about Lucid Emacs.
`alt.lucid-emacs.help`	Q&A and general discussion of Lucid Emacs.
`alt.lycra`	The WunderFabrik.
`alt.magic`	For discussion about stage magic.
`alt.magick`	For discussion about supernatural arts.
`alt.manga`	Like rec.arts.manga, only different.
`alt.mcdonalds`	Can I get fries with that?
`alt.med.cfs`	Chronic fatigue syndrome information.
`alt.meditation`	General discussion of meditation.
`alt.meditation.transcendental`	Contemplation of states beyond the teeth.
`alt.messianic`	Messianic traditions.
`alt.military.cadet`	Preparing for the coming apocalypse.
`alt.mindcontrol`	Are you sure those thoughts are really your own?
`alt.misanthropy`	Go away.
`alt.missing-kids`	Locating missing children.
`alt.motd`	The messages of the day.

continues

Newsgroup	Description
alt.motherjones	Mother Jones magazine.
alt.msdos.programmer	For the serious MS/DOS programmer (no forsale ads).
alt.mud	Like rec.games.mud, only different.
alt.music.alternative	For groups having 2 or less Platinum-selling albums.
alt.music.amy-grant	Discussion about Amy Grant and her music.
alt.music.bela-fleck	Bela and the Flecktones.
alt.music.billy-joel	Discussion of Billy Brinkley, er, Joel.
alt.music.blues-traveler	For "All fellow travelers."
alt.music.canada	Oh, Canada, eh?
alt.music.deep-purple	Discussions about Deep Purple and related artists.
alt.music.enya	Gaelic set to spacey music.
alt.music.filk	SF/fantasy related folk music.
alt.music.france	Continental music.
alt.music.hardcore	Could be porno set to music.
alt.music.james-taylor	JT!
alt.music.jewish	Jewish music.
alt.music.marillion	A progressive band. The Silmarillion is a book.
alt.music.nin	Nine Inch Nails.
alt.music.pat-mccurdy	Milwaukee's music at its finest.
alt.music.pearl-jam	The music of the alternative rock band Pearl Jam.
alt.music.peter-gabriel	Discussion of the music of Peter Gabriel.
alt.music.prince	So my Prince came. Make him go away.
alt.music.progressive	Yes, Marillion, Asia, King Crimson, etc.

Newsgroup	Description
`alt.music.queen`	He's dead, Jim.
`alt.music.rush`	For Rushheads.
`alt.music.ska`	Discussions of ska (skank) music, bands, and suchlike.
`alt.music.synthpop`	Depeche Mode, Erasure, Pet Shop Boys, and much more!
`alt.music.techno`	Bring on the bass!
`alt.music.tmbg`	They Might Be Giants.
`alt.music.u2`	Another group for the band U2. See also alt.fan.u2.
`alt.music.world`	Discussion of music from around the world.
`alt.my.head.hurts`	So don't do that.
`alt.mythology`	Zeus rules.
`alt.native`	People indigenous to an area before modern colonisation.
`alt.necromicon`	Big time death wish.
`alt.netgames.bolo`	Like rec.games.bolo, only different.
`alt.news-media`	Don't believe the hype.
`alt.news.macedonia`	News concerning Macedonia in the Balkan Region.
`alt.nick.sucks`	Like alt.life.sucks, only Nick's sucks worse.
`alt.non.sequitur`	Richard Nixon.
`alt.nuke.the.USA`	Last one out is a radioactive egg.
`alt.obituaries`	A place to note the passage of the noteworthy.
`alt.online-service`	Large commercial online services, and the Internet.
`alt.online-service.delphi`	Run! It's the Delphioids!
`alt.org.toastmasters`	Public speaking and Toastmasters International.

continues

Newsgroup	Description
alt.os.multics	30 years old and going strong.
alt.out-of-body	Out of Body Experiences.
alt.overlords	Omnipotent Overlords of the Omniverse. Inflated egos.
alt.pagan	Discussions about paganism & religion.
alt.pantyhose	Stockings are sexier.
alt.paranet.abduct	"They replaced Jim-Bob with a look-alike!"
alt.paranet.paranormal	"If it exists, how can supernatural be beyond natural?"
alt.paranet.psi	"How much pressure can you generate with your brain?"
alt.paranet.science	"Maybe if we dissect the psychic ..."
alt.paranet.skeptic	"I don't believe they turned you into a newt."
alt.paranet.ufo	"Heck, I guess naming it 'UFO' identifies it."
alt.paranormal	Phenomena which are not scientifically explicable.
alt.parents-teens	Parent-teenager relationships.
alt.party	Parties, celebration and general debauchery.
alt.pave.the.earth	Damn the environmentalists, full speed ahead!
alt.peeves	Discussion of peeves & related.
alt.personals	Do you really want to meet someone this way?
alt.personals.ads	Geek seeks Dweeb. Object: low-level interfacing.
alt.personals.bi	Personals by or seeking bisexuals.
alt.personals.bondage	Are you tied up this evening?

Newsgroup	Description
alt.personals.misc	Dweeb seeks Geek. Object: low-level interfacing.
alt.personals.poly	Hi there, do you multiprocess?
alt.personals.spanking	Oedipus gives this group a thumbs up.
alt.pets.rabbits	Coneys abound. See also alt.fan.john-palmer.
alt.philosophy.objectivism	A product of the Ayn Rand corporation.
alt.plastic.utensils.spork.spork.spork	Like alt.utensils.spork, only longer.
alt.politics.british	Politics and a real Queen, too.
alt.politics.clinton	Discussing Slick Willie & Co.
alt.politics.correct	A Neil Bush fan club.
alt.politics.datahighway	Electronic interstate infrastructure.
alt.politics.drinking-age	Regarding age restrictions for alcohol use.
alt.politics.economics	War == Poverty, & other discussions.
alt.politics.elections	All about the process of electing leaders.
alt.politics.greens	Green party politics & activities worldwide.
alt.politics.homosexuality	As the name implies.
alt.politics.libertarian	The libertarian ideology.
alt.politics.org.batf	Politics of the U.S. firearms (etc.) regulation agency.
alt.politics.org.misc	Political organizations.
alt.politics.perot	Discussion of the non-candidate.
alt.politics.radical-left	Who remained after the radicals left?

continues

Newsgroup	Description
`alt.politics.reform`	Political reform.
`alt.politics.sex`	Not a good idea to mix them, sez Marilyn & Profumo.
`alt.politics.socialism.trotsky`	Trotskyite socialism discussions.
`alt.politics.usa.constitution`	U.S. Constitutional politics.
`alt.politics.usa.misc`	Miscellaneous USA politics.
`alt.politics.usa.republican`	Discussions of the USA Republican Party.
`alt.polyamory`	For those who maintain multiple love relationships.
`alt.postmodern`	Postmodernism, semiotics, deconstruction, and the like.
`alt.president.clinton`	Will the CIA undermine his efforts?
`alt.prisons`	Can I get an alt.* feed in the slammer?
`alt.privacy`	Privacy issues in cyberspace.
`alt.prose`	Postings of original writings, fictional & otherwise.
`alt.psychoactives`	Better living through chemistry.
`alt.psychology.help`	An alt.support group away from home.
`alt.psychology.personality`	Personality taxonomy, such as Myers-Briggs.
`alt.pub-ban.homolka`	About the publication ban on the Karla Homolka trial.
`alt.pub.coffeehouse.amethyst`	Realistic place to meet and chat with friends.
`alt.pub.dragons-inn`	Fantasy virtual reality pub similar to alt.callahans.
`alt.pud`	"Discussion of the TFiLE PuD!@#@#!@$!" Whatever.

Newsgroup	Description
alt.punk	Burning them keeps insects away.
alt.ql.creative	The "Quantum Leap" tv show.
alt.quotations	Quotations, quips, .sig lines, witticisms, et al.
alt.radio.digital	News & Talk about Digital Audio Broadcasting (DAB).
alt.radio.networks.npr	U.S. National Public Radio: shows, stories, hosts, etc.
alt.radio.pirate	Hide the gear, here comes the magic station-wagons.
alt.radio.scanner	Discussion of scanning radio receivers.
alt.rap	For fans of rap music.
alt.rave	Techno-culture: music, dancing, drugs, dancing, etc.
alt.recovery	For people in recovery programs (e.g., AA, ACA, GA).
alt.recovery.codependency	Mutually destructive relationships.
alt.religion.all-worlds	Grokking the Church of All Worlds from Heinlein's book.
alt.religion.christian	Unmoderated forum for discussing Christianity.
alt.religion.eckankar	Eckankar, the religion of the Light and Sound of God.
alt.religion.emacs	Emacs. Umacs. We all macs.
alt.religion.kibology	He's Fred, Jim.
alt.religion.monica	Discussion about net-venus Monica and her works.
alt.religion.scientology	He's dead, Jim.
alt.religion.sexuality	The politics of sexuality and religion.

continues

Newsgroup	Description
alt.revenge	Two wrongs trying to make a right.
alt.revisionism	"It CAN'T be that way 'cause here's the FACTS".
alt.revolution.counter	Discussions of counter-revolutionary issues.
alt.rhode_island	A little state with apparently world-wide interest.
alt.rock-n-roll	Counterpart to alt.sex and alt.drugs.
alt.rock-n-roll.acdc	Dirty deeds done dirt cheap.
alt.rock-n-roll.aerosmith	Lead singer looks like an ugly lady.
alt.rock-n-roll.classic	Classic rock, both the music and its marketing.
alt.rock-n-roll.hard	Music where stance is everything.
alt.rock-n-roll.metal	For the headbangers on the net.
alt.rock-n-roll.metal.death	"Death metal" and newgroup overkill.
alt.rock-n-roll.metal.gnr	"Axl Rose" is an anagram for "Oral Sex".
alt.rock-n-roll.metal.heavy	Non-sissyboy metal bands.
alt.rock-n-roll.metal.ironmaiden	Sonic torture methods.
alt.rock-n-roll.metal.metallica	Sort of like Formica with more hair.
alt.rock-n-roll.metal.progressive	Slayer teams up with Tom Cora.
alt.rock-n-roll.oldies	Discussion of rock and roll music from 1950-1970.
alt.rock-n-roll.stones	Gathering plenty of moss by now.
alt.romance	Discussion about the romantic side of love.
alt.romance.chat	Talk about no sex.
alt.rush-limbaugh	Fans of the conservative activist radio announcer.

Newsgroup	Description
alt.satanism	Not such a bad dude once you get to know him.
alt.satannet	Don't piss me off.
alt.satannet.barney	Discussion of that big, purple, plush agent of Satan.
alt.satellite.tv.europe	All about European satellite tv.
alt.save.the.earth	Environmentalist causes.
alt.sb.programmer	Programming the Sound Blaster PC sound card.
alt.sci.physics. new-theories	Scientific theories you won't find in journals.
alt.sci.planetary	Studies in planetary science.
alt.sci.sociology	People are really interesting when you watch them.
alt.scooter	Motor scooters (Vespas, Lambrettas, etc.).
alt.security	Security issues on computer systems.
alt.security.index	Pointers to good stuff in alt.security. (Moderated)
alt.security.pgp	The Pretty Good Privacy package.
alt.sega.genesis	Another addiction.
alt.self-improve	Self-improvement in less than 14 characters.
alt.sewing	A group that is not as it seams.
alt.sex	Postings of a prurient nature.
alt.sex.bestiality	Happiness is a warm puppy.
alt.sex.bestiality.barney	For people with big, purple newt fetishes.
alt.sex.bondage	Tie me, whip me, make me read the net!
alt.sex.exhibitionism	So you want to be a star.

continues

Newsgroup	Description
alt.sex.fetish.diapers	They're dry and secure all day, too.
alt.sex.fetish.fa	Supposedly for fans of fat, not the 4th diatonic tone.
alt.sex.fetish.fashion	Rubber, leather, chains, and other fetish clothing.
alt.sex.fetish.feet	Kiss them. Now.
alt.sex.fetish.hair	Hair, hair, everywhere. Palms even.
alt.sex.fetish.orientals	The mysteries of Asia are a potent lure.
alt.sex.fetish.watersports	They don't mean hottub polo.
alt.sex.masturbation	Where one's SO is oneself.
alt.sex.motss	Jesse Helms would not subscribe to this group.
alt.sex.movies	Discussing the ins and outs of certain movies.
alt.sex.pictures	Gigabytes of copyright violations.
alt.sex.pictures.female	Copyright violations featuring mostly females.
alt.sex.services	The oldest profession.
alt.sex.spanking	Bondage for beginners.
alt.sex.stories	For those who need it *now*.
alt.sex.stories.d	For those who talk about needing it *now*.
alt.sex.strip-clubs	Discussion of strip clubs, exotic dancers, etc.
alt.sex.wanted	Requests for erotica, either literary or in the flesh.
alt.sex.wizards	Questions for only true sex wizards.
alt.sex.zoophilia	Having sex with animals and respecting them too. (Moderated)
alt.sexual.abuse.recovery	Helping others deal with traumatic experiences.

Newsgroup	*Description*
`alt.sexy.bald.captains`	More Stardrek.
`alt.shenanigans`	Practical jokes, pranks, randomness, etc.
`alt.showbiz.gossip`	A misguided attempt to centralize gossip.
`alt.shut.the.hell.up.geek`	Group for Usenet motto.
`alt.silly-group.im-matt`	I'm Dave, but you don't see me making a group about it.
`alt.silly-group.lampreys`	Jawless parasitical fish.
`alt.skate-board`	Discussion of all apsects of skate-boarding.
`alt.skinheads`	The skinhead culture/anti-culture.
`alt.skunks`	Enthusiasts of skunks and other mustelidae.
`alt.slack`	Posting relating to the Church of the Subgenius.
`alt.smokers`	Puffing on tobacco.
`alt.snail-mail`	Mail sent on paper. Some people still do that.
`alt.snowmobiles`	For bikers who don't like two wheels in snow and ice.
`alt.society.anarchy`	Societies without rulers.
`alt.society.ati`	The Activist Times Digest. (Moderated)
`alt.society.civil-liberties`	Individual rights.
`alt.society.civil-liberty`	Same as alt.society.civil-liberties.
`alt.society.conservatism`	Social, cultural, and political conservatism.
`alt.society.generation-x`	Lifestyles of those born 1960-early-1970s.
`alt.soft-sys.corel.draw`	The Corel Draw graphics package.

continues

Newsgroup	Description
`alt.soulmates`	Richard Bach and his herculean odds.
`alt.sources`	Alternative source code, unmoderated. Caveat Emptor.
`alt.sources.amiga`	Source code for the Amiga.
`alt.sources.index`	Pointers to source code in alt.sources.*. (Moderated)
`alt.sources.mac`	Source file newsgroup for the Apple Macintosh computers.
`alt.sources.wanted`	Requests for source code.
`alt.spam`	What is that stuff that doth jiggle in the breeze?
`alt.spleen`	Venting as a biological function.
`alt.sport.bowling`	In the gutter again.
`alt.sport.darts`	Look what you've done to the wall!
`alt.sport.foosball`	Table soccer and dizzy little men.
`alt.sport.lasertag`	Indoor splatball with infrared lasers.
`alt.sport.officiating`	Problems related to officiating athletic contests.
`alt.sport.paintball`	Splat, you're it.
`alt.sport.pool`	Knock your balls into your pockets for fun.
`alt.sport.racquetball`	All aspects of indoor racquetball and related sports.
`alt.sport.squash`	With the proper technique, vegetables can go very fast.
`alt.sports.baseball.` `atlanta-braves`	Atlanta Braves major league baseball.
`alt.sports.baseball.` `balt-orioles`	Baltimore Orioles major league baseball.
`alt.sports.baseball.` `chicago-cubs`	Chicago Cubs major league baseball.

Newsgroup	Description
`alt.sports.baseball.` `cinci-reds`	Cincinnati Reds major league baseball.
`alt.sports.baseball.` `houston-astros`	Houston Astros major league baseball.
`alt.sports.baseball.` `la-dodgers`	Los Angeles Dodgers baseball talk.
`alt.sports.baseball.` `montreal-expos`	Montreal Expos major league baseball.
`alt.sports.baseball.ny-mets`	New York Mets baseball talk.
`alt.sports.baseball.` `ny-yankees`	New York Yankees baseball talk.
`alt.sports.baseball.` `oakland-as`	Oakland A's major league baseball.
`alt.sports.baseball.` `phila-phillies`	Philadelphia Phillies baseball talk.
`alt.sports.baseball.` `sf-giants`	San Francisco Giants baseball talk.
`alt.sports.baseball.` `tor-bluejays`	Toronto Blue Jays baseball talk
`alt.sports.basketball.` `ivy.penn`	Basketball at Penn State.
`alt.sports.basketball.` `nba.nj-nets`	New Jersey Nets NBA basketball.
`alt.sports.football.` `mn-vikings`	Minnesota Vikings football talk.
`alt.sports.football.pro.` `buffalo-bills`	Buffalo Bills NFL football talk.
`alt.sports.football.` `pro.car-panthers`	Carolina Panthers NFL football talk.
`alt.sports.football.pro.` `dallas-cowboys`	Dallas Cowboys NFL football talk.
`alt.sports.football.pro.` `gb-packers`	Green Bay Packers NFL football talk.

continues

Newsgroup	Description
`alt.sports.football.pro.miami-dolphins`	Miami Dolphins NFL football talk.
`alt.sports.football.pro.ne-patriots`	New England Patriots NFL football talk.
`alt.sports.football.pro.ny-giants`	New York Giants NFL football.
`alt.sports.football.pro.sea-seahawks`	Seattle Seahawks NFL football.
`alt.sports.football.pro.sf-49ers`	San Francisco 49ers NFL football talk.
`alt.sports.football.pro.wash-redskins`	Washington Redskins football talk.
`alt.sports.hockey.nhl.buffalo-sabres`	Buffalo Sabres NHL hockey talk
`alt.sports.hockey.nhl.chi-blackhawks`	Chicago Black Hawks NHL hockey talk.
`alt.sports.hockey.nhl.hford-whalers`	Hartford Whalers NHL hockey talk.
`alt.sports.hockey.nhl.la-kings`	For discussion of the Los Angeles Kings.
`alt.sports.hockey.nhl.mtl-canadiens`	Montreal Canadiens NHL hockey talk.
`alt.sports.hockey.nhl.nj-devils`	New Jersey Devils NHL hockey talk.
`alt.sports.hockey.nhl.ny-rangers`	New York Rangers NHL hockey talk.
`alt.sports.hockey.nhl.tor-mapleleafs`	Toronto Maple Leafs NHL hockey talk.
`alt.sports.hockey.nhl.vanc-canucks`	Vancouver Canucks NHL hockey talk.
`alt.sports.hockey.nhl.wash-capitals`	Washington Capitals NHL hockey talk.
`alt.sports.hockey.nhl.winnipeg-jets`	Winnipeg Jets NHL Hockey talk.

Newsgroup	*Description*
alt.stagecraft	Technical theatre issues.
alt.starfleet.rpg	Starfleet role playing stories.
alt.startrek.creative	Stories and parodies related to Star Trek.
alt.startrek.klingon	Ack! What is that thing on your head?!
alt.stupidity	Discussion about stupid newsgroups.
alt.suicide.holiday	Talk of why suicides increase at holidays.
alt.super.nes	Like rec.games.video.nintendo, only different.
alt.supermodels	Discussing famous & beautiful models.
alt.support	Dealing with emotional situations & experiences.
alt.support.arthritis	Helping people with stiff joints.
alt.support.attn-deficit	Info/Discus of Attention Deficit Disorder
alt.support.big-folks	Sizeism can be as awful as sexism or racism.
alt.support.cancer	Emotional aid for people with cancer.
alt.support.diet	Seeking enlightenment through weight loss.
alt.support.eating-disord	People over the edge about weight loss.
alt.support.mult-sclerosis	Living with multiple sclerosis.
alt.support.obesity	Support/resources to treat obesity. (Moderated)
alt.support.tinnitus	Coping with ringing ears and other head noises.

continues

Newsgroup	Description
`alt.surfing`	Riding the ocean waves.
`alt.surrealism`	Surrealist ideologies and their influences.
`alt.sustainable.agriculture`	Such as the Mekong delta before Agent Orange.
`alt.swedish.chef.bork.bork.bork`	The beginning of the end.
`alt.sys.amiga.demos`	Code and talk to show off the Amiga.
`alt.sys.amiga.uucp`	AmigaUUCP.
`alt.sys.amiga.uucp.patches`	Patches to the AmigaUUCP system.
`alt.sys.intergraph`	Support for Intergraph machines.
`alt.sys.pc-clone.gateway2000`	A PC clone vendor.
`alt.sys.pdp8`	A great old machine.
`alt.sys.perq`	PERQ graphics workstations.
`alt.sys.sun`	Technical discussion of Sun Microsystems products.
`alt.taiwan.republic`	Like soc.culture.taiwan, only different.
`alt.tasteless`	Truly disgusting.
`alt.tasteless.jokes`	Sometimes insulting rather than disgusting or humorous.
`alt.test`	Alternative subnetwork testing.
`alt.test.test`	More from the people who brought you "BBS systems."
`alt.thrash`	Thrashlife.
`alt.timewasters`	A pretty good summary of making the list of alt groups.
`alt.toolkits.xview`	The X windows XView toolkit.
`alt.toys.hi-tech`	Optimus Prime is my hero.
`alt.toys.lego`	Snap 'em together.

Newsgroup	Description
alt.toys.transformers	From robots to vehicles and back again.
alt.transgendered	Boys will be girls, and vice-versa.
alt.travel.road-trip	Ever go to Montreal for pizza—from Albany?
alt.true-crime	Criminal acts around the world.
alt.tv.animaniacs	Steven Spielberg's Animaniacs!
alt.tv.babylon-5	Casablanca in space.
alt.tv.barney	He's everywhere. Now appearing in several alt groups.
alt.tv.beakmans-world	Some sort of science and comedy show.
alt.tv.beavis-n-butthead	Uh huh huh huh uh uh huh uh huh.
alt.tv.bh90210	Fans of "Beverly Hills 90210" TV show.
alt.tv.dinosaurs.barney.die.die.die	Squish the saccharine newt.
alt.tv.eek-the-cat	Fans of the television show "Eek The Cat"
alt.tv.game-shows	Just look at these wonderful prizes.
alt.tv.infomercials	30 minutes to sell you a vacuum hair cutting system.
alt.tv.kids-in-hall	The Kids in the Hall comedy skits.
alt.tv.la-law	For the folks out in la-law land.
alt.tv.mash	Nothing like a good comedy about war and dying.
alt.tv.max-headroom	Blipverts will kill ya.
alt.tv.melrose-place	Cat fights and sleaziness, Wednesdays on FOX.
alt.tv.mst3k	Hey, you robots! Down in front!
alt.tv.muppets	Miss Piggy on the tube.
alt.tv.mwc	"Married... With Children".

continues

Newsgroup	*Description*
alt.tv.northern-exp	For the TV show with moss growing on it.
alt.tv.prisoner	The Prisoner television series from years ago.
alt.tv.red-dwarf	The British sci-fi/comedy show.
alt.tv.ren-n-stimpy	Some change from Lassie, eh?
alt.tv.rockford-files	But he won't do windows.
alt.tv.saved-bell	Saved by the Bell, a sitcom for teens.
alt.tv.seinfeld	A funny guy.
alt.tv.simpsons	Don't have a cow, man!
alt.tv.simpsons.itchy-scratchy	The alter egos of Ren and Stimpy.
alt.tv.snl	Saturday Night Live, older but not better.
alt.tv.talkshows.late	Discussion of late night talk shows
alt.tv.taz-mania	What a devil of a newsgroup.
alt.tv.time-traxx	Back from the future in Time Traxx.
alt.tv.tiny-toon	Discussion about the "Tiny Toon Adventures" show.
alt.tv.tiny-toon.fandom	Apparently one fan group could not bind them all.
alt.tv.twin-peaks	Discussion about the popular (and unusual) TV show.
alt.tv.x-files	Extra-terrestrial coverup conspiracies.
alt.usage.english	English grammar, word usages, and related topics.
alt.usage.german	Questions and answers about the German language.
alt.usenet.kooks	I have a theory about why we have such crazy theories.
alt.usenet.offline-reader	Getting your fix offline.

Newsgroup	Description
`alt.utensils.spork`	People fascinated by dual purpose eating utensils.
`alt.uu.comp.os.linux.questions`	Usenet University helps with LINUX.
`alt.uu.future`	Does Usenet University have a viable future?
`alt.uu.lang.russian.misc`	Learning Russian from Usenet University.
`alt.vampyres`	Discussion of vampires and related writings, films, etc.
`alt.video.laserdisc`	LD players and selections available for them.
`alt.visa.us`	Discussion/information on visas pertaining to US.
`alt.war`	Not just collateral damage.
`alt.war.civil.usa`	Discussion of the U.S. Civil War (1861-1865).
`alt.war.vietnam`	Discussion of all aspects of the Vietnam War.
`alt.wedding`	Til death or our lawyers do us part.
`alt.wesley.crusher.die.die.die`	Like alt.ensign.wesley.die.die.die, only not.
`alt.whine`	Why me?
`alt.winsock`	Windows Sockets.
`alt.wired`	Wired Magazine.
`alt.wolves`	Discussing wolves & wolf-mix dogs.
`alt.zines`	Small magazines, mostly noncommercial.
`alt.znet.aeo`	Atari Explorer Online magazine. (Moderated)
`alt.znet.pc`	Z*NET International ASCII Magazines (Weekly). (Moderated)

You should make submissions to the moderated alt groups to the addresses listed in the companion posting of moderator addresses.

You can join the "alt subnet" by finding a site in your area that carries the groups. Either send mail to the administrators of the sites you connect to or post something to a local "general" or "wanted" newsgroup for your area. If no sites nearby are getting them, you can get them from uunet or psi.

bit

The bit collection of newsgroups are distributed by a collection of sites that choose to carry them. The bit newsgroups are redistributions of the more popular BitNet LISTSERV mailing lists. Contact Jim McIntosh at jim@american.edu for more information. Following is a list of the current bit newsgroups:

Newsgroup	*Description*
bit.admin	bit.* Newgroups Discussions.
bit.general	Discussions Relating to BitNet/ Usenet.
bit.lang.neder-l	Dutch Language and Literature List. (Moderated)
bit.listserv.3com-l	3Com Products Discussion List.
bit.listserv.9370-l	IBM 9370 and VM/IS specific topics List.
bit.listserv.ada-law	ADA Law Discussions.
bit.listserv.advanc-l	Geac Advanced Integrated Library System Users.
bit.listserv.advise-l	User Services List.
bit.listserv.aix-l	IBM AIX Discussion List.
bit.listserv.allmusic	Discussions on all forms of Music.
bit.listserv.appc-l	APPC Discussion List.
bit.listserv.apple2-l	Apple II List.
bit.listserv.applicat	Applications under BITNET.

Newsgroup	Description
`bit.listserv.arie-l`	RLG Ariel Document Transmission Group.
`bit.listserv.ashe-l`	Higher Ed Policy and Research.
`bit.listserv.asm370`	IBM 370 Assembly Programming Discussions.
`bit.listserv.autism`	Autism and Developmental Disabilities List.
`bit.listserv.autocat`	Library Cataloging and Authorities List.
`bit.listserv.axslib-l`	Library Access for People with Disabilities.
`bit.listserv.banyan-l`	Banyan Vines Network Software Discussions.
`bit.listserv.big-lan`	Campus-Size LAN Discussion Group. (Moderated)
`bit.listserv.billing`	Chargeback of computer resources.
`bit.listserv.biosph-l`	Biosphere, ecology, Discussion List.
`bit.listserv.bitnews`	BITNET News.
`bit.listserv.blindnws`	Blindness Issues and Discussions. (Moderated)
`bit.listserv.buslib-l`	Business Libraries List.
`bit.listserv.c+health`	Computers and Health Discussion List.
`bit.listserv.c18-l`	18th Century Interdisciplinary Discussion.
`bit.listserv.c370-l`	C/370 Discussion List.
`bit.listserv.candle-l`	Candle Products Discussion List.
`bit.listserv.catala`	Catalan Discussion List.
`bit.listserv.catholic`	Free Catholics Mailing List.
`bit.listserv.cdromlan`	CD-ROM on Local Area Networks.
`bit.listserv.cfs.newsletter`	Chronic Fatigue Syndrome Newsletter. (Moderated)

continues

Newsgroup	Description
bit.listserv.christia	Practical Christian Life. (Moderated)
bit.listserv.cics-l	CICS Discussion List.
bit.listserv.cinema-l	Discussions on all forms of Cinema.
bit.listserv.circplus	Circulation Reserve and Related Library Issues.
bit.listserv.cmspip-l	VM/SP CMS Pipelines Discussion List.
bit.listserv.coco	Tandy Color Computer List.
bit.listserv.csg-l	Control System Group Network.
bit.listserv.cumrec-l	CUMREC-L Administrative computer use. (Moderated)
bit.listserv.cw-email	Campus-Wide E-mail Discussion List.
bit.listserv.cwis-l	Campus-Wide Information Systems.
bit.listserv.cyber-l	CDC Computer Discussion.
bit.listserv.dasig	Database Administration.
bit.listserv.db2-l	DB2 Database Discussion List.
bit.listserv.dbase-l	Discussion on the use of the dBase IV.
bit.listserv.deaf-l	Deaf List.
bit.listserv.decnews	Digital Equipment Corporation News List.
bit.listserv.dectei-l	DECUS Education Software Library Discussions.
bit.listserv.devel-l	Technology Transfer in International Development.
bit.listserv.disarm-l	Disarmament Discussion List.
bit.listserv.domain-l	Domains Discussion Group.
bit.listserv.down-syn	Downs Syndrome Discussion Group.

Newsgroup	Description
bit.listserv.dsshe-l	Disabled Student Services in Higher Education.
bit.listserv.earntech	EARN Technical Group.
bit.listserv.easi	Computer Access for People with Disabilities.
bit.listserv.edi-l	Electronic Data Interchange Issues.
bit.listserv.edtech	EDTECH - Educational Technology. (Moderated)
bit.listserv.edusig-l	EDUSIG Discussions.
bit.listserv.emusic-l	Electronic Music Discussion List.
bit.listserv.endnote	Bibsoft Endnote Discussions.
bit.listserv.envbeh-l	Forum on Environment and Human Behavior.
bit.listserv.erl-l	Educational Research List.
bit.listserv.ethics-l	Discussion of Ethics in Computing.
bit.listserv.ethology	Ethology List.
bit.listserv.euearn-l	Computers in Eastern Europe.
bit.listserv.film-l	Film making and reviews List.
bit.listserv.fnord-l	New Ways of Thinking List.
bit.listserv.frac-l	FRACTAL Discussion List.
bit.listserv.free-l	Fathers Rights and Equality Discussion List.
bit.listserv.games-l	Computer Games List.
bit.listserv.gaynet	GayNet Discussion List. (Moderated)
bit.listserv.gddm-l	The GDDM Discussion List.
bit.listserv.geodesic	List for the Discussion of Buckminster Fuller.
bit.listserv.geograph	Geography List.
bit.listserv.gguide	BITNIC GGUIDE List.
bit.listserv.gophern	Lets go Gopherin.

continues

Newsgroup	Description
bit.listserv.govdoc-l	Discussion of Government Document Issues.
bit.listserv.graph-ti	Discussion of the TI-8x Series Calculators.
bit.listserv.gutnberg	GUTNBERG Discussion List. (Moderated)
bit.listserv.hellas	The Hellenic Discussion List. (Moderated)
bit.listserv.help-net	Help on BitNet and the Internet.
bit.listserv.hindu-d	Hindu Digest. (Moderated)
bit.listserv.history	History List.
bit.listserv.hytel-l	HYTELNET Discussions. (Moderated)
bit.listserv.i-amiga	Info-Amiga List.
bit.listserv.ibm-hesc	IBM Higher Education Consortium.
bit.listserv.ibm-main	IBM Mainframe Discussion List.
bit.listserv.ibm-nets	BITNIC IBM-NETS List.
bit.listserv.ibm7171	Protocol Converter List.
bit.listserv.ibmtcp-l	IBM TCP/IP List.
bit.listserv.idms-l	CA-IDMS Discussions.
bit.listserv.india-d	India Interest Group. (Moderated)
bit.listserv.ingrafx	Information Graphics.
bit.listserv.innopac	Innovative Interfaces Online Public Access.
bit.listserv.ioob-l	Industrial Psychology.
bit.listserv.ipct-l	Interpersonal Computing and Technology List. (Moderated)
bit.listserv.isn	ISN Data Switch Technical Discussion Group.
bit.listserv.jes2-l	JES2 Discussion group.
bit.listserv.jnet-l	BITNIC JNET-L List.

Newsgroup	Description
bit.listserv.l-hcap	Handicap List. (Moderated)
bit.listserv.l-vmctr	VMCENTER Components Discussion List.
bit.listserv.lawsch-l	Law School Discussion List.
bit.listserv.liaison	BITNIC LIAISON.
bit.listserv.libref-l	Library Reference Issues. (Moderated)
bit.listserv.libres	Library and Information Science Research. (Moderated)
bit.listserv.license	Software Licensing List.
bit.listserv.linkfail	Link failure announcements.
bit.listserv.lis-l	Library and Information Science Students.
bit.listserv.literary	Discussions about Literature.
bit.listserv.lstsrv-l	Forum on LISTSERV.
bit.listserv.mail-l	BITNIC MAIL-L List.
bit.listserv.mailbook	MAIL/MAILBOOK subscription List.
bit.listserv.mba-l	MBA Student curriculum Discussion.
bit.listserv.mbu-l	Megabyte University - Computers and Writing.
bit.listserv.mdphd-l	Dual Degree Programs Discussion List.
bit.listserv.medforum	Medical Student Discussions. (Moderated)
bit.listserv.medlib-l	Medical Libraries Discussion List.
bit.listserv.mednews	Health Info-Com Network Newsletter. (Moderated)
bit.listserv.mideur-l	Middle Europe Discussion List.
bit.listserv.mla-l	Music Library Association.

continues

Newsgroup	Description
bit.listserv.muslims	Islamic Information and News Network. (Moderated)
bit.listserv.netnws-l	NETNWS-L Netnews List.
bit.listserv.nettrain	Network Trainers List.
bit.listserv.new-list	NEW-LIST - New List Announcements. (Moderated)
bit.listserv.next-l	NeXT Computer List.
bit.listserv.nodmgt-l	Node Management.
bit.listserv.notabene	Nota Bene List.
bit.listserv.notis-l	NOTIS/DOBIS Discussion group List.
bit.listserv.novell	Novell LAN Interest Group.
bit.listserv.omrscan	OMR Scanner Discussion.
bit.listserv.os2-l	OS/2 Discussion.
bit.listserv.ozone	OZONE Discussion List.
bit.listserv.pacs-l	Public-Access Computer System Forum. (Moderated)
bit.listserv.page-l	IBM 3812/3820 Tips and Problems Discussion List.
bit.listserv.pagemakr	PageMaker for Desktop Publishers.
bit.listserv.pakistan	Pakistan News Service. (Moderated) (Moderated)
bit.listserv.physhare	K-12 Physics List.
bit.listserv.pmail	Pegasus Mail Discussions.
bit.listserv.pmdf-l	PMDF Distribution List.
bit.listserv.pns-l	Pakistan News Service Discussions. (Moderated)
bit.listserv.politics	Forum for the Discussion of Politics.
bit.listserv.postcard	Postcard Collectors Discussion Group.
bit.listserv.power-l	POWER-L IBM RS/6000 POWER Family.

Newsgroup	Description
`bit.listserv.powerh-l`	PowerHouse Discussion List.
`bit.listserv.psycgrad`	Psychology Grad Student Discussions.
`bit.listserv.qualrs-l`	Qualitative Research of the Human Sciences.
`bit.listserv.relusr-l`	Relay Users Forum.
`bit.listserv.rra-l`	Romance Readers Anonymous. (Moderated)
`bit.listserv.rscs-l`	VM/RSCS Mailing List.
`bit.listserv.rscsmods`	The RSCS modifications List.
`bit.listserv.s-comput`	SuperComputers List.
`bit.listserv.script-l`	IBM vs. Waterloo SCRIPT Discussion Group.
`bit.listserv.scuba-l`	Scuba diving Discussion List.
`bit.listserv.seasia-l`	Southeast Asia Discussion List.
`bit.listserv.seds-l`	Interchapter SEDS Communications.
`bit.listserv.sfs-l`	VM Shared File System Discussion List.
`bit.listserv.sganet`	Student Government Global Mail Network.
`bit.listserv.simula`	The SIMULA Language List.
`bit.listserv.slart-l`	SLA Research and Teaching.
`bit.listserv.slovak-l`	Slovak Discussion List.
`bit.listserv.snamgt-l`	SNA Network Management Discussion.
`bit.listserv.sos-data`	Social Science Data List.
`bit.listserv.spires-l`	SPIRES Conference List.
`bit.listserv.sportpsy`	Exercise and Sports Psychology.
`bit.listserv.sqlinfo`	Forum for SQL/DS and Related Topics.

continues

Newsgroup	Description
bit.listserv.tbi-support	St. Johns Traumatic Brain Injury Support List.
bit.listserv.tech-l	BITNIC TECH-L List.
bit.listserv.techwr-l	Technical Writing List.
bit.listserv.tecmat-l	Technology in Secondary Math.
bit.listserv.test	Test Newsgroup.
bit.listserv.tex-l	The TeXnical topics List.
bit.listserv.tn3270-l	tn3270 protocol Discussion List.
bit.listserv.toolb-l	Asymetrix Toolbook List.
bit.listserv.trans-l	BITNIC TRANS-L List.
bit.listserv.transplant	Transplant Recipients List.
bit.listserv.travel-l	Tourism Discussions.
bit.listserv.tsorexx	REXX for TSO List.
bit.listserv.ucp-l	University Computing Project Mailing List.
bit.listserv.ug-l	Usage Guidelines.
bit.listserv.uigis-l	User Interface for Geographical Info Systems.
bit.listserv.urep-l	UREP-L Mailing List.
bit.listserv.usrdir-l	User Directory List.
bit.listserv.uus-l	Unitarian-Universalist List.
bit.listserv.valert-l	Virus Alert List. (Moderated)
bit.listserv.vfort-l	VS-Fortran Discussion List.
bit.listserv.vm-util	VM Utilities Discussion List.
bit.listserv.vmesa-l	VM/ESA Mailing List.
bit.listserv.vmslsv-l	VAX/VMS LISTSERV Discussion List.
bit.listserv.vmxa-l	VM/XA Discussion List.
bit.listserv.vnews-l	VNEWS Discussion List.
bit.listserv.vpiej-l	Electronic Publishing Discussion List.

Newsgroup	Description
`bit.listserv.vse-l`	VSE/ESA Discussions.
`bit.listserv.wac-l`	Writing Across the Curriculum.
`bit.listserv.win3-l`	Microsoft Windows Version 3 Forum.
`bit.listserv.words-l`	English Language Discussion Group.
`bit.listserv.wpcorp-l`	WordPerfect Corporation Products Discussions.
`bit.listserv.wpwin-l`	WordPerfect for Windows.
`bit.listserv.wx-talk`	Weather Issues Discussions.
`bit.listserv.x400-l`	x.400 Protocol List.
`bit.listserv.xedit-l`	VM System Editor List.
`bit.listserv.xerox-l`	The Xerox Discussion List.
`bit.listserv.xmailer`	Crosswell Mailer.
`bit.listserv.xtropy-l`	Extopian List.
`bit.mailserv.word-mac`	Word Processing on the Macintosh.
`bit.mailserv.word-pc`	Word Processing on the IBM PC.
`bit.org.peace-corps`	International Volunteers Discussion Group.
`bit.software.international`	International Software List. (Moderated)
`bit.tech.africana`	Information Technology and Africa.

ClariNet

The ClariNet hierarchy consists of newsgroups gatewayed from commercial news services and other "official" sources. A feed of the ClariNet groups requires payment of a fee and execution of a license. You can obtain more information by sending mail to `info@clarinet.com`.

Newsgroup	Description
clari.biz.commodity	Commodity news and price reports. (Moderated)
clari.biz.courts	Lawsuits and business related legal matters. (Moderated)
clari.biz.economy	Economic news and indicators. (Moderated)
clari.biz.economy.world	Economy stories for non-US countries. (Moderated)
clari.biz.features	Business feature stories. (Moderated)
clari.biz.finance	Finance, currency, corporate finance. (Moderated)
clari.biz.finance.earnings	Earnings & dividend reports. (Moderated)
clari.biz.finance.personal	Personal investing & finance. (Moderated)
clari.biz.finance.services	Banks and financial industries. (Moderated)
clari.biz.invest	News for investors. (Moderated)
clari.biz.labor	Strikes, unions and labor relations. (Moderated)
clari.biz.market	General stock market news. (Moderated)
clari.biz.market.amex	American Stock Exchange reports & news. (Moderated)
clari.biz.market.dow	Dow Jones NYSE reports. (Moderated)
clari.biz.market.ny	NYSE reports. (Moderated)
clari.biz.market.otc	NASDAQ reports. (Moderated)
clari.biz.market.report	General market reports, S&P, etc. (Moderated)
clari.biz.mergers	Mergers and acquisitions. (Moderated)

Newsgroup	*Description*
clari.biz.misc	Other business news. (Moderated)
clari.biz.products	Important new products & services. (Moderated)
clari.biz.top	Top business news. (Moderated)
clari.biz.urgent	Breaking business news. (Moderated)
clari.canada.biz	Canadian Business Summaries. (Moderated)
clari.canada.features	Alamanac, Ottawa Special, Arts. (Moderated)
clari.canada.general	Short items on Canadian News stories. (Moderated)
clari.canada.gov	Government related news (all levels). (Moderated)
clari.canada.law	Crimes, the courts and the law. (Moderated)
clari.canada.newscast	Regular newscast for Canadians. (Moderated)
clari.canada.politics	Political and election items. (Moderated)
clari.canada.trouble	Mishaps, accidents, and serious problems. (Moderated)
clari.feature.dave_barry	Columns of humourist Dave Barry. (Moderated)
clari.feature.dilbert	The daily comic strip "Dilbert" (MIME/uuencoded GIF). (Moderated)
clari.feature.mike_royko	Chicago Opinion Columnist Mike Royko. (Moderated)
clari.feature.miss_manners	Judith Martin's Humourous Etiquette Advice. (Moderated)
clari.local.alberta.briefs	Local news Briefs. (Moderated)
clari.local.arizona	Local news. (Moderated)

continues

Newsgroup	Description
clari.local.arizona.briefs	Local news Briefs. (Moderated)
clari.local.bc.briefs	Local news Briefs. (Moderated)
clari.local.california	Local news. (Moderated)
clari.local.california. briefs	Local news Briefs. (Moderated)
clari.local.chicago	Local news. (Moderated)
clari.local.chicago.briefs	Local news Briefs. (Moderated)
clari.local.florida	Local news. (Moderated)
clari.local.florida.briefs	Local news Briefs. (Moderated)
clari.local.georgia	Local news. (Moderated)
clari.local.georgia.briefs	Local news Briefs. (Moderated)
clari.local.headlines	Various local headline summaries. (Moderated)
clari.local.illinois	Local news. (Moderated)
clari.local.illinois.briefs	Local news Briefs. (Moderated)
clari.local.indiana	Local news. (Moderated)
clari.local.indiana.briefs	Local news Briefs. (Moderated)
clari.local.iowa	Local news. (Moderated)
clari.local.iowa.briefs	Local news Briefs. (Moderated)
clari.local.los_angeles	Local news. (Moderated)
clari.local.los_angeles. briefs	Local news Briefs. (Moderated)
clari.local.louisiana	Local news. (Moderated)
clari.local.manitoba.briefs	Local news Briefs. (Moderated)
clari.local.maritimes. briefs	Local news Briefs. (Moderated)
clari.local.maryland	Local news. (Moderated)
clari.local.maryland.briefs	Local news Briefs. (Moderated)
clari.local.massachusetts	Local news. (Moderated)
clari.local.massachusetts. briefs	Local news Briefs. (Moderated)

Newsgroup	Description
`clari.local.michigan`	Local news. (Moderated)
`clari.local.michigan.briefs`	Local news Briefs. (Moderated)
`clari.local.minnesota`	Local news. (Moderated)
`clari.local.minnesota.briefs`	Local news Briefs. (Moderated)
`clari.local.missouri`	Local news. (Moderated)
`clari.local.missouri.briefs`	Local news Briefs. (Moderated)
`clari.local.nebraska`	Local news. (Moderated)
`clari.local.nebraska.briefs`	Local news Briefs. (Moderated)
`clari.local.new_england`	Local news. (Moderated)
`clari.local.new_hampshire`	Local news. (Moderated)
`clari.local.new_jersey`	Local news. (Moderated)
`clari.local.new_jersey.briefs`	Local news Briefs. (Moderated)
`clari.local.new_york`	Local news. (Moderated)
`clari.local.new_york.briefs`	Local news Briefs. (Moderated)
`clari.local.nyc`	Local news (New York City). (Moderated)
`clari.local.nyc.briefs`	Local news Briefs. (Moderated)
`clari.local.ohio`	Local news. (Moderated)
`clari.local.ohio.briefs`	Local news Briefs. (Moderated)
`clari.local.ontario.briefs`	Local news Briefs. (Moderated)
`clari.local.oregon`	Local news. (Moderated)
`clari.local.oregon.briefs`	Local news Briefs. (Moderated)
`clari.local.pennsylvania`	Local news. (Moderated)
`clari.local.pennsylvania.briefs`	Local news Briefs. (Moderated)
`clari.local.saskatchewan.briefs`	Local news Briefs. (Moderated)
`clari.local.sfbay`	Stories datelined San Francisco Bay Area. (Moderated)

continues

Newsgroup	Description
clari.local.texas	Local news. (Moderated)
clari.local.texas.briefs	Local news Briefs. (Moderated)
clari.local.utah	Local news. (Moderated)
clari.local.utah.briefs	Local news Briefs. (Moderated)
clari.local.virginia+dc	Local news. (Moderated)
clari.local.virginia+dc.briefs	Local news Briefs. (Moderated)
clari.local.washington	Local news. (Moderated)
clari.local.washington.briefs	Local news Briefs. (Moderated)
clari.local.wisconsin	Local news. (Moderated)
clari.local.wisconsin.briefs	Local news Briefs. (Moderated)
clari.matrix_news	Monthly journal on the Internet. (Moderated)
clari.nb.apple	Newsbytes Apple/Macintosh news. (Moderated)
clari.nb.business	Newsbytes business & industry news. (Moderated)
clari.nb.general	Newsbytes general computer news. (Moderated)
clari.nb.govt	Newsbytes legal and government computer news. (Moderated)
clari.nb.ibm	Newsbytes IBM PC World coverage. (Moderated)
clari.nb.review	Newsbytes new product reviews. (Moderated)
clari.nb.telecom	Newsbytes telecom & online industry news. (Moderated)
clari.nb.top	Newsbytes top stories (crossposted). (Moderated)
clari.nb.trends	Newsbytes new developments & trends. (Moderated)

Newsgroup	Description
clari.nb.unix	Newsbytes Unix news. (Moderated)
clari.net.admin	Announcements for news admins at ClariNet sites. (Moderated)
clari.net.announce	Announcements for all ClariNet readers. (Moderated)
clari.net.newusers	Online info about ClariNet. (Moderated)
clari.net.products	New ClariNet products. (Moderated)
clari.net.talk	Discussion of ClariNet — only unmoderated group.
clari.news.almanac	Daily almanac - quotes, 'this date in history' etc. (Moderated)
clari.news.arts	Stage, drama & other fine arts. (Moderated)
clari.news.aviation	Aviation industry and mishaps. (Moderated)
clari.news.books	Books & publishing. (Moderated)
clari.news.briefs	Regular news summaries. (Moderated)
clari.news.bulletin	Major breaking stories of the week. (Moderated)
clari.news.canada	News related to Canada. (Moderated)
clari.news.cast	Regular U.S. news summary. (Moderated)
clari.news.children	Stories related to children and parenting. (Moderated)
clari.news.consumer	Consumer news, car reviews, etc. (Moderated)
clari.news.demonstration	Demonstrations around the world. (Moderated)

continues

Newsgroup	Description
`clari.news.disaster`	Major problems, accidents & natural disasters. (Moderated)
`clari.news.economy`	General economic news. (Moderated)
`clari.news.election`	News regarding both US and international elections. (Moderated)
`clari.news.entertain`	Entertainment industry news & features. (Moderated)
`clari.news.europe`	News related to Europe. (Moderated)
`clari.news.features`	Unclassified feature stories. (Moderated)
`clari.news.fighting`	Clashes around the world. (Moderated)
`clari.news.flash`	Ultra-important once-a-year news flashes. (Moderated)
`clari.news.goodnews`	Stories of success and survival. (Moderated)
`clari.news.gov`	General Government related stories. (Moderated)
`clari.news.gov.agency`	Government agencies, FBI etc. (Moderated)
`clari.news.gov.budget`	Budgets at all levels. (Moderated)
`clari.news.gov.corrupt`	Government corruption, kickbacks, etc. (Moderated)
`clari.news.gov.international`	International government-related stories. (Moderated)
`clari.news.gov.officials`	Government officials & their problems. (Moderated)
`clari.news.gov.state`	State government stories of national importance. (Moderated)
`clari.news.gov.taxes`	Tax laws, trials etc. (Moderated)
`clari.news.gov.usa`	US Federal government news. (High volume). (Moderated)

Newsgroup	Description
`clari.news.group`	Special interest groups not covered in their own group. (Moderated)
`clari.news.group.blacks`	News of interest to black people. (Moderated)
`clari.news.group.gays`	Homosexuality & Gay Rights. (Moderated)
`clari.news.group.jews`	Jews & Jewish interests. (Moderated)
`clari.news.group.women`	Women's issues and abortion. (Moderated)
`clari.news.headlines`	Hourly list of the top U.S./World headlines. (Moderated)
`clari.news.hot.east_europe`	News from Eastern Europe. (Moderated)
`clari.news.hot.laquake`	News on the L.A. Earthquake. (Moderated)
`clari.news.hot.somalia`	News from Somalia. (Moderated)
`clari.news.hot.ussr`	News from the Soviet Union. (Moderated)
`clari.news.interest`	Human interest stories. (Moderated)
`clari.news.interest.animals`	Animals in the news. (Moderated)
`clari.news.interest.history`	Human interest stories & history in the making. (Moderated)
`clari.news.interest.people`	Famous people in the news. (Moderated)
`clari.news.interest.people.column`	Daily "People" column — tidbits on celebs. (Moderated)
`clari.news.interest.quirks`	Unusual or funny news stories. (Moderated)
`clari.news.issues`	Stories on major issues not covered in their own group. (Moderated)

continues

Newsgroup	Description
`clari.news.issues.civil_rights`	Freedom, Racism, Civil Rights Issues. (Moderated)
`clari.news.issues.conflict`	Conflict between groups around the world. (Moderated)
`clari.news.issues.family`	Family, Child abuse, etc. (Moderated)
`clari.news.labor`	Unions, strikes. (Moderated)
`clari.news.labor.strike`	Strikes. (Moderated)
`clari.news.law`	General group for law related issues. (Moderated)
`clari.news.law.civil`	Civil trials & litigation. (Moderated)
`clari.news.law.crime`	Major crimes. (Moderated)
`clari.news.law.crime.sex`	Sex crimes and trials. (Moderated)
`clari.news.law.crime.trial`	Trials for criminal actions. (Moderated)
`clari.news.law.crime.violent`	Violent crime & criminals. (Moderated)
`clari.news.law.drugs`	Drug related crimes & drug stories. (Moderated)
`clari.news.law.investigation`	Investigation of crimes. (Moderated)
`clari.news.law.police`	Police & law enforcement. (Moderated)
`clari.news.law.prison`	Prisons, prisoners & escapes. (Moderated)
`clari.news.law.profession`	Lawyers, Judges, etc. (Moderated)
`clari.news.law.supreme`	U.S. Supreme court rulings & news. (Moderated)
`clari.news.lifestyle`	Fashion, leisure, etc. (Moderated)
`clari.news.military`	Military equipment, people & issues. (Moderated)
`clari.news.movies`	Reviews, news and stories on movie stars. (Moderated)

Newsgroup	Description
`clari.news.music`	Reviews and issues concerning music & musicians. (Moderated)
`clari.news.politics`	Politicians & politics. (Moderated)
`clari.news.politics.people`	Politicians & Political Personalities. (Moderated)
`clari.news.religion`	Religion, religious leaders, televangelists. (Moderated)
`clari.news.sex`	Sexual issues, sex-related political stories. (Moderated)
`clari.news.terrorism`	Terrorist actions & related news around the world. (Moderated)
`clari.news.top`	Top US news stories. (Moderated)
`clari.news.top.world`	Top international news stories. (Moderated)
`clari.news.trends`	Surveys and trends. (Moderated)
`clari.news.trouble`	Less major accidents, problems & mishaps. (Moderated)
`clari.news.tv`	TV news, reviews & stars. (Moderated)
`clari.news.urgent`	Major breaking stories of the day. (Moderated)
`clari.news.weather`	Weather and temperature reports. (Moderated)
`clari.sfbay.briefs`	Twice daily news roundups for SF Bay Area. (Moderated)
`clari.sfbay.entertain`	Reviews and entertainment news for SF Bay Area. (Moderated)
`clari.sfbay.fire`	Stories from Fire Depts. of the SF Bay. (Moderated)
`clari.sfbay.general`	Main stories for SF Bay Area. (Moderated)
`clari.sfbay.misc`	Shorter general items for SF Bay Area. (Moderated)

continues

Newsgroup	Description
clari.sfbay.police	Stories from the Police Depts. of the SF Bay. (Moderated)
clari.sfbay.roads	Reports from Caltrans and the CHP. (Moderated)
clari.sfbay.short	Very short items for SF Bay Area. (Moderated)
clari.sfbay.weather	SF Bay and California Weather reports. (Moderated)
clari.sports.baseball	Baseball scores, stories, stats. (Moderated)
clari.sports.baseball.games	Baseball games & box scores. (Moderated)
clari.sports.basketball	Basketball coverage. (Moderated)
clari.sports.basketball. college	College basketball coverage. (Moderated)
clari.sports.features	Sports feature stories. (Moderated)
clari.sports.football	Pro football coverage. (Moderated)
clari.sports.football. college	College football coverage. (Moderated)
clari.sports.football.games	Coverage of individual pro games. (Moderated)
clari.sports.hockey	NHL coverage. (Moderated)
clari.sports.misc	Other sports, plus general sports news. (Moderated)
clari.sports.motor	Racing, Motor Sports. (Moderated)
clari.sports.olympic	The Olympic Games. (Moderated)
clari.sports.tennis	Tennis news & scores. (Moderated)
clari.sports.top	Top sports news. (Moderated)
clari.tw.aerospace	Aerospace industry and companies. (Moderated)
clari.tw.computers	Computer industry, applications and developments. (Moderated)

Newsgroup	*Description*
clari.tw.defense	Defense industry issues. (Moderated)
clari.tw.education	Stories involving Universities & colleges. (Moderated)
clari.tw.electronics	Electronics makers and sellers. (Moderated)
clari.tw.environment	Environmental news, hazardous waste, forests. (Moderated)
clari.tw.health	Disease, medicine, health care, sick celebs. (Moderated)
clari.tw.health.aids	AIDS stories, research, political issues. (Moderated)
clari.tw.misc	General technical industry stories. (Moderated)
clari.tw.nuclear	Nuclear power & waste. (Moderated)
clari.tw.science	General science stories. (Moderated)
clari.tw.space	NASA, Astronomy & spaceflight. (Moderated)
clari.tw.stocks	Regular reports on computer & technology stock prices. (Moderated)
clari.tw.telecom	Phones, Satellites, Media & general Telecom. (Moderated)
clari.world.africa	Translated reports from Africa. (Moderated)
clari.world.americas	News on the Americas, usually outside the USA and Canada. (Moderated)
clari.world.asia	News from Asia and the Pacific Rim. (Moderated)
clari.world.europe.eastern	Translated reports from Eastern Europe. (Moderated)

continues

Newsgroup	Description
`clari.world.europe.western`	Stories on western Europe. (Moderated)
`clari.world.mideast`	News from the Middle East. (Moderated)

K12

K12Net is a collection of conferences devoted to K–12 educational curriculum, language exchanges with native speakers, and classroom-to-classroom projects designed by teachers. The conferences are privately distributed among FidoNet-compatible electronic bulletin board systems in Africa, Asia, Australia, Europe, and North America, and are also available from `uunet.uu.net` as Usenet newsgroups in the hierarchy `k12.*`.

Classroom-to-classroom projects are featured in the K12 "Channels," which are periodically reassigned based on usage and appropriate project length. They comprise the `k12.sys` hierarchy.

Forums for casual conversation among students are divided by grade level in the `k12.chat` hierarchy; an area also exists for teachers to exchange general ideas about using telecommunications in education.

Newsgroups	Description
`k12.ed.art`	Arts & crafts curricula in K-12 education.
`k12.ed.business`	Business education curricula in grades K-12.
`k12.ed.comp.literacy`	Teaching computer literacy in grades K-12.
`k12.ed.health-pe`	Health and Physical Education curricula in grades K-12.
`k12.ed.life-skills`	Home Economics, career education, and school counseling.
`k12.ed.math`	Mathematics curriculum in K-12 education.

Newsgroup	Description
k12.ed.music	Music and Performing Arts curriculum in K-12 education.
k12.ed.science	Science curriculum in K-12 education.
k12.ed.soc-studies	Social Studies and History curriculum in K-12 education.
k12.ed.special	Educating students with handicaps and/or special needs.
k12.ed.tag	K-12 education for gifted and talented students.
k12.ed.tech	Industrial arts & vocational education in grades K-12.
k12.library	Implementing info technologies in school libraries.
k12.lang.art	The art of teaching language skills in grades K-12.
k12.lang.deutsch-eng	Bilingual German/English practice with native speakers.
k12.lang.esp-eng	Bilingual Spanish/English practice with native speakers.
k12.lang.francais	French practice with native speakers.
k12.lang.russian	Bilingual Russian/English practice with native speakers.
k12.sys.projects	Discussion of potential projects.
k12.sys.channel0	Current projects.
k12.sys.channel1	Current projects.
k12.sys.channel2	Current projects.
k12.sys.channel3	Current projects.
k12.sys.channel4	Current projects.
k12.sys.channel5	Current projects.
k12.sys.channel6	Current projects.

continues

Newsgroup	Description
k12.sys.channel7	Current projects.
k12.sys.channel8	Current projects.
k12.sys.channel9	Current projects.
k12.sys.channel10	Current projects.
k12.sys.channel11	Current projects.
k12.sys.channel12	Current projects.
k12.chat.elementary	Casual conversation for elementary students, grades K-5.
k12.chat.junior	Casual conversation for students in grades 6-8.
k12.chat.senior	Casual conversation for high school students.
k12.chat.teacher	Casual conversation for teachers of grades K-12.

For more information, contact one of the members of the K12Net Council of Coordinators. They are as follows:

Jack Crawford at jack@rochgate.fidonet.org

Janet Murray at jmurray@psg.com

Rob Reilly at rreilly@athena.mit.edu

Mort Sternheim at sternheim@phast.umass.edu

Louis Van Geel at lvg@psg.com

Appendix

PDIAL List

This appendix contains the text of Peter Kaminski's PDIAL List, a large but certainly not complete list of organizations that provide full Internet access, usually for a fee. I am including Peter's list for you because it's an invaluable resource for locating Internet providers near you. Neither Peter nor I make any claims about the completeness or accuracy of this list, however; I provide it merely as an aid.

> **Tip:** Hayden Books has worked out a deal with one of the providers, Northwest Nexus, for two weeks of free access time. This deal is certainly worth comparing with other providers (and be aware that the listings don't always carry complete or updated data), but I think you'll find that the Northwest Nexus offer is extremely attractive for initial Internet access (see appendix F for the details).

```
<< nwnexus >>
name — — — — —> Northwest Nexus Inc.
dialup — — — —> contact for numbers
area codes — —> 206
local access —> WA: Seattle
long distance -> provided by user
```

```
services ———> UUCP, SLIP, PPP, feeds, dns
fees —————> $10/month for first 10 hours + $3/hr; $20 start-up
email ————> info@nwnexus.wa.com
voice ————> 206-455-3505
ftp more info -> nwnexus.wa.com:/NWNEXUS.info.txt
```

I also recommend that you briefly look at the rates for the commercial services such as AppleLink ($37.00 per hour at 9600 bps) and CompuServe ($22.80 per hour at 9600 bps) in chapter 7, "Email Gateways," because they help bring home what a good deal some of these Internet providers give you.

The Public Dialup Internet Access List

Copyright 1992-1993 Peter Kaminski. Do not modify. Freely distributable for non-commercial purposes. Please contact me if you wish to distribute commercially or in modified form.

I make no representations about the suitability or accuracy of this document for any purpose. It is provided "as is" without express or implied warranty. All information contained herein is subject to change.

Contents:

-00- Quick Start!
-01- Area Code Summary: Providers With Many Local Dialins (1-800, PDN)
-02- Area Code Summary: US/Canada Metro and Regional Dialins
-03- Area Code Summary: International Dialins
-04- Alphabetical List of Providers
-05- What *Is* The Internet?
-06- What The PDIAL Is
-07- How People Can Get The PDIAL (This List)
-08- Appendix A: Other Valuable Resources
-09- Appendix B: Finding Public Data Network (PDN) Access Numbers
-10- Providers: Get Listed in PDIAL!

-00- Quick Start!

THE INTERNET is a global cooperative information network which can give you instant access to millions of people and terabytes of data. Providers listed in the PDIAL provide inexpensive public access to the Internet using your regular modem and computer.

[Special note: the PDIAL currently lists only providers directly connected to the Internet. Much of the Internet can still be explored through systems with only Internet email and USENET netnews connections, but you need to check other BBS lists to find them.]

GET A GUIDE: I highly recommend obtaining one of the many good starter or guide books to the Internet. Think of them as travel guides to a new and different country, and you wouldn't be far off. See section -08- below for more details.

CHOOSING A PROVIDER: Phone charges can dominate the cost of your access to the Internet. Check first for providers with metro or regional dialins that are a local call for you (no per-minute phone charges). If there aren't any, move on to comparing prices for PDN, 800, and direct-dial long distance charges. Make sure to compare all your options. Calling long distance out-of-state or across the country is often cheaper than calling 30 miles away.

If you're not in North America and have no local provider, you may still be able to use one of the providers listed as having PDN access. Contact the individual providers with PDN access (see listings below) to find out.

INFORMATION CHANGES: The information listed in the PDIAL changes and expands rapidly. If this edition is more than 2 months old, consider obtaining a new one. You can use the Info Deli email server, which will provide you with updates and other information. Choose from the commands below and just email them to <info-deli-server@netcom.com>.

  "Send PDIAL" — receive the current PDIAL
  "Subscribe PDIAL" — receive new editions of the PDIAL automatically
  "Subscribe Info-Deli-News" — news of Info Deli changes and additions

See section -07- below for more details and other ways to obtain the PDIAL.

CHECK IT OUT: Remember, the PDIAL is only a summary listing of
the resources and environment delivered by each of the various
providers. Contact the providers that interest you by email or
voice phone and make sure you find out if they have what you
need.

Then GO FOR IT! Happy 'netting!

-01- Area Code Summary: Providers with Many Local Dialins (1-800, PDN)

        800 class cns crl csn dial-n-cerf-usa hookup.net IGC jvnc OARnet
        PDN delphi holonet hookup.net IGC michnet millennium novalink portal
        PDN psi-world-dial psilink tmn well world

"PDN" means the provider is accessible through a public data network
(check the listings below for which network); note that many PDNs listed
offer access outside North America as well as within North America. Check
with the provider or the PDN for more details.

"800" means the provider is accessible via a "toll-free" US phone number.

The phone company will not charge for the call, but the service
provider will add a surcharge to cover the cost of the 800 service. This may be more expensive than other long-distance options.

-02- Area Code Summary: US/ Canada Metro and Regional Dialins

If you are not local to any of these providers, it's still likely
you are able to access those providers available through a public
data network (PDN). Check the section above for providers with
wide area access.

        201 jvnc-tiger
        202 CAPCON clarknet express michnet tmn

```
203 jvnc-tiger
205 nuance
206 eskimo GLAIDS halcyon netcom nwnexus olympus
212 echonyc maestro mindvox panix pipeline
213 crl dial-n-cerf kaiwan netcom
214 metronet netcom
215 jvnc-tiger PREPnet
216 OARnet wariat
217 prairienet
301 CAPCON clarknet express michnet tmn
302 ssnet
303 cns csn netcom nyx
305 gate.net
310 class crl dial-n-cerf kaiwan netcom
312 InterAccess mcsnet netcom xnet
313 michnet MSen
401 anomaly ids jvnc-tiger
403 PUCnet UUNET-Canada
404 crl netcom
407 gate.net
408 a2i netcom portal
410 CAPCON clarknet express
412 PREPnet telerama
415 a2i class crl dial-n-cerf IGC netcom portal well
416 hookup.net UUNET-Canada uunorth
419 OARnet
503 agora.rain.com netcom teleport
504 sugar
508 anomaly nearnet northshore novalink
510 class crl dial-n-cerf holonet netcom
512 realtime
513 fsp OARnet
514 CAM.ORG UUNET-Canada
516 jvnc-tiger
517 michnet
519 hookup.net UUNET-Canada uunorth
602 crl Data.Basix evergreen indirect
603 MV nearnet
604 UUNET-Canada
609 jvnc-tiger
613 UUNET-Canada uunorth
614 OARnet
616 michnet
617 delphi nearnet netcom northshore novalink world
619 cg57 class crash.cts.com cyber dial-n-cerf netcom
703 CAPCON clarknet express michnet netcom tmn
```

```
704 concert Vnet
707 crl
708 InterAccess mcsnet xnet
713 blkbox nuchat sugar
714 class dial-n-cerf express kaiwan netcom
717 PREPnet
718 maestro mindvox netcom panix pipeline
719 cns csn oldcolo
804 wyvern
810 michnet MSen
814 PREPnet
815 InterAccess mcsnet xnet
817 metronet
818 class dial-n-cerf netcom
905 UUNET-Canada
906 michnet
907 alaska.edu
908 express jvnc-tiger
910 concert
916 netcom
919 concert Vnet
```

These are area codes local to the dialups, although some prefixes
in the area codes listed may not be local to the dialups. Check
your phone book or with your phone company.

-03- Area Code Summary: International Dialins

If you are not local to any of these providers, there is still a
chance you are able to access those providers available through a
public data network (PDN). Check section -01- above for providers with wide area access, and send email to them to ask about
availability.

```
+44 (0)81 Demon dircon ibmpcug
      +49 Individual.NET
   +49 23 ins
  +49 069 in-rhein-main
  +49 089 mucev
    +61 2 connect.com.au
    +61 3 connect.com.au
     +301 Ariadne
   +353 1 IEunet
```

-04- PDIAL Alphabetical List of Providers

Fees are for personal dialup accounts with outgoing Internet access; most sites have other classes of service with other rate structures as well. Most support email and netnews along with the listed services.

"Long distance: provided by user" means you need to use direct dial long distance or other long distance services to connect to the provider.

```
<< a2i >>
name — — — — —> a2i communications
dialup — — — —> 408-293-9010 (v.32bis), 415-364-5652 (v.32bis), 408-293-9020
        (PEP); login 'guest'
area codes — —> 408, 415
local access —> CA: West and South SF Bay Area
long distance -> provided by user
services — — —> shell (SunOS UNIX and MS-DOS), ftp, telnet, irc, feeds,
        domains and host-less domains, virtual ttys, gopher
fees — — — — —> $20/month or $45/3 months or $72/6 months
email — — — —> info@rahul.net
voice — — — —> 408-293-8078 voicemail
ftp more info -> ftp.rahul.net:/pub/BLURB
```

```
<< agora.rain.com >>
name — — — — —> RainDrop Laboratories
dialup — — — —> 503-293-1772 (2400) 503-293-2059 (v.32, v.32 bis) 'apply'
area codes — —> 503
local access —> OR: Portland, Beaverton, Hillsboro, Forest Grove, Gresham,
        Tigard, Lake Oswego, Oregon City, Tualatin, Wilsonville
long distance -> provided by user
services — — —> shell, ftp, telnet, gopher, usenet
fees — — — — —> $6/month (1 hr/day limit)
email — — — —> info@agora.rain.com
voice — — — —>n/a
ftp more info -> agora.rain.com:/pub/gopher-data/agora/agora
```

```
<< alaska.edu >>
name — — — — —> University Of Alaska Southeast, Tundra Services
dialup — — — —> 907-789-1314
area codes — —> 907
local access —> All Alaskan sites with local UACN access — Anchorage,
        Barrow, Fairbanks, Homer, Juneau, Keni, Ketchikan, Kodiak,
        Kotzebue, Nome, Palmer, Sitka, Valdez
```

```
long distance -> provided by user
services — — —> Statewide UACN Mail, Internet, USENET, gopher, Telnet, FTP
fees — — — —> $20/month for individual accounts, discounts for 25+ and 50+
         to public, gov't and non-profit organizations.
email — — — —> JNJMB@acad1.alaska.edu
voice — — — —> 907-465-6453
fax — — — —> 907-465-6295
ftp more info -> n/a


<< anomaly >>
name  — — — —> Anomaly - Rhode Island's Gateway To The Internet
dialup — — — —> 401-331-3706 (v.32) or 401-455-0347 (PEP)
area codes — —> 401, 508
local access —> RI: Providence/Seekonk Zone
long distance -> provided by user
services — — —> shell, ftp, telnet, SLIP
fees — — — —> Commercial: $125/6 months or $200/year; Educational: $75/6
          months or $125/year
email — — — —> info@anomaly.sbs.risc.net
voice — — — —> 401-273-4669
ftp more info -> anomaly.sbs.risc.net:/anomaly.info/access.zip


<< Ariadne >>
name  — — — —> Ariadne - Greek Academic and Research Network
dialup — — — —> +301 65-48-800 (1200 - 9600 bps)
area codes — —> +301
local access —> Athens, Greece
long distance -> provided by user
services — — —> e-mail, ftp, telnet, gopher, talk, pad(EuropaNet)
fees — — — — —> 5900 drachmas per calendar quarter, 1 hr/day limit.
email — — — —> dialup@leon.nrcps.ariadne-t.gr
voice — — — —> +301 65-13-392
fax — — — — —> +301 6532910
ftp more info -> n/a


<< blkbox >>
name  — — — —> The Black Box
dialup — — — —> (713) 480-2686 (V32bis/V42bis)
area codes — —> 713
local access —> TX: Houston
long distance -> provided by user
services — — —> shell, ftp, telnet, SLIP, PPP, UUCP
fees — — — — —> $21.65 per month or $108.25 for 6 months
email — — — —> info@blkbox.com
voice — — — —> (713) 480-2684
```

ftp more info -> n/a

<< CAM.ORG >>
name — — — — —> Communications Accessibles Montreal
dialup — — — —> 514-931-7178 (v.32 bis), 514-931-2333 (2400bps)
area codes — —> 514
local access —> QC: Montreal, Laval, South-Shore, West-Island
long distance -> provided by user
services — — —> shell, ftp, telnet, gopher, wais, WWW, irc, feeds, SLIP,
         PPP, AppleTalk, FAX gateway
fees — — — — —> $25/month Cdn.
email — — — —> info@CAM.ORG
voice — — — —> 514-931-0749
ftp more info -> ftp.CAM.ORG

<< CAPCON >>
name — — — — —> CAPCON Library Network
dialup — — — —> contact for number
area codes — —> 202, 301, 410, 703
local access —> District of Columbia, Suburban Maryland & Northern Virginia
long distance -> various plans available/recommended; contact for details
services — — —> menu, archie, ftp, gopher, listservs, telnet, wais, whois,
         full day training and 'CAPCON Connect User Manual'
fees — — — — —> $35 start-up + $150/yr + $24/mo for first account from an
         institution; $35 start-up + $90/yr + $15/mo for additional
         users (member rates lower); 20 hours/month included,
         additional hours $2/hr
email — — — —> capcon@capcon.net
voice — — — —> 202-331-5771
fax — — — — —> 202-797-7719
ftp more info -> n/a

<< cg57 >>
name — — — — —> E & S Systems Public Access *Nix
dialup — — — —> 619-278-8267 (V.32bis, TurboPEP), 619-278-8267 (V32)
         619-278-9837 (PEP)
area codes — —> 619
local access —> CA: San Diego
long distance -> provided by user
services — — —> shell, ftp, irc, telnet, gopher, archie, bbs (UniBoard)
fees — — — — —> bbs (FREE), shell - $30/3 months, $50/6 months, $80/9
         months, $100/year
email — — — —> steve@cg57.esnet.com
voice — — — —> 619-278-4641
ftp more info -> n/a

```
<< clarknet >>
name  — — — — —>  Clark Internet Services, Inc. (ClarkNet)
dialup — — — —> 410-730-9786, 410-995-0271, 301-596-1626, 301-854-0446,
          301-621-5216 'guest'
area codes — —> 202, 301, 410, 703
local access —> MD: Baltimore; DC: Washington; VA: Northern VA
long distance -> provided by user
services — — —> shell, menu, ftp, telnet, irc, gopher, hytelnet, www, WAIS,
         SLIP/PPP, ftp space, feeds (UUCP & uMDSS), dns, Clarinet
fees — — — — —> $23/month or $66/3 months or $126/6 months or $228/year
email — — — —> info@clark.net
voice — — — —> Call 800-735-2258 then give 410-730-9764 (MD Relay Svc)
fax — — — — —> 410-730-9765
ftp more info -> ftp.clark.net:/pub/clarknet/fullinfo.txt


<< class >>
name  — — — — —>  Cooperative Library Agency for Systems and Services
dialup — — — —> contact for number; NOTE: CLASS serves libraries and
         information distributors only
area codes — —> 310, 415, 510, 619, 714, 818, 800
local access —> Northern and Southern California or anywhere (800) service
          is available
long distance -> 800 service available at $6/hour surcharge
services — — —> menus, mail, telnet, ftp, gopher, wais, hytelnet, archie,
         WWW, IRC, Unix shells, SLIP, etc. Training is available.
fees — — — — —> $4.50/hour + $150/year for first account + $50/year each
          additional account + $135/year CLASS membership. Discounts
          available for multiple memberships.
email — — — —> class@class.org
voice — — — —> 800-488-4559
fax — — — — —> 408-453-5379
ftp more info -> n/a


<< cns >>
name  — — — — —>  Community News Service
dialup — — — —> 719-520-1700 id 'new', passwd 'newuser'
area codes — —> 303, 719, 800
local access —> CO: Colorado Springs, Denver; continental US/800
long distance -> 800 or provided by user
services — — —> UNIX shell, email, ftp, telnet, irc, USENET, Clarinet,
          gopher, Commerce Business Daily
fees — — — — —> $2.75/hour; $10/month minimum + $35 signup
email — — — —> service@cscns.com
voice — — — —> 719-592-1240
ftp more info -> cscns.com


<< concert >>
```

```
name  — — — — —> CONCERT-CONNECT
dialup — — — —> contact for number
area codes — —> 704, 910, 919
local access —> NC: Asheville, Chapel Hill, Charlotte, Durham, Greensboro,
        Greenville, Raleigh, Winston-Salem, Research Triangle Park
long distance -> provided by user
services — — —> UUCP, SLIP
fees — — — — —> SLIP: $150 educational/research or $180 commercial for first
        60 hours/month + $300 signup
email — — — —> info@concert.net
voice — — — —> 919-248-1999
ftp more info -> ftp.concert.net


<< connect.com.au >>
name  — — — — —> connect.com.au pty ltd
dialup — — — —> contact for number
area codes — —> +61 3, +61 2
local access —> Australia: Melbourne, Sydney
long distance -> provided by user
services — — —> SLIP, PPP, ISDN, UUCP, ftp, telnet, NTP, FTPmail
fees — — — — —> AUS$2000/year (1 hour/day), 10% discount for AUUG members;
        other billing negotiable
email — — — —> connect@connect.com.au
voice — — — —> +61 3 5282239
fax — — — — —> +61 3 5285887
ftp more info -> ftp.connect.com.au


<< crash.cts.com >>
name  — — — — —> CTS Network Services (CTSNET)
dialup — — — —> 619-637-3640 HST, 619-637-3660 V.32bis, 619-637-3680 PEP
        'help'
area codes — —> 619
local access —> CA: San Diego, Pt. Loma, La Jolla, La Mesa, El Cajon, Poway,
        Ramona, Chula Vista, National City, Mira Mesa, Alpine, East
        County, new North County numbers, Escondido, Oceanside, Vista
long distance -> provided by user
services — — —> Unix shell, UUCP, Usenet newsfeeds, NNTP, Clarinet, Reuters,
        FTP, Telnet, SLIP, PPP, IRC, Gopher, Archie, WAIS, POPmail,
        UMDSS, domains, nameservice, DNS
fees — — — — —> $10-$23/month flat depending on features, $15 startup,
        personal $20-> /month flat depending on features, $25
        startup, commercial
email — — — —> info@crash.cts.com (server), support@crash.cts.com (human)
voice — — — —> 619-637-3637
fax — — — — —> 619-637-3630
ftp more info -> n/a
```

```
<< crl >>
name  — — — — —>  CR Laboratories Dialup Internet Access
dialup — — — —> 415-389-UNIX
area codes — —> 213, 310, 404, 415, 510, 602, 707, 800
local access —> CA: San Francisco Bay area + San Rafael, Santa Rosa, Los
        Angeles, Orange County; AZ: Phoenix, Scottsdale, Tempe, and
        Glendale; GA: Atlanta metro area; continental US/800
long distance -> 800 or provided by user
services — — —> shell, ftp, telnet, feeds, SLIP, WAIS
fees — — — — —> $17.50/month + $19.50 signup
email — — — —> info@crl.com
voice — — — —> 415-381-2800
ftp more info -> n/a


<< csn >>
name  — — — — —>  Colorado SuperNet, Inc.
dialup — — — —> contact for number
area codes — —> 303, 719, 800
local access —> CO: Alamosa, Boulder/Denver, Colorado Springs, Durango, Fort
        Collins, Frisco, Glenwood Springs/Aspen, Grand Junction,
        Greeley, Gunnison, Pueblo, Telluride; anywhere 800 service
        is available
long distance -> provided by user or 800
services — — —> shell or menu, UUCP, SLIP, 56K, ISDN, T1; ftp, telnet, irc,
        gopher, WAIS, domains, anonymous ftp space, email-to-fax
fees — — — — —> $1/hour off-peak, $3/hour peak ($250 max/month) + $20
        signup, $5/hr surcharge for 800 use
email — — — —> info@csn.org
voice — — — —> 303-273-3471
fax — — — — —> 303-273-3475
ftp more info -> csn.org:/CSN/reports/DialinInfo.txt
off-peak — — —> midnight to 6am


<< cyber >>
name  — — — — —>  The Cyberspace Station
dialup — — — —> 619-634-1376 'guest'
area codes — —> 619
local access —> CA: San Diego
long distance -> provided by user
services — — —> shell, ftp, telnet, irc
fees — — — — —> $15/month + $10 startup or $60 for six months
email — — — —> help@cyber.net
voice — — — —> n/a
ftp more info -> n/a


<< Data.Basix >>
```

```
name  — — — — —> Data Basix
dialup — — — —> 602-721-5887
area codes — —> 602
local access —> AZ: Tucson
long distance -> provided by user
services — — —> Telnet, FTP, NEWS, UUCP; on-site assistance
fees — — — — —> $25 monthly, $180 yearly; group rates available
email — — — —> info@Data.Basix.com (automated); sales@Data.Basix.com (human)
voice — — — —> 602-721-1988
ftp more info -> Data.Basix.COM:/services/dial-up.txt


<< Demon >>
name  — — — — —> Demon Internet Systems (DIS)
dialup — — — —> +44 (0)81 343 4848
area codes — —> +44 (0)81
local access —> London, England
long distance -> provided by user
services — — —> ftp, telnet, SLIP/PPP
fees — — — — —> GBPounds 10.00/month; 132.50/year (inc 12.50 startup
        charge). No on-line time charges.
email — — — —> internet@demon.co.uk
voice — — — —> +44 (0)81 349 0063
ftp more info -> n/a


<< delphi >>
name  — — — — —> DELPHI
dialup — — — —> 800-365-4636 'JOINDELPHI password:INTERNETSIG'
area codes — —> 617, PDN
local access —> MA: Boston; KS: Kansas City
long distance -> Sprintnet or Tymnet: $9/hour weekday business hours, no
        charge nights and weekends
services — — —> ftp, telnet, feeds, user groups, wire services, member
        conferencing
fees — — — — —> $10/month for 4 hours or $20/month for 20 hours + $3/month
        for Internet services
email — — — —> walthowe@delphi.com
voice — — — —> 800-544-4005
ftp more info -> n/a


<< dial-n-cerf >>
name  — — — — —> DIAL n' CERF or DIAL n' CERF AYC
dialup — — — —> contact for number
area codes — —> 213, 310, 415, 510, 619, 714, 818
local access —> CA: Los Angeles, Oakland, San Diego, Irvine, Pasadena, Palo
          Alto
long distance -> provided by user
```

```
services  — — —>  shell, menu, irc, ftp, hytelnet, gopher, WAIS, WWW,
terminal
          service, SLIP
```
fees — — — — —> $5/hour ($3/hour on weekend) + $20/month + $50 startup OR
          $250/month flat for AYC
email — — — —>help@cerf.net
voice — — — —> 800-876-2373 or 619-455-3900
ftp more info -> nic.cerf.net:/cerfnet/dial-n-cerf/
off-peak — — —> Weekend: 5pm Friday to 5pm Sunday

<< dial-n-cerf-usa >>
```
name  — — — — —> DIAL n' CERF USA
```
dialup — — — —> contact for number
area codes — —> 800
local access —> anywhere (800) service is available
long distance -> included
```
services  — — —> shell, menu, irc, ftp, hytelnet, gopher, WAIS, WWW, terminal
          service, SLIP
```
fees — — — — —> $10/hour ($8/hour on weekend) + $20/month
email — — — —>help@cerf.net
voice — — — —> 800-876-2373 or 619-455-3900
ftp more info -> nic.cerf.net:/cerfnet/dial-n-cerf/
off-peak — — —> Weekend: 5pm Friday to 5pm Sunday

<< dircon >>
```
name  — — — — —> The Direct Connection
```
dialup — — — —> +44 (0)81 317 2222
area codes — —> +44 (0)81
local access —> London, England
long distance -> provided by user
```
services  — — —> shell or menu, UUCP feeds, SLIP/PPP, ftp, telnet, gopher,
        WAIS, Archie, personal ftp/file space, email-to-fax
```
fees — — — — —> Subscriptions from GBPounds 10 per month, no on-line
          charges. GBPounds 7.50 signup fee.
email — — — —>helpdesk@dircon.co.uk
voice — — — —> +44 (0)81 317 0100
fax — — — — —> +44 (0)81 317 0100
ftp more info -> n/a

<< echonyc >>
```
name  — — — — —> Echo Communications
```
dialup — — — —> (212) 989-8411 (v.32, v.32 bis) 'newuser'
area codes — —> 212
local access —> NY: Manhattan
long distance -> provided by user
```
services  — — —> shell, ftp, telnet, gopher, archie, wais, SLIP/PPP
```

```
fees ——————> Commercial: $19.95/month; students/seniors: $13.75/
month
email ——————> horn@echonyc.com
voice ——————> 212-255-3839
ftp more info -> n/a
```

<< eskimo >>
```
name ——————> Eskimo North
dialup ——————> 206-367-3837 300-14.4k, 206-362-6731 for 9600/14.4k,
          206-742-1150 World Blazer
area codes ——> 206
local access —> WA: Seattle, Everett
long distance -> provided by user
services ————> shell, ftp, telnet
fees ——————> $10/month or $96/year
email ——————> nanook@eskimo.com
voice ——————> 206-367-7457
ftp more info -> n/a
```

<< evergreen >>
```
name ——————> Evergreen Communications
dialup ——————> (602) 955-8444
area codes ——> 602
local access —> AZ
long distance -> provided by user or call for additional information
services ————> ftp, telnet, gopher, archie, wais, www, uucp, PPP
fees ——————> individual: $239/yr; commercial: $479/yr; special
          educational rates
email ——————> evergreen@libre.com
voice ——————> 602-955-8315
fax ———————> 602-955-5948
ftp more info -> n/a
```

<< express >>
```
name ——————> Express Access - A service of Digital Express Group
dialup ——————> 301-220-0462, 410-766-1855, 703-281-7997, 714-377-9784,
          908-937-9481 'new'
area codes ——> 202, 301, 410, 703, 714, 908
local access —> Northern VA, Baltimore MD, Washington DC, New Brunswick NJ,
          Orange County CA
long distance -> provided by user
services ————> shell, ftp, telnet, irc, gopher, hytelnet, www, Clarinet,
        SLIP/PPP, archie, mailing lists, autoresponders, anonymous
          FTP archives
fees ——————> $25/month or $250/year
```

```
email ————> info@digex.net
voice ————> 800-969-9090, 301-220-2020
ftp more info -> n/a
```

<< fsp >>
```
name —————> Freelance Systems Programming
dialup ————> (513) 258-7745 to 14.4 Kbps
area codes ——> 513
local access —> OH: Dayton
long distance -> provided by user
services ———> shell, ftp, telnet, feeds, email, gopher, archie, SLIP, etc.
fees —————> $20 startup and $1 per hour
email ————> fsp@dayton.fsp.com
voice ————> (513) 254-7246
ftp more info -> n/a
```

<< gate.net >>
```
name —————> CyberGate, Inc
dialup ————> 305-425-0200
area codes ——> 305, 407
local access —> South Florida, expanding in FL
long distance -> provided by user
services ———> shell, UUCP, SLIP/PPP, leased, telnet, FTP, IRC, archie,
          gopher, etc.
fees —————> $17.50/mo on credit card; group discounts; SLIP/PPP:
            $17.50/mo + $2/hr
email ————> info@gate.net or sales@gate.net
voice ————> 305-428-GATE
fax —————> 305-428-7977
ftp more info -> n/a
```

<< GLAIDS >>
```
name —————> GLAIDS NET (Homosexual Network)
dialup ————> 206-322-0621
area codes ——> 206
local access —> WA: Seattle
long distance -> provided by user
services ———> BBS, Gopher, ftp, telnet
fees —————> $10/month. Scholarships available. Free 7 day trial.
          Visitors are welcome.
email ————> tomh@glaids.wa.com
voice ————> 206-323-7483
ftp more info -> GLAIDS.wa.com
```

<< halcyon >>
```
name —————> Halcyon
dialup ————> 206-382-6245 'new', 8N1
```

```
area codes ——> 206
local access —> Seattle, WA
long distance -> provided by user
services ———> shell, telnet, ftp, bbs, irc, gopher, hytelnet
fees —————> $200/year, or $60/quarter + $10 start-up
email ————> info@halcyon.com
voice ————> 206-955-1050
ftp more info -> halcyon.com:/pub/waffle/info
```

<< holonet >>
```
name —————> HoloNet
dialup ————> 510-704-1058
area codes ——> 510, PDN
local access —> Berkeley, CA
long distance -> [per hour, off-peak/peak] Bay Area: $0.50/$0.95; PSINet A:
          $0.95/$1.95; PSINet B: $2.50/$6.00; Tymnet: $3.75/$7.50
services ———> ftp, telnet, irc, games
fees —————> $2/hour off-peak, $4/hour peak; $6/month or $60/year minimum
email ————> info@holonet.net
voice ————> 510-704-0160
ftp more info -> holonet.net:/info/
off-peak ———> 5pm to 8am + weekends and holidays
```

<< hookup.net >>
```
name —————> HookUp Communication Corporation
dialup ————> contact for number
area codes ——> 800, PDN, 416, 519
local access —> Ontario, Canada
long distance -> 800 access across Canada, or discounted rates by HookUp
services ———> shell or menu, UUCP, SLIP, PPP, ftp, telnet, irc, gopher,
          domains, anonymous ftp space
fees —————> Cdn$14.95/mo for 5 hours; Cdn$34.95/mo for 15 hrs;
          Cdn$59.95/mo for 30 hrs; Cdn$300.00/yr for 50 hrs/mo;
          Cdn$299.00/mo for unlimited usage
email ————> info@hookup.net
voice ————> 519-747-4110
fax —————> 519-746-3521
ftp more info -> n/a
```

<< ibmpcug >>
```
name —————> UK PC User Group
dialup ————> +44 (0)81 863 6646
area codes ——> +44 (0)81
local access —> London, England
long distance -> provided by user
services ———> ftp, telnet, bbs, irc, feeds
fees —————> GBPounds 15.50/month or 160/year + 10 startup (no time
                charges)
```

```
email — — — —> info@ibmpcug.co.uk
voice — — — —> +44 (0)81 863 6646
ftp more info -> n/a
```

`<< ids >>`
```
name  — — — —> The IDS World Network
dialup — — — —> 401-884-9002, 401-785-1067
area codes — —> 401
local access —> East Greenwich, RI; northern RI
long distance -> provided by user
services — — —> ftp, telnet, SLIP, feeds, bbs
fees — — — —> $10/month or $50/half year or $100/year
email — — — —> sysadmin@ids.net
voice — — — —> 401-884-7856
ftp more info -> ids.net:/ids.net
```

`<< IEunet >>`
```
name  — — — —> IEunet Ltd., Ireland's Internet Services Supplier
dialup — — — —> +353 1 6790830, +353 1 6798600
area codes — —> +353 1
local access —> Dublin, Ireland
long distance -> provided by user, or supplied by IEunet
services — — —> DialIP, IPGold, EUnet Traveller, X400, X500, Gopher, WWW,
          FTP, FTPmail, SLIP/PPP, FTP archives
fees — — — — —> IEP25/month Basic
email — — — —> info@ieunet.ie, info@Ireland.eu.net
voice — — — —> +353 1 6790832
ftp more info -> ftp.ieunet.ie:/pub
```

`<< IGC >>`
```
name  — — — —> Institute for Global Communications/IGC Networks
(PeaceNet,
          EcoNet, ConflictNet, LaborNet, HomeoNet)
dialup — — — —> 415-322-0284 (N-8-1), 'new'
area codes — —> 415, 800, PDN
local access —> CA: Palo Alto, San Francisco
long distance -> [per hour, off-peak/peak] SprintNet: $2/$7; 800: $11/$11
services — — —> telnet, local newsgroups for environmental, peace/social
          justice issues; NO ftp
fees — — — — —> $10/month + $3/hr after first hour
email — — — —> support@igc.apc.org
voice — — — —> 415-442-0220
ftp more info -> igc.apc.org:/pub
```

`<< indirect >>`
```
name  — — — —> Internet Direct, Inc.
```

```
dialup — — — —> 602-274-9600 (Phoenix); 602-321-9600 (Tucson); 'guest'
area codes — —> 602
local access —> AZ: Phoenix, Tucson
long distance -> provided by user
services — — —> Shell/menu, UUCP, Usenet, NNTP, FTP, Telnet, SLIP,
PPP, IRC,
          Gopher, WAIS, WWW, POP, DNS, nameservice, QWK (offline
          readers)
fees — — — — —> $20/month (personal); $30/month (business)
email — — — —> info@indirect.com (automated); support@indirect.com (human)
voice — — — —> 602-274-0100 (Phoenix), 602-324-0100 (Tucson)
ftp more info -> n/a
```

```
<< Individual.NET >>
name  — — — — —> Individual Network e.V. (IN)
dialup — — — —> contact for number
area codes — —> +49
local access —> Germany: Berlin, Oldenburg, Bremen, Hamburg, Krefeld, Kiel,
          Duisburg, Darmstadt, Dortmund, Hannover, Ruhrgebiet, Bonn,
          Magdeburg, Duesseldorf, Essen, Koeln, Paderborn, Bielefeld,
          Aachen, Saarbruecken, Frankfurt, Braunschweig, Dresden, Ulm,
          Erlangen, Nuernberg, Wuerzburg, Chemnitz, Muenchen,
          Muenster, Goettingen, Wuppertal, Schleswig, Giessen,
          Rostock, Leipzig and other
long distance -> provided by user
services — — —> e-mail, usenet feeds, UUCP, SLIP, ISDN, shell, ftp, telnet,
          gopher, irc, bbs
fees — — — — —> 15-30 DM/month (differs from region to region)
email — — — —> in-info@individual.net
voice — — — —> +49 2131 64190 (Andreas Baess)
fax — — — — —> +49 2131 605652
ftp more info -> ftp.fu-berlin.de:/pub/doc/IN/
```

```
<< in-rhein-main >>
name  — — — — —> Individual Network - Rhein-Main
dialup — — — —> +49-69-39048414, +49-69-6312934 (+ others)
area codes — —> +49 069
local access —> Frankfurt/Offenbach, Germany
long distance -> provided by user
services — — —> shell (Unix), ftp, telnet, irc, gopher, uucp feeds
fees — — — — —> SLIP/PPP/ISDN: 40 DM, 4 DM / Megabyte
email — — — —> info@rhein-main.de
voice — — — —> +49-69-39048413
ftp more info -> n/a
```

```
<< ins >>
name  — — — — —> INS - Inter Networking Systems
```

```
dialup — — — —>  contact for number
area codes — —>  +49 23
local access —>  Ruhr-Area, Germany
long distance ->  provided by user
services — — —>  e-mail,uucp,usenet,slip,ppp,ISDN-TCP/IP
fees — — — —>  fees for commercial institutions and any others:
        uucp/e-mail,uucp/usenet:$60/month; ip:$290/month minimum
email — — — —> info@ins.net
voice — — — —> +49 2305 356505
fax — — — — —> +49 2305 25411
ftp more info -> n/a
```

```
<< InterAccess >>
name — — — — —>  InterAccess
dialup — — — —> 708-671-0237
area codes — —> 708, 312, 815
local access —> Chicagoland metropolitan area
long distance -> provided by user
services — — —> ftp, telnet, SLIP/PPP, feeds, shell, UUCP, DNS, ftp space
fees — — — — —> $23/mo shell, $26/mo SLIP/PPP, or $5/mo +$2.30/hr
email — — — —> info@interaccess.com
voice — — — —> (800) 967-1580
fax — — — — —> 708-671-0113
ftp more info -> interaccess.com:/pub/interaccess.info
```

```
<< jvnc >>
name — — — — —> The John von Neumann Computer Network - Tiger Mail &
Dialin'
        Terminal
dialup — — — —> contact for number
area codes — —> 800
local access —> anywhere (800) service is available
long distance -> included
services — — —> email and newsfeed or terminal access only
fees — — — — —> $19/month + $10/hour + $36 startup (PC or Mac SLIP software
        included)
email — — — —> info@jvnc.net
voice — — — —> 800-35-TIGER, 609-897-7300
fax — — — — —> 609-897-7310
ftp more info -> n/a
```

```
<< jvnc-tiger >>
name — — — — —> The John von Neumann Computer Network - Dialin' Tiger
dialup — — — —> contact for number
area codes — —> 201, 203, 215, 401, 516, 609, 908
local access —> Princeton & Newark, NJ; Philadelphia, PA; Garden City, NY;
        Bridgeport, New Haven, & Storrs, CT; Providence, RI
```

```
long distance -> provided by user
services ———> ftp, telnet, SLIP, feeds, optional shell
fees —————> $99/month + $99 startup (PC or Mac SLIP software in-
cluded —
                  shell is additional $21/month)
email ————> info@jvnc.net
voice ————> 800-35-TIGER, 609-897-7300
fax —————> 609-897-7310
ftp more info -> n/a
```

<< kaiwan >>
```
name —————> KAIWAN Public Access Internet Online Services
dialup ————> 714-539-5726, 310-527-7358
area codes ——> 213, 310, 714
local access —> CA: Los Angeles, Orange County
long distance -> provided by user
services ———> shell, ftp, telnet, irc, WAIS, gopher, SLIP/PPP, ftp space,
         feeds, dns, 56K leasd line
fees —————> $15.00/signup + $15.00/month or $30.00/quarter (3 month) or
          $11.00/month by credit card
email ————> info@kaiwan.com
voice ————> 714-638-2139
ftp more info -> kaiwan.com: /pub/KAIWAN
```

<< maestro >>
```
name —————> Maestro
dialup ————> (212) 240-9700 'newuser'
area codes ——> 212, 718
local access —> NY: New York City
long distance -> provided by user
services ———> shell, ftp, telnet, gopher, wais, irc, feeds, etc.
fees —————> $15/month or $150/year
email ————> info@maestro.com (autoreply); staff@maestro.com,
         rkelly@maestro.com, ksingh@maestro.com
voice ————> 212-240-9600
ftp more info -> n/a
```

<< mcsnet >>
```
name —————> MCSNet
dialup ————> (312) 248-0900 V.32, 0970 V.32bis, 6295 (PEP), follow prompts
area codes ——> 312, 708, 815
local access —> IL: Chicago
long distance -> provided by user
services ———> shell, ftp, telnet, feeds, email, irc, gopher, hytelnet, etc.
fees —————> $25/month or $65/3 months untimed, $30/3 months for 15
          hours/month
email ————> info@genesis.mcs.com
```

```
voice — — — —> (312) 248-UNIX
ftp more info -> genesis.mcs.com:/mcsnet.info/
```

<< metronet >>
name — — — — —> Texas Metronet
dialup — — — —> 214-705-2901/817-261-1127 (V.32bis),214-705-
2929(PEP),'info'
                  or 214-705-2917/817-261-7687 (2400) 'signup'
area codes — —> 214, 817
local access —> TX: Dallas, Fort Worth
long distance -> provided by user
services — — —> shell, ftp, telnet, SLIP, PPP, uucp feeds
fees — — — —> $5-$45/month + $10-$30 startup
email — — — —> info@metronet.com
voice — — — —> 214-705-2900, 817-543-8756
fax — — — — —> 214-401-2802 (8am-5pm CST weekdays)
ftp more info -> ftp.metronet.com:/pub/metronetinfo/

<< michnet >>
name — — — — —> Merit Network, Inc. — MichNet project
dialup — — — —> contact for number or telnet hermes.merit.edu and type
        'help' at 'Which host?' prompt
area codes — —> 202, 301, 313, 517, 616, 703, 810, 906, PDN
local access —> Michigan; Boston, MA; Wash. DC
long distance -> SprintNet, Autonet, Michigan Bell packet-switch network
services — — —> telnet, SLIP, PPP, outbound SprintNet, Autonet and Ann Arbor
        dialout
fees — — — — —> $35/month + $40 signup ($10/month for K-12 & libraries in
        Michigan)
email — — — —> info@merit.edu
voice — — — —> 313-764-9430
ftp more info -> nic.merit.edu:/

<< millennium >>
name — — — — —> Millennium Online
dialup — — — —> contact for numbers
area codes — —> PDN
local access —> PDN private numbers available
long distance -> PDN
services — — —> shell, ftp, telnet, irc, feeds, gopher, graphical bbs
        (interface required)
fees — — — — —> $10 monthly/.10 per minute domestic .30 internationally
email — — — —> jjablow@mill.com
voice — — — —> 800-736-0122
ftp more info -> n/a

<< mindvox >>
```
```

```
name  — — — — —> MindVOX
dialup  — — — —> 212-989-4141 'mindvox' 'guest'
area codes  — —> 212, 718
local access  —> NY: New York City
long distance -> provided by user
services  — — —> conferencing system ftp, telnet, irc, gopher, hytelnet,
                 Archives, BBS
fees  — — — — —> $15-$20/month.  No startup.
email  — — — —> info@phantom.com
voice — — — —> 212-989-2418
ftp more info -> n/a
```

<< MSen >>
```
name  — — — — —> MSen
dialup — — — —> contact for number
area codes — —> 313, 810
local access —> All of SE Michigan (313, 810)
long distance -> provided by user
services — — —> shell, WAIS, gopher, telnet, ftp, SLIP, PPP, IRC, WWW,
         Picospan BBS, ftp space
fees — — — — —> $20/month; $20 startup
email — — — —> info@msen.com
voice — — — —> 313-998-4562
fax — — — — —> 313-998-4563
ftp more info -> ftp.msen.com:/pub/vendor/msen
```

<< mucev >>
```
name  — — — — —> muc.de e.V.
dialup — — — —> contact for numbers
area codes — —> +49 089
local access —> Munich/Bavaria, Germany
long distance -> provided by user
services — — —> mail, news, ftp, telnet, irc, gopher, SLIP/PPP/UUCP
fees — — — — —> From DM 20. — (Mail only) up to DM 65. — (Full Account with
          PPP)
email — — — —> postmaster@muc.de
voice — — — —>
ftp more info -> ftp.muc.de:public/info/muc-info.*
```

<< MV >>
```
name  — — — — —> MV Communications, Inc.
dialup — — — —> contact for numbers
area codes — —> 603
local access —> Many NH communities
long distance -> provided by user
services — — —> shell, ftp, telnet, gopher, SLIP, email, feeds, dns,
         archives, etc.
```

```
fees — — — —> $5.00/mo minimum + variable hourly rates.  See sched-
ule.
email — — — —> info@mv.com
voice — — — —> 603-429-2223
ftp more info -> ftp.mv.com:/pub/mv


<< nearnet >>
name — — — — —> NEARnet
dialup — — — —> contact for numbers
area codes — —> 508, 603, 617
local access —> Boston, MA; Nashua, NH
long distance -> provided by user
services — — —> SLIP, email, feeds, dns
fees — — — — —> $250/month
email — — — —> nearnet-join@nic.near.net
voice — — — —> 617-873-8730
ftp more info -> nic.near.net:/docs


<< netcom >>
name — — — — —> Netcom Online Communication Services
dialup — — — —> 206-547-5992, 214-753-0045, 303-758-0101, 310-842-8835,
              312-380-0340, 404-303-9765, 408-241-9760, 408-459-9851,
              415-328-9940, 415-985-5650, 503-626-6833, 510-274-2900,
              510-426-6610, 510-865-9004, 617-237-8600, 619-234-0524,
              703-255-5951, 714-708-3800, 818-585-3400, 916-965-1371
area codes — —> 206, 213, 214, 303, 310, 312, 404, 408, 415, 503, 510,
            617, 619, 703, 714, 718, 818, 916
local access —> CA: Alameda, Irvine, Los Angeles, Palo Alto, Pasadena,
            Sacramento, San Diego, San Francisco, San Jose, Santa Cruz,
            Walnut Creek; CO: Denver; DC: Washington; GA: Atlanta; IL:
            Chicago; MA: Boston; OR: Portland; TX: Dallas; WA: Seattle
long distance -> provided by user
services — — —> shell, ftp, telnet, irc, WAIS, gopher, SLIP/PPP, ftp space,
            feeds, dns
fees — — — — —> $19.50/month + $20.00 signup
email — — — —> info@netcom.com
voice — — — —> 408-554-8649, 800-501-8649
fax — — — — —> 408-241-9145
ftp more info -> ftp.netcom.com:/pub/netcom/


<< northshore >>
name — — — — —> North Shore Access
dialup — — — —> 617-593-4557 (v.32bis, v.32, PEP) 'new'
area codes — —> 617, 508
local access —> MA: Wakefield, Lynnfield, Lynn, Saugus, Revere, Peabody,
            Salem, Marblehead, Swampscott
long distance -> provided by user
```

```
services — — —> shell (SunOS UNIX), ftp, telnet, archie, gopher, wais,
www,
                   UUCP feeds
fees — — — —> $9/month includes 10 hours connect, $1/hr thereafter,
higher
                   volume discount plans also available
email — — — —> info@northshore.ecosoft.com
voice — — — —> 617-593-3110 voicemail
ftp more info -> northshore.ecosoft.com:/pub/flyer
```

<< novalink >>
name — — — — —> NovaLink
dialup — — — —> (800) 937-7644 'new' or 'info', 508-754-4009 2400, 14400
area codes — —> 508, 617, PDN
local access —> MA: Worcester, Cambridge, Marlboro, Boston
long distance -> CPS: $1.80/hour 2400, 9600; SprintNet $1.80/hour nights and
          weekends
services — — —> ftp, telnet, gopher, shell, irc, XWindows, feeds, adult,
          user groups, FAX, Legends of Future Past
fees — — — — —> $12.95 sign-up (refundable and includes 2 hours), + $9.95/mo
          (includes 5 daytime hours) + $1.80/hr
email — — — —> info@novalink.com
voice — — — —> 800-274-2814
ftp more info -> ftp.novalink.com:/info

<< nuance >>
name — — — — —> Nuance Network Services
dialup — — — —> contact for number
area codes — —> 205
local access —> AL: Huntsville
long distance -> provided by user
services — — —> shell (Unix SVR4.2), ftp, telnet, gopher, SLIP, PPP, ISDN
fees — — — — —> personal $25/mo + $35 start-up, corporate: call for options
email — — — —> staff@nuance.com
voice — — — —> 205-533-4296 voice/recording
ftp more info -> ftp.nuance.com:/pub/NNS-INFO

<< nuchat >>
name — — — — —> South Coast Computing Services, Inc.
dialup — — — —> (713) 661-8593 (v.32) - (713) 661-8595 (v.32bis)
area codes — —> 713
local access —> TX: Houston metro area
long distance -> provided by user
services — — —> shell, ftp, telnet, gopher, Usenet, UUCP feeds, SLIP,
          dedicated lines, domain name service; FULL time tech support
fees — — — — —> dialup - $3/hour, UUCP - $1.50/hour or $100/month unlimited,
          dedicated - $120, unlimited access
```
```

```
email —————> info@sccsi.com
voice —————> 713-661-3301
ftp more info -> sccsi.com:/pub/communications/*
```

```
<< nwnexus >>
name —————> Northwest Nexus Inc.
dialup —————> contact for numbers
area codes ——> 206
local access —> WA: Seattle
long distance -> provided by user
services ———> UUCP, SLIP, PPP, feeds, dns
fees —————> $10/month for first 10 hours + $3/hr; $20 start-up
```
email ————> info@nwnexus.wa.com
voice ————> 206-455-3505
ftp more info -> nwnexus.wa.com:/NWNEXUS.info.txt

```
<< nyx >>
name —————> Nyx, the Spirit of the Night; Free public internet
```
access

        provided by the University of Denver's Math & Computer
        Science Department
dialup ————> 303-871-3324
area codes ——> 303
local access —> CO: Boulder/Denver
long distance -> provided by user
services ———> shell or menu; semi-anonymous accounts; ftp, news, mail
fees —————> none; donations are accepted but not requested
email ————> aburt@nyx.cs.du.edu
voice ————> login to find current list of volunteer 'voice' helpers
ftp more info -> n/a

```
<< OARnet >>
name —————> OARnet
```
dialup ————> send e-mail to nic@oar.net
area codes ——> 614, 513, 419, 216, 800
local access —> OH: Columbus, Cincinnati, Cleveland, Dayton
long distance -> 800 service
services ———> email, ftp, telnet, newsfeed
fees —————> $4.00/hr to $330.00/month; call for code or send email
email ————> nic@oar.net
voice ————> 614-292-8100
fax —————> 614-292-7168
ftp more info -> n/a

```
<< oldcolo >>
name —————> Old Colorado City Communications
```
dialup ————> 719-632-4111 'newuser'

```
area codes — —> 719
local access —> CO: Colorado Springs
long distance -> provided by user
services — — —> shell, ftp, telnet, AKCS, home of the NAPLPS conference
fees — — — — —> $25/month
email — — — —> dave@oldcolo.com / thefox@oldcolo.com
voice — — — —> 719-632-4848, 719-593-7575 or 719-636-2040
fax — — — — —> 719-593-7521
ftp more info -> n/a
```

<< olympus >>
```
name — — — — —> Olympus - The Olympic Peninsula's Gateway To The
Internet
dialup — — — —> contact voice number below
area codes — —> 206
local access —> WA:Olympic Peninsula/Eastern Jefferson County
long distance -> provided by user
services — — —> shell, ftp, telnet, pine, hytelnet
fees — — — — —> $25/month + $10 startup
email — — — —> info@pt.olympus.net
voice — — — —> 206-385-0464
ftp more info -> n/a
```

<< panix >>
```
name — — — — —> PANIX Public Access Unix
dialup — — — —> 212-787-3100 'newuser'
area codes — —> 212, 718
local access —> New York City, NY
long distance -> provided by user
services — — —> shell, ftp, telnet, gopher, wais, irc, feeds
fees — — — — —> $19/month or $208/year + $40 signup
email — — — —> alexis@panix.com, jsb@panix.com
voice — — — —> 212-877-4854 [Alexis Rosen], 212-691-1526 [Jim Baumbach]
ftp more info -> n/a
```

<< pipeline >>
```
name — — — — —> The Pipeline
dialup — — — —> 212-267-8606 'guest'
area codes — —> 212, 718
local access —> NY: New York City
long distance -> provided by user
services — — —> Windows interface or shell/menu; all IP services
fees — — — — —> $15/mo. (inc. 5 hrs) or $20/20 hrs or $35 unlimited
email — — — —> info@pipeline.com, staff@pipeline.com
voice — — — —> 212-267-3636
ftp more info -> n/a
```

<< portal >>

```
name  — — — —>  The Portal System
dialup  — — — —>  408-973-8091 high-speed, 408-725-0561 2400bps; 'info'
area codes  — —>  408, 415, PDN
local access  —>  CA: Cupertino, Mountain View, San Jose
long distance ->  SprintNet: $2.50/hour off-peak, $7-$10/hour peak;
Tymnet:
                    $2.50/hour off-peak, $13/hour peak
services  — — —>  shell, ftp, telnet, IRC, UUCP, feeds, bbs
fees  — — — —>  $19.95/month + $19.95 signup
email  — — — —>  cs@cup.portal.com, info@portal.com
voice  — — — —>  408-973-9111
ftp more info ->  n/a
off-peak  — — —>  6pm to 7am + weekends and holidays
```

<< prairienet >>
name — — — —> Prairienet Freenet
dialup — — — —> (217) 255-9000 'visitor'
area codes — —> 217
local access —> IL: Champaign-Urbana
long distance -> provided by user
services — — —> telnet, ftp, gopher, IRC, etc.
fees — — — —> Free for Illinois residents, $25/year for non-residents
email — — — —> jayg@uiuc.edu
voice — — — —> 217-244-1962
ftp more info -> n/a

<< PREPnet >>
name — — — —> PREPnet
dialup — — — —> contact for numbers
area codes — —> 215, 412, 717, 814
local access —> PA: Philadelphia, Pittsburgh, Harrisburg
long distance -> provided by user
services — — —> SLIP, terminal service, telnet, ftp
fees — — — —> $1,000/year membership. Equipment-$325 onetime fee plus
          $40/month
email — — — —> prepnet@cmu.edu
voice — — — —> 412-268-7870
fax — — — —> 412-268-7875
ftp more info -> ftp.prepnet.com: /prepnet/general/

<< psilink >>
name — — — —> PSILink - Personal Internet Access
dialup — — — —> North America: send email to classa-na-numbers@psi.com and
          classb-na-numbers@psi.com; Rest of World: send email to
          classb-row-numbers@psi.com
area codes — —> PDN
local access —>

```
long distance -> [per hour, off-peak/peak] PSINet A: included; PSINet B:
                 $6/$2.50; PSINet B international: $18/$18
services ———> email and newsfeed, ftp
fees —————> 2400: $19/month; 9600: $29/month (PSILink software
included)
email ————> all-info@psi.com, psilink-info@psi.com
voice ————> 703-620-6651
fax —————> 703-620-4586
ftp more info -> ftp.psi.com:/
```

```
<< psi-world-dial >>
name —————> PSI's World-Dial Service
dialup ————> send email to numbers-info@psi.com
area codes ——> PDN
local access —>
long distance -> [per hour, off-peak/peak] V.22bis: $1.25/$2.75; V.32:
        $3.00/$4.50; 14.4K: $4.00/$6.50
services ———> telnet, rlogin, tn3270, XRemote
fees —————> $9/month minimum + $19 startup
email ————> all-info@psi.com, world-dial-info@psi.com
voice ————> 703-620-6651
fax —————> 703-620-4586
ftp more info -> ftp.psi.com:/
off-peak ———> 8pm to 8am + weekends and holidays
```

```
<< PUCnet >>
name —————> PUCnet Computer Connections
dialup ————> 403-484-5640 (v.32 bis) 'guest'
area codes ——> 403
local access —> AB: Edmonton and surrounding communities in the Extended
        Flat Rate Calling Area
long distance -> provided by user
services ———> shell, menu, ftp, telnet, archie, gopher, feeds, USENET
fees —————> Cdn$25/month (20 hours connect time) + Cdn$6.25/hr (ftp &
        telnet only) + $10 signup
email ————> info@PUCnet.com (Mail responder) or pwilson@PUCnet.com
voice ————> 403-448-1901
fax —————> 403-484-7103
ftp more info -> n/a
```

```
<< realtime >>
name —————> RealTime Communications (wixer)
dialup ————> 512-459-4391 'new'
area codes ——> 512
local access —> TX: Austin
long distance -> provided by user
services ———> shell, ftp, telnet, irc, gopher, feeds, SLIP, UUCP
```

```
fees —————> $75/year.  Monthly and quarterly rates available.
email ————> hosts@wixer.bga.com
voice ————> 512-451-0046 (11am-6pm Central Time, weekdays)
fax —————> 512-459-3858
ftp more info -> n/a


<< ssnet >>
name —————> Systems Solutions
dialup ————> contact for info
area codes ——> 302
local access —> Wilminton, Delaware
long distance -> provided by user
services ———> shell, UUCP, SLIP, PPP, ftp, telnet, irc, gopher,
archie,
                mud, etc.
fees —————> full service  $25/month $20/startup; personal slip/ppp
              $25/month + $2/hour, $20/startup; dedicated slip/ppp
          $150/month, $450/startup
email ————> sharris@marlin.ssnet.com
voice ————> (302) 378-1386, (800) 331-1386
ftp more info -> n/a


<< sugar >>
name —————> NeoSoft's Sugar Land Unix
dialup ————> 713-684-5900
area codes ——> 504, 713
local access —> TX: Houston metro area; LA: New Orleans
long distance -> provided by user
services ———> bbs, shell, ftp, telnet, irc, feeds, UUCP
fees —————> $29.95/month
email ————> info@NeoSoft.com
voice ————> 713-438-4964
ftp more info -> n/a


<< teleport >>
name —————> Teleport
dialup ————> 503-220-0636 (2400) 503-220-1016 (v.32, v.32 bis) 'new'
area codes ——> 503
local access —> OR: Portland, Beaverton, Hillsboro, Forest Grove, Gresham,
        Tigard, Lake Oswego, Oregon City, Tualatin, Wilsonville
long distance -> provided by user
services ———> shell, ftp, telnet, gopher, usenet, ppp, WAIS, irc, feeds,
          dns
fees —————> $10/month (1 hr/day limit)
email ————> info@teleport.com
voice ————> 503-223-4245
ftp more info -> teleport.com:/about
```

```
<< telerama >>
name — — — —> Telerama Public Access Internet
dialup — — — —> 412-481-5302 'new' (2400)
area codes — —> 412
local access —> PA: Pittsburgh
long distance -> provided by user
services — — —> telnet, ftp, irc, gopher, ClariNet/Usenet, shell/menu,
uucp
fees — — — —> 66 cents/hour 2400bps; $1.32/hour 14.4K bps; $6 min/
month
email — — — —> info@telerama.pgh.pa.us
voice — — — —> 412-481-3505
ftp more info -> telerama.pgh.pa.us:/info/general.info


<< tmn >>
name — — — — —> The Meta Network
dialup — — — —> contact for numbers
area codes — —> 703, 202, 301, PDN
local access —> Washington, DC metro area
long distance -> SprintNet: $6.75/hr; FTS-2000; Acunet
services — — —> Caucus conferencing, email, shell, ftp, telnet, bbs, feeds
fees — — — — —> $20/month + $15 signup/first month
email — — — —> info@tmn.com
voice — — — —> 703-243-6622
ftp more info -> n/a


<< UUNET-Canada >>
name — — — — —> UUNET Canada, Inc.
dialup — — — —> contact for numbers
area codes — —> 416, 905, 519, 613, 514, 604, 403
local access —> ON: Toronto, Ottawa, Kitchener/Waterloo, London, Hamilton,
        QC: Montreal,  AB: Calgary,  BC: Vancouver
long distance -> provided by user
services — — —> terminal access to telnet only, UUCP (e-mail/news),
        SLIP/PPP, shared or dedicated basis, from v.32bis to 56k+
fees — — — — —> (All Cdn$ + GST) TAC: $6/hr, UUCP: $20/mo + $6/hr, IP/UUCP:
        $50/mo + $6/hr, ask for prices on other services
email — — — —> info@uunet.ca
voice — — — —> 416-368-6621
fax — — — — —> 416-368-1350
ftp more info -> ftp.uunet.ca


<< uunorth >>
name — — — — —> UUnorth
dialup — — — —> contact for numbers
area codes — —> 416, 519, 613
```

```
local access —> ON: Toronto
long distance -> provided by user
services — — —> shell, ftp, telnet, gopher, feeds, IRC, feeds, SLIP,
PPP
fees — — — — —> (All Cdn$ + GST) $20 startup + $25 for 20 hours off-
peak +
                $1.25/hr OR $40 for 40 hours up to 5/day + $2/hr OR
$3/hr
email — — — —> uunorth@uunorth.north.net
voice — — — —> 416-225-8649
fax — — — — —> 416-225-0525
ftp more info -> n/a
```

```
<< Vnet >>
name — — — — —> Vnet Internet Access, Inc.
dialup — — — —> 704-347-8839, 919-406-1544, 919-851-1526 'new'
area codes — —> 704, 919
local access —> NC: Charlotte, RTP, Raleigh, Durham, Chappel Hill.
Winston
                Salem/Greensboro
long distance -> Available for $3.95 per hour through Global Access.
Contact
                Vnet offices for more information.
services — — —> shell, ftp, telnet, hytelnet, irc, gopher, WWW, wais,
        usenet, clarinet, NNTP, DNS, SLIP/PPP, UUCP, POPmail
fees — — — — —> $25/month individual. $12.50 a month for telnet-in-only.
        SLIP/PPP/UUCP starting at $25/month.
email — — — —> info@char.vnet.net
voice — — — —> 704-374-0779
ftp more info -> n/a
```

```
<< well >>
name — — — — —> The Whole Earth 'Lectronic Link
dialup — — — —> 415-332-6106 'newuser'
area codes — —> 415, PDN
local access —> Sausalito, CA
long distance -> Compuserve Packet Network: $4/hour
services — — —> shell, ftp, telnet, bbs
fees — — — — —> $15.00/month + $2.00/hr
email — — — —> info@well.sf.ca.us
voice — — — —> 415-332-4335
ftp more info -> n/a
```

```
<< wariat >>
name — — — — —> APK- Public Access UNI* Site
dialup — — — —> 216-481-9436 (V.32bis, SuperPEP on separate rotary)
```

```
area codes ——> 216
local access —> OH: Cleveland
long distance -> provided by user
services ———> shell, ftp, telnet, archie, irc, gopher, feeds,
              BBS(Uniboard1.10)
fees ————> $15/20 hours, $35/monthly, $20 signup
email ————> zbig@wariat.org
voice ————> 216-481-9428
ftp more info -> n/a


<< world >>
name ————> The World
dialup ————> 617-739-9753 'new'
area codes ——> 617, PDN
local access —> Boston, MA
long distance -> Compuserve Packet Network: $5.60/hour
services ——> shell, ftp, telnet, irc
fees ————> $5.00/month + $2.00/hr or $20/month for 20 hours
email ————> office@world.std.com
voice ————> 617-739-0202
ftp more info -> world.std.com:/world-info/description


<< wyvern >>
name ————> Wyvern Technologies, Inc.
dialup ————> (804) 627-1828 Norfolk, (804) 886-0662 (Peninsula)
area codes ——> 804
local access —> VA: Norfolk, Virginia Beach, Portsmouth, Chesapeake,
Newport
              News, Hampton, Williamsburg
long distance -> provided by user
services ——> shell, menu, ftp, telnet, uucp feeds, irc, archie,
gopher,
              UPI news, email, dns, archives
fees ————> $15/month or $144/year, $10 startup
email ————> system@wyvern.com
voice ————> 804-622-4289
fax ————> 804-622-7158
ftp more info -> n/a


<< xnet >>
name ———|——> XNet Information Systems
dialup ————> (708) 983-6435 V.32bis and TurboPEP
area codes ——> 312, 708, 815
local access —> IL: Chicago, Naperville, Hoffman Estates
long distance -> provided by user
```

```
services ———> shell, telnet, hytelnet, ftp, irc, gopher, www,
wais,
                SLIP/PPP, dns, uucp feeds, bbs
fees ————> $45/3 months or $75/6 months
email ————> info@xnet.com
voice ————> (708) 983-6064
ftp more info -> ftp.xnet.com:/xnet.info/
```

-05- What *Is* the Internet?

The Internet is a global cooperative network of university, corporate, government, and private computers, all communicating with
each other by means of something called TCP/IP (Transmission
Control Protocol/Internet Protocol). Computers directly on the
Internet can exchange data quickly and easily with any other
computer on the Internet to download files, send email, provide
remote logins, etc.

Users can download files from publicly accessible archive sites
("anonymous FTP"); login into remote computers (telnet or
rlogin); chat in real-time with other users around the world
(Internet Relay Chat); or use the newest information retrieval
tools to find a staggering variety of information (Wide Area
Information Servers, Gopher, World Wide Web).

Computers directly on the Internet also exchange email directly
and very quickly; email is usually delivered in seconds between
Internet sites.

Sometimes the Internet is confused with other related networks or
types of networking.

First, there are other ways to be "connected to the Internet"
without being directly connected as a TCP/IP node. Some computers connect via UUCP or other means at regular intervals to an
Internet site to exchange email and USENET newsgroups, for instance. Such a site can provide email (though not as quickly as
a directly connected systems) and USENET access, but not Internet
downloads, remote logins, etc.

"email" (or "Internet email", "netmail") can be exchanged with a
wide variety of systems connected directly and indirectly to the
Internet. The email may travel solely over the Internet, or it
may traverse other networks and systems.

"USENET" is the collection of computers all over the world that exchange USENET news — thousands of "newsgroups" (like forums, or echos) on a wide range of topics. The newsgroup articles are distributed all over the world to USENET sites that wish to carry them (sometimes over the Internet, sometimes not), where people read and respond to them.

The "NSFNET" is one of the backbones of the Internet in the US. It is funded by the NSF, which restricts traffic over the NSFNET to "open research and education in and among US research and instructional institutions, plus research arms of for-profit firms when engaged in open scholarly communication and research." Your Internet provider can give you more details about acceptable use, and alternatives should you need to use the Internet in other ways.

-06- What the PDIAL Is

This is the PDIAL, the Public Dialup Internet Access List.

It is a list of Internet service providers offering public access dialins and outgoing Internet access (ftp, telnet, etc.). Most of them provide email and USENET news and other services as well.

If one of these systems is not accessible to you and you need email or USENET access, but *don't* need ftp or telnet, you have many more public access systems from which to choose. Public access systems without ftp or telnet are *not* listed in this list, however. See the nixpub (alt.bbs, comp.misc) list and other BBS lists.

Some of these providers offer time-shared access to a shell or BBS program on a computer connected directly to the Internet, through which you can FTP or telnet to other systems on the Internet. Usually other services are provided as well. Generally, you need only a modem and terminal or terminal emulator to access these systems. Check for "shell", "bbs", or "menu" on the "services" line.

Other providers connect you directly to the Internet via SLIP or PPP when you dial in. For these you need a computer system capable of running the software to interface with the Internet, e.g., a Unix machine, PC, or Mac. Check for "SLIP", or "PPP" on the services line.

While I have included all sites for which I have complete infor-

mation, this list is surely incomplete. If you have any additions or corrections please send them to me at one of the addresses listed in section -10-.

-07- How People Can Get the PDIAL (This List)

EMAIL:

    From the Information Deli archive server (most up-to-date):
       To receive the current edition of the PDIAL, send email containing
       the phrase "Send PDIAL" to "info-deli-server@netcom.com".

       To be put on a list of people who receive future editions as they
       are published, send email containing the phrase "Subscribe PDIAL"
       to "info-deli-server@netcom.com".

       To receive both the most recent and future editions, send both
       messages.

       From time to time, I'll also be sending out news and happenings
       that relate to the PDIAL or The Information Deli. To receive
       the Info Deli News automatically, send email containing the
       phrase "Subscribe Info-Deli-News" to "info-deli-server@netcom.com".

    From the news.answers FAQ archive:
       Send email with the message "send usenet/news.answers/pdial" to
       "mail-server@rtfm.mit.edu". For help, send the message "help" to
       "mail-server@rtfm.mit.edu".

USENET:

    The PDIAL list is posted semi-regularly to alt.internet.access.wanted,
    alt.bbs.lists, alt.online-service, ba.internet, and news.answers.

FTP ARCHIVE SITES (PDIAL and other useful information):

    Information Deli FTP site:
       ftp.netcom.com:/pub/info-deli/public-access/pdial [192.100.81.100]

    As part of a collection of public access lists:
       VFL.Paramax.COM:/pub/pubnet/pdial [128.126.220.104]
       (used to be GVL.Unisys.COM)

From the Merit Network Information Center Internet information archive:
    nic.merit.edu:/internet/providers/pdial [35.1.1.48]

As part of an Internet access compilation file:
  liberty.uc.wlu.edu:/pub/lawlib/internet.access [137.113.10.35]

As part of the news.answers FAQ archive:
    rtfm.mit.edu:/pub/usenet/news.answers/pdial [18.70.0.209]

-08- Other Valuable Resources

InterNIC Internet Help Desk

The US National Science Foundation has funded Information, Registration, and Directory services for the Internet, and they are available to all Internet users. The most useful branch for PDIAL readers is Information Services, which provides all sorts of information to help Internet users.
Contact Information Services by:

voice: 800-444-4345 (US)
voice: +1 (619) 455-4600
fax: +1 (619) 455-4640
email: mailserv@is.internic.net, put "SEND HELP" in body
email: info@internic.net
gopher: gopher gopher.internic.net / telnet gopher.internic.net
ftp: is.internic.net
postal: InterNIC Information Services
         General Atomics
         PO Box 85608
         San Diego, CA 92186-9784 USA

Internet Guide Books

Connecting To The Internet; Susan Estrada; O'Reilly & Associates; ISBN 1-56592-061-9 (A how-to on selecting the right IP provider, from dialup to dedicated.)

A DOS User's Guide to the Internet — E-mail, Netnews and File Transfer with UUCP; James Gardner; MKS; ISBN 0-13-106873-3 ("Internet" in the title is misleading — covers UUCP connections only.)

The Electronic Traveller — Exploring Alternative Online Systems; Elizabeth Powell Crowe; Windcrest/McGraw-Hill; ISBN 0-8306-4498-9. (A good tour of various personal IP and other types of providers, but some data is seriously out of date.)

Internet Basics; Steve Lambert, Walt How; Random House; ISBN 0-679-75023-1

The Internet Companion; Tracy LaQuey, Jeanne C. Ryer; Addison-Wesley; ISBN 0-201-62224-6

The Internet Companion Plus; Tracy LaQuey, Jeanne C. Ryer; Addison-Wesley; ISBN 0-201-62719-1

The Internet Complete Reference; Harley Hahn, Rick Stout; Osborne; ISBN 0-07-881980-6

The Internet Directory; Eric Brawn; Fawcett Columbine; ISBN 0-449-90898-4 (Phone book style listing of resources.)

The Internet for Dummies; John R. Levine, Carol Baroudi; IDG Books Worldwide; ISBN 1-56884-024-1 (Lots of useful information, but much of it is intermediate level, not "dummy".)

Internet: Getting Started; April Marine, Susan Kirkpatrick, Vivian Neou, Carol Ward; PTR Prentice Hall; ISBN 0-13-289596-X

The Internet Guide for New Users; Daniel P. Dern; McGraw-Hill; ISBN 0-07-016511-4 (Good, very thorough guide for new users.)

The Internet Navigator; Paul Glister; John Wiley & Sons; ISBN 0-471-59782-1 (Good, comprehensive guide for new users.)

The Internet Roadmap; Bennet Falk; Sybex; ISBN 0-7821-1365-6

Internet Starter Kit for the Macintosh With Disk; Adam C. Engst; Hayden Books; ISBN 1-56830-064-6

The Mac Internet Tour Guide; Michael Fraase; Ventana Press; ISBN 1-56604-062-0

Navigating the Internet; Richard J. Smith, Mark Gibbs; SAMS Publishing; ISBN 0-672-30362-0

Welcome to... Internet — From Mystery to Mastery; Tom Badgett, Corey Sandler; MIS:Press; ISBN 1-55828-308-0

The Whole Internet User's Guide & Catalog; Ed Krol; O'Reilly & Associates; ISBN 1-56592-025-2 (Good all around guide.)

Zen & the Art of the Internet: A Beginner's Guide; Brendan P. Kehoe;
PTR Prentice Hall; ISBN 0-13-010778-6

Other BBS/Internet Provider Lists

FSLIST — The Forgotten Site List. USENET: alt.internet.access.wanted;
ftp: freedom.nmsu.edu:/pub/docs/fslist/ or login.qc.ca:/pub/fslist/

nixpub — public access Unixes. USENET: comp.bbs.mis, alt.bbs;
email: to <mail-server@bts.com>, body containing "get PUB nixpub.long";
ftp: VFL.Paramax.COM:/pub/pubnetc/nixpub.long

-09- Finding Public Data Network (PDN) Access Numbers

Here's how to get local access numbers or information for the various
PDNs. Generally, you can contact the site you're calling for help, too.

IMPORTANT NOTE: Unless noted otherwise, set your modem to 7E1 (7 data
bits, even parity, 1 stop bit) when dialing to look up access numbers by
modem as instructed below.

BT Tymnet

For information and local access numbers, call 800-937-2862 (voice) or
215-666-1770 (voice).

To look up access numbers by modem, dial a local access number, hit <cr> and 'a', and
enter "information" at the "please log in:" prompt.

Compuserve Packet Network

You do NOT have to be a Compuserve member to use the CPN to dial other
services.

For information and local access numbers, call 800-848-8199 (voice).

To look up access numbers by modem, dial a local access number, hit <cr>
and enter "PHONES" at the "Host Name:" prompt.

PSINet

For information, call 800-82PSI82 (voice) or 703-620-6651 (voice), or send email to "all-info@psi.com". For a list of local access numbers send email to "numbers-info@psi.com".

-10- Providers: Get Listed in PDIAL!

NEW SUBMISSION/CORRECTION PROCEDURES:

The PDIAL will be undergoing expansion in both breadth (how many and what kinds of public access providers) and depth (how much information is carried for each provider). To collect the data, I will be emailing a questionnaire to providers already on the PDIAL, and to any providers who wish to be added. Corrections can also be submitted via update questionnaires.

To be listed in the PDIAL, retrieve the PDIAL questionnaire by sending email to <info-deli-server@netcom.com> containing the command "Send PDIAL-Q". The questionnaire will not be available until 15 Dec 1993, but requests received before then will be queued and honored when it is available.

Appendix

The nixpub List

This appendix contains the text of Phil Eschallier's nixpub list, another large but certainly not complete list of organizations that provide Internet access, often for a fee. The nixpub list differs from Peter Kaminski's PDIAL list in that not all of the sites on the nixpub list offer full Internet access. Some may offer only email and Usenet news, or perhaps only email. Many of the sites on the nixpub list are worth checking into, however, because they may provide access at an attractive rate and with a local call. As you can see by the Updated Last column, many of these sites haven't updated their listings in some time, and therefore, the details may differ from what you read here.

```
=============================================================================
NixPub Long Listing — March 04, 1994
Public/Open Access UNIX (*NIX) Sites [both Fee and No Fee]
=============================================================================
Sites Listed <146>
** Sites with multiple locations are only counted once **

    a2i       aa7bq      abode      actrix     admiral    agora
    alphacm   amaranth   anomaly    anubis     aquila     atrium
    bdt       bigtex     blkbox     bluemoon   btr        bucket
    cellar    cg57       chinet     cinnet     clinet     cns
```

colmiks	conexch	coyote	cpumagic	crash	cruzio
cyber	cyberspace	ddsw1	debug	deeptht	dhw68k
digex	dircon	dorsai	echo	edsi	eskimo
ExNet	exuco1	fullfeed	gagme	genesis	gorn
grebyn	grex	halcyon	hcserv	HoloNet	ibmpcug
ichlibix	indirect	infocom	isys-hh	ixgch	jabber
jack	kilowatt	kralizec	latour	loft386	lopez
lunapark	lunatix	m-net	m2xenix	madnix	magnus1
magpie	marob	maynard	medsys	metronet	micor
mindlink	mindvox	mixcom	mugnet	mv	ncoast
nervous	netcom	netlink	northshore	nuchat	nucleus
nyx	oaknet	odbffm	oldcolo	pallas	panix
pnet51	polari	portal	quack	quake	r-node
rgm	ritz	rock	sactoh0	sashimi	satelnet
schunix	scuzzy	sdf	seanews	sir-alan	sixhub
skypoint	solaria	stanton	starnet	sugar	sytex
szebra	teleport	telerama	telesys	tmsoft	tnc
tnl	tronsbox	tutor	ukelele	unixuser	uunet
uuwest	vicstoy	vpnet	wa9aek	wariat	wb3ffv
well	wet	WinNET	woodowl	world	wybbs
wyvern	xmission				

===

Updated		System			Speed	
Last	Telephone #	Name	Location		Range	Hours

11/93 201-432-0060   ritz   Jersey City   NJ 300-FAST 24
 Gateway2000 486/66 EISA, 16mb RAM, 900 meg disk space, BSDI/386 unix.
 5 dialins, all support MNP 3-5 and v.42/v.42bis. 4 modems are AT&T
 Dataport (14.4kbps/v.32bis) and one is a Telebit T2000 (19.2kbps/PEP).
 Shells supported: ash, csh, ksh, tcsh. Internet email / Mailers
 supported: elm, pine. Full USENET feed / Newsreaders supported: tin,
 trn. Editors supported: emacs, vi. RIP interface coming soon.
 Contact: ritz@mordor.com

03/94 201-759-8450   tronsbox Belleville   NJ 300-FAST 24
 Generic 386, UNIX 3.2; Provides shell for some users, USENET, E-Mail
 (feeds available) at $15 a month flat;
 Multiple line (-8568 300 - 2400 baud).

12/93 203-230-4848   colmiks Hamden   CT 2400-FAST 24
 Linux. Public Access Unix site. Internet mail and Usenet news are
 available. News becomes stale in one week. Low monthly fee; no per hour
 connect charges and no setup fees. First month is free. Unix account

with choice of two shells and three newsreaders. In addition, new members
can select three new Usenet newsgroups that Colmik's is not currently
receiving. Login as 'newuser'. For more info, contact mps@colmiks.com.

03/93 203-661-1279   admiral   Greenwich   CT 300-FAST 24
   SCO Unix 3.2.2. (HST/V32) 203-661-2873, (PEP/V32) 203-661-1279, (V32)
   203-661-0450, (MNP6) 203-661-2967. Magpie BBS for local conversation
   and Waffle for Internet mail/Usenet news. Interactive chat and games.
   BBS name is "The Grid." Willing to give newsfeeds and mail access.
   Shell (tcsh, ksh avail) accounts available at no charge. Direct connect
   to Internet site (Yale) via UUCP. 230 megs disk space. For more information
   contact uunet!admiral!doug (Doug Fields) or fields-doug@cs.yale.edu.

03/94 206-328-4944   polari   Seattle   WA 300-FAST 24
   Equip ???; 8-lines, Trailblazer on 206-328-1468; $50/year (flat rate);
   Multi-user games, chat, full USENET.
   Contact: bruceki%polari.uucp@sumax.seattleu.edu

03/94 206-367-3837   eskimo   Seattle   WA 300-FAST 24
   Sun 3/180 SUN/OS 4.1.1_U1 - Everett Tel 206-742-1150 Fast 206-362-6731
   14 Lines including TB World:lazer and TB-3000. Free 2-week trial account.
   Rates $10/month or $96/year.   Everybody gets their choice of sh, csh, tcsh,
   ksh, bash, or zsh. Full Usenet News feed 7 day expire. Unique real-time
   conference, message and files system. UUCP mail and news feeds available.
   Home of the Western Washington BBS List. Many applications online.
   Lots of Unix source code archived online. Internet ftp/telnet coming soon!

03/94 206-382-6245   halcyon   Seattle   WA 300-FAST 24
   ULTRIX 4.1, (PEP/V.32) 206-382-6245; monthly and annual fee schedules
   available. 56kBaud commercial Internet link to the T-3 backbone; NNTP
   news feed. Waffle bbs available. Irc server, archie and gopher clients,
   hytelnet, spop; dialup or telnet: login as 'bbs' and provide account
   information. For more information, contact: info@remote.halcyon.com,
   or call voice (PST, USA) +1 206 426 9298

03/94 206-747-6397   seanews   Redmond   WA 1200-FAST 24
   Xenix 386 2.3.2. SEANEWS is a free public service, providing
   access to Usenet and Internet mail. There are no games, very limited
   files, etc. However SEANEWS does have up-to-date Usenet news and
   excellent mail-handling capability.

03/94 212-420-0527   magpie   NYC   NY 300-FAST 24
   ? - UNIX SYSV - 2, Magpie BBS, no fee, Authors: Magpie/UNIX; No Shell;
   Multi-line (using Telebit Worldblazers) plus anonymous uucp;
   Contact: Steve Manes, manes@magpie.com

```
03/94 212-675-7059     marob     NYC           NY 300-FAST 24
   386 SCO-XENIX 2.2, XBBS, no fee, limit 60 min;  Telebit Trailblazer (9600
   PEP) only 212-675-8438;
   Contact: {philabs¦rutgers¦cmcl2}!phri!marob!clifford

03/94 212-787-3100     panix     New York City  NY 1200-FAST 24
   2 Sparc10/40 & 2 Sparc2, 176MB RAM, 12GB disk, Cisco routers, Annex 64-port
   term servers. Use any of 6 shells or our own custom-written menu system. 119
   dialins, all support MNP3-5 & V.42/V.42bis. 62 are V.32bis Zyxels (14.4kbps
   and higher), the rest 2400bps. We are a full internet site with high-speed
   (T1) line- telnet to panix.com (198.7.0.2). Full UseNet; (t)rn, nn, GNUs,
   Tin. Elm, Pine, MM, other mail readers. Vi, Emacs, Jove, Pico, other editors.
   Compile your own code (C/C++). $10/mn or 100/yr for basic, $9 per month add'l
   for telnet/ftp/gopher/www/etc. Feeds, domains, IP, more.
       NEW: SLIP or PPP service for only $35/month on 10 (soon 30) new lines.
           24 local numbers in Long island (516) 626-7863.
       COMING SOON: Local numbers in N.J. (201) and Westchester (914).
                   4-processor CPU upgrade. And, as usual, more lines.
       Contact: Alexis Rosen (alexis@panix.com) 212-877-4854, or Jim Baumbach
       (jsb@panix.com). Or email/finger info@panix.com, 212-787-6160.

03/94 212-989-4141     mindvox   New York       NY 1200-FAST 24
   Sparc10/51, SparcServer, 2 TurboSparcs, 256MB Ram, 15GB Disk, 96 dialups,
   32 additional Hayes V.FC modems @ 212-645-8065.  More high-speed lines
   added every month.  No startup fees.  Conference-oriented system with
   CyberPunk/Creative Arts focus.  Custom Interface.  Wired, Mondo 2000,
   aXcess and others host online conferences.  We are a full internet site
   with a high-speed leased line connection, telnet to phantom.com (198.67.3.2)
   and login as "guest" for a tour.  Telnet, ftp, gopher, www, lynx, wais, irc,
   ddial, SLIP, PPP, newsfeeds, QWK, POP3.  Prices go from $10-$17.50 per month
   for full access, discounts for pre-payment are available.
       Contact: info@phantom.com, gopher phantom.com, or 800-MindVox

09/93 212-989-8411     echo      NYC            NY 300-FAST 24
   Equip ???, OS ???;  A full Internet site with a highspeed leased line:
   telnet to echonyc.com (198.67.15.1).  Members have full access to shell,
   Usenet, telnet, ftp, gopher et al.  $19.95/month, $13.95/month for
   students and seniors.  We are a public computer conferencing system with
   1500 members (40% female) and full Internet access.
   Contact: horn@echonyc.com (Voice: (212) 255-3839)

03/94 214-248-9811     sdf       Dallas         TX 300-FAST 24
   i386/25 isc 2.0.1; sdf.lonestar.org; 8-line rotary, 2400 bps, 14.4k, PEP;
   No Fees;  Shell account and UUCP mail/news feeds available;  Providing
   access to Internet E-Mail, 1600+ USENET newsgroups, online games, pro-
   gramming utilities and more.
   login 'info' for registration information.
   contact: smj@sdf.lonestar.org
```

03/94 214-705-2901   metronet   Dallas   TX 300-FAST 24
HP-UX 8.07, HP 9000/705; Texas Metronet Communications Service.
10 14.4k dialups (7052901), 10 2400 dialups (7052917). Offers shell
accounts w/ ftp, telnet, irc, UseNet, etc. Also UUCP and SLIP. Flat
monthly fees from $10-$50, depending on service type. telnet connections
to feenix.metronet.com welcome. For more information login as info/info,
or mail info@metronet.com, or call voice at 7052900.

11/93 215-348-9727   jabber   Doylestown   PA 300-FAST 24
80486DX/33, ISC 386/ix 4.0; WorldBlazer (TurboPEP & V.32[bis]) on dial in
line, T3000s (V.32[bis]) on -8129 & -1932; No fee services: "*NIX Depot"
BBS, BBS for UNIX/Xenix users; Fee services: UUCP feeds, providing access
to Internet E-mail and full USENET News (2750+ groups);
Anonymous UUCP available for access to the latest nixpub lists,
please see the footer of this list for more details.
Contact: Phil Eschallier (phil@bts.com).
   anon-uucp: ogin: nuucp (No passwd)

02/94 216-481-9445   wariat   Cleveland   OH 300-FAST 24
ISC Unix SysV/386; USR DS on 481-9445, T-3000 on 481-9425. Shell and
UUCP/Internet mail access available. News and mail feeds are
available; also, DOS and UNIX files. Anonymous uucp: login: nuucp,
no password; request /x/files/ls-lR.Z; nuucp account does not allow
mail exchange; UnixBBS distribution point. BBS free (with e-mail)
for shell/uucp/newsfeed donation requested. For details, e-mail to:
zbig@wariat.org (Zbigniew Tyrlik)

03/94 216-582-2460   ncoast   Cleveland   OH 1200-FAST 24
80386 Mylex, SCO Xenix; 600 meg. storage; XBBS and Shell; USENET
(newsfeeds available), E-Mail; donations requested; login as "bbs"
for BBS and "makeuser" for new users.
Telebit used on 216-237-5486.

03/93 217-789-7888   pallas   Springfield   IL 300-FAST 24
AT&T 6386, 600 meg disk space; 4 lines w/ USRobotics Dual Standard modems;
BBS available at no fee (UBBS), shell access for $50/year; E-Mail, Usenet;
"guest" login available.

03/94 301-220-0462   digex   Greenbelt   MD 300-2400 24
Express Access Online Communications. Local to Washington, Baltimore,
Annapolis and Northern Virginia (area code 703); Baltimore dialup
410-766-1855, Gaithersburg/Damascus 301-570-0001. SunOS shell, full
Usenet, and e-mail $15/month or $150/year; Internet services incl.
Telnet, FTP, IRC with news/mail $25/month or $250/year; includes
unlimited usage 3am - 3pm and 1 hour between 3pm and 3am. Login as
new (no password) for info and account application, major credit
cards accepted. Telnet to digex.com or mail to info@digex.com for
more info; voice phone 800-969-9090 (or 301-220-2020).

03/94 303-871-3324   nyx   Denver   CO 300-FAST 24
A sort of "social experiment" aimed at providing Internet access to the
public with minimal operational costs with a "friendly" front end (a
home-made menu system). Completely donation and volunteer
operated, no user fees at all. Log in as 'new' to create an account.
Equipment: Sun SparcServer II + Pyramid 90x, ~6Gb disk space, 16 phone
lines (+ network logins; usually ~50 users logged in). Public domain
file area, private file area, games, full USENET news, internet e-mail.
Provides shell and more network access with proof of identity.
Contact: Andrew Burt, aburt@nyx.cs.du.edu

02/94 305-434-7340   satelnet Fort Lauderdale FL 300-FAST 24
MIPS RISCserver RC3260, UNIX (RISCos 4.52). Login "new" for
1 week of free access. Rates: $17/month or $60 for 4 months ($15/mo).
Full internet access (telnet, ftp, gopher, irc, etc), unix shell access,
usenet (nn, tin, rn, trn), e-mail (elm, pine, mail). Any other PD software
installed upon request.
Contact: root@sefl.satelnet.org

03/94 309-676-0409   hcserv   Peoria   IL 300-FAST 24
SGI 4d70 SysV and 386BSD - Public Access UNIX Systems - Mult.Lines/ 1.8GB
Access fee structure based on usage and a $0.02 a minute connection with
a cap of $20.00 a month. Shells (sh,csh,bash,tcsh,zsh), Compilers C and
Fortran, games, File and Pic. Libs., UUCP and USENET access with various
news readers, U.S. Patent and USPS Stamp databases, general timesharing
and programmed on-line applications. Three gateways including AT&T mail
services with outgoing FAX. Self register.
    Contact: Victoria Kee {uunet!hcserv!sysop   sysop%hcserv@uunet.uu.net}

11/93 312-248-0900   ddsw1   Chicago   IL 300-FAST 24
Intel Machines, BSDI/DELL; guest users have free BBS access; fee for
shell, Usenet, Internet, unlimited use, and offsite mail; Authors
of AKCS bbs; 6.5GB storage, fee varies with service classification,
V.32bis & PEP available. Newsfeeds and mail connections available;
Full Internet services including SLIP, PPP, and leased circuits
Contact: Karl Denninger (karl@MCS.COM) or voice/fax at 312-248-UNIX

03/94 312-282-8606   gagme   Chicago   IL 300-FAST 24
80486 - Linux. World Wide Access (TM) Full Internet Access now
available! Full netnews, E-mail, ftp, telnet, IRC, MUD, and so much
more! Shell and BBS options. Multiple V.32bis and PEP lines. More
lines added as needed. UUCP feeds also available. Send mail to or
finger info@wwa.com for more information.

03/94 312-283-0559   chinet   Chicago   IL 300-FAST 24
'386, SysVr3.2.1; Multiple lines including Telebit and HST;
Picospan BBS (free), USENET at $50/year (available to guests on
weekends).

02/94 313-623-6309   nucleus   Clarkston   MI 1200-2400 24
   AMI 80386 - ESIX 5.3.2, large online sources archive accessible by
   anonymous UUCP, login: nuucp, nucleus!/user/src/LISTING lists
   available public domain/shareware source code.
   Contact: jeff@nucleus.mi.org

03/93 313-761-3000   grex   Ann Arbor   MI 300-FAST 24
   Sun 2/170 with SunOS 3.2. Full Usenet feed, Internet e-mail, shell
   accounts, on-line games, PicoSpan, UUCP accounts. Voluntary
   donation ($6/month or $60/year) for coop membership and Usenet
   posting access. 6 lines, 300MB. Cooperatively owned & operated by
   Cyberspace Communications.
   Contact: info@cyberspace.org

03/94 313-996-4644   m-net   Ann Arbor   MI 300-2400 24
   486 - BSDI, open access; run by Arbornet, tax-exempt nonprofit; donations
   tax deductible; dues for extended access; user supported; 15 lines;
   Picospan conferencing; 500 MB disk; Internet e-mail; UUCP available;
   free shell access, C compiler, multiuser party, games (including nethack,
   empire, rotisserie baseball); M-Net 10 year anniversary in June, 1993!
   Access from the Internet: telnet m-net.ann-arbor.mi.us
   contact: help@m-net.ann-arbor.mi.us

03/93 401-455-0347   anomaly   Esmond   RI 300-FAST 24
   Informtech 486 mongrel; SCO Open Desktop 1.1; Trailblazer+ (0347) and
   v.32 T2500 (401-331-3706) dialins. Directly connected to the Internet:
   IP Address: 155.212.2.2, or 'anomaly.sbs.risc.net'. Current fees: $15/mo.
   includes complete Internet access. Mail and USENET Newsfeeds available,
   limited feeds for non-PEP sites. SCO software archive site, anonymous
   UUCP login: xxcp, pass: xenix. Anonymous FTP also supported. Software
   listing & download directions in anomaly!~/SOFTLIST

02/94 403-569-2882   debug   Calgary   AB 300-FAST 24
   386, SCO-Xenix; Login: gdx; Telebit, HST, V.32bis, MNP-5 supported;
   6 phone lines: (403) 569-2882, 569-2883, 569-2884, 569-2885, 569-2886;
   System runs modified GDX BBS software; Services: Usenet, Internet email,
   IRC, local-chat, 50+ games, legal-forms, programming, ftp-via-email,
   and much more; Fee: $10/month-3hrs/day to $25/month-24hrs/day;
   Visa & Amex accepted. Demo accounts with limited access are free.
   Contact: Rob Franke root@debug.cuc.ab.ca

03/94 407-299-3661   vicstoy   Orlando   FL 1200-2400 24
   ISC 386/ix 2.0.2. Partial USENET, e-mail (feeds available); Login as
   bbs, no passwd (8N1); Free shell access; Orlando BBS list, games;
   cu to Minix 1.5.10 system (weather permitting); USENET includes
   Unix/Minix source groups. Contact: uunet!tarpit!bilver!vicstoy!vickde
   or vickde@vicstoy.UUCP (Vick De Giorgio).

```
03/94 408-241-9760      netcom      San Jose        CA 1200-FAST 24
     UNIX, Sun Network SunOS 4.1;  Netcom - Online Communication Services;
     70 Telebit lines V.32/V.42  9600/2400/;  USENET (16 days), Lrg archive,
     News/Mail Feeds, Shell, Internet (ftp, telnet, irc),  Slip Connections,
     Local access via CALNet San Jose,  Palo Alto, Red Wd Cty, San Fran,
     Oklnd, Berkly, Alameda, Pleasanton, Los Angeles, and Santa Cruz;
     Fee $17.50/mo + Reg fee of $15.00.  Login: guest (510)865-9004,
     (408)241-9760,(408)459-9851,(310)842-8835,(415)424-0131,(510)426-6860;
     Just Say No to connect fees, Login as guest (no password).

03/94 408-245-7726      uuwest      Sunnyvale       CA 300-FAST  24
     SCO-XENIX, Waffle. No fee, USENET news (news.*, music, comics, telecom, etc)
     The Dark Side of the Moon BBS. This system has been in operation since 1985.
     Login: new Contact: (UUCP) ames!uuwest!request (Domain) request@darkside.com

03/94 408-249-9630      quack       Santa Clara     CA 300-FAST  24
     Sun 4/75, SunOS 4.1.3; 3 lines: First two are Zyxel U-1496E (300-2400,
     v.32bis/v.42bis), third is a Worldblazer (same and add PEP); Internet
     connectivity; Shell - $10/mo; New users should login as 'guest';
     Contact: postmaster@quack.kfu.com

08/93 408-293-9010      a2i         San Jose        CA 1200-FAST 24
     Usenet/Email/Internet/SunOS (Unix).  20 lines.  Dial 408-293-9010
     (v.32bis, v.32) or 408-293-9020 (PEP) and log in as "guest".  Or
     telnet to a2i.rahul.net, 192.160.13.1.  Or send any message to
     info@rahul.net; a daemon will auto-reply.  $12/month for 6-month.

04/93 408-423-4810      deeptht     Santa Cruz      CA 300-FAST  24
     4 dialin lines (2 2400 at 423-4810, 2 v32 at 423-1767), 486/40+32M,
     2 GB disk space including a large part of the uunet source archives,
     SCO UNIX 3.2v4.1, C/Pascal/Fortran/BASIC compilers, TinyMud, rn/trn.
     Domain name: deeptht.armory.com (and alias armory.com).

02/94 408-423-9995      cruzio      Santa Cruz      CA 1200-2400 24
     Tandy 4000, Xenix 2.3.*, Caucus 3.*;  focus on Santa Cruz activity
     (ie directory of community and government organizations, events, ...);
     USENET Support;  Multiple lines;  no shell; fee: $15/quarter.
     Contact: ...!uunet!cruzio!chris

02/94 408-458-2289      gorn        Santa Cruz      CA 300-FAST  24
     Everex 386, SCO xenix 2.3.2;  2 lines, -2837 telebit for PEP connects;
     Standard shell access, games, email injection into the internet, up to
     date archive of scruz-sysops information, upload/download, usenet news
     including scruz.* hierarchy for santa cruz area information;  UUCP set
     up on as-requested;  No charge, donations accepted; newuser:  log in as
     "gorn" and fill out online form.
     Contact: falcon@gorn.echo.com
```

03/94 408-725-0561   portal   Cupertino   CA 300-FAST 24
Networked Suns (SunOS), multiple lines, shell or "online menu" access;
Live Internet; fees: $19.95/mn; conferencing, multi-user chats, computer
special interest groups; E-Mail/USENET; UUCP service also available.
Contact: Customer Service (cs@portal.com).

03/94 408-739-1520   szebra   Sunnyvale   CA 300-FAST 24
386PC, AT&T SVR4v3; Trailblazer+; Full Usenet News, email (Internet & UUCP),
first time users login: bbs, shell access/files storage/email available
(registration required); GNU, X11R4 and R5 source archives. viet-net/SCV
and VNese files/sftware archives.
contact: tin@szebra.Saigon.COM or {claris,zorch,sonyusa}!szebra!tin

03/93 410-661-2598   wb3ffv   Baltimore   MD 1200-FAST 24
80486, UNIX V.3.2.x; XBBS for HAM radio enthusiasts; 1.6 Gigabytes online;
Multiple lines, dial in - TB WorldBlazer, 2475 - USR HST DS V.32bis/42bis,
2648 - Tb+ PEP; Some USENET; Anon-UUCP available; Login as bbs (8-N-1).

12/93 410-893-4786   magnus1   Belair   MD 300-FAST 24
Equip Unisys S/Series, UNIX 3.3.2; ksh, csh, sh; Multiple lines;
$60.00/yr; E-Mail/USENET,ftp, telnet,finger; 'C', Pascal, Fortran, Cobol,
Basic development systems; Interactive chat and games; Files for download;
USA Today, Online Magazines, Daily Business News; PC Catalog; Local Online
Forums as well; as Technical Help; Clarinet News; No limits.
Contact cyndiw@magnus1.com

03/94 412-481-5302   telerama Pittsburgh   PA 300-FAST 24
Telerama Public Access Internet. 4.3 bsd. Multiple lines. Hourly fee
includes telnet, ftp, e-mail, Usenet, ClariNet/UPI, gopher, IRC, games,
compilers, editors, shell or menu navigation and 1 meg disk quota. Also
offering SLIP, UUCP and commercial accounts. Fees: $20/mo (personal),
$50/mo (commercial); Registration: login as new. FTP info from
telerama.pgh.pa.us; /info/telerama.info
Contact: Kristen McQuillin, info@telerama.pgh.pa.us. 412/481-3505 voice.

03/94 414-241-5469   mixcom   Milwaukee   WI 1200-FAST 24
80386, SCO UNIX 3.2; MIX (Milwaukee Internet eXchange); $9/mo
access to Internet services including email, Usenet BBS and file
archives; MIX has comprehensive and easy to use menus, along with
shell access; Multiple lines; login as 'newuser' password 'newuser'.
Contact: Dean Roth (sysop@mixcom.com) [414-962-8172 voice]

03/93 414-321-9287   solaria   Milwaukee   WI 300-2400 24
Sun 3/60LE, SunOS 4.1. Internet E-mail, limited USENET news, shell access,
Telebit WorldBlazer soon. Feeds available. Donations requested,
registration required. One hop off of the Internet.
Contact: jgreco@solaria.mil.wi.us (Joe Greco) or log in as "help"

```
06/93 414-342-4847      solaria    Milwaukee      WI 300-FAST  24
  Sun 3/60LE, SunOS 4.1.  Internet E-mail, limited USENET news, shell access,
  feeds available,  donations requested, registration required.
  One hop off of the Internet.
  Contact: jgreco@solaria.mil.wi.us (Joe Greco) or log in as "help"

06/93 414-734-2499      edsi       Appleton       WI 300-FAST  24
  IBM PS/2 Model 55SX, SCO Xenix 2.3.2;  Running STARBASE II Software.
  Enterprise Data Systems Incorporated (Non-profit).  100+ local rooms,
  PLUS USENET, Multi Channel Chat, 9 ports, $15 yr, flat rate for full
  access to net news (no alternet yet), mail.  The Fox Valley's only public
  access Unix based BBS.
  Contact: Chuck Tomasi (chuck@edsi.plexus.COM)

03/94 415-332-6106      well       Sausalito      CA 1200-FAST 24
  6-processor Sequent Symmetry (i386); Internet, UUCP and USENET
  access; multiple lines; access via CPN and Internet (well.sf.ca.us);
  PICOSPAN BBS; $15/mo + $2/hr (CPN or 9600 +$4/hr);
  Contact (415) 332-4335

03/94 415-826-0397      wet        San Francisco  CA 1200-FAST 24
  386 SYS V.3.  Wetware Diversions.  $15 registration, $0.01/minute.
  Public Access UNIX System:  uucp, PicoSpan bbs, full Usenet News,
  Multiple lines (6), shell access.  Newusers get initial credit!
  contact:{ucsfcca¦hoptoad¦well}!wet!editor (Eric Swanson)

03/94 415-949-3133      starnet    Los Altos      CA 300-FAST  24
  SunOS 4.1. 8-lines. MNP1-5 and v42/bis, or PEP on all lines.
  Shell access for all users.  USENET—900+ groups.  E-mail (feeds
  available).  smart mail.  Publically available software (pd/shareware).
  $12/mo. Contact: admin@starnet.uucp or ...!uunet!apple!starnet!admin

03/94 415-967-9443      btr        Mountain View  CA 300-FAST  24
  Sun (SunOS UNIX), shell access, e-mail, netnews, uucp, can access by
  Telenet PC Pursuit, multiple lines, Telebit, flat rate: $12.50/month.
  For sign-up information please send e-mail to Customer Service at
  cs@btr.com or ..!{decwrl,fernwood,mips}!btr!cs
  or call 415-966-1429 Voice.

03/93 416-249-5366      r-node     Etobicoke      ON 300-FAST  24
  80386, ISC SV386; SupraModem2400 on Dial-in line, Worldblazer and
  Cardinal2400 on other two lines; No fee services: Uniboard BBS for
  BBS users; shell access for those who ask; Fee services: access
  to subsequent lines, unlimited dl/ul access; full USENET News and
  International E-mail access through Usenet/Internet mail; Free
  UUCP connections;
  Contact: Marc Fournier (marc@r-node.gts.org)
```

03/93 416-461-2608   tmsoft   Toronto   ON 300-FAST 24
   NS32016, Sys5r2, shell; news+mail $30/mo, general-timesharing $60/mo
   All newsgroups. Willing to setup mail/news connections.
   Archives:comp.sources.{unix,games,x,misc}
   Contact: Dave Mason <mason@tmsoft> / Login: newuser

03/94 503-220-1016   teleport Portland   OR 300-FAST 24
   SPARCstations, SunOS 4.1.3, 5.5GB disk; 30 lines and support PEP/V.32
   and V.32bis; E-Mail/USENET; Shell access for $120 / year includes
   choice of shell, full news feed, complete internet (ftp, telnet, irc,
   mud) access; apply with "new" or email info@teleport.com

03/94 503-293-1772   agora   PDX   OR 1200-FAST 24
   Intel Unix V/386, $6/mo or $60/yr, news, mail, ftp, telnet, irc.
   Six lines with trunk-hunt, all V.32bis. Agora is part of RAINet.
   Contact: Alan Batie, batie@agora.rain.com

03/94 503-297-3211   m2xenix   Portland   OR 300-FAST 24
   '386/20, Xenix 2.3. 2 Lines (-0935); Shell accounts available, NO BBS;
   No fee; E-mail, USENET News, program development.
   Contact: ...!uunet!m2xenix!news or on Fido at 297-9145

03/94 503-632-7891   bucket   Portland   OR 300-FAST 24
   Tektronix 6130, UTek 3.0(4.2bsd-derived). Bit Bucket BBS no longer
   online. Modem is Telebit Trailblazer+ (PEP). Users interested in
   access to Unix should send EMail to rickb@pail.rain.com. $30/year
   access fee includes USENET News, EMail (fast due to local Internet
   access), and access to all tools/utilities/games. Internet 'ftp'
   available upon request. UUCP connections (1200, 2400, 9600V.32,
   9600PEP, 19200PEP) available (through another local system which is
   not publicly available) to sites which will poll with reasonable
   regularity and reliability.

06/93 508-664-0149   genesis   North Reading MA 300-FAST 24
   SVR3 UNIX; Internet mail; Usenet News; No Fees; Shell access and menu
   system; Three lines; One hop from the Internet; HST and V.32bis; UUCP
   feeds available. Contact: steve1@genesis.nred.ma.us (steve belczyk).
   Automated reply: info@genesis.nred.ma.us

09/93 508-853-0340   schunix   Worcester   MA 2400-FAST 24
   Sparc 2, 1.9GB; Email, Shell, Full UseNet, C/C++, over 11GB on CD's,
   $5/month $3/hr, $10/mn 5hrs incl. $2/hr, uucp-feeds call,
   login:guest for info, Free BBS inside of schunix, login:pbbs,
   Contact: Robert Schultz (schu@schunix.com) 508-853-0258
   SCHUNIX 8 Grove Heights Drive, Worcester, MA 01605

03/93 510-294-8591   woodowl   Livermore   CA 1200-FAST 24
   Xenix/386 3.2.1. Waffle BBS, Usenet Access; Reasonable users welcome.
   No fee; For more information contact: william@woodowl.UUCP,
   lll-winken!chumley!woodowl!william, or call and just sign up on system.

01/94 510-530-9682   bdt   Oakland   CA 1200-FAST 24
   Sun 4, SunOS 4.1; BBS access to Usenet news, E-mail (Internet and
   UUCP). QWK support. PEP/V.32 on 510-530-6915. First time users
   login: bbs. Unix, Atari ST, and IBM-PC sources and PD/shareware.
   $35 annual fee. 30-day free trial. Newsfeeds and UUCP access by
   special arrangement. Contact: David Beckemeyer david@bdt.com

03/94 510-623-8652   jack   Fremont   CA 300-FAST 24
   Sun 4/470 running Solaris 2.2 offers downloading of netnews archives
   and all uploaded software. Each user can log in as bbs or as the account
   which they create for themselves. This is a free Public Access Unix
   System that is part of a network of 4 machines. The primary phone line
   is on a rotary to five other lines.

02/94 510-704-1058   HoloNet   Berkeley   CA 1200-FAST 24
   DECstations, ULTRIX; Commercial network, over 850 cities; Custom shell;
   Full Internet, IRC, telnet, USENET, USA Today Decisionline, games;
   $2/hr off-peak; Telnet: holonet.net, Info server: info@holonet.net,
   Contact: support@holonet.net

03/94 512-346-2339   bigtex   Austin   TX FAST   24
   SysVr3.2 i386, anonymous shell, no fee, anonymous uucp ONLY,
   Telebit 9600/PEP; Mail links available. Carries GNU software.
   anon uucp login: nuucp NO PASSWD, file list /usr3/index
   anon shell login: guest NO PASSWD, chroot'd to /usr3
   Contact: james@bigtex.cactus.org

03/93 513-779-8209   cinnet   Cincinnati   OH 1200-FAST 24
   80386, ISC 386/ix 2.02, Telebit access, 1 line; $7.50/Month; shell
   access, Usenet access; news feeds available;
   login: newacct password: new user to register for shell access

03/93 514-435-8896   ichlibix   Blainville Queb CA 300-FAST 24
   80386, ISC 2.2.1; 2400 bps modem on dial in, HST DS on -2650; BBS
   program is Ubbs (RemoteAccess Clone) - named Soft Stuff, no shell;
   No fees required but are recommended for more access ($25 - $75/yr);
   Files for both dos and UNIX + a lot of binaries for ISC; Possibility
   to send/receive UUCP mail from the BBS

02/94 515-945-7000   cyberspace Jefferson   IA 300-FAST 24
   SUNOS: FREE SERVICE, no time limits; T1 (1.536MB) Internet Link, Full
   News Feed, Irc, Archie, Lynx, WWW, telnet
   ncftp, and more. FREE Unix Shell, PPP & Slip Accounts.

06/93 516-586-4743   kilowatt Deer Park   NY 2400-FAST 24
Consensys SVR4 running on a clone 80486-33. 516-586-4743 for Telebit World-
Blazer, 516-667-6142 for a Boca V.32bis. Providing FREE USENET email/news
to the general public. FREE feeds available with a selection of all of
alt, biz, comp, rec, talk, sci, soc, and vmsnet newsgroups ... using UUCP
or QWK-packets. Contact: Arthur Krewat 516-253-2805 krewat@kilowatt.UUCP
or krewat@kilowatt.linet.org Telnet/Ftp not available here, so don't
even ask!

03/93 517-487-3356   lunapark E. Lansing   MI 1200-2400 24
Compaq 386/20 SCO-UNIX 3.2, lunabbs bulletin board & conferencing
system, no fee, login: bbs password: lunabbs. Primarily UNIX software
with focus on TeX and Postscript, also some ATARI-ST and IBM-PC stuff
2400/1200 —> 8 N 1
Contact: ...!{mailrus,uunet}!frith!lunapark!larry

03/93 517-789-5175   anubis   Jackson   MI 300-1200 24
Equip ???, OS ???; 1200 baud dial-in (planning on 19.2kbps);
UUCP connections to the world, PicoSpan BBS software, Teleconferencing,
C programming compiler, 3 public dial-in lines, Online games;
Contact: Matthew Rupert (root@anubis.mi.org).

03/93 518-237-2163   tnl   Troy   NY 300-FAST 24
80386 w/ SCO XENIX. No Fee. Full shell, USENET, BBS, games, optional menus,
2 hr limit. Login as 'new' for an account, no valid. "The Northern Lights."
Contact: norstar@tnl.com   (Daniel Ray)

03/93 518-346-8033   sixhub   upstate   NY 300-2400 24
PC Designs GV386. hub machine of the upstate NY UNIX users group (*IX)
two lines reserved for incoming, bbs no fee, news & email fee $15/year
Smorgasboard of BBS systems, UNaXcess and XBBS online,
Citadel BBS now in production. Contact: davidsen@sixhub.uucp.

09/93 602-274-9600   indirect Phoenix   AZ 300-FAST 24
Sun/SunOS + multiple 486/50's; Live internet, multiple lines (up to 14.4k);
E-Mail/USENET, 5mb disk quota, shell or menu system, multi-user games, offline news readers (personal $20/mo, business $30/mo); UUCP feeds available
($20-$45/mo); SLIP/PPP connection at speeds up to 14.4k - demand/dedicated
lines (leased line connections to 24kbps) (basic rates $150/mo).
Contact: info@indirect.com

03/93 602-293-3726   coyote   Tucson   AZ 300-FAST 24
FTK-386, ISC 386/ix 2.0.2; Waffle BBS, devoted to embedded systems
programming and u-controller development software; E-Mail/USENET;
UUCP and limited USENET feeds available;
Contact: E.J. McKernan (ejm@datalog.com).
     bbs: ogin: bbs   (NO PWD)
     uucp: ogin: nuucp (NO PWD)

```
09/93 602-321-9600     indirect   Tucson        AZ 300-FAST  24
   Refer to primary entry (Phoenix, AZ) for system/services details.


03/94 602-649-9099     telesys    Mesa          AZ 1200-FAST 24
   SCO UNIX V/386 3.2.4; Telebit WorldBlazers; TeleSys-II Unix based BBS
   (no fee) login: bbs; Unix archives available via BBS or ANON UUCP;
   Shell Accounts available for full access USENET, email (fees);
   Phoenix Matchmaker with more than 9000 members (fees) login: bbs
   Regional supplier of USENET Newsfeeds; uucp-anon: nuucp NOPWD;
   Contact: kreed@tnet.com  or  ...!ncar!noao!enuucp!telesys!kreed


02/94 602-991-5952     aa7bq      Scottsdale    AZ 300-2400  24
   Sun 4, SunOS 4.1.2; NB bbs system; 900 meg online; Primarily Ham Radio
   related articles from usenet (Rec.radio.amateur.misc), complete Callsign
   Database, Radio and scanner modifications, frequency listings, shell access
   by permission, No fees, Free classified ads, Local e-mail only.
   Login: bbs (8N1) or
   Login: callsign for callsign database only.  Don't use MNP!
   For additional info contact Fred.Lloyd@West.Sun.COM


03/93 603-429-1735     mv         Litchfield    NH 1200-FAST 24
   80386; ISC UNIX; MV is on the Internet (mv.MV.COM, host 192.80.84.1);
   mail connections and news feeds via uucp; domain registrations;
   membership in "domain park" MV.COM; domain forwarding; archives of
   news and mail software for various platforms; mailing lists;
   area topics; $7/month for 1 hour/month; $20/month for 3 hours/month
   $2/hour thereafter; blocks of 30 hours for $20 month - First month free
   up to 20 hours.
   Voice: 603-429-2223; USMail: MV Communications Inc, PO Box 4963
   Manchester NH 03108; Or dial the modem and login as "info" or "rates".


03/93 603-448-5722     tutor      Lebanon       NH 300-FAST  24
   Altos 386 w/ System V 3.1; Limited newsfeed; E-Mmail and USENET available
   via UUCP.
   Contact: peter.schmitt@dartmouth.edu


03/93 604-576-1214     mindlink   Vancouver     BC 300-FAST  24
   80386 w/ SCO Xenix; 14 lines, 660 Meg disk space, TB+ & 9600 HST available;
   No shell; Fee of $45/year for BBS access; E-Mail, USENET, hundreds of megs
   of file downloads; Operating since 1986.

02/94 605-348-2738     loft386    Rapid City    SD 300-FAST  24
   80386 SYS V/386 Rel 3.2, Usenet mail/news via UUNET, UUNET archive access.
   NO BBS! News feeds available. 400 meg hd. Fees: $10/month or $25/quarter.
   Call (605) 343-8760 and talk to Doug Ingraham to arrange an account or email
   uunet!loft386!dpi
```

03/93 606-233-2051   lunatix   Lexington   KY 300-2400   24
    SCO Unix 3.2.2. 2 2400 baud lines. V32bis later in the fall.
    Home grown Pseudo BBS software. Multiuser games, Full USENET Feed on
    tap, USENET Feeds available. Shells available, No Fees.

03/93 608-246-2701   fullfeed   Madison   WI FAST   24
    Sun SPARC station SLC, 16Mb RAM, 1Gb disk, SunOS 4.1.1, Telebit
    WorldBlazers; operated by FullFeed Communications; USENET/E-Mail,
    UUCP plus other digital communication services; login: fullfeed;
    UUCP starts at $24/month, shells cost $16/month; No-cost, limited-term,
    evaluation accounts are setup over the telephone; FullFeed plans to offer
    Internet connections (SLIP, PPP, 56Kbps) within 6 months.
    Contact "SYSop@FullFeed.Com" or call +1-608-CHOICE-9 (voice).

03/93 608-273-2657   madnix   Madison   WI 300-2400   24
    486, MST UNIX SysV/386, shell, no fee required, USENET news, mail, login: bbs
    Contact: ray@madnix.uucp

03/94 610-539-3043   cellar   Trooper/Oaks   PA 300-FAST   24
    DTK 486/33, SCO Unix 3.2, Waffle BBS - The Cellar BBS, no shell; USR
    Dual-Standard modems, five lines and growing. BBS is free; net news
    (full feed) and net mail by subscription. $10/mo, $55/6-mo, or $90/yr.
    Fancies itself to be more of a colorful "electronic community" than the
    best plug into the net, and as such, it features a lively local message
    base. But it also generally carries the latest Linux distribution,
    just to prove it hasn't forgotten its hacker roots.
    Contact: Tony Shepps (toad@cellar.org).

08/93 612-458-3889   skypoint   Newport   MN 300-FAST   24
    Unixware System V R4.2. VGA Graphics BBS/OIS using Sentience BBS
    software from Cyberstore - Sentience uses the RIP graphics protocol; 4
    lines are Courier 14.4 Modems, 1 Worldblazer; Full News Feed 7 day expire,
    Clarinet Feed Site, USA Today, Board Watch, News Bytes, Internet Mail, Real
    time games and conferences; Unix, DOS, Windows and OS/2 source and binary
    archives on CDROMS and 2.1 Gigabytes of Disk; $45 dollars year basic
    services $85 dollars a year for full access, $100 a year for Unix shell
    account and access to full development tools; Will provide Clarinet and
    USENET News Feeds; Will add Fidonet and other networks in the near future;
    Login as 'guest'.
    Contact: info@skypoint.com

03/94 612-473-2295   pnet51   Minneapolis   MN 300-2400   24
    Equip ?, Xenix, multi-line, no fee, some Usenet news, email, multi-threaded
    conferencing, login: pnet id: new, PC Pursuitable
    UUCP: {rosevax, crash}!orbit!pnet51!admin

```
04/93 613-724-9817    latour    Ottawa      ON 300-FAST 24
    Sun 3/60, SunOS 4.1, 8meg Ram, 660 meg of disk; 2nd line v.32[bis];
    No BBS;  Unix access rather than usenet;  Login as guest for a shell
    (send mail to postmaster asking for an account);
    Anon uucp is login as 'anonuucp' (/bin/rmail is allowed) —
    Grab ~uucp/README[.Z] for an ls-lR.

03/93 613-837-3029    micor     Orleans     ON 300-FAST 24
    386/25, 600 Meg, Xenix 2.3.2, USENET, email, 2 phone lines
    fee required to get more than 15 mins/day of login and to access
    additional phone lines.
    Available:  bbs accounts (waffle) or shell accounts.
    Contact: michel@micor.ocunix.on.ca or michel@micor.uucp, Michel Cormier.

03/94 614-868-9980    bluemoon  Reynoldsburg OH 300-FAST 24
    Sun 4/75, SunOS;  2.2gb;  Leased line to the Internet;  Multiple lines,
    HST Dual on -9980 & -9982, Telebit T2500 on -9984;  2gb disk space;
    Bluemoon BBS — supporting UNIX, graphics, and general interest;  Full
    USENET, gated Fidonet conferences, E-Mail;
    Contact: grant@bluemoon.uucp (Grant DeLorean).

03/93 615-288-3957    medsys    Kingsport    TN 1200-FAST 24
    386 SCO-UNIX 3.2, XBBS;  No fee, limit 90 min;  Telebit PEP, USENET, 600mb;
    login: bbs   password: bbs
    anon uucp —> medsys Any ACU (speed) 16152883957 ogin: nuucp
    Request /u/xbbs/unix/BBSLIST.Z for files listing
    Contact: laverne@medsys (LaVerne E. Olney)

03/93 616-457-1964    wybbs     Jenison      MI 300-FAST 24
    386 - SCO-XENIX 2.3.2, two lines, XBBS for new users, mail in for shell
    access, usenet news, 150 meg storage, Telebit. Interests: ham radio, xenix
    AKA: Consultants Connection  Contact: danielw@wyn386.mi.org
    Alternate phone #: 616-457-9909 (max 2400 baud). Anonymous UUCP available.

09/93 617-593-4557    northshore Lynn       MA 300-FAST 24
    Sun SPARCstation, SunOS 4.1.3;  Telebit Worldblazer modems (v.32bis, v.32,
    2400, 1200 baud);  Eco Software, Inc;  GNU, archie, gopher, wais, etc. -
    any software you need, we'll add it;  $9/month for 10 hours connect time,
    3 Mb disk quota (additional usage: connect - $1/hour, disk - $1/Mb/month);
    UUCP feeds available;  Hours: 7 days/week, 24 hours/day (except Friday
    15:00-18:00 for backups).
    Contact: info@northshore.ecosoft.com (Voice: (617) 593-3110).

03/94 617-739-9753    world     Brookline    MA 300-FAST 24
    Sun 4/280, SunOS 4.0.3;  Shell, USENET, E-Mail, UUCP, IRC, Alternet
    connection to the Internet, and home of the Open Book Initiative (text
    project), multiple lines; fees: $5/mo + $2/hr or $20/20hrs per month;
    Contact: geb@world.std.com
```

11/93 619-278-8267   cg57   San Diego   CA 1200-FAST 24
  i386 Unix ISC 3.2 R4.0, UniBoard BBS Software (login as bbs); Worldblazer
  on dial-in, -3905 Telebit Trailblazer Plus, -9837 Practical Peripherals
  (V32); BBS is free; Over 800 meg of downloadable software
  (UNIX/FreeBSD/386BSD/Linux/NETBSD and DOS systems + Soundblaster files);
  Shell accounts available for $30 for 3 months with access to ftp/telnet/
  irc/gopher/archie/etc. Full (USENET) news feed, and selected Fidonet
  uucp accounts available. cg57.esnet.com is on the internet (198.180.239.3)
  Anonymous uucp - login: nuucp (no password). Get file ls-lR.Z for
  complete files listing.
  Contact: steve@cg57.esnet.com

03/94 619-453-1115   netlink   San Diego   CA 1200-FAST 24
  The Network Information eXchange (NIX). i386 Unix system, provides
  access to email, over 1000 Usenet newsgroups, and file archives
  through Waffle BBS interface (no shell). Multiple lines, NO FEE for basic
  access (E-mail only). Higher access available to contributing members.
  Mail feeds available. Login: nix   Contact: system@netlink.nix.com

04/94 619-634-1376   cyber   Encinitas   CA 300-FAST 24
  Equip ???; Multiple lines [HST16.8/V.32]; The Cyberspace Station;
  On the Internet (telnet to CYBER.NET [192.153.125.1]); A Public Access
  Unix service with full Internet connectivity; E-Mail/USENET,
  International communications, hunting for files, and interactive chatting;
  Login on as "guest" and send feedback (Don't forget to leave a phone number
  where you can be reached).
  Contact: info@cyber.net

03/94 619-637-3640   crash   San Diego   CA 12-FAST   24
  CTSNET Public Access Unix. A network of 486-66/DX2 64mb+32mb, SCO
  Unix 3.2v4.1 machines, 41 lines; HST: 619-593-6400, 637-3640,
  220-0836; V32/V32.bis: 619-593-7300, 637-3660, 220-0853; PEP:
  619-593-9500, 637-3680, 220-0857. V42.bis most lines, All modems at
  38,400bps, Telebits at 19,200/38,400bps. 8N1 only. International
  Usenet (6600+ groups), Clarinet News Service, Reuters News, worldwide
  email, shell and uucp accounts. 3.5gb disk. Direct Internet T1
  dedicated. Shell accounts $18 per month flat, newfeeds, SLIP, PPP,
  other svcs. Contact bblue@crash.cts.com, support@ctsnet.cts.com,
  info@crash.cts.com

03/94 703-281-7997   grebyn   Vienna   VA 300-2400 24
  Networked Vax/Ultrix. $30/month for 25 hours. $1.20 connect/hr after 25
  hours. 1 MB disk quota. $2/MB/month additional quota. USENET News.
  Domain mail (grebyn.com). Full Internet IP connectivity expected in the
  summer of 1992. Mail to info@grebyn.com, voice 703-281-2194.

04/93 703-528-4380   sytex   Arlington   VA 300-FAST 24
  ISC Unix, UUCP, Waffle BBS, 5 lines. Login as "bbs". Mail, usenet news,
  ftp available via ftp-requests though UUnet. Serving Washington DC,
  Northern Virginia, Southern Maryland. First year startup Charter member
  accounts available for $120. Gives fullest access as the system develops.

06/93 703-551-0095   ukelele   Woodbridge   VA 300-FAST 24
  Genuine Computing Resources. SVR4/386. Calling area includes
  District of Columbia, Fairfax Cty, Prince William Cty, Manassas, and
  Dumfries, VA. Shell, Full Usenet, Internet E-Mail. $15/month
  for access to (703)551 exchange, $10/month for (703)878 access.
  All lines V.32bis or higher. You get 1 hour/day connect time and
  1.5MB disk storage. Direct Internet connectivity expected soon
  without rate increase for existing users. Login as 'guest' or
  send mail to info@gcr.com for further details. For human interaction
  send mail to cjl@gcr.com. News and mail feeds also considered.

03/94 703-803-0391   tnc   Fairfax Station VA 300-FAST 24
  Zenith Z-386, SCO Xenix; 120 MB HDD; 12 lines, tb+ for UUCP only;
  "The Next Challenge"; Usenet, mail, Unique (sysop written) multi-user
  space game; No Shell; Free and user supported —> No fee for light mail
  and usenet; Subscription required for game and unlimited mail and usenet
  at $25 / year;
  Contact: Tom Buchsbaum (tom@tnc.UUCP or uunet!tnc!tom).

03/94 708-367-1871   sashimi   Vernon Hills   IL 300-FAST 24
  80486 - SVR4. World Wide Access (TM) Full Internet Access now
  available! Full netnews, E-mail, ftp, telnet, IRC, MUD, and so much
  more! Shell and BBS options. Multiple V.32bis lines. More
  lines added as needed. UUCP feeds also available. Send mail to or
  finger info@wwa.com for more information.

03/93 708-425-8739   oaknet   Oak Lawn   IL 300-FAST 24
  386 Clone running AT&T System V release 3.2.1, no access charges.
  Free shell accounts, USENET news, and internet email...
  Contact: jason@oaknet.chi.il.us, Jason Vanick (708)499-0905 (human).

03/94 708-833-8126   vpnet   Villa Park   IL 1200-FAST 24
  386 Clone - Interactive Unix R2.2 (3.2), Akcs linked bbs FREE, including many selected Usenet groups. Shells are available for a minimum
  $60/year contribution; under 22, $30. Includes access to our FULL
  Usenet feed. Well connected. Five lines including three Trailblazers.
  Two hunt groups - V.32 modems call 708-833-8127 (contributors only).
  Contact: lisbon@vpnet.chi.il.us, Gerry Swetsky (708)833-8122 (human).

03/93 708-879-8633   unixuser   Batavia   IL 300-FAST 24
  386, w/ Linux/Waffle; v.32[bis] support; Linux downloads; Limited free

use; Paid subscribers get Internet mail access, some USENET groups;
Subscription is $25/year; CDROM disk available - changes monthly;
Shell accounts are available.

03/93 708-983-5147   wa9aek   Lisle   IL 1200-FAST 24
   80386, UNIX V.3.2.3; XBBS for HAM radio enthusiasts; 1.5 Gigabytes online;
   Multiple lines, dial in - USR HST DS V.32bis/42bis, 8138 - Tb T2500;
   Login as bbs (8-N-1).

03/94 713-480-2686   blkbox   Houston   TX 300-FAST 24
   486/33, SCO Open Desktop; 5 lines, all V32[bis]/V42[bis]; E-Mail/USENET
   (4500+ groups); 25 online adventure games, IRC, SLIP/PP; $21.65 / month
   for full shell access.
   Contact: Marc Newman (mknewman@blkbox.com)

03/94 713-668-7176   nuchat   Houston   TX 300-FAST 24
   i486/25, UHC Unix SVR4, 2.5 Gigs online, ** 56kb internet connection
   **, 7 lines (2 Trailblazers, 5 Worldblazers), full Usenet news feed,
   personal accounts ($3/hour), UUCP feeds (several options), dedicated
   lines available w/ unlimited usage @$120/month (SLIP or any protocol
   you like). Full internet access (ftp, telnet, gopher, archie).

03/94 713-684-5900   sugar   Houston   TX 300-FAST 24
   486/AT, SCO UNIX, 16+ lines (V.22, V.32, PEP, TurboPEP), Usenet news, email,
   Clarinet, complete *.sources and *.binaries archives, dial-up SLIP, access
   to Internet (FTP, telnet, ...), varying fees for shell access, news feeds.

03/94 714-635-2863   dhw68k   Anaheim   CA 1200-FAST 24
   Unistride 2.1; Trailblazer access; 2nd line -1915; No fee; USENET News;
   /bin/sh or /bin/csh available

03/94 714-821-9671   alphacm   Cypress   CA 1200-FAST 24
   386 - SCO-XENIX, no fee, Home of XBBS, 90 minutes per login, 4 lines,
   Trailblazer pluses in use.
     uucp-anon: ogin: nuucp NO PASSWD

03/94 714-842-5851   conexch   Santa Ana   CA 300-2400 24
   386 - SCO Xenix - Free Unix guest login and PC-DOS bbs login, one
   hour initial time limit, USENET news, shell access granted on request &
   $25/quarter donation. Anon uucp: ogin: nuucp NO PASSWD. List of
   available Unix files resides in /usr3/public/FILES.

03/94 714-894-2246   stanton   Irvine   CA 300-2400 24
   80386-25, SCO Xenix-386, 320mb disk, 2400/1200/300 MNP supported; E-Mail &
   USENET; Fixed fee $20/yr; X11R4 archive and many packages ported to Xenix
   386; C development system (XENIX/MSDOS), PROCALC 1-2-3 clone, FOXBASE+;
   anon uucp: ogin: nuucp, no word

```
03/93 716-634-6552      exuco1     Buffalo        NY 300-FAST  -24
   SGI Iris Indigo;  2 Lines, both Telebit WorldBlazers (on a hunt) [PEP
   Answer sequence last]; "The Buffalo Computer Society", Western New York's
   first Public Access UNIX; Mon - Fri 6:00pm - 7:00am EST, 24 Hours on
   Weekends;  No Fee;  E-Mail/USENET
   Come March '93 — will be running on several DEC Vaxen running BSD 4.3,
   and MANY MANY MANY more lines.

04/93 718-729-5018      dorsai     NYC            NY 300-FAST  24
   80386, ISC 386/ix, Waffle bbs;  Live Internet connection; 3 phone lines
   (V.32bis for contributors);  no shell (yet);  BBS with over 250 non-Usenet
   newsgroups, 1.2 gb of mac, ibm, amiga, cp-m, appleII, cbm files;  BBS is
   free, $25/yr for UseNet access, (180 min/day), $50/yr for extended gold
   access (300 min/day);  $?? for platinum access (i.e. ftp/telnet/irc/etc);
   Full news and mail feed from uupsi; login through bbs.
   Contact: postmaster@dorsai.com

02/94 719-520-1700      cns        Colorado Spring CO 300-2400  24
   Sun 3/260,  SunOS; 22 lines (on rollover); $35 signup fee, CNS has national
   800 service for $8/hr (incl Alaska, Hawaii, Virgin Islands and Puerto Rico),
   In Colo Springs/Denver (719/303) and telnet: $2.75/hr;
   CNS offers dialup, uucp, slip, xwindows xremote; CNS offers 56K and T1
   access directly to the T3 ANS backbone nationally
   Information at 1-800-748-1200 (voice)
     or write to info@cscns.com for automated response
     or write to service@cscns.com for operator response

03/93 719-632-4111      oldcolo    Colorado Spring CO 1200-FAST 24
   386 - SCO-XENIX frontend, 2 CT Miniframes backend, e-mail conferencing,
   databases, Naplps Graphics, USENET news;  7 lines 8N1, 2400 on -2906,
   USR Dual 9600 on -2658;  Self registering for limited free access
   (political, policy, marketplace)
   Subscriptions $10, $15, $18 per month for full use.
   Dave Hughes SYSOP.

01/94 801-539-0900      xmission   Salt Lake City UT 300-FAST  24
   Sun Sparc Classic, Solaris; T1 Connection into Internet Backbone; 10 (at
   the moment) incoming phone lines (ZyXEL 19.2K 1496E+ modems on all lines);
   tin, nn, rn newsreaders;  gopher, lynx, www navigators;  hytelnet, telnet,
   ncftp, ftp;  zmodem, ymodem, xmodem, kermit protocols;  PPP and UUCP
   connections with all accounts;  gnu software and compilers;  assisted
   "menus" or shell access;  "Big Dummy's Guide to the Internet" hypertexted
   online;  nethack, mdg, and robohunt multiplayer games.
   $5 introductory rate for the first month ... Individuals: $19/mn ($102/6mns),
   Small businesses: $29/mn ($162/6mns), BBS accounts: $39/mn ($216/6mns).
   Voice Support at 801-539-0852
```

04/93 804-627-1828   wyvern   Norfolk   VA 1200-FAST 24
  Multiple 486/66 networked, SVR4. Ten v.32bis lines. Shell accounts,
  mail, and news feeds available. Gigs of disk space with lots of
  games, programming languages, news. Modest fees. We provide full
  Internet services, including ftp, telnet, IRC, archie, etc. We can
  provide uucp email and news feeds, and can include your machine in
  our domain park.
  login as guest, no password, to register for full access.
  Contact: Wyvern Technologies, Inc. at (804) 622-4289,
                                 or system@wyvern.wyvern.com
                                 (uunet!wyvern!system)

03/93 812-333-0450   sir-alan   Bloomington   IN 1200-FAST 24
  SCO UNIX 3.2; no fee; TB+ on 333-0450 (300-19.2K); archive site for
  comp.sources.[games,misc,sun,unix,x], some alt.sources, XENIX(68K/286/386)
  uucp-anon: ogin: nuucp password: anon-uucp
  uucp-anon directory: /u/pdsrc, /u/pubdir, /u/uunet, help in /u/pubdir/HELP
  Contact: miikes@iuvax.cs.indiana.edu (812-855-3974 days 812-333-6564 eves)

01/94 812-476-7564   aquila   Evansville   IN 2400-FAST 24
  SCO Unix; Email/News provider to the Tri-State area; Supports regional
  BBSs; Has satellite downlink for 2500+ Usenet newsgroups. No fee for
  mail, low fee for news;
  The Aquila System, PO Box 4912, Evansville IN 47724-0912.
  Contact: kilroy@aquila.nshore.org

03/93 814-353-0566   cpumagic   Bellefonte   PA 1200-FAST 24
  80386, ESIX 4.0.3a (SVR4); Dual Standard (v.32/v.32bis/HST);
  The Centre Programmers Unit BBS, custom BBS software (Micro Magic);
  Files available: UNIX, GNU, X, ESIX, MSDOS tools and libraries;
  No fee but up/download ratios enforced.
  Contact: Mike Loewen at mloewen@cpumagic.scol.pa.us
            or ... psuvax1!cpumagic!mloewen

11/93 815-874-3998   maynard   Rockford   IL 300-FAST 24
  USL UnixWare SysVr4.2; Provides shell, USENET, E-Mail, uuftp
  sources, BBS, games, chat and more. $5 Email only
  $10 Email USENET. UUCP available Contact troy@maynard.chi.il.us

03/94 818-287-5115   abode   El Monte   CA 2400-FAST 24
  XENIX 2.3.3; 2400-9600 Baud (Telebit T1000 PEP); Fee of $40 per year;
  Users get access to shell account, C compiler, email, usenet news,
  games, etc. For more information send email to contact name below
  or login as 'guest'.
  Contact: eric@abode.ttank.com (cerritos.edu!ttank!abode!eric)

```
03/94 818-367-2142    quake    Sylmar        CA 300-FAST  24
  ESIX/386 3.2D running Waffle;  Telebit WorldBlazer on dial-in line,
  818-362-6092 has Telebit T2500;  Usenet (1000+ groups), Email
  (registered as quake.sylmar.ca.us), UUCP/UUPC connections;  Rare Bird
  Advisories, Technomads, more;  $5 a month if paid a year at a time.
  New users login as "bbs", then "new".  One week free to new users.

03/94 818-793-9108    atrium    Pasadena      CA 300-FAST  24
  LINUX; Internet E-mail, Usenet Newsgroups (5,400+), MUD, Chat.
  Contact: sysop@atrium.ucm.org; multi-lines V.32bis; login "mm"

06/93 900-468-7727    uunet    Falls Church   VA 300-FAST  24
  Sequent S81, Dynix 3.0.17(9);  UUNET Communication Services;  No Shell;
  Anonymous UUCP, fee $0.40/min — billed by the telephone company,
  login: uucp (no passwd);  Multiple lines, PEP and V.32 available;
  grab "uunet!~/help for more info" ...
  Full internet mail and USENET access via subscriber UUCP accounts.
  Contact: info@uunet.uu.net or call [voice] 703-204-8000.

03/93 904-456-2003    amaranth  Pensacola     FL 1200-FAST 24
  ISC Unix V/386 2.2.1 TB+ on dialin. XBBS no fee. limited NEWS, E-mail
  For more info: Jon Spelbring jsspelb@amaranth.UUCP

03/93 906-228-4399    lopez    Marquette      MI 1200-2400 24
  80386, SCO Xenix 2.3.4; Running STARBASE II Software.  Great White North
  UPLink, Inc. (Non Profit) 100+ local rooms, PLUS USENET, Multi Channel Chat,
  5 ports, $30 yr, flat rate for full access to net news, mail.
  Upper Michigan's ORIGINAL BBS (since 1983)
  Contact: Gary Bourgois ...rutgers!sharkey!lopez!flash (flash@lopez.UUCP)

08/93 908-937-9481    digex    New Brunswick  NJ 300-FAST  24
  Refer to primary entry (Greenbelt, MD) for system/services details.
  Telnet to cnj.digex.com or mail to info@cnj.digex.com for more info;
  voice phone 1-800-969-9090.

03/94 916-649-0161    sactoh0  Sacramento     CA 1200-FAST 24
  3B2/310 SYVR3.2; SAC_UNIX, sactoh0.SAC.CA.US;  $2/month;  3 lines,
  v.32 on 722-6519, TB+ on 649-0161, 2400/1200 baud on 722-5068;
  USENET, E-Mail, some games; login: new
  Contact: root@sactoh0.SAC.CA.US   or   ..ames!pacbell!sactoh0!root

02/94 916-923-5013    rgm      Sacramento     CA 1200-FAST 24
  486SX-25. 200mb. Coherent 386 v4.0.1; Dedicated incoming HST line. Full
  Bourne/Korn shell access for all users.  Internet mail, limited Usenet
  (requests encouraged). Mail & news feeds available.  $2/mo. for light
  mail/news users.  login: new; Contact root@rgm.com
```

03/94 919-248-1177   rock   RTP   NC 300-FAST 24
  SparcStation 1+, SunOS 4.1; Fee: $50 installation, $30/month. Full
  internet access (FTP, TELNET, etc). Netnews (includes vmsnet, u3b, alt)
  and E-Mail. No limit on time, 5 meg disk quotas enforced. 56Kbps and
  T1 internet connections also available. Phone number depends on location
  within North Carolina (PC Pursuit also available).
  Contact: info@concert.net

11/93 +31-1720-42580   mugnet   Alphen a/d Rijn NL 300-FAST 24
  386 PC/AT, LINUX — Mugnet int. hobbiest network, Worldblazer 300-19.2k
  + V42bis + V32; No Fee services : all good stuff for Linux Fee services:
  UUCP feeds, internet E-mail mugnet domain.
  SUITABLE FOR BUSINESS USE TOO
  Own distribution of Linux/Pro, supplied on disks/tape/removable pack
  or downloadable. Anonymous guest account. Bash Shell Access on Linux
  system, UUCP News and Mail Feeds.
  Contact: root@nic.nl.mugnet.org,
  Voice +31 1720 40005 , Fax: +31 1720 30979

04/93 +358-0-455-8331   clinet   Espoo   FI 300-FAST 24
  Sun 3/60 16M/1G + Motorola M8[48]00-hybrid 32M/300M (terminal server,
  mostly), SunOS (4.1.1); Multi-line -8331 (V32bisMNP), -8332 (V32MNP)
  & -8778 (V32), 4 lines starting at -8688 (V22bis); custom software
  (locally written), conferences, menu system, other stuff; TCP/IP
  connected with IRC, USENET (all groups), E-Mail, shell access, common
  UNIX software, programming; $10/mo including at least 1hr of daily
  time ($0.25/hr if all lines busy). login as 'new'. Since 1987.
  Contact: clinet@clinet.fi.

09/93 +39-541-27135   nervous   Rimini (Fo)   IT 300-FAST 24
  386/33, 1GB, Unix System V; Menu driven BBS, no shell. This system is
  the official UniBoard Development Site; latest UniBoard releases/fixes
  are available here. Also, lots of unix sources (& erotic images) as well
  as USENET & Fidonet conferences, are available on line.
  Contact: pizzi@nervous.com
  Foreign callers need to send email to the above address to gain access to
  most board options.

04/93 +41-61-8115492   ixgch   Kaiseraugst   CH 300-FAST 24
  80386, SCO XENIX SV2.3.3, USR-DS (-V.32); Host: ixgch.xgp.spn.com (Ixgate
  Switzerland); Organization: XGP Switzerland & SPN Swiss Public Network;
  Public UI: PubSh (Public Shell), free!; Services among others: UUCP feeds
  for Internet Mail and Usenet News, Swiss BBS-List Service, Ixgate-Archive
  (RFCs,NIC-docs,non-comp-areas etc.), anonymous UUCP, CHAT conference, TALK
  software and more. BTW: V.32bis connections soon!
  General info: mail to service@spn.com (Subject: help).
  Contact: sysadm@xgp.spn.com (...!gator!ixgch!sysadm)

04/93 +44-734-34-00-55 infocom   Berkshire   UK 300-FAST 24
    80486, SCO UNIX 3.2.2; BBS, Teletext pages; 2nd line 32-00-55; Internet
    Mail/USENET at HOME using FSUUCP (DOS)/UUCP; Max 60.00 + V.A.T. per annum,
    this will also be the charge when internet access (i.e. ftp & telnet
    arrive shortly), this level includes UUCP Login & a BBS Login account, if
    you choose UUCP transfers this can save a lot of connection charges from
    those nasty telephone companies.
    File Upload & Download, no quotas; Some services are free and some are pay;
    login as 'new' (8-N-1) ... on-line registration, password sent by mail;
    Contact: sysop@infocom.co.uk or mail <information@infocom.co.uk> with
    "general" in the subject line or Fax +44 734 32 09 88

03/94 +44 81 244 6677   ExNet   London   UK 300-2400 24
    SunOS 4.1, V32/V42b soon. Mail, news and UNIX shell (/usr/ucb/mail,
    ream; rn; sh, csh, tcsh, bash) UK#5 per month. 500 USENET groups
    currently and expanding. All reasonable mail and USENET use free.
    Beginner's pack available. Mail for contract and charges documents.
    One month free trial period possible. ***Mail and news feeds.***
    SUITABLE FOR BUSINESS USE TOO.
    Contact: HelpEx@exnet.co.uk, or voice +44 81 244 0077 GMT 1300-2300.

08/93 +44-81-317-2222   dircon   London   UK 300-FAST 24
    UNIX SysV3.2; The Direct Connection multi-user on-line service; Full
    Internet Connectivity (including TELNET, FTP, GOPHER, IRC, etc), USENET
    News conferencing with a choice of newsreaders, Internet electronic mail
    with an outgoing FAX gateway, 24 hour computer newswire, download areas,
    chat/talk facilities, personal file areas with access to a choice of shells
    (including Unix). UUCP and TCP-IP (PPP or SLIP) connections are also
    available. Login as 'demo' to sign-up.
    EMAIL Contact: helpdesk@dircon.co.uk (+44-81-317 0100 [voice]).

12/93 +44-81-863-6646   ibmpcug   London   UK 300-FAST 24
    486 PC/AT, SCO Unix — IBM-PC User Group; Multiple lines,
    300-19.2k + V42bis + V32; Fee: ~50 pounds sterling per year,
    unlimited use; Internet Access (FTP, Telnet and IRC) as well as News
    and Mail services via UUCP; Shell Access available as an option.
    UUCP News and Mail Feeds
    Contact: info@ibmpcug.co.uk, Voice +44 81 863 1191

12/93 +44-81-863-6646   WinNET   London   UK 300-FAST 24
    486 PC/AT, SCO Unix — IBM-PC User Group; Multiple lines,
    300-19.2k + V42bis + V32; Fee: from 6.75 pounds sterling per month,
    (3.25 per hour) includes custom Windows 3.x Software;
    Software available for download vai anon ftp from ftp.ibmpcug.co.uk
    or via dial up link login as winnet (no password).

Internet Access (optional FTP, Telnet and IRC) as well as News
and Mail services via UUCP; Shell Access available as an option.
UUCP News and Mail Feeds
Contact: info@ibmpcug.co.uk, or request@win-uk.net Voice +44 81 863 1191

04/93 +49-30-694-61-82 scuzzy   Berlin   DE 300-FAST 24
    80486/33, ISC 3.0; HST 14400/v.42bis on the first, HST 14400/V.32bis/V.42bis
    Modems on other dial-in lines; Large library of source code including
    386BSD, GNU, TeX, and X11 — will distribute on tapes (grab /src/TAPES
    for the order form, /src/SERVICE for info about support for Free Software).
    Bulletin Board System with possible full Internet access, i.e. email,
    USENET, IRC, FTP, telnet (grab /src/BBS for info, or login as 'guest');
    Login as 'archive' for x/y/z-modem and kermit transfers; Anonymous UUCP
    available, grab /src/README for initial info;
    Contact: src@contrib.de (Heiko Blume)
       anon uucp: ogin: nuucp   word: nuucp

02/94 +49-40-4915655   isys-hh   Hamburg   DE 300-FAST 24
    Intel 2*80486 >2GB Disk - Unix System V 3.2v4.2 & Linux 0.99PL14,
    multiple lines w/ V.32bis, ISDN +49-40-40192183,
    Shells: msh, sh, csh, ksh, bash; nn & tin for newsreaders, ELM for mail,
    anon. UUCP: ogin: nuucp (no password) get ~/ls-lgR.[Z¦z¦F]
    Contact: mike@isys-hh.hanse.de (Michael 'Mike' Loth)

04/93 +49-69-308265   odbffm   Frankfurt/Main DE 300-FAST 24
    Altos 386/2000, Telebit Modem, Public Access Unix; only shell accounts,
    no bbs software. Mail and news access (currently via UUCP, Internet
    planned).
    Contact: oli@odb.rhein-main.de, voice +49 69 331461, fax +49 69 307682

04/93 +61-2-837-1183   kralizec   Sydney   AU 1200-FAST 24
    Sun 3/50, SunOS 4.0; 470mb disk; V.32/MNP-5 modem; Dialup access to
    Internet E-mail & USENET; mail-based FTP. 80 - 100 Mb software online
    for download. Full C-shell access to all members. No joining fee. Usage
    fee $50 for 50 hours connect time. Voice number +61-2-837-1397.
    Home of IXgate - Internet to Fidonet gateway - also Fido 713/602.
    Contact: nick@kralizec.zeta.org.au

04/93 +64-4-389-5478   actrix   Wellington   NZ 300-FAST 24
    Zenith 386/33MHz w/ ISC 386/ix 2.02; Actrix Information Exchange —
    New Zealand's first Public Access UNIX. 750 Mb disk; 3 lines, USR
    Courier HST (T2500 due December 1990, X25 in '91). Fee: NZ$54 p.a. -
    offers heavily modified XBBS with USEnet and Fidonet, e-mail (elm),
    hundreds of file areas divided into sections for UNIX, MS-DOS, Amiga,
    Atari, Apple //, Macintosh, CP/M etc. Shell w/ many extras available
    via 'Enhanced subscription'. Planned to join APC (PeaceNet/EcoNet);
    Contact: paul@actrix.gen.nz (Paul Gillingwater) PO Box 11-410, Wgtn, NZ

```
===============================================================================
NOTE: The information in this document is kept as current as possible ...
      however, you use this data at your own risk and cost.
===============================================================================
Lists are available via any of the following:
     o  Anonymous uucp from jabber.
            +1 215 348 9727 [Telebit access]
            login: nuucp  NO PWD   [no rmail permitted]
            long list: /usr/spool/uucppublic/nixpub.long
            short list: /usr/spool/uucppublic/nixpub.short
            (also available from the "*NIX Depot" BBS)
     o  Mail server on jabber
            mail to mail-server@bts.com
            body containing:
               get PUB nixpub.long
            or
               get PUB nixpub.short
     o  The nixpub-list electronic mailing list.  To subscribe to
        the list:
            mail to mail-server@bts.com
            body containing:
               subscribe NIXPUB-LIST Your Name
     o  USENET, regular posts to:
            comp.misc
            comp.bbs.misc
            alt.bbs
     o  Anonymous ftp from VFL.Paramax.COM [128.126.220.104]
            under ~/pub/pubnet/{nixpub.long,nixpub.short}
===============================================================================
The "nixpub" listings are (C) Copyright 1993-94, Bux Technical Services.
This publication is released for unlimited redistribution over any
electronic media providing it remains in its original form.  Publishing,
removing this copyright notice, or in any way revising this document's
contents is forbidden without written consent from the owner.
===============================================================================


 —

 .
```

Appendix

Glossary

A

addressing   A method of identifying a resource (such as a program) or a piece of information (such as a file) on a network. Methods of addressing vary considerably from network to network.

ADJ   The Boolean ADJACENT operator used by WAIS to indicate that the two words on either side of the ADJ tag should sit next to each other in found documents.

Adventure   One of the earliest text adventure games written for computers. It is the forerunner of the popular Zork series from Infocom.

America Online   A popular commercial information service with a graphical interface.

AND   The Boolean AND operator used by WAIS to indicate that found documents must contain both terms in the question.

AOL   Shorthand for America Online. Each letter is pronounced separately.

AppleTalk A local area network protocol Apple developed to connect computers and peripherals over various different types of wiring.

.ARC An older DOS archiving format.

Archie An invaluable Internet service that maintains and allows users to search a large database of materials stored on anonymous FTP sites.

archive site A site that archives files for users to retrieve, either via FTP or email.

ARPA Advanced Research Projects Agency. The governmental organization responsible for creating the beginnings of the Internet.

ARPAnet The proto-Internet network created by ARPA.

ASCII American Standard Code for Information Interchange. In the context of a file, an ASCII file is one that contains only "text" characters—numbers, letters, and standard punctuation. Although ASCII text can contain international characters available in Windows, these characters are not commonly supported by Internet services such as email, Gopher, and FTP. In FTP, a command that tells FTP that you will be transferring text files (which is the default).

atob (pronounced "a to b") A UNIX program that turns ASCII files into binary files. The btoa program does the reverse.

B

bandwidth Information theory used to express the amount of information that can flow through a given point at any given time. Some points have narrow bandwidth (indicating not much information can flow through at one time), and others have high bandwidth (indicating a great deal of information can flow through at one time). This term is commonly used in reference to "wasted bandwidth," indicating that some (or most) of the information flowing by a point is of no use to a user. This term can include overloading a site's network connection (thus curtailing other users' use of the lines) or including lengthy signature files in Usenet postings or discussion groups. "Wasted bandwidth" is often relative: what one person views as waste might be essential to another.

bang The exclamation point! Used in UUCP path-style addressing, which isn't all that common anymore.

baud A measure of modem speed equal to one signal per second. 300 baud equals 300 bits per second (bps), but at higher speeds one signal can contain more than one bit, so a 9600 baud modem is not a 9600 bps modem. (The terms are often incorrectly used interchangeably). See also **bps**.

BBS Bulletin Board System. A computer system that provides its users files for downloading and areas for electronic discussions. Bulletin board systems usually are run by and for local users, although many now provide Internet, UUCP, or FidoNet mail.

Binary In the context of a file, any file that contains nontextual data. (Images and applications are examples of binary files.) In FTP, a command that tells FTP to transfer information as an arbitrary stream of bits rather than as a series of textual characters.

BITNET An academic large-scale computer network, primarily connecting academic institutions. BITNET is often expanded as the "Because It's Time" Network. Mark Williamson notes, "Actually, it seems that the definitive answer to what the BIT stands for is `It has varied, and depends on whom you asked and when.'"

BIX The online commercial information service called the BYTE Information Exchange, although I have never heard anyone use the full name in favor of BIX.

body The part of an email message where you type your message, as opposed to the header or the signature.

bounce What email does when it doesn't go through.

bps Bits per second. The measurement of modem transmission speed. Not comparable to baud after 300 bps.

Brownian motion With apologies to Douglas Adams, the best example is indeed a really hot cup of tea. It has something to do with internal movement within a hot liquid.

btoa (pronounced "b to a") A UNIX program that turns binary files into ASCII files for transmission via email. The atob program decodes such files.

BTW Abbreviation for "By the way."

C

Call For Votes   What you do after discussing whether a new newsgroup should be created. Abbreviated CFV.

CEO   Chief Executive Officer. The head honcho of a company who has little time to learn computer systems. CEOs generally earn a lot more money than you or I do.

CERN   The birthplace of the World-Wide Web, although in real life they do high energy physics research. Located in Geneva, Switzerland.

CFV   See **Call For Votes**.

charter   The document that lays out what topics a newsgroup will cover, what its name will be, and other relevant details.

chat script   A simple conversation (you hope) between your computer and your host machine that allows you to log in automatically. Chat scripts usually involve a series of send and expect strings. Your host sends a login prompt; your computer responds with your username. Your host sends a password prompt; your computer responds with your password.

CIM   See **CompuServe Information Manager**.

CIS   CompuServe Information Service, or something similar. Wags often replace the *S* with a $.

ClariNet   An alternate hierarchy of newsgroups that uses the same transmission routes as Usenet, but that carries commercial information from UPI and others. You or your provider must pay to read ClariNet news.

client   The program or computer that requests information from a server computer or program. Used in terms of client/server computing.

CMS   Conversational Monitor System. The part of the operating system on certain IBM mainframes with which you interact. Not at all conversational.

command line   Where you type commands to an operating system like DOS or UNIX. Command-line operating systems can be powerful but are often a pain to work with, especially for those used to a graphical interface.

compress   Generically, to make a file smaller by removing redundant information. Specifically, the UNIX program that does just that. Files compressed with the UNIX compress command end with a .Z suffix. (Always capital Z.) May be decompressed with UNIX command uncompress.

CompuServe   One of the oldest and largest commercial services. Sometimes abbreviated as **CIS**.

CompuServe Information Manager   A decent graphical program for the Windows (and Mac) that puts a nice face on CompuServe. Generally abbreviated **CIM** or **WinCIM**.

connect time   The amount of time you are actually connected to and using a computer. Because connect or telephone charges are based on this amount of time, you want to keep it as low as possible.

CREN   Corporation for Research and Educational Networking.

cross-posted   What happens to a Usenet posting when you put several newsgroup names in the Newsgroups line. More efficient than posting multiple individual copies.

D

daemons   Small programs in UNIX that run frequently to see whether something has happened: if so, they act as they were programmed; if not, they go back to sleep.

DARPA   Defense Advanced Research Projects Agency. Replaced ARPA and has a more military bent.

DEC   Digital Equipment Corporation. Also known as Digital, this company produces the popular VAX line of computers and the VMS operating system.

dial up   To call another computer via modem. The term is often lumped together as one word.

dialup   A connection or line reached by modem, as in "a dialup line."

digestified   The process by which individual postings to a mailing list or newsgroup are concatenated into a single file, usually with a specific format.

directed information   Information specifically aimed at you.

domain   A level of hierarchy in a machine's full nodename. For instance, `tidbits.com` is in the `com` domain along with many other machines.

domain name server   A computer that keeps track of names of other machines and their numeric IP addresses. When you refer to a machine by name, therefore, your domain name server translates that information appropriately into the numeric IP address necessary to make the connection.

domain name system   The system that makes it possible for you to think in terms of names such as `tidbits.com`, whereas computers think in terms of `192.135.191.128`.

DOS   The ubiquitous operating system that is frequently enhanced by Microsoft Windows. Currently at release 6.2.

download   To retrieve a file from another machine, usually a host machine, to your machine.

downstream   Usenet neighbors that are downstream from you get most of their news from your machine, in contrast to machines upstream from you.

E

80x86   The class of processors brought to you by Intel Corporation. These chips are the heart and soul of DOS and Windows. Frequently, the initial 80 is dropped in casual conversation: "My 486 sports more megahertz than yours."

electronic mail or **email**   Messages that travel through the networks rather than being committed to paper and making the arduous journey through the U.S. Postal Service.

emoticons   Another name for **smileys**.

Ethernet   A network specification developed by DEC, Intel, and Xerox, which provides 10 megabits per second transmission speeds (theoretically). Think of this as 1000 times faster than a 9600 bps modem. Most PCs can use Ethernet by adding an Ethernet expansion card.

Eudora   A thoroughly nice email program written by Steve Dorner. Specifically, a POP and SMTP email client program.

expire   After a certain amount of time, Usenet postings can be set to expire, which means that they will be deleted even if they haven't been read so that they don't waste space.

F

FAQ   Frequently Asked Question. Lists of these questions and answers to them are often posted in newsgroups to reduce the number of novice questions. Read a FAQ list before asking a question, to make sure yours isn't a frequently asked one.

Fax   Slang for facsimile. A technology that takes paper from the sender and makes more paper that looks just like it at the recipient's end. You can use fax modems to eliminate the paper step at one end or both, but they may be less reliable than stand-alone fax machines. Email is cleaner, often cheaper, more environmentally friendly, and the results are more useful in other programs. However, you can't easily send signatures or existing paper documents via email.

Federal Express   A company that can transport paper mail overnight for a hefty sum of money. Email is far faster and cheaper.

feed   Shorthand for a connection to another machine that sends you mail and news. I might say, "I have a mail feed from Ed's machine."

filename extension   A three-letter (usually) code at the end of a filename that indicate file type. Common extensions include .txt for text files, .exe for application files, and .ini for initialization files.

fileserver or **file server**   A machine that provides files via a network. Perhaps because of time spent working on BITNET, I tend to use it as a synonym for mailserver, or a machine that returns files that are requested via email.

file site   Another name for archive site or FTP site. A computer on which files are stored for anyone on the Internet to retrieve.

finger   A program that helps you find out information about someone else on the Internet.

flame war   A conflagration in which lots of people jump in on different sides of an argument and start insulting each other. Fun to watch briefly, but a major waste of bandwidth.

flaming   The act of calling into question someone's thoughts, beliefs, and parentage simply because you don't agree with them. Don't do it.

followup   An article on Usenet posted in reply to another article. The subject should stay the same so that readers can tell the two articles are related.

Freenet   An organization whose goal it is to provide free Internet access in a specific area, often by working with local schools and libraries. Ask around to see if a Freenet has sprung up in your area. The first and still-prominent example is the Cleveland Freenet. Freenet also refers to the specific Freenet software and the information services that use it.

freeware   Software that you can distribute freely and use for free, but for which the author often retains the copyright, which means that you can't modify the software.

FTP   File Transfer Protocol. One of the main ways in which you retrieve information from other machines on the Internet.

FYI   Abbreviation for "For your information."

G

GIF   Graphics Interchange Format. A platform-independent file format developed by CompuServe, the GIF format is commonly used to distribute graphics on the Internet. Mighty battles have been waged over the pronunciation of this term, and although Robin Williams notes that it's pronounced "jiff" in her book *Jargon*, both of my glossary proofreaders flagged it as being pronounced with a hard *g*, as in "graphics." I surrender, pronounce it as you want.

.gif   The filename extension generally given to GIF files.

GNU   In a circular reference, GNU stands for "GNU's Not UNIX." Developed by Richard Stallman and the Free Software Foundation, GNU is (or will be, when finished) a high-quality operating system like UNIX that is free of charge and freely modifiable by its users. GNU software is distributed at no cost with source code. Many GNU applications and utilities are mainstays of the UNIX community.

Gopher   An information retrieval system created by the University of Minnesota. In wide acceptance on the Internet, Gopher is one of the most useful resources available.

.gz   A extension used by the gzip compression program, GNU's version of ZIP, under UNIX.

H

header   The part of an email message or Usenet posting that contains information about the message, such as who it's from, when it was sent, and so on. Headers are mainly interesting when something doesn't work.

host   The large computer you connect to for your Internet access.

HTML   HyperText Markup Language. The language used to mark up text files with links for use with World-Wide Web browsers.

HTTP   HyperText Transport Protocol. The protocol used by the World-Wide Web.

hypertext   A term created by Ted Nelson to describe non-linear writing in which you follow associative paths through a world of textual documents.

HYTELNET   Stands for HyperTelnet. HYTELNET is essentially a database of Telnet sites and other Internet resources that can link to other programs when you want to connect to a site you've found. Interesting, but not as useful as Gopher.

I

IAB   Internet Architecture Board.

IBM   International Business Machines. IBM remains one of the most powerful companies in the computer industry despite numerous problems in recent years. Developer of numerous mainframes and operating systems, many of which are still in use today. Co-developed OS/2 with Microsoft (who has since bowed out in favor of Windows NT).

IETF   Internet Engineering Task Force.

IMAP   A new protocol for the storage and retrieval of email, much like POP, the Post Office Protocol. It's not in wide use yet.

IMHO   Abbreviation for "In my humble opinion."

information agent   A software program (currently only an interface to frequently updated databases) that can search numerous databases for information that interests you without your having to know what it is searching. Archie and Veronica are current examples of information agents.

interactive   You use the Internet interactively when you are working on it personally, browsing Gopherspace or searching an Archie database.

internet   With a lowercase *i*, an internet is a group of connected networks.

Internet   The collection of all the connected networks in the world, although it is sometimes better called WorldNet or just the Net. More specifically, the Internet is the set of networks that communicate via TCP/IP. If you're still confused, go back and read chapters 1 through 7.

Internet Architecture Board   A group of invited volunteers that manages certain aspects of the Internet, such as standards and address allocation.

Internet Engineering Task Force   A volunteer organization that meets regularly to discuss problems facing the Internet.

IP   Internet Protocol. The main protocol used on the Internet.

IP address   A four-part number that uniquely identifies a machine on the Internet. For instance, my IP address for `tidbits.com` is `192.135.191.128`. People generally use the name instead.

IRC   Internet Relay Chat. A world-wide network of people who spend their time talking to each other in real-time over the Internet rather than talking to other people in person.

IRS   Internal Revenue Service. If you live in the United States and you're not aware of them, you might want to watch out.

ISOC   The Internet Society. ISOC is a membership organization that supports the Internet and is the governing body to which the IAB reports.

J

JANET Joint Academic Network. JANET is Great Britain's national network, and in true British fashion, JANET addresses work backwards from normal Internet addresses in that they work from largest domain to the smallest, as in `joe@uk.ac.canterbury.cc.trumble`. Luckily, most gateways to JANET perform the necessary translations automatically.

jargon The sometimes incomprehensible language used to talk about specialized topics. If you need help with computer jargon, check out *Jargon*, by Robin Williams, a light-hearted and detailed trip through the world of jargon.

Jolt cola All the sugar and twice the caffeine of normal colas. First suggested as a joke by George Carlin, later developed and marketed by Carlin and a food industry entrepreneur.

jordanism An attempt at sounding intelligent, but ending up wasting peoples' time and coming off like an idiot.

JPEG Joint Photographic Experts Group. A group that has defined a compression scheme that reduces the size of image files by up to 20 times at the cost of slightly reduced image quality.

.jpeg A filename extension used to mark JPEG-compressed images.

K

Kermit A file transfer protocol named after the popular Kermit the Frog. Kermit is generally slower than XMODEM, YMODEM, and the top-of-the-line ZMODEM.

Knowledge Navigator A video of John Sculley's anthropomorphic vision of an information agent. Information agents will probably be more successful if they don't look like people because computers cannot currently meet the high expectations we have of people.

L

LAN   See **local area network**.

leaf site   A machine on Usenet that talks to only one other machine instead of passing news onto other machines.

LISTSERV   A powerful program for automating mailing lists. It currently requires an IBM mainframe, but that requirement may change in the near future.

local area network   Often abbreviated LAN. Two or more computers connected together via network cables. A Windows for Workgroup setup is a typical local area network.

login   The process by which you identify yourself to a host computer, usually involving a userid and a password.

lurkers   Not a derogatory term. People who merely read discussions online without contributing to them.

M

mail gateway   A machine that exists on two networks, such as the Internet and BITNET, and that can transfer mail between them.

mailing list   A list of people who all receive postings sent to the group. Mailing lists exist on all sorts of topics.

man pages   The UNIX manual pages. You must go to the man pages to find out more about a UNIX command. Accessed through use of the man command followed by the command whose description you want to view.

MCI   A large telecommunications company that provides an email system called MCI Mail. It's apparently not Windows friendly but can be used efficiently to receive Internet email.

Microsoft   That programming machine out in Redmond, Washington that continues to define trends in personal computers. Their applications division include some of the most popular software to date, including Word, Excel, PowerPoint, and Works. Their systems division, of course, is responsible for bringing Windows and Windows NT to the world.

MIME   Multipurpose Internet Mail Extensions. MIME is a new Internet standard for transferring nontextual data, such as audio messages or pictures, via email.

mirror site   An FTP site that contains exactly the same contents as another site. Mirror sites help distribute the load on a single popular site.

modem   Stands for modulator-demodulator, because that's what it does, technically. In reality, a modem allows your computer to talk to another computer over the phone lines.

moderator   An overworked volunteer who reads all of the submissions to a mailing list or newsgroup to make sure they are appropriate before posting them.

monospaced font   A font whose characters are all the same width. Courier New is the most common monospaced font in Windows, but you can find others like Letter Gothic, Courier, and Orator. You generally want to use a monospaced font when reading text on the Internet.

MTU   Maximum Transmission Unit. A number that your system administrator must give you so that you can configure SLIP.

MUD   Multi-User Dungeon, or sometimes Multi-User Dimension. A text-based alternate reality where you can grow to a level at which you can modify the environment. Mostly used for games, and extremely addictive.

MX record   Mail Exchange record. An entry in a database that tells domain name servers where they should route mail so that it gets to you.

N

NavCIS   A program designed for efficient reading of discussions on CompuServe. Not a good front-end for email of any sort, but extremely useful for automating the retrieval of messages and for reading and replying offline.

NCSA   National Center for Supercomputing Applications. A group that has produced a great deal of public domain software for the scientific community. They wrote NCSA Telnet and have completed NCSA Mosaic for Windows, X-Windows, and Macintosh.

net heavies   Those system administrators who run large sites on the Internet. Although they don't necessarily have official posts, they wield more power than most people on the nets.

NetBEUI   Stands for NetBIOS Extended User Interface. It is the common networking protocol of Windows for Workgroups. Meant for small local area networks, it is sometimes difficult to get a PC to "talk" NetBEUI and anything else.

NetBIOS   Network Basic Input/Output System. NetBIOS is a very basic applications interface to allow an application to communicate on a network.

NetWare   The most popular of PC local area networks by Novell, Inc. Rather than using TCP/IP as its "standard" protocol for intercomputer communications, it uses IPX/SPX. It is sometimes difficult to get a PC to "talk" TCP/IP and IPX/SPX at the same time.

Network Information Center   An organization that provides information about a network.

news   Synonymous with Usenet news, or sometimes just Usenet.

newsgroup   A discussion group on Usenet devoted to talking about a specific topic. Currently, around 4,000 newsgroups exist.

.newsrc   The file that UNIX newsreaders use to keep track of which messages in which newsgroups you've read.

newsreader   A program that helps you read news and provides capabilities for following or deleting threads.

NIC   See **Network Information Center**.

nickname   An easy-to-remember shortcut for an email address.

nixpub list   A list of public access Internet providers from Phil Eschallier.

nn   A popular UNIX newsreader.

NNTP   Net News Transport Protocol. A transmission protocol for the transfer of Usenet news.

nodename   The name of a machine, like `tidbits.com`.

noninteractive Noninteractive use of the Internet is automated by a program, so the information is transferred much faster than you can read it interactively, and then you peruse it offline.

NOT The Boolean operator NOT, which WAIS uses to limit the found documents to ones that contain one term but not another.

Notepad Windows application that allows you to view (and edit) ASCII text files. Typically use with files of the .txt extension.

NREN National Research and Education Network. The successor to the NSFNET.

NSF National Science Foundation. The creators of the NSFNET.

NSFNET National Science Foundation Network. The current high-speed networking linking users with supercomputer sites around the country. Also called the interim NREN.

O

offline Actions performed when you aren't actually connected to another computer.

online Actions performed when you are connected to another computer.

P

PDIAL list Peter Kaminski's list of public providers that offer full Internet access.

Pentium Class of processor brought to you by Intel Corporation. It is the lastest entry in the long list of processors of the 80x86 family. Think of it as an 80586 (hence Pent-ium—for five).

PEP Packetized Ensemble Protocol. Telebit's proprietary method of increasing throughput when two of Telebit's modems connect to each other.

PKZIP or PKUNZIP Suite of utilities from PKWARE for compressing and uncompressing DOS and Windows files. Uses the .zip extension.

POP   Post Office Protocol. A protocol for the storage and retrieval of email. Eudora uses POP.

port   In software, the act of converting code so that a program runs on more than one type of computer. In networking, a number that identifies a specific "channel" used by network services. For instance, Gopher generally uses port 70 but is occasionally set to use other ports on various machines.

post   To send a message to a discussion group or list.

PPP   Point to Point Protocol. A protocol similar to SLIP that allows your computer to pretend it is a full Internet machine using only a modem and a normal telephone line.

Program Group   A mechanism in the Windows Program Manager that allows you to collect like applications. For instance, you could have a group consisting of all WinSock applications. Groups are not nestable in that you cannot have groups within groups.

Program Item   An executable entity in the form of an icon that lives in a Program Group of the Windows Program Manager. Typically, double-clicking on these will launch applications, but in some cases it can launch documents or batch files.

Program Manager   Windows default shell or interface. The Program Manager, unless you've replaced it with something better, like PC Tools for Windows, allows you to launch other Windows applications.

proportionally spaced font   A font whose characters vary in width, so that a *W* is wider than an *i*. Proportionally spaced fonts often work poorly when reading text on the Internet.

protocol   A language that computers use when talking to each other.

public access provider   An organization that provides Internet access for individuals or other organizations, often for a fee.

public domain   Software that you can use freely, distribute freely, and modify in any way you want. See also **freeware** and **shareware**.

Q

quoting   The act of including parts of an original message in a reply.

The standard character used to set off a quote from the rest of the text is a column of > (greater-than) characters along the left margin.

R

ranking   The method by which WAIS displays found documents in order of possible utility.

rec.humor.funny   A popular moderated newsgroup devoted to jokes judged funny by the group's moderator. Set up by Brad Templeton because the rec.humor group had become so overrun with jokes that no one found funny, and discussions about how unfunny they all were.

relevance feedback   A method WAIS uses to "find me more documents like this one."

Request for Comments   Documents containing the standards, proposed standards, and other necessary details regarding the operation of the Internet.

Request for Discussion   The part of the newsgroup creation process where you propose a group and discussion starts.

RFC   See **Request for Comments**.

RFD   See **Request for Discussion**.

rn   A popular, if aging, UNIX newsreader. Perhaps the most common newsreader available under UNIX—if a UNIX machine has a newsfeed, it will almost certainly have rn.

root directory   The topmost directory that you can see. Under DOS the root directory is typically **c:**. Each volume or disk drive will have its own root directory.

rot13   A method of encoding possible offensive postings on Usenet so that those who don't want to be offended can avoid accidentally seeing the posting. Works by converting each letter to a number (a = 1, b = 2, etc.), adding 13 to the number, and then converting back into a letter, rendering the file unreadable with deciphering.

RTFM   Read the f***ing manual. Used frequently throughout Usenet as a standard flame whenever a stupid question is posed.

S

scripting language   A programming language to instruct how one computer should communicate with another computer. Typically, you would use a scripting language to cause your computer to automatically connect to a host computer, validate your user id and password, and then processes desired commands (like initiate SLIP).

self-extracting archive   A compressed file or files encapsulated in a decompression program, so you don't need any other programs to expand the archive.

server   A machine that makes services available on a network. A file server makes files available. A WAIS server makes full-text information available through the WAIS protocol, although WAIS uses the term *source* interchangeably with server.

shareware   A method of software distribution in which the software may be freely distributed, and you may try it before paying. If you decide to keep and use the program, you send your payment directly to the shareware author.

shell   A common interface—either command-based or graphical. Typical UNIX shells are csh, ksh, and sh. The Macintosh shell is the Finder; DOS shell is command.com; and Windows' is the Program Manager.

signature   Several lines automatically appended to your email messages, usually listing your name and email address, sometimes along with witty sayings and ASCII graphics. Keep them short, and leave out the ASCII graphics.

.sit   The filename extension used by files compressed by StuffIt.

SLIP   Serial Line Internet Protocol. Like PPP, a protocol that lets your computer pretend it is a full Internet machine using only a modem and a normal phone line. SLIP is older and less flexible than PPP but currently somewhat more prevalent.

smileys   Collections of characters meant to totally replace body language, intonation, and complete physical presence. ;-)

SMTP   Simple Mail Transport Protocol. The protocol used on the Internet to transfer mail. Eudora uses SMTP to send mail.

snail mail The standard name on the Internet for paper mail because email can travel across the country in seconds, whereas my birthday present from my parents took a week once.

SoftPC A software program that enables you to run DOS or Windows software on a UNIX machine, Macintosh, or PowerPC.

source In WAIS jargon, a database of information. Also sometimes called a server.

StuffIt A family of programs originally developed by Raymond Lau and now published by Aladdin Systems. Version 1.5.1 was originally shareware, and Aladdin has maintained a shareware version, now called StuffIt Lite. Typically used only in the Macintosh world, the extension is **.sit**.

system administrator The person who runs your host machine or network. Also known as the network administrator or just plain administrator. Be very nice to this person.

T

T1 A high-speed network link used on the Internet (1.54 Megabits/second).

T3 An even higher speed network link used on the Internet (45 Megabits/second).

.tar The filename extension used by files made into an archive by the UNIX tar program.

TCP Transmission Control Protocol.

TCP/IP The combination of Transmission Control Protocol and Internet Protocol.

Ted Nelson The man who coined the term *hypertext*.

Telnet Both a terminal emulation protocol that lets you log in to other machines, and programs that implement this protocol on various platforms.

terminal A piece of hardware that lets you interact with a character-based operating system such as UNIX.

Terminal emulator   Software that allows one computer to act like a dedicated terminal, such as a VT-100 to another computer.

Text   In terms of files, a file that contains only characters from the ASCII character set. In terms of FTP, a mode that assumes the files you will be transferring contain only ASCII characters. You set this mode in FTP with the ASCII command.

thread   A group of messages in a Usenet discussion group that all share the same subject and topic, so you can easily read the entire thread or delete it, depending on your specific newsreader.

TidBITS   A free weekly newsletter distributed solely over computer networks. TidBITS focuses on the Macintosh and the world of electronic communications. I'm the editor, so I think it's neat. Send email to `info@tidbits.com` for subscription information.

timeout   After a certain amount of idle time, some connections will disconnect, hanging up the phone in the case of a SLIP connection.

TurboGopher   From the University of Minnesota, a fast rodent-like program that enables you to browse through Gopherspace.

.txt   The filename extension generally used for straight text files that you can read (as opposed to text files that have been encoded by uuencode).

U

undirected information   Information that is broadcast out without regard as to who reads it. Usenet and mailing lists are undirected.

UNIX   An extremely popular operating system in wide use on computers on the Internet. Other operating systems work fine on the Internet, but UNIX is probably the most common.

UPI   United Press International. ClariNet gets much of their news from UPI.

upload   To send a file to another machine.

upstream   Machines that send you most of your Usenet news are said to be upstream from you. Machines that get most of their news from you are downstream.

Usenet An anarchic network of sorts, composed of thousands of discussion groups on every imaginable topic.

Usenet news The news that flows through Usenet. Sometimes abbreviated Usenet or news.

userid The name you use to log in to another computer. Synonymous with username.

username See **userid**. They're the same.

.uu The filename extension generally used by uuencoded files.

UUCP UNIX to UNIX CoPy. UUCP is a small pun on the fact that the UNIX copy command is cp. UUCP is a transmission protocol that carries email and news.

.uud A filename extension sometimes used by uuencoded files.

uudecode A UNIX program for decoding files in the uuencode format, turning them from ASCII back into binary files.

.uue Yet another filename extension sometimes used by uuencoded files.

uuencode A UNIX program that turns binary files into ASCII files for transmission via email.

V

v.32bis Currently the fastest standard modem protocol. v.Fast and v.32terbo, although faster, have not become standardized. Almost all v.32bis modems support all sorts of other protocols, including v.42 error correction and v.42bis data compression. Don't worry about the specifics; just try to match protocols with the modems you call.

VAT Value Added Tax. A thoroughly unpleasant tax paid by residents of countries such as France and Great Britain. You realize how cheap things in the United States are after hearing about prices in other countries over the Internet.

Veronica An information agent that searches a database of Gopher servers to find items that interest you.

vi An extremely powerful UNIX editor with the personality of a junkyard dog. Much-beloved by many UNIX aficionados.

VMS   DEC's main operating system for their Vax computers.

VT-100   Originally, a dedicated terminal built by DEC to interface to mainframes. The VT-100 became a standard for terminals, and as a result almost all terminal emulation programs can emulate the VT-100. The VT-100s make excellent footstools these days and will be outlived only by terminals made long ago by DataMedia that could withstand being dropped out a window without losing a connection.

W

WAIS   Wide Area Information Servers. A set of full-text databases containing information on hundreds of topics. You can search WAIS using natural language queries and use relevance feedback to refine your search.

WAN   See **wide-area network**.

wide-area network   A group of geographically separated computers connected via dedicated lines or satellite links. The Internet enables small organizations to simulate a wide-area network without the cost of one.

wildcards   Special characters such as * and ? that can stand in for other characters during text searches in some programs. The * wildcard generally means "match any other *characters* in this spot," whereas the ? wildcard generally means "match any other *character* in this spot."

Windows   Extremely popular operating system for personal computers. Released in 1986 with poor reception. But, it redeemed itself in 1989 with the release of Windows 3.0 by providing such revolutionary features as overlapping window panes and better memory management (yes, we can get over that 640K limit).

Windows for Workgroups   Version of Windows that supports local area networks. Resources, such as disks and printers, can be shared among users within a workgroup. Windows for Workgroups also includes workgroup software such as electronic mail and scheduling.

Windows NT   Windows New Technology. The 32-bit, multi-tasking version of Windows. Code was generalized to run on a plethora of microprocessors, including Intel 80x86, Pentium, DEC's Alpha, and PowerPC.

WinSock Windows Sockets (WinSock) is a TCP/IP extension to the Windows Applications Interface (API). It essentially allows Windows applications to run independently of the hardware underneath. It's just like the device independence you gain with a Windows graphics program. It can run independently of your video board.

World-Wide Web The newest and most ambitious of the special Internet services. The World-Wide Web provides full text access to documents marked up with the HyperText Markup Language, along with links to Gopher and WAIS. World-Wide Web browsers can display styled text and graphics. Often abbreviated WWW.

worm A program that infiltrates a computer system and copies itself many times, filling up memory and disk space and crashing the computer. The most famous worm of all time was released accidentally by Robert Morris over the Internet and brought down whole sections of the Internet.

WWW See **World-Wide Web**.

X–Z

Xerox PARC The Xerox research lab that invented the graphical interface, among many other things, including the mouse and Ethernet.

XMODEM A common file transfer protocol.

YMODEM Another common file transfer protocol.

.Z The filename extension used by files compressed with the UNIX compress program.

.z A filename extension used by files compressed with the UNIX gzip program.

.ZIP The filename extension used by files compressed into the ZIP format common on PCs.

ZMODEM The fastest and most popular file transfer protocol.

Appendix

Special Internet Access Offer

What would a book about the Internet be if it didn't provide some means of getting on the Internet for those people who aren't already connected? Not much, and to remedy that situation Hayden Books has worked out a deal for readers of this book with Northwest Nexus, Inc., a commercial Internet provider based in Bellevue, Washington. In fact, I'm especially pleased that we were able to work with Northwest Nexus, since I've obtained my Internet access from them for quite some time now. They're good folks, and I've always been happy with their service. Here's what they say about themselves. (The following section provides general information about Northwest Nexus, some of which won't apply to people using our special offer. Further down in this appendix is information specific to our offer—including how to get online. That's important, so make sure you don't skip it!)

Northwest Nexus, Inc.

Northwest Nexus offers a wide range of low-cost options to give both private individuals and companies access to the vast resources of the Internet: millions of people interacting on thousands of subjects, and data available from countless sources, including the U.S. Government, universities, research labs, and private corporations.

Our Company

Northwest Nexus was incorporated in Washington State in 1987 and has steadily grown over the years to now serve several thousand accounts. Customers have included such organizations as GTE, Immunex Corporation, McCaw Cellular, Microsoft, Nintendo of America, Traveling Software, US West, and many smaller businesses, professional organizations, consultants and individuals.

Our current staff has over 100 combined years of experience in computer and network operations, network engineering, and business. As we grow, we're continually adding staff and equipment to meet your needs.

Although our primary target market is the Puget Sound area, we also serve customers throughout the United States and around the world.

Our Services

Shell Service: Log on to one of our Shell servers and you can explore the Internet using either the traditional UNIX command line interface or a variety of menu-based interfaces such as Gopher and Hytelnet.

SLIP/PPP Service: With the right software, you can put any computer (including Macintoshes and Windows PCs) directly on the Internet—while still keeping your familiar point-and-click interface. Services for both dedicated and dynamic IP address assignment are available.

UUCP Service: Using a pre-set schedule, or whenever required, your computer can connect to our UUCP relay system and collect any mail or other files waiting for your site. A free preassigned wa.com sub-domain is included to identify your site. If you would like your own custom domain name, we can arrange it for an additional setup fee.

Dedicated Service: From 56 KB to T-1, we offer reliable, economical high-speed connections using either Frame Relay or dedicated lines. For your convenience, domain name and net number registrations are included. We can also order your circuit for you if you prefer.

Access to Usenet news is included with all service types. Electronic mail can be set up for all service types and is included free with all accounts except "Classic" (dedicated IP address) dialup SLIP/PPP.

If you're not sure what kind of connection you need, please give us a call and we can help you determine which one will work best and be most cost-effective for you. More detailed information, including pricing, is also available on sheets describing each individual service.

Our Network

Northwest Nexus dial-in lines are a local call from all prefixes in the Seattle metropolitan area, Seattle's Eastside, Everett, parts of Snohomish County, Tacoma, Olympia, and Shelton. New service areas are added periodically. If you are located outside the Puget Sound region, please call our office for available options to standard long-distance charges for your area.

US West Frame Relay service may be used for Frame Relay access to Northwest Nexus within the Puget Sound region. We can also connect with several other carriers in other areas; please call for details.

Our network is monitored 7 days a week, 24 hours a day by professional staff to ensure the reliability of your connection.

What You Need To Connect

Hardware: You can access the Internet through Northwest Nexus from almost any personal computer, workstation, or mini-computer. For Shell service, you can even use a simple terminal. For all connections except leased-line service, you will also need a modem and a regular telephone line. Leased-line connections require a CSU/DSU, a router of the appropriate speed and protocol, and a digital circuit of the appropriate speed and type.

Software: Each type of connection requires different software. Shell service is the simplest; if you don't have an actual terminal, you can use almost any (many are free). SLIP/PPP and UUCP services require software that supports these protocols; there are several packages available for many types of computers.

If you're not sure what kind of hardware or software to choose, please give us a call. We can recommend proven combinations to get you started on the net.

We Make Internet Easy

To sign up for Internet service, ask a question or get detailed information and pricing for each service, please contact us by phone, postal mail or email:

Northwest Nexus, Inc.
P.O. Box 40597
Bellevue, WA 98015-4597
206-455-3505

or

1-800-539-3505 (US and Canada)
FAX: 206-455-4672

`info@nwnexus.wa.com`

The Special Connection Offer

Folks that purchase this book can take advantage of a special connection, because Northwest Nexus is making dial-up accounts available at a special flat rate. This means that you can use NetManage's Chameleon Sampler and the rest of the software on the disk pretty much right away. If you peruse the PDIAL list, you'll see prices as high as $100 for a signup fee, and connect rates in the range of $20 per month plus about $2 for each hour of connect time. At that rate, your bill can add up fast.

In contrast, Northwest Nexus has created one of the only flat rate accounts. You pay $20 to sign up, and $22.50 per month (billed in advance on a quarterly basis—they have to keep their overhead low to be able to offer such low prices, and billing monthly is expensive) for as many hours as you want to use it each month. In addition, since Northwest Nexus realizes that you should be allowed to try something before buying, they are making the first two weeks available for free to allow you to configure your software and giving you time to "surf the net." If after two weeks you don't want to keep the account for any reason, just call Northwest Nexus at (800) 539-3505 and ask them to deactivate your account, at which point you pay nothing. (It's possible you may receive an automatically generated bill before that time. Just call Northwest Nexus if that happens and they'll straighten everything out for you).

There is a catch. There is always a catch. The catch is that you have to call Northwest Nexus in Washington State, and that will be a long distance phone call for everyone outside of the Puget Sound area. In our investigations, we were unable to find a provider that offered connections with local numbers throughout the country or via an 800 number (some had 800 numbers but charged $8 per hour or more for you to use them, which is more expensive than a normal long distance call). So with Northwest Nexus, you do have to make that long distance call, but at least you aren't charged additionally for your connect time on their machines.

One way around the long distance charges (and I really don't know any details here) is that some specialized telecommunications companies offer deals whereby you pay a certain amount per month that allows you to make a certain number of 30 minute calls per month, for instance, for $.50 per call. Details will vary widely, but do some poking around and you may be able to find a company in your area that can help. Calling the operators of local bulletin boards is a good place to start. You might also try looking in the Yellow Pages for telecommunications companies.

How to Activate Your Account

So here's how to activate an account. You call a UNIX machine called `halcyon.com`, log in, and sign up online by providing your name and address and all those details. This process requires a terminal emulation program like Terminal, which ships with Windows. Below, I'll run you through the login process, noting any quirks and making sure you know how to respond to all the prompts. Within 72 business hours, Northwest Nexus will activate your account, at which point you can configure NetManage's Chameleon Sampler as I've outlined below. (Read chapter

10, "Windows Sockets (WinSock) Access," for more details, but the information below is what you must use to configure Chameleon for Northwest Nexus.) If your account isn't active when you call back after 72 business hours, call Northwest Nexus at 800-539-3505 to check on your account status.

You still must return the original coupon included with the book to Northwest Nexus via snail mail (that is, regular U.S. Postal Service mail, stamps and all) so that they know that you really bought a copy, but you can do that after going through the initial setup process. Sending in the coupon is important: it indicates that you're a honest-to-goodness purchaser of this book, and that as such you are entitled to the two free weeks of online service. **So make sure to send in the coupon!**

Once your account is active, you're ready to log in for the first time using Chameleon. I recommend you use Ping for the first test, since it requires the least configuration.

Signup Process

> **Note:** in the following discussion, italic is used to indicate text that you should replace with your own information. For instance, replace *Sally Q. Public* with your own name.

Don't be alarmed by the excessive detail in these instructions. I want everyone to be able to get onto the Internet as quickly as possible, so I've made no assumptions on peoples' abilities.

This process requires a terminal emulation program. But hey, Windows comes with Terminal, so you should be all set. So bring up the Terminal program by double-clicking on its icon. It can be found in the Accessories Group of the Program Manager.

Bring up the Communications dialog box. It can be found in the Settings menu. As in figure F.1, set the Data Bits to 8, the Stop Bits to 1, the Parity to None, and Flow Control to Xon/Xoff. The other two values depend on your configuration and it varies from machine to machine.

Enter your modem's maximum baud rate. If your modem is a 14.4K (or V.32bis), then enter 19200. Don't worry that they don't match. You're only configuring the speed that you are talking to the modem, not the speed that the modem will actually connect.

Then enter your modem's port, as shown in figure F.1. It is probably COM1 or COM2.

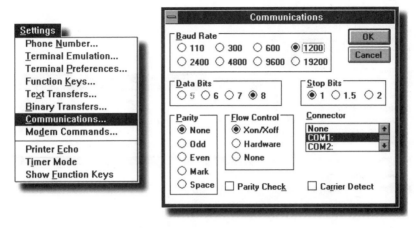

Figure F.1 *Terminal Communications Settings*

Next bring up the Phone Number dialog box. It can also be found in the Settings menu. As in figure F.2, enter the appropriate values. Northwest Nexus's phone number is 206-382-6245. Be sure to lop off the area code if you are calling from Northwest Nexus' local calling area (Seattle, Washington). You may need to prefix the number with a '1', if you need to dial 1 for a long distance call. Also, you'll need to prefix the phone number with the appropriate codes for getting an outside line should you be working for a company that has a PBX (usually 9 followed by a comma ',' which pauses for a short time until an outside line is obtained). And, if you have call waiting, you should disable it. Otherwise an incoming call **will** disrupt your session (US West customers would enter *70 as a prefix, for example).

You may want to increase the Timeout value if your modem is slow to connect with the ones at Northwest Nexus. I know that the Hayes Ultra takes anywhere from 30 to 45 seconds including dialing time, so I had to increase it.

The next set of settings deals with the idiosyncrasies of modems. Suffice to say that most modems support or emulate the Hayes command set (ways of communicating and configuring your modem), so simply insure that the values that you see in the Modem Commands dialog box of the Settings menu match the ones in figure F.3. If you have trouble, try changing the modem type. Don't even bother changing the entries in the Command section unless you are **very** familiar with modems and modem communications.

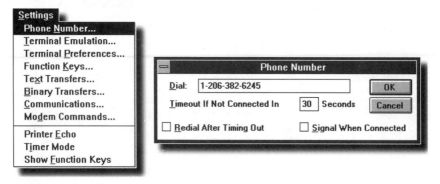

Figure F.2   *Terminal Phone Number Settings.*

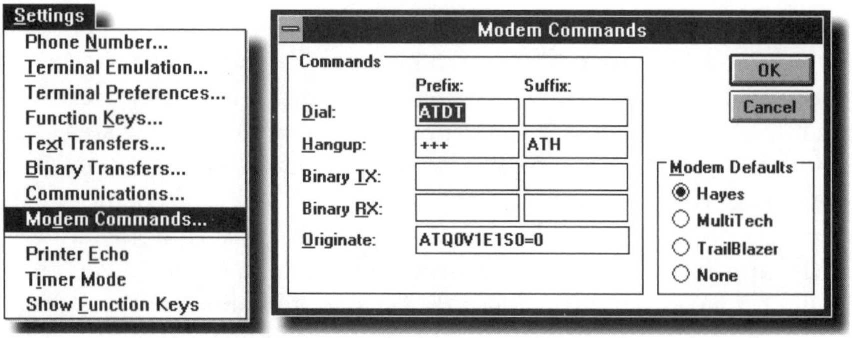

Figure F.3   *Terminal Modem Commands.*

Finally, enter values for Terminal Emulation dialog box that you get from the Settings menu as shown in figure F.4. It really doesn't matter which setting you select because all of them will work. Humor my instructions and select VT-100 (ANSI). This will ensure that all my instructions work *as advertised*.

Finally! Dial Northwest Nexus by choosing the Dial menu item from the Phone menu. Terminal will then issue commands to your modem and dial out.

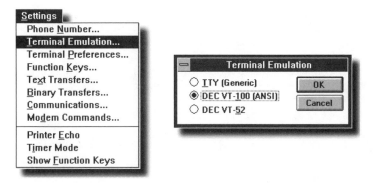

Figure F.4 *Terminal Emulation setting.*

```
CONNECT 14400
```

When the modems connect, you see a statement like the one above, although depending on your modem, the speed may be lower. Hit Enter to get to the login screen.

```
To establish an account, log in as "new" (no password needed)
login: new
```

Log in as new, as the onscreen instructions say—you won't need a password at this point.

```
Last login: Fri Sep  3 14:32:25 from DS200B
ULTRIX V4.1 (Rev. 52) System #5: Thu Mar 19 06:18:19 PST 1992
UWS V4.1 (Rev. 197)
                halcyon.com, Public Access Internet
      Seattle: 382-6245   Lynnwood: 672-4554   Shelton: 427-0102
          Eastside: 455-8455 Tacoma: 927-5834 Olympia: 456-0770
              "A World of Information at your Fingertips"
              P.O. Box 40597, Bellevue, WA 98015-4597 USA
            ralphs@halcyon.com, +1-206-455-3505 (1-800-539-3505)
This system participates in the Acceptable Use Policies of the
National Science Foundation and/or Advanced Network & Services,
Inc. and will offer help in investigating illegal and inappropriate
usage of this machine as it connects to other Internet sites, up to
and including, but not limited to, keystroke monitoring.
Type 'help' for general information... 'help goodies' for new stuff
Terminal recognized as vt100 (Generic vt100)
Halcyon is a fee-based, commercial system. Please disconnect
now if you do not wish to subscribe.
```

```
This system provides a means to access all Internet services, in
addition to providing email and newsgroup capabilities. Many
applications are available online to assist in utilizing these
services and more.
Our office phone is +1 206 455 3505. Feel free to call with
any questions or concerns. US and Canadian callers may use
1 800 539 3505.
Again, this is a commercially-operated system. Users will be
billed for their access.
Thank you for considering halcyon.com as your information gate-
way.
Ralph Sims, System Administrator (halcyon.com)
NWNEXUS, Inc., P.O. Box 40597, Bellevue, WA 98105-4597
Do you want to open an account (Yes/No)? Yes
```

Answer **Yes** to the question about opening an account. Also note the phone numbers and addresses above, but ignore the rates, since they don't apply to this special offer.

```
Your Full Name: Sally Q. Public
```

Type *your* full name, not Sally Q. Public!

```
Daytime Phone Number: 206/555-1234
Evening Phone Number: 206/555-6789
```

Please enter both of your phone numbers here. Northwest Nexus doesn't plan on calling you if they can avoid it, but if you need help setting up your account, they must be able to reach you by telephone.

```
    Enter Address Like This:
        12345 Main Street South
        Apt #452
        Seattle, WA  98101 USA

Address Line 1: 999 Elm Street
Address Line 2: Apt #333
Address Line 3: Seattle, WA 98100 USA
```

Enter your address on the lines provided. If you only have two lines in your address, hit Return on the third line.

```
Please select a login name this identifies you when you login.
This can not be more then 8 characters long.
Login name will be converted to lower case.
Login name: sallyp
```

Remember that your login name is *lowercase*. In order for you to configure Chameleon correctly, the login name must be lowercase.

Here comes the first part that requires a small amount of creativity. You have to think of a unique login name here, so using your first name very likely won't work. However, this will also act as your email userid, so make it something intelligible. Read chapter 5, "Addressing and Email," for some thoughts on email userids—combinations like first name and last initial (as I've shown above) or first initial and last name work fine and are often unique.

```
Please select a secret password, it will not show on the screen.
Password: <- I typed Adam, but it didn't show up.
```

Here I typed my first name, which is a password that many people use because it's easy to remember and type. Unfortunately, crackers know this, and it's one of the first things they try when breaking into an account. Because of this security risk, this machine refuses to take simple passwords, so you have to make up something completely unintelligible. Write this password down first and store it somewhere safe!

```
A UNIX system password should be at least 5 characters long and
include
at least one upper case letter (A-Z), digit (0-9) or punctuation
character
(such as   .  , or  -  ).
Passwords will NOT be accepted that:
     * Are less than 5 characters long.
     * Are composed entirely of uppercase or lowercase letters,
       numbers, or are simply capitalized.
     * Matches anything in your UNIX account information, such as
your login
       name or an item from your "finger" data entry.
     * Are found in the hackers' dictionary of common passwords.
     * Have less than 5 different characters.
     * Fail any of these tests when reversed, pluralized, or trun-
cated.
Please select a secret password, it will not show on the screen.
Password:   <- I typed qw12er34, but it didn't show up.
Password Again: <- I typed the password again as a check.
```

For a password I entered *qw12er34*, which is completely meaningless but easy to type and difficult to guess. (A better and more mnemonic strategy for thinking of these passwords is to use the first letters of a phrase like "Take me out to the ball game," which would translate to a password of *tmo2tbg*.) You have to enter the password twice, to make sure you've got it right. Write it down after the first time to make sure you don't forget, especially since you need it later. Without this password, you won't be able to log in again.

```
Now you can leave up to three lines of information you want the
System
Operator to know about you.
Line 1: TISK Windows
Line 2: Please set up a SLIP account for me to use with Chameleon
Line 3: (leave this line blank)
```

OK, pay attention. This is a free-form entry area, but you must enter some specific information to take advantage of the special offer and to get Northwest Nexus to set up a SLIP account for you.

In the first line, enter TISK Windows, exactly as I have done. In the second line, type the sentence I typed above, just to make sure that Northwest Nexus knows that you are taking advantage of the special offer and that you want the SLIP account. Leave the third line blank.

```
Your Information
— — — — — — — — — — — — — — — — — —
[1] Full Name: Sally Q. Public
[2] Daytime #: 206/555-1234
    Evening #: 206/555-6789
[3] Address:   999 Elm Street
               Apt #333
               Seattle, WA 98100 USA
[4] Login:     sallyp
Select 1, 2, 3, 4 to Change, E to End or A to Abort: E
```

Once you finish, you get a chance to check and re-enter your information if it's wrong. If you choose to re-enter a piece of information, the entry process will be exactly the same as it was the first time around. To save your entry, type **E**. If you get cold feet and decide that you don't want to set up this account after all, type **A**.

```
Please wait....
Please wait....
```

```
    Thank you for selecting halcyon.com as your information
provider.
    Your account should be activated within 72 hours. If you are
    able to log in with your new userid and password, then every-
thing has been set up and ready to go, generally within 72 hours.
If you are not able to log in, call us by phone and we will in-
vestigate the problem.
    Our office number is +1 206 455 3505, and is monitored 24
hours a day. US and Canadian callers may use 1 800 539 3505.
        Ralph Sims, ralphs@halcyon.com
```

A few seconds later, your modem will hang up, since you can't use anything until Northwest Nexus activates your account. Now you have to sit tight for a couple days before you can call back using NetManage's Chameleon Sampler.

Configuring NetManage's Chameleon Sampler

Let's jump forward briefly and assume you're ready to configure Chameleon. In chapter 10, I mention over and over that you have to get a bunch of information from your system administrator. One advantage of working with Northwest Nexus is that much of that information exists right here. I'm not going to explain the process in great detail here—that information is in chapter 10—but I will tell you what information goes where and provide screen shots of the Custom application of Chameleon so you can see exactly how it should be set up.

Installation

The first thing you want to do is install the NetManage Chameleon sampler software. You do this by inserting the floppy into your drive and choosing Run from the File menu of the Program Manager. Type **a:\setup** (or **b:\setup**, depending on the location of your 3 1/2" floppy drive). Click OK and you're on your way. Installation is typical of other Windows applications, so you should have no problems.

Tip: Chameleon loads its WinSock Dynamic Link Library (winsock.dll) in its own directory, which defaults to c:\netmanag. If you plan on using other WinSock compliant software (and believe me you will), then you should copy or move this file from c:\netmanag to your Windows System directory, which is typically c:\windows\system.

Caution: Chameleon alters your **autoexec.bat** file by placing its default directory into the path. Some people are pretty picky about the search path and the things that go in it. It won't cause any problems, but I thought you'd like to know.

When Setup is complete, you'll have a new Program Group called Chameleon Sampler (see figure F.5). It should be the foremost window under the Program Manager, and you'll notice lots of neat applications there for you to start exploring the Internet.

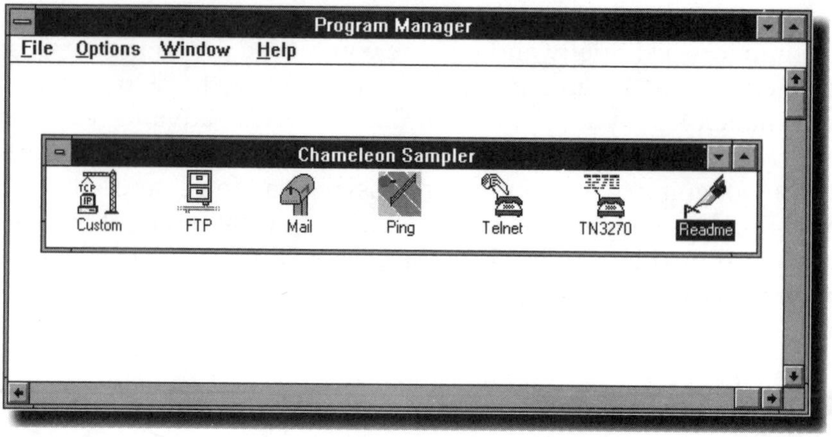

Figure F.5   Program Manager, Chameleon Sampler group.

Custom

You'll now need to invoke NetManage's WinSock called Newt. You do this by launching the Custom application. Keep this in mind. As a SLIP user, each time you want to connect to the Internet, you'll need to launch Custom and keep it running (and thus Newt running) until you are completely finished with the Internet—and I hope that isn't at 5:00 A.M.

I've included on disk nearly all the information required to attach to Northwest Nexus. You do this by selecting Open from the File Menu of Custom (see figure F.6) and selecting **nwnexus.cfg**. This file contains nearly all the technical Internet information necessary to connect.

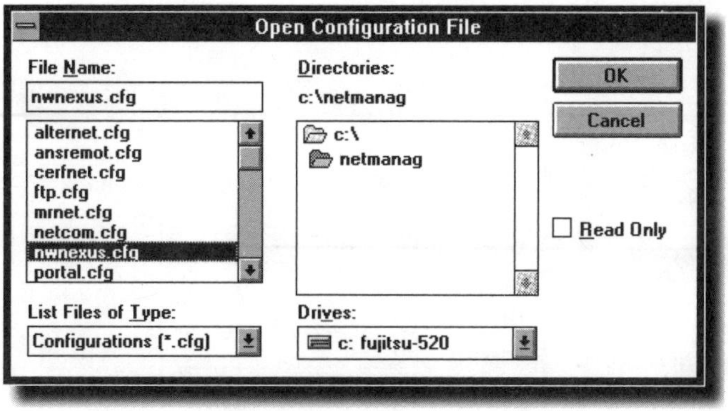

Figure F.6 Custom Open Configuration.

Now let's set up those portions of the configuration that I couldn't anticipate. We'll start with the serial port of your computer. Start by bringing up the Port Setting dialog box from the Setup menu (see figure F.7). Should doing this look vaguely familiar? It is. You entered similar values for Terminal when you signed up for an account just a few days ago (or whenever you obtained your user id and password).

Enter your modem's maximum baud rate. If your modem is a 14.4K or V.32bis, then enter 19200. Don't worry that they don't match. You're only configuring the speed that you are talking to the modem, not the speed that the modem will actually connect.

Then enter your modem's port. It is probably COM1 or COM2.

Now you need to let Custom know what type of modem you are using. Bring up the Modem Settings dialog box from the Setup menu (see figure F.8).

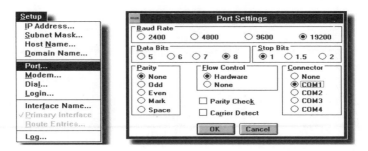

Figure F.7   Custom Port Settings.

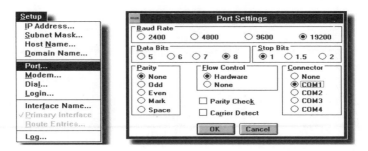

Figure F.8   Custom Modem Settings.

For most modems, a Modem Default of **Hayes** will suffice.

Next bring up the Dial Settings from the Setup menu (see figure F.9).

Enter the same phone number that you used when you dialed Northwest Nexus to obtain your user ID and password. Also, check the Signal When Connected checkbox. It will let you know when you've successfully connected to halcyon.com by beeping once.

You can probably leave the rest of the values alone.

Now you need to tell Custom your user ID and password. Bring up the Login Settings dialog box from the Setup menu (see figure F.10).

User ID and passwords are case sensitive, so be careful when you type in your values. You can leave the Startup Command edit box blank.

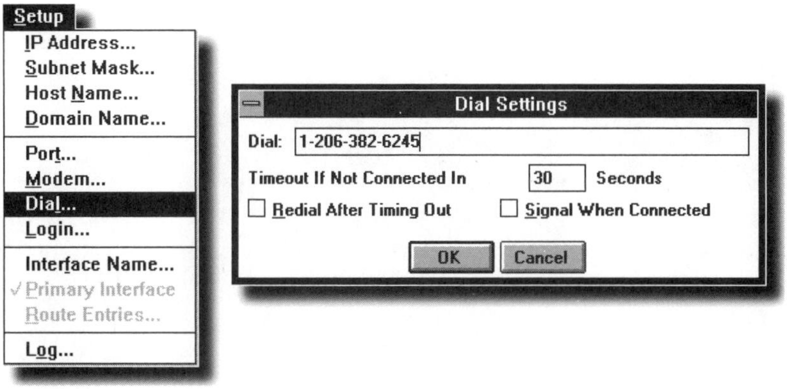

Setup
IP Address...
Subnet Mask...
Host Name...
Domain Name...

Port...
Modem...
Dial...
Login...

Interface Name...
√ Primary Interface
Route Entries...

Log...

Dial Settings

Dial: 1-206-382-6245

Timeout If Not Connected In   30   Seconds
☐ Redial After Timing Out   ☐ Signal When Connected

OK   Cancel

Figure F.9   *Custom Dial Settings.*

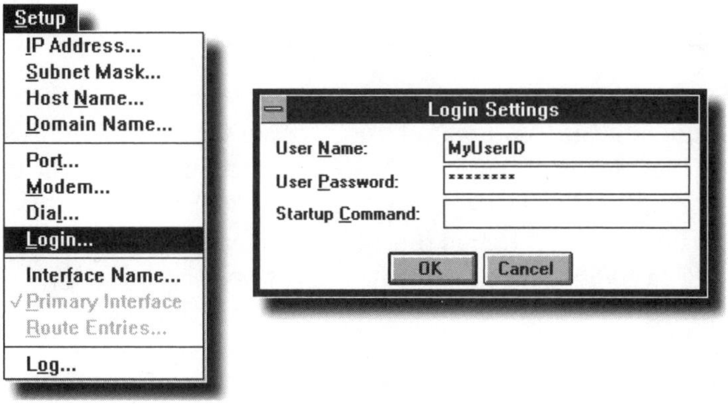

Setup
IP Address...
Subnet Mask...
Host Name...
Domain Name...

Port...
Modem...
Dial...
Login...

Interface Name...
√ Primary Interface
Route Entries...

Log...

Login Settings

User Name: MyUserID
User Password: ********
Startup Command:

OK   Cancel

Figure F.10   *Custom Login Settings.*

Finally, save your configuration by selecting Save from the File menu. It will overwrite the nwnexus.cfg file with your new information so you never have to type them here again. Whew!

Now you're ready to connect to the Internet. You might notice that the Connect menu is dimmed. Now that you've given Custom enough information, you need to get Custom to reinitialize. Do this by exiting Custom and then re-launching it. If you opened any other Chameleon applications, quit those applications until the Newt icon disappears from your Desktop before restarting Custom. Voilà! The Connect menu is now available and you'll be connected to Northwest Nexus in a matter of minutes.

> **Tip:** Before connecting, bring up the Log Window in the Settings menu. This will allow you to watch your computer communicate with your modem and therefore with `halcyon.com`. If either your computer or modem runs into trouble, you'll be able to see what's really going on.

Click on the Connect menu. There are no menu items in that menu so it will simply start the connection process. In a matter of seconds, you'll be connected to the Internet and then the world will be your oyster.

Email

When configuring Eudora to send and receive email, you mainly need to know your POP account, which runs from a machine called `halcyon.com` and uses your user ID. So, in my example above, Sally Q. Public's POP account for Eudora (and this is the account everyone should send email to as well) is `sallyp@halcyon.com`. You don't need to fill in SMTP Server or Return Address fields, since Eudora generates those automatically for you on the fly.

Timeouts

Also, keep in mind that if your connection is idle for too long and Northwest Nexus hangs up the line, you must quit any WinSock-based programs that are running, since if you connect again with Custom without doing so, you will receive a different IP address and will confuse the heck out of the programs already running.

Northwest Nexus Gateway Script

Here's the `slip.ini` entry for Northwest Nexus should you ever need to refer to it. `slip.ini` is the initialization file that Custom uses.

```
[NW Nexus]
SCRIPT=login: $u$r word: $p$r to $- -i
TYPE=CSLIP
```

Northwest Nexus Terms & Conditions

Terms and Conditions—Effective February 12, 1994

1. You understand and accept these Terms and Conditions and agree to pay for these services according to the Billing Policies currently in effect.

2. If we do not receive your payment when due, your account may be terminated. Termination of your account does not remove your responsibility under this agreement to pay all fees incurred up to the date the account was canceled including any collection fees incurred by Northwest Nexus Inc.

3. Northwest Nexus Inc. makes no warranties of any kind, whether expressed or implied, including any implied warranty of merchantability or fitness of this service for a particular purpose. Northwest Nexus Inc. takes no responsibility for any damages suffered by you including, but not limited to, loss of data from delays, nondeliveries, misdeliveries, or service interruptions caused by Northwest Nexus' own negligence or your errors and/or omissions.

4. Northwest Nexus' services may only be used for lawful purposes. Transmission of any material in violation of any US or state regulation is prohibited. This includes, but is not limited to: copyrighted material, threatening or obscene material, or material protected by trade secret. You agree to indemnify and hold harmless Northwest Nexus Inc. from any claims resulting from your use of this service which damages you or another party. At our discretion, we may revoke your access for inappropriate usage.

5. Use of any information obtained via this service is at your own risk. Northwest Nexus specifically denies any responsibility for the accuracy or quality of information obtained through our services.

6. We may list your contact information in relevant directories.

7. If you use another organization's networks or computing resources, you are subject to their respective permission and usage policies.

8. These Terms and Conditions are subject to change without notice. A current copy will always be available online through our "help" facility. Continued usage of your account after a new policy has gone into effect constitutes acceptance of that policy. We encourage you to regularly check the policy statement for any changes. (The effective date at the top will be updated to indicate a new revision.)

9. You will notify Northwest Nexus of any changes in account contact information such as your address.

10. You are responsible for how your account is used. You may allow others to use it, bearing in mind that you are fully responsible for what they do.

11. Per-session time limits are currently set at two hours; you may log back in after a two-hour "offline" time. This applies to the `halcyon.com` machines only.

12. Disk storage is limited to 5 megabytes. Excess storage is not permitted on the user drives; use of **/scratch** for excess files is permitted. This applies only to the `halcyon.com` machines.

13. Northwest Nexus Inc. reserves the right to cancel this service and reimburse you with any unused fees where appropriate on a pro-rata basis.

14. You may cancel your account at any time upon prior written notice to us. You will still be responsible for any fees incurred up to the date of termination of the service. We will reimburse you for any unused fees where appropriate on a pro-rata basis.

15. These Terms and Conditions supercede all previous representations, understandings or agreements and shall prevail notwithstanding any variance with terms and conditions of any order submitted.

Index

GO AHEAD. PLUG YOURSELF INTO
PRENTICE HALL COMPUTER PUBLISHING.
Introducing the PHCP Forum on CompuServe®

Yes, it's true. Now, you can have CompuServe access to the same professional, friendly folks who have made computers easier for years. On the PHCP Forum, you'll find additional information on the topics covered by every PHCP imprint—including Que, Sams Publishing, New Riders Publishing, Alpha Books, Brady Books, Hayden Books, and Adobe Press. In addition, you'll be able to receive technical support and disk updates for the software produced by Que Software and Paramount Interactive, a division of the Paramount Technology Group. It's a great way to supplement the best information in the business.

WHAT CAN YOU DO ON THE PHCP FORUM?

Play an important role in the publishing process—and make our books better while you make your work easier:

- Leave messages and ask questions about PHCP books and software—you're guaranteed a response within 24 hours
- Download helpful tips and software to help you get the most out of your computer
- Contact authors of your favorite PHCP books through electronic mail
- Present your own book ideas
- Keep up to date on all the latest books available from each of PHCP's exciting imprints

JOIN NOW AND GET A FREE COMPUSERVE STARTER KIT!

To receive your free CompuServe Introductory Membership, call toll-free, **1-800-848-8199** and ask for representative **#597**. The Starter Kit Includes:

- Personal ID number and password
- $15 credit on the system
- Subscription to CompuServe Magazine

HERE'S HOW TO PLUG INTO PHCP:

Once on the CompuServe System, type any of these phrases to access the PHCP Forum:

GO PHCP	**GO BRADY**
GO QUEBOOKS	**GO HAYDEN**
GO SAMS	**GO QUESOFT**
GO NEWRIDERS	**GO PARAMOUNTINTER**
GO ALPHA	

Once you're on the CompuServe Information Service, be sure to take advantage of all of CompuServe's resources. CompuServe is home to more than 1,700 products and services—plus it has over 1.5 million members worldwide. You'll find valuable online reference materials, travel and investor services, electronic mail, weather updates, leisure-time games and hassle-free shopping (no jam-packed parking lots or crowded stores).

Seek out the hundreds of other forums that populate CompuServe. Covering diverse topics such as pet care, rock music, cooking, and political issues, you're sure to find others with the sames concerns as you—and expand your knowledge at the same time.

Coupon

Northwest Nexus Terms & Conditions

Terms and Conditions—Effective February 12, 1994

1. You understand and accept these Terms and Conditions and agree to pay for these services according to the Billing Policies currently in effect.

2. If we do not receive your payment when due, your account may be terminated. Termination of your account does not remove your responsibility under this agreement to pay all fees incurred up to the date the account was canceled including any collection fees incurred by Northwest Nexus Inc.

3. Northwest Nexus Inc. makes no warranties of any kind, whether expressed or implied, including any implied warranty of merchantability or fitness of this service for a particular purpose. Northwest Nexus Inc. takes no responsibility for any damages suffered by you including, but not limited to, loss of data from delays, nondeliveries, misdeliveries, or service interruptions caused by Northwest Nexus' own negligence or your errors and/or omissions.

4. Northwest Nexus' services may only be used for lawful purposes. Transmission of any material in violation of any US or state regulation is prohibited. This includes, but is not limited to: copyrighted material, threatening or obscene material, or material protected by trade secret. You agree to indemnify and hold harmless Northwest Nexus Inc. from any claims resulting from your use of this service which damages you or another party. At our discretion, we may revoke your access for inappropriate usage.

5. Use of any information obtained via this service is at your own risk. Northwest Nexus specifically denies any responsibility for the accuracy or quality of information obtained through our services.

6. We may list your contact information in relevant directories.

7. If you use another organization's networks or computing resources, you are subject to their respective permission and usage policies.

8. These Terms and Conditions are subject to change without notice. A current copy will always be available on-line through our "help" facility. Continued usage of your account after a new policy has gone into effect constitutes acceptance of that policy. We encourage you to regularly check the policy statement for any changes. (The effective date at the top will be updated to indicate a new revision.)

9. You will notify Northwest Nexus of any changes in account contact information such as your address.

10. You are responsible for how your account is used. You may allow others to use it, bearing in mind that you are fully responsible for what they do.

11. Per-session time limits are currently set at two hours; you may log back in after a two-hour "offline" time. This applies to the `halcyon.com` machines only.

12. Disk storage is limited to 5 megabytes. Excess storage is not permitted on the user drives; use of **/scratch** for excess files is permitted. This applies only to the `halcyon.com` machines.

13. Northwest Nexus Inc. reserves the right to cancel this service and reimburse you with any unused fees where appropriate on a pro-rata basis.

14. You may cancel your account at any time upon prior written notice to us. You will still be responsible for any fees incurred up to the date of termination of the service. We will reimburse you for any unused fees where appropriate on a pro-rata basis.

15. These Terms and Conditions supercede all previous representations, understandings or agreements and shall prevail notwithstanding any variance with the terms and conditions of any order submitted.

Northwest Nexus Internet Access Offer

What would a book about the Internet be if it didn't provide some means of getting on the Internet for those people who aren't already connected? Not much, and to remedy that situation, Hayden Books has worked out a deal for readers of this book with Northwest Nexus, Inc., a commercial Internet provider based in Bellevue, Washington.

Northwest Nexus has created a flat rate SLIP account. You pay $20 to sign up, and $22.50 per month (billed in advance on a quarterly basis) for as many hours as you want to use it each month. In addition, they are making the first two weeks available for free to allow you to get connected. If after two weeks you don't want to keep the account for any reason, just call Northwest Nexus at (800) 539-3505 and ask them to deactivate your account, at which point you pay nothing. (It's possible you may receive an automatically generated bill before that time. Just call Northwest Nexus if that happens and they'll straighten everything out for you).

One thing to keep in mind is that you have to call Northwest Nexus (in Washington State) to connect, and that will be a long distance phone call for everyone outside of the Puget Sound area. However, this is a good deal even with long-distance fees—and the two free weeks just sweetens the pot.

Details for setting up an account are provided in Appendix F, "Special Internet Access Offer." The important fact is that after you set up the account, you'll have to send *this page* (not a copy!) to Northwest Nexus to confirm that you bought this book. Just tear out the page, and drop it in the mail. If you don't, you won't get the special deal, so make sure you fill out and send in this page. It's not tough!

Please set up an account for me!

Full Name: _____

Daytime Phone #: _____

Evening Phone #: _____

Address: _____

_____

_____

Requested Login: _____

Please tear out this page (do not send a copy!) and mail it to:

Northwest Nexus Inc.
ATTN: Hayden Books Special Offer
P.O. Box 40597
Bellevue, WA 98015-4597

If you have questions, contact Northwest Nexus at (206) 455-3505 or toll-free at (800) 539-3505 (U.S. and Canada).

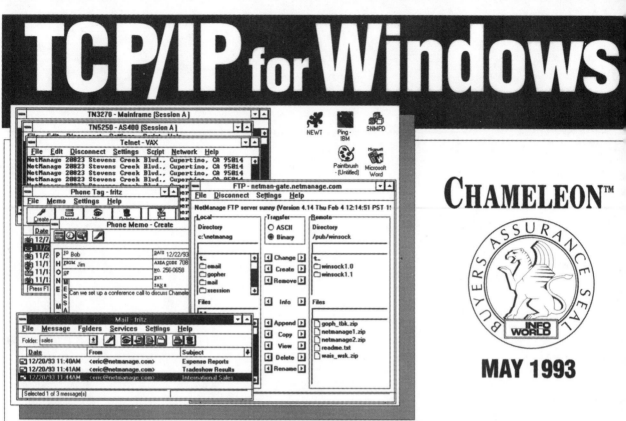

The Internet Starter Kit Disk

The Internet Starter Kit for Windows disk contains all the software you need to access the Internet! Read Chapter 10 and Appendix F for instructions on installing Chameleon.

Chameleon Sampler—NetManage's Chameleon Sampler contains everything you need to connect to the Internet. Not only does it contain WinSock and provisions to get SLIP and PPP access to the Internet, but it also contains a plethora of very capable applications including: **Telnet**, **TN 3270**, **FTP**, **Ping**, and **Mail**. With this basic set of tools, you can download and use virtually any DOS or Windows program publicly available on the Internet.

Eudora 1.4—Eudora is the most popular email program for Internet on Windows and Macintosh. Created by Steve Dorner of QUALCOMM, Eudora is flexible enough to work via dialup or direct-connect. Even better, Eudora comes completely free of charge. Eudora can be found on the **\extras** directory of the supplied diskette. Simply copy **eudora14.exe** using the Windows File Manager to a directory on your hard drive, perhaps **c:\eudora**. Then open the MS-DOS prompt (in the Main Group of Program Manager), move to that directory (e.g., `cd \eudora`), and type `eudora`. This is a self-extracting archive that will create **weudora.exe**. **eudora14.exe** can be deleted to save disk space. You now install Eudora as a Program Item under Program Manager. Read Chapter 10 for more in-depth instructions.

WinVN—This is an NNTP newsreader for Microsoft Windows 3.1. You can use it to read and post Usenet News. WinVN can be found on the **\extras** directory of the supplied diskette. Simply copy **!winvn.exe** using the Windows File Manager to a directory on your hard drive, perhaps **c:\winvn**. Open the MS-DOS prompt (in the Main Group of Program Manager), move to that directory (e.g., `cd \winvn`), and type `!winvn`. This is a self-extracting archive that will create **winvn.exe**. **!winvn.exe** can be deleted to save disk space. You now install WinVN as a Program Item under Program Manager. Hint: If you're taking advantage of the Northwest Nexus deal, use `nwfocus.wa.com` as your NNTP (Server) when you configure WinVN. You can leave all other values the same.

WinSock Gopher—This is a Windows Socket client for Gopher and can be found on the **\extras** directory of the supplied diskette. Copy **wsg-09g.exe** using the Windows File Manager to a directory on your hard drive, perhaps **c:\gopher**. Then open the MS-DOS prompt (in the Main Group of Program Manager), move to that directory (e.g., `cd \gopher`), and type `wsg-09g`. This is a self-extracting archive that will create **wsgopher.exe**. **wsg-09g.exe** can be deleted to save disk space. You now can install WSGopher as a Program Item under Program Manager. WSGopher is ready to go, nothing more is really necessary. It is recommended that you read the **install.txt** file included in the archive.

The Rest of the Best

I wanted to put more programs on the disk, I really did. But since I seem to have collected about 25M of software in the course of my testing, including ten disks would barely have been enough. So, I had a talk with the folks at Northwest Nexus, and they agreed to set up an FTP site for me that everyone on the Internet could access. That way you will have a single site to visit for the latest and greatest. The FTP site is called `ftp.halcyon.com`, and you don't need a special user ID or password to log in.

Here's a quick tutorial on connecting to the FTP site after you have installed and configured the Chameleon Sampler. Launch FTP. Click on Connect, and then fill in `ftp.halcyon.com` for the host and your email address for the password. Click on the OK button and you should be connected to `ftp.halcyon.com`. Once you are there, type `/pub/tiskwin` into the Remote Directory dialog box and click on change arrow pointing at the remote side. In a couple of seconds you'll see the list of files on halcyon on the right hand side. You can retrieve them by just selecting them with your mouse and clicking on the copy arrow pointing toward your own machine.